Chinese Culture Through Legends and Fiction

I0585720

This is a collection of selected and translated Chinese legends and tales arranged under specific topics important to Chinese culture, with an introduction and reading guide for each piece.

Comprised of 4 parts covering Confucian culture, Daoist culture, Buddhist culture and topics beyond the Three Teachings, the sources featured in this anthology include legends, fictional works, historical texts, as well as philosophical texts of ancient China, ranging from the Han 漢 dynasty (206 BCE–220 CE) to the Qing 清 dynasty (1644–1911).

Helping its readers learn about Chinese customs, traditions, and values by immersing them in the wonderful world of traditional China, with the compelling legends and tales revealing the fascinating meshwork of Chinese culture, this book is an invaluable text for students and scholars of Chinese literature, culture and history, as well as general readers with an interest in China.

Zhenjun Zhang is Professor of Chinese in the Department of World Languages, Cultures, and Media at St. Lawrence University, USA, and co-editor (with Victor H. Mair) of *Routledge Handbook of Traditional Chinese Literature* (2025).

Chinese Culture Through Legends and Fiction

A Guided Reader

Zhenjun Zhang

Routledge
Taylor & Francis Group

LONDON AND NEW YORK

Designed cover image: Getty Images

First published 2025
by Routledge
4 Park Square, Milton Park, Abingdon, Oxon OX14 4RN

and by Routledge
605 Third Avenue, New York, NY 10158

Routledge is an imprint of the Taylor & Francis Group, an informa business

© 2025 Zhenjun Zhang

British Library Cataloguing-in-Publication Data
A catalogue record for this book is available from the British Library

ISBN: 978-1-032-79161-6 (hbk)
ISBN: 978-1-032-79163-0 (pbk)
ISBN: 978-1-003-49082-1 (ebk)

DOI: 10.4324/9781003490821

Typeset in Times New Roman
by Apex CoVantage, LLC

Contents

Chinese Dynasty Chronology

Shang	ca. 1554–1045 BCE
Western Zhou	ca. 1045–771 BCE
Eastern Zhou	770–256 BCE
Spring and Autumn Period	770–481 BCE
Warring States Period	475–221 BCE
Qin	221–207 BCE
Western Han	206 BCE–8 CE
Xin	9–25 CE
Eastern Han	25–220
Three Kingdoms	220–280
Wei	220–265
Shu	221–263
Wu	222–280
Western Jin	265–316
Eastern Jin	317–420
Southern and Northern Dynasties	386–589
Southern Dynasties	420–589
[Liu] Song	420–479
Southern Qi	479–502
Southern Liang	502–557
Southern Chen	557–589
Northern Dynasties	386–581
Northern Wei	386–534
Eastern Wei	534–550
Western Wei	535–556
Northern Qi	550–577
Northern Zhou	557–581
Sui	581–618
Tang	618–907
Five Dynasties	907–960
Northern Song Dynasty	960–1127
Southern Song Dynasty	1127–1279
Yuan Dynasty	1260–1358
Ming Dynasty	1368–1644
Qing Dynasty	1644–1911

Terms Regarding Weights and Measures

Dou 斗, a decaliter
Hu 斛, bushel, 10 *dou* before the Tang dynasty; 5 *dou* since the Song dynasty
Sheng 升, pint, 1/10 of *dou*
Jin 斤, catty, half a kilogram
Liang 兩, 1/10 of jin
Dan 石, bushel, 10 dou
Yi 鎰, 24 *liang*
Chi 尺, foot
Cun 寸, inch, 1/10 *chi*
Duan 端, 20 *chi*
Fen 分, 1/3 centimeter
Li 里, half a kilometer, or approximately one-third of a mile
Zhang 丈, pole, 10 *chi*, approximately 3 1/3 meters
Pi 匹, bolt [of silk cloth], 40 feet and 4 *zhang*

Introduction

I. The Rational for Compiling This Anthology

From generation to generation, national cultures have been and continue to be transmitted through the universal mediums of folklore and literature. Chinese culture is no exception. A fascinating and effective way to learn about Chinese customs, traditions, and values is to immerse oneself in Chinese culture via its legends and fiction.

This is a collection of selected and translated Chinese legends and tales arranged under specific topics important to Chinese culture, with an introduction and reading guide for each piece. It aims to help readers, especially college students, learn about Chinese culture by immersing them in the world of traditional China. The compelling tales selected for this collection reveal the fascinating meshwork of Chinese culture, a network familiar to many Chinese.

It has been my wish to put together such an anthology since I started teaching Chinese history and culture courses at Grinnell College, and especially when I began teaching at St. Lawrence University a decade ago. In my teaching, I found that directly learning about concepts and customs was sometimes tedious for students; they were much more interested in learning through reading stories. They always became excited and enthusiastic when discussing legendary figures and the themes of fiction. However, a collection of such works was not available in print. Thus, I started to translate some stories for my students myself. This anthology is the result of my effort over the past ten years.

II. The Focus and Organization of This Anthology

"Culture" is a broad term referring to "the integrated pattern of human knowledge, belief, and behavior that depends upon the capacity for learning and transmitting knowledge to succeeding generations,"[1] "the way of life, especially the general customs and beliefs, of a particular group of people at a particular time,"[2] and in sociology "the languages, customs, beliefs, rules, arts, knowledge, and collective identities and memories developed by members of all social groups that make their social environments meaningful."[3]

"Chinese culture" is a term that consists of numerous facts, including Chinese languages, archaeology, history, society, economy, relationships with foreign countries, philosophy, religions, practices, literature, arts, science, technology, medicine, cuisine, etc. As the online *New World Encyclopedia* says,

> The Culture of China (Chinese: 中國文化) is home to one of the world's oldest and most complex civilizations covering a history of over 5,000 years. The nation covers a large geographical region with customs and traditions varying greatly between towns, cities, and provinces. Chinese culture (Chinese: 中華文化) is a broad term used to describe the cultural foundation, even among Chinese-speaking regions outside of mainland China.
>
> Chinese culture underwent several turning points and renewals throughout its long unfolding but it was already rich and essential in the period of antiquity called the pre-Qin period that saw the brutal unification of China by Shi Huangdi. A major shift happened from the Shang dynasty which was still connected with barbarian practices to the Zhou dynasty when culture started to flourish.
>
> The antique period saw the creation of language, the emergence of philosophy, science, and technology with a great intelligence and diversity that contrast with the chaos that plagued China during the Warring States period, particularly from the third century to the first century B.C.E.[4]

The task of this anthology is not providing a nuanced picture of the complex whole of Chinese culture by touching upon as much of it as possible in different types of texts, as the *Hawai'i Reader in Traditional Chinese Culture* (edited by Victor Mair and others) does. On the contrary, it selects only stories bearing important themes that reflect the basic teachings in Chinese culture and the most popular beliefs and practices in traditional China, from the very beginning to modern China, which started in 1911 when the Republic of China was established.

Classic Chinese philosophy is known for its "various masters and hundred schools" (*zhuzi baijia* 諸子百家), such as Legalism (*fajia* 法家), which promotes governing by law and regulations; Moism (*Mojia* 墨家), which promotes impartial love; Egoism (Yang Zhu school 楊朱學派), which values self or individual; and *Yin-Yang* schools (*yinyang jia* 陰陽家), which has synthesized the concepts of yin and yang with the Five Elements (*wuxing* 五行), etc. But the major foundation of Chinese culture that shaped the basic ethics of the Chinese people is the so-called "Three Teachings" or "Three Doctrines" (*sanjiao* 三教): Confucianism (*Rujia* 儒家), which promotes benevolence and ritual and has long been considered conventional value; Daoism (*Daojia* 道家), which promotes individualism and being harmonious with the Dao; and Buddhism (*Fojiao* 佛教), a foreign religion that was introduced to China from India.

Confucianism exists at the core of Chinese culture, and because of this it has almost become the substitutive term of Chinese culture. The core of Confucian teachings is the power of relationships between people, specifically the Five Relationships (wulun 五倫). As the noted Chinese scholar He Lin 賀麟 (1902–1992)

remarked, "For thousands of years, the Five Confucian Relationships have endured as one of the most powerful concepts shaping the moral lives of Chinese people. These relationships lie at the core of our ethical code; they constitute the regulatory framework for the Chinese ethnicity."[5]

Similarly, Daoism and Buddhism have also played important roles in shaping the ways in which the Chinese think and behave. The seeking of spiritual freedom and individuality from Daoism, as well as the concepts of incarnation, karmic retribution, and the sense of emptiness from Buddhism, are all deeply rooted in Chinese minds. Beyond the Confucian system of cosmology, there are also heaven and earth, the system of Daoist deities, the immortal land, the Buddhist heavens, and the western paradise and hells – all are facets of Chinese culture. The literature of the "Three Teachings" is populated by loyal vassals and filial sons, carefree wanderers, and arrogant, self-aggrandizing scholars, as well as the descended goddesses, divine Taoist priests and Buddhist monks, and the merciful Bodhisattvas.

This anthology is comprised of four major sections, the first three of which are the cultures of Confucianism, Daoism, and Buddhism. While the Three Doctrines exerted influence on each other throughout the last two millennia, the selections here are focused on the basic teachings of each. As such, tracing their influence on each other is beyond the scope of this anthology.

Of course, there is more to Chinese culture than just the Three Doctrines. So the fourth section covers many additional concepts, characters, and practices. Specifically, writings on knights-errant, warriors, ungrateful men, appreciative friends, ghost wives, and spirit maidens are included in this "special topics" section.

III.   Sources and Selection Criteria

The sources for this anthology include legends, fictional works, and historical texts, as well as philosophical texts of ancient China, ranging from the Han 漢 dynasty (206 BCE–220 CE) to the Qing 清 dynasty (1644–1911).[6]

In terms of source genres, a few works come from historical texts such as Sima Qian's 司馬遷 (145–86? BCE) *Shiji* 史記 (The Grand Scribe's Records) and Ban Gu's 班固 (32–92) *Han shu* 漢書 (History of the Han) as well as philosophical texts such as *Zhuangzi* and *Liezi* 列子. Most are tales in classical Chinese, including *zhiguai* 志怪 (accounts of anomalies) and *chuanqi* 傳奇 (transmission of marvels).

Zhiguai is a genre of brief prose narratives about extraordinary phenomena, people, and events. These narratives discuss other species – the supernatural beings such as deities, ghosts, monsters, goblins, and immortals; other spheres – the realms beyond the human world such as heaven, the underworld, immortal lands, and exotic territories; cross-boundary oddities such as omens, thaumaturgy, metamorphoses, trafficking between humans and supernatural beings, and interactions of humans with humanized beasts; as well as human world oddities such as legendary figures, strange creatures, natural wonders, and other marvels. They were most popular in the Han, Wei 魏 (220–265) and Six Dynasties 六朝 period (220–589).[7] Noted collections include Gan Bao's 干寶 (fl.335–349) *Soushen ji* 搜神記 (In Search of the Supernatural), Tao Qian's 陶潛 (365–427) *Soushen houji* 搜神後記

(A Sequel to In Search of the Supernatural), and Liu Yiqing's 劉義慶 (403–444) *Youming lu* 幽明錄 (Records of the Hidden and Visible Realms), etc. The *zhiguai* genre lasted until the Qing dynasty when *Liaozhai zhiyi* 聊齋志異 (Strange Tales from Make-Do Studio), the masterpiece by Pu Songling 蒲松齡 (1640–1715) appeared.

Chuanqi 傳奇, a more sophisticated genre starting in the Tang 唐 (618–907), features much more elaborate plots, polished language, and significantly, the "conscious creation" by its author.[8] Apart from many independently transmitted pieces such as "Huo Xiaoyu" and "Li Wa zhuan," noted collections include Pei Xing's 裴 鉶 *Chuanqi* 傳奇, Niu Sengru's 牛僧孺 (779–848) *Xuanguai lu* 玄怪錄 (Records of the Mysterious Anomalies), and Li Fuyan's 李復言 (775–833) *Xu Xuanguai lu* 續玄怪錄 (A Sequel to Records of the Mysterious Anomalies), etc.

In addition, some legends, or "biographies," come from the *zazhuan* 襍傳 (miscellaneous biographies) genre – unofficial biographies such as Liu Xiang's 劉向 (79–8 BCE) *Lienü zhuan* 列女傳 (Biographies of Exemplary Women), Huangfu Mi's 皇甫謐 (215–282) *Gaoshi zhuan* 高士傳 (Biographies of High-minded Gentlemen), Ge Hong's 葛洪 (280–340) *Shenxian zhuan* 神仙傳 (Biographies of Divine Immortals), and Huijiao's 慧皎 (497–554) *Gaoseng zhuan* 高僧傳 (Biographies of Eminent Monks).

The works included in this anthology are all written in classical Chinese. The only exception is Feng Menglong's 馮夢龍 (1574–1646) "Yu Boya Smashes His Zither in Gratitude to an Appreciative Friend" from his *Jingshi tongyan* 警世通言 (Stories to Caution the World), which is an example of short stories (*huaben* 話本) in vernacular Chinese and is much longer than the classical tales.[9] The reasons why I do not include more stories written in vernacular Chinese are as follows: (1) compared with the vernacular short stories that flourished after the Song 宋 (960–1279) and Yuan 元 (1260–1368) dynasties, the classical tales are much shorter and provide more information within the same parameters; and (2) this is purposely done because of my experience in teaching a course, "Chinese Culture through Fiction and Film." I have used the *Traditional Chinese Stories: Themes and Variants* (edited by Y. W. Ma and Joseph S. M. Lau) as the required textbook. The readings on one theme are over 40 large pages, which is too long for many students now. By selecting and translating the same stories in classical Chinese, I intend to reduce student workload in reading and give them more time to ponder on the readings.

IV.   Translation, Annotation, and Reading Guide

The legends and tales presented in this anthology are all translated by me, though some of them have been rendered and appeared in the publications of others as well as my own, such as the *Hidden and Visible Realms: Classical Chinese Tales of the Supernatural in Early Medieval China* (Columbia University Press, 2018) and the *Anthology of Tang and Song Tales* (World Scientific, 2020, co-edited with Victor Mair).

The reasons why I chose to retranslate those works that are already translated instead of including earlier translations by others are as follows: (1) to avoid copyright issues with other publishers; (2) many old translations use Wade-Giles romanization instead of pinyin; (3) in my translation, I tried to correct mistakes found in earlier translations; and (4) most important of all, by putting together such a collection, I hope to save instructors time and effort in finding and copying these stories from different books for their students. I have strived to render the stories literally and fluently, though it is always challenging to harmonize these two approaches to translation. In addition to the translations, detailed footnotes are provided on cultural and literary contexts, historical figures and events, as well as some important terms to help readers understand the stories. Furthermore, in order to help readers to better understand the overall topics, their places in Chinese culture, and their relationship with the stories included in their respective sections, at the beginning of each section and each topic I include a brief introduction and at the end I give further readings for more information.

Although this anthology is designed as a textbook or a complementary textbook for college students taking a Chinese culture class, its target audience also includes general readers. I hope all readers will find this book especially valuable as a companion to understanding traditional China and the Chinese people.

Zhenjun Zhang
Potsdam, New York
Oct 1, 2023

Notes

1 www.merriam-webster.com/dictionary/culture.
2 Cambridge English Dictionary: https://dictionary.cambridge.org/us/dictionary/english/culture.
3 American Sociological Association: www.asanet.org/topics/culture.
4 New World Encyclopedia: www.newworldencyclopedia.org/entry/Culture_of_China.
5 He Lin, "A New Discussion of the Five Relationships," *Strategies of a Warring State* 3 (1940), cited in He Huaihong, *Social Ethics in the Changing China: Moral Decay or Ethic Awaking?* (Washington, DC: Brookings Institution Press, 2015), p. 6.
6 The *Liezi*, attributed to Liezi who lived in the fifth century BCE, was most likely composed much later (approximately 300 CE).
7 See "Introduction" in Zhenjun Zhang, *Hidden and Visible Realms: Early Medieval Chinese Tales of the Supernatural and the Fantastic* (New York: Columbia University Press, 2018), pp. xxv–xxvi.
8 See "Introduction" in Victor Mair and Zhenjun Zhang, *Anthology of Tang and Song Tales: The Tang Song cuanqi ji of Lu Xun* (Singapore: World Scientific, 2020), pp. xvii–xxvi.
9 See Patrick Hannan, *The Chinese Vernacular Story* (Cambridge, MA: Harvard University Press, 1969).

Part I

Confucian Culture

Confucianism, established by Confucius 孔子 (ca. 551–479 BCE) and developed by Mencius 孟子 (372–289 BCE), Xunzi 荀子 (ca. 313–238 BCE), and other later philosophers, has long been considered the "conventional value system" in Chinese culture.

The most important Confucian texts include the Four Books: *The Analects [of Confucius]* (Lunyu 論語), *The Mencius* (Mengzi), *The Great Learning* (Daxue 大學), and *The Doctrine of the Golden Mean* (Zhongyong 中庸), as well as the Five Classics: *The Classic of Odes* (Shijing 詩經), *The Book of Documents* (Shangshu 尚書), *The Classic of Rites* (Liji 禮記), *The Classic of Changes* (Yijing 易經), and *The Spring and Autumn Annals* (Chunqiu 春秋), all of which are said to be compiled or revised by Confucius.

Since the royal house of the Western Han 西漢 (206 BCE–8 CE) accepted it as the ruling ideology, Confucianism has played the leading role in governing and regulating the society as well as shaping the ethics of the Chinese people. For this reason, Confucianism has almost become the substitute term of Chinese culture.

The Eastern Zhou 東周 period (770–256 BCE) was an era of turbulence. In order to regulate society, philosophers offered different remedies, such as the non-action approach by Daoists Laozi 老子 (fl. 6th BCE) and Zhuangzi 莊子 (ca. 369–286 BCE), universal love by Mozi 墨子 (c. 470–c. 391 BCE), and punishment and law by Legalists such as Shang Yang 商鞅 (ca. 390–338 BCE) and Han Fei 韓非 (ca. 280–233 BCE). Differing from the above schools, the ideal of Confucianism is maintaining a harmonious society similar to how it was in the Western Zhou period 西周 (ca. 1045–771 BCE); to achieve this goal, Confucius promoted the twin concepts of humanity (*ren* 仁) and propriety or ritual (*li* 禮), which are both ethical codes used to regulate people's behavior.

The concept of *ren* has been interpreted in English as "goodness," "humanity," "benevolence," and "love."

All these interpretations, however, share two notions: every human being has the capacity to possess *ren*, and *ren* manifests itself when a virtuous person treats others with humaneness. Confucians associated the humane individual with the *junzi*, or cultured gentleman, whose exemplary behaviour distinguishes him from the petty person (*xiaoren*; literally a "small person," like

DOI: 10.4324/9781003490821-1

a child). One could say that within the Confucian worldview, *ren* is *ren*: embodying the virtue of humaneness requires that one become an ethically mature human being.[1]

According to Confucius, *ren* is the most important moral quality a man must possess:

> If the gentleman forsakes benevolence, in what way can he make a name for himself?
> The gentleman never deserts benevolence, not even for as long as it takes to eat a meal.
> If he hurries and stumbles, one may be sure that it is in benevolence that he does so.[2]

The concept of *li* is often rendered "ritual," "proper conduct," or "propriety." As the *Encyclopedia Britannica* says,

> Originally *li* denoted court rites performed to sustain social and cosmic order. Confucians, however, reinterpreted it to mean formal social roles and institutions that, in their view, the ancients had abstracted from cosmic models to order communal life. From customary patterns, *li* came to mean conventional norms, yielding a new concept of an internalized code of civility that defined proper human conduct. It is this concept that is both celebrated throughout the early corpus of Confucian literature and codified in the Confucian classic called the *Liji* ("Record of Rites"). Transcending mere politeness or convention, *li* is central to Confucian human-centred religiousness. A derivative of natural order, *li* retains a cosmic role in its enchantment of human experience by harmonizing it with nature.[3]

Confucius believed that disorder in society is the result of people neglecting their social roles, and thus the best way to govern is to encourage everyone to fulfill their social roles. The need to enforce social roles gave birth to the conventional Confucian formula for social relations, the five relationships (*wulun* 五倫) derived from *ren* and *li*: the relationship between ruler and subject, father and son, husband and wife, older brother and younger brother, as well as friend and friend.

In the transmission of Confucian teachings and Confucianism's process of shaping the moral lives of Chinese people, the five human relations have played an important role by providing "the regulatory framework for the Chinese ethnicity."[4]

The legends and tales selected in this section are arranged under six categories: loyal subjects/vassals, filial sons, chaste wives, respectful brothers, trustworthy friends, and dutiful individuals. The last category is beyond the scope of the Five Confucian Relationships, but it represents important relationships between individuals and their families as well as society in Confucianism.

Notes

1 Encyclopedia Britannica: https://www.britannica.com/topic/ren.
2 D. C. Lau, trans., *The Analects* (London: Penguin Books, 1979), p. 72.
3 Encyclopedia Britannica: https://www.britannica.com/topic/li-Chinese-philosophy.
4 See He Huaihong, *Social Ethics in the Changing China: Moral Decay or Ethic Awaking* (Washington, DC: Brookings Institution Press, 2015), p. 6.

Further Readings

Hsu, Dau-Lin. "The Myth of the Five Human Relationships of Confucius." *Monumenta Serica* 29 (1970–1971): 27–37.
Hall, David I. and Roger T. Ames. *Thinking Through Confucius*. Albany, NY: State University of New York Press, 1987.
Nivison, David. *The Ways of Confucianism: Investigations of Chinese Philosophy*. Chicago, IL: Open Court, 1996.
Tu, Wei-Ming. "Probing the 'Three Bonds' and 'Five Relationships' in Confucianism." In Walter H. Slote and George A. de Vos, eds. *Confucianism and Family*. Albany, NY: State University of New York Press, 1998, pp. 121–36.

1 Loyal Subjects

The relationship between ruler and subject is the first of the five Confucian Relationships.

In early Confucian texts, mutual duty exists between ruler and subject. For instance, Confucius says in Chapter 3 of the *Analects*, "The ruler should employ the services of his subjects according to the rites. A subject should serve his ruler with loyalty" 君使臣以禮，臣事君以忠. *Mencius* defines the Five Constant Virtues (*wuchang* 五常) as "love between father and son, duty between ruler and subject, distinction between husband and wife, precedence between old over young, and faith between friends."[1] The "duty between ruler and subject" here seems also to be a mutual commitment.

During the Han dynasty, however, the Five Constant Virtues were directly combined with the Three Cardinal Guides (*sangang* 三綱). The Han Confucians said bluntly: The lord is the cardinal guide of subjects, the father is the cardinal guide of sons, and the husband is the cardinal guide of wives.[2] Thus the mutual duty between ruler and subject changed into just the subjects' obligation – loyalty to the ruler, reflecting the arbitrariness of the ruler under the monarchical system.

During the 2000-year history of imperial China, loyalty – to serve only one ruler and never betray him – has been the leading virtue among the four dominant virtues: loyalty, filiality, integrity, and righteousness or duty (*zhong xiao jie yi* 忠孝節義).

The ideal of most Chinese intellectuals during imperial China was to become the mentor of one's ruler and help him to rule. In order to correct mistakes or misbehavior of the ruler, a subject would offer admonishment at the risk of his own life. However, when the loyalty of a subject was not reciprocated, namely, when the effort to realize his ideal failed, the subject would unavoidably fall into a dilemma – one that all Confucian intellectuals had to face: give up his belief and ambition or give up his life.

Since the loyalty of a subject is seen more clearly under adverse circumstances, almost all of the well-known loyal subjects are tragic heroes, as is seen in the four historical stories next.

DOI: 10.4324/9781003490821-2

Boyi and Shuqi[3]

Both Boyi 伯夷 and Shuqi 叔齊 were sons of the Lord of Guzhu.[4] Their father intended to establish Shuqi, his youngest son, as the heir.

After his death, however, Shuqi tried to yield the throne to his elder brother Boyi.

Boyi refused, saying, "It was our father's order that you inherit the throne." So he fled the state.

Unwilling to be enthroned, Shuqi also fled.

Thus the people of the state enthroned the middle son.

At this point, Boyi and Shuqi heard that Jichang,[5] the Lord of the West (*xibo*), was good at looking after the elderly. They thought, "Why not go and follow him?"

Having arrived there, they found that the Lord of the West had died; his son, King Wu of Zhou 周 (r. 1046–1043 BCE), had taken up the ancestral tablet of his father, whom he honored with the posthumous title of King Wen (1152–1056 BCE),[6] and was marching east to attack the emperor of the Yin [Shang] 殷[商] dynasty (c. 1554–1045 BCE).

Boyi and Shuqi clutched the reins of King Wu's horse and reprimanded him, saying, "The mourning for your father is not yet completed and here you take up shield and spear – can this conduct be called filial? As a subject you seek to assassinate your sovereign – can this conduct be called humane?" The king's attendants wished to strike them down, but the king's counselor, the Grand Duke,[7] interposed, saying, "These are righteous men," and he sent them away unharmed.

After this, King Wu conquered and pacified the people of the Yin and the world honored the house of Zhou as its ruler. But Boyi and Shuqi were filled with outrage and considered it unrighteous to eat the grain of Zhou (c. 1045–221 BCE). They fled to Shouyang Mountain,[8] where they lived as recluses and gathered ferns to eat. At the point of starvation, they composed a song:

> We climb this western hill
> and pick its ferns;
> replacing violence with violence,
> he will not see his own fault.
> Emperors Shennong, Yü Shun, and Xia,[9]
> great men gone so long ago –
> whom shall we turn to now?
> Ah – let us be off,
> for our fate has run out!

They died of starvation on Shouyang Mountain. When we examine this song, do we find any rancor or not?

(Sima Qian 司馬遷 (145–86? BCE), *Shiji* 史記
[Records of the Historian], Chapter 61)

The Death of Bigan[10]

When Emperor Yi passed away, his son, Xin辛, ascended the throne. This was Emperor Xin. People under heaven all called him Zhow 紂.[11]

Emperor Zhow was inherently clever and quick-minded, with keen eyes and sharp hearing. His physical strength surpassed ordinary men, capable of fighting with ferocious beasts bare-handed. His wisdom was sufficient to reject all remonstrances, and his speech was good enough to conceal his faults. He was arrogant to his ministers due to his capabilities. He belittled all people under heaven because of his fame. He believed that all others were inferior to him.

Zhow indulged in drinking and excessive pleasure and was given to women. He pampered Daji and followed only what she would say.[12] Thus he ordered the musician Juan to make new licentious songs, the Northern Ward dances, and decadent music; he increased taxes to increase the funds needed to maintain the Deer Terrace[13] and to fill the grain stores in the Giant Bridge; he gathered dogs, horses, and rare items to fill his palaces; and he expanded his royal parks and terraces at the Sand Hill, placing more animals and birds inside. Neglecting the ghosts and spirits, Zhow gathered people to play at Shaqiu. He made a pool of wine and a forest of hanging meat, urging naked men and women to chase each other and drink alcohol all night long.

Popular discontent was seething, and some feudal lords betrayed Zhow. Thus Zhow increased the punishments, among which was branding-like torture. He made the Lord of the West, named Ji Chang, the Marquis of Jiu 九,[14] and the Marquis of E鄂 the Three Dukes. Marquis Jiu had a beautiful daughter, whom he gave to Zhow. Since the girl disliked licentiousness, Zhow became angry and killed her. The Marquis of Jiu was also chopped into meat sauce. The Marquis of E argued with Zhow stubbornly with fierce words, thus Zhow made him into dried meat. Hearing of this, the Lord of the West secretly sighed. This was heard by Hu, the Marquis of Chong 崇, who reported it to Zhow. Then Zhow imprisoned the Lord of the West at Youli.[15] The subjects of the Lord of the West, such as Hongyao, gathered beautiful girls, rare curios, and nice horses to send to Zhow as gifts, so Zhow released the Lord of the West. Having come out of the prison, the Lord of the West offered Zhow the land west of the Luo River to request abolition of the branding-like penalty. Zhow approved this and also granted him bows, arrows, axes, and tomahawks, enabling him to attack and become the Lord of the West.

Yet Zhow used Fei Zhong 費中 to run the state affairs. Fei Zhong was good at flattering and fond of profit, so the people of Yin were not close to him. Zhow then used Wu Lai, who was good at defaming and slandering. Because of him, the feudal lords became estranged even more. After returning, the Lord of the West secretly strove after virtue and practiced good deeds. Many of the feudal lords betrayed Zhow and went over and pledged allegiance to him. As the Lord of the West grew stronger, Zhow gradually lost his power and importance.

Prince Bigan remonstrated with Zhow, but he would not listen. Shang Rong was a worthy man loved by the commoners, but Zhow deposed him.

When the Lord of the West attacked the Ji State and destroyed it, King Zhow's vassal Zuyi 祖伊 blamed the Zhow State [under the Lord of the West]. In fear, he ran away and told Zhow this: "Heaven has already terminated the fate of our Yin [Shang]dynasty. Neither observations of the people nor divination through the big turtle showed good omens. It is not that the deceased kings do not help the descendants of Yin. Rather, it is Your Majesty who has been licentious and cruel, thereby seeking self-destruction. Therefore, Heaven abandoned us. Thus, everyone cannot eat and sleep peacefully, do not consider and understand Heaven's will, and do not follow the common law. Now, there is no one in our country who does not want you to die. They say: 'Why doesn't Heaven send down punishment? Why doesn't the person with the great mandate come?' Your Majesty, what can you do now?" King Zhow said, "Was I not born under the mandate of Heaven?"

Zuyi went back home, saying, "There is no way to remonstrate with Zhow."

After the death of the Lord of the West, King Wu of Zhou launched an eastward expedition. When he reached Mengjin,[16] the feudal lords who betrayed Yin and allied with Zhou were about 800. All of them said, "We can attack King Zhow now." King Wu of Zhou said, "You do not know the mandate of Heaven." So they withdrew.

King Zhow was endlessly licentious. The Viscount of Wei remonstrated with him several times,[17] but he would not listen. So the Viscount of Wei left with the Grand Tutor and the Lesser Tutor.

Bigan said with a deep sigh, "If one's lord has faults but one does not reprimand him, then he is not loyal; and if one does not say anything because of fear of death, he is not brave. In the case that the lord is at fault, one will reprimand him; if his remonstration is not accepted, then he dies. This is perfect loyalty." So he remonstrated with the king without leaving for three days.[18] King Zhow became angry, saying, "I heard that the sage's heart has seven holes." Then he cut open Bigan's chest to look at his heart.

Fear came upon the Viscount of Ji,[19] so he pretended to be mad and dressed as a slave. King Zhow imprisoned him again. Carrying the sacrificial vessels, the Grand Tutor and Lesser Tutor fled to the Zhou State. Thereupon, King Wu led the feudal lords to attack King Zhow. King Zhow also sent troops to resist at Muye.

On the day of Jiazi,[20] King Zhow's troops were defeated, and he ran into the palace, ascended the Deer Terrace, put on his precious jade-decorated clothes, and threw himself into a fire and died. King Wu of Zhou cut off King Zhow's head and hung it on the pole of a white flag, killed Daji, released the Viscount of Ji from jail, and rebuilt Bigan's tomb with full honors.

(From Sima Qian, *Shiji*, Chapter 3)

The Heir Apparent Shensheng

Consort Li 驪姬 slandered Shensheng, the Heir Apparent, to Duke Xian [of Jin 晉] (d. 651 BCE). Duke Xian was about to kill him.

Prince Chong'er said to Shensheng,[21] "He is not doing this because you are guilty. Why don't you offer an explanation? If you do, you would surely avoid the punishment."

Shensheng replied, "I should not. If I do, Consort Li would certainly be blamed. Our ruler is aged now. Without Consort Li, he would not be able to sleep at ease and any food would be tasteless to him. How could I allow our ruler to be filled with regret until his death?"

Chong'er said, "If you don't present explanation, you had better leave immediately."

Shensheng said, "I should not do that either! To avoid punishment by leaving the state is to disgrace our ruler. If I expose our father's fault and fawn on the feudal lords at the same time, who would allow me to enter their state? To be afflicted with the royal clan inside and be distressed with escaping outside, it would compound my misbehavior. I heard that a loyal vassal does not expose his ruler's faults, a wise man does not compound his misbehavior, and a brave man does not seek to escape from death. Thus, I will face the punishment with my body!"

Thereupon, he was killed by the sword.

Hearing of this, a gentleman said, "The heir apparent, this is your fate by Heaven."

The Classic of Odes reads:

A few elegant lines
May be made out to be shell-embroidery.
Those slanderers,
Have gone to great excess.[22]

(From Liu Xiang 劉向 (79–8 BCE), *Shuo yuan* 說苑 Chapter 4)

Qu Yuan: The Tragic Hero

Qu Yuan 屈原 (c. 340–278 BCE), who was named Ping, shared the same surname with the Chu 楚 royal house and served as the Left Assistant (*zuotu*) to King Huai 懷 of Chu (r. 229–299 BCE). He was known for his encyclopedic knowledge and amazingly good memory, insightful in the reasons for national stability and turmoil, and adept at speech. Entering the imperial court, he discussed state affairs with the king in order to issue orders; going out of it, he received guests and communicated with the feudal lords. The king trusted him very much.

Grand Master Shangguan 上官 held the same rank as Qu Yuan did in the court. Striving for the king's favor, he was jealous of Qu's ability. Once, King Huai of Chu assigned Qu Yuan to write up an edict. Before his draft was finalized, Shangguan saw it and wanted to take it away [to finalize]. Qu Yuan refused to give him the draft. Thus Shangguan slandered him to the king, saying, "Your Majesty assigned Qu Ping to write edicts. Everyone knew that when an edict had been issued, Ping would brag of his own merit, saying that nobody but he himself can do it." Enraged, the king alienated Qu Ping.

Qu Ping was grieved that the king was incapable of distinguishing between truth or lies of what he heard, that his perception could be so easily clouded by slander, that a petty evil man could harm justice, and honest and upright people could not be tolerated. Therefore, seized by grief and sorrow, he wrote "Lisao." "Lisao" means "encountering sorrow."

Heaven is the origin of mankind; parents are the root of people. When people are desperate, they will go back to their origin: when they are extremely tired and exhausted, they always call upon heaven; when they are ill or sorrowful, they always call their parents. Qu Ping was upright and he had exhausted his loyalty and wisdom in serving his lord; however, the slanderer sowed discord between him and the king. His situation can be said to be desperate. He was honest but was suspect, and he was loyal but was defamed. How could there be no resentment? Qu Yuan's writing "Lisao" was likely due to his grievances.

The poems in "Airs of the States" are lustful but not excessive; the poems in the "Lesser Elegntiae" express the feelings of resentment and sarcasm but not to provoke riots. As for the poem "Lisao," it can be said to possess the features of both. The earliest ruler it praises is Di Ku 帝嚳,[23] the most recent one is Duke Huan 桓 of Qi (r. 685–643 BCE),[24] and between them are King Tang 湯 of Shang (c. 1675–1646 BCE)[25] and King Wu 武 of Zhou (b.–1043 BCE). By praising them, it criticizes the current political affairs of Chu. The broadness and profoundness of ethics, as well as the reasons for stability and turmoil, are all manifested in detail. His writing is succinct, his words are subtle, his ambition is pure, and his behavior is upright. Although he describes the small and ordinary things, his purpose is extremely broad. Although he lists things that are close at hand, the significance of the expression is far-reaching. His ambition was pure, therefore he used fragrant grass and flowers as metaphors; his behavior was upright, thus he was not tolerated by the evil men even after his death. He freed himself from the dirty muddy water, getting rid of filthiness as if he had shelled, floating away from the worldly dust without being stained, and keeping clean as a lotus flower emerging from the mud. I assume that he deserves it if we liken the glory of his ambition to that of the Sun and the Moon.

After Qu Yuan was alienated, the State of Qin intended to attack Qi. Qi formed an alliance with Chu and kept a close relationship with Chu. Worried about this, King Hui 惠 of Qin (356–311 BCE) ordered Zhang Yi 張儀 (d. 309 BCE) to pretend to leave Qin and bring handsome gifts, as a token to serve Chu, saying, "Qin hates Qi very much, but Qi has allied with Chu. If Chu can truly break off ties with Qi, Qin is willing to offer Chu the six hundred *li* of land at Shang and Wu/Yu."

Coveting the land, Kung Huai of Chu therefore believed Zhang Yi. He broke off close relations with Qi and sent an envoy to Qin to accept the land that Zhang Yi had promised. Zhang Yi deceived the envoy of Chu, saying, "I had promised the King of Chu six *li*. I did not hear anything about six hundred *li*."

The envoy of Chu returned and told King Huai about this. Enraged, King Huai launched a punitive expedition against Qin. Qin sent troops to attack the Chu army and crushed them near the rivers of Dan and Xi.[26] They beheaded more than 80,000 Chu soldiers, captured the Chu general Qu Hong, and consequently seized the area of Hanzhong in Chu.[27]

King Huai of Chu sent all his soldiers deep into the territory of Qin to attack the Qin army and battled them at Lantian.[28] Hearing this news, the State of Wei launched a surprise attack against Chu, and their army reached Deng.[29] The Chu army was terrified, so they withdrew from Qin. Since the State of Qi was still unhappy with what Chu had done to them, they did not rescue Chu. Thus the State of Chu was in dire straits.

Next year, Qin wanted to make peace with Chu by ceding the Hanzhong region that they took in the battle. King Huai of Chu replied, "I do not want the land returned, but I will be content with getting Zhang Yi." Hearing this, Zhang Yi said, "It is worth it to replace the land of Hanzhong with one person; I request to go to Chu."

When Zhang Yi arrived in the State of Chu, he again bribed the powerful minister Jin Shang, and he also engaged in sophistry with Zheng Xiu, the favorite consort of King Huai. Surprisingly, King Huai listened to Zheng Xiu's words and released Zhang Yi in the end. At that time, Qu Yuan had been estranged and no longer served in court. After he returned from Qi as an envoy, he admonished King Huai by saying, "Why didn't you kill Zhang Yi?" In regret, King Huai sent soldiers after Zhang Yi, but it was too late.

After this, the feudal lords of all the states jointly attacked Chu, defeated the Chu army, and killed its general, Tang Mei 唐昧 (d. 301 BCE). At that time, King Zhao 昭 of Qin (r. 306–251 BCE) intended to make peace with Chu through marriage. He also wanted to meet King Huai of Chu. King Huai of Chu intended to go. Qu Ping said, "Qin is a state as fierce as tigers and wolves. It is not to be trusted, so it is better not to go." But King Huai's young son, Zilan 子蘭, persuaded King Huai to go, saying, "Why should we cut off a friendship with Qin?" In the end, King Huai went to Qin.

Upon entering Wuguan,[30] Qin troops in ambush blocked the retreat route of King Huai, then detained him, and forced him to cede land [to Qin]. King Huai became enraged. He refused the request and fled to the State of Zhao. But Zhao did not accept him.

He returned to Qin again and eventually died there. His body was later sent back to Chu for burial. His oldest son, Prince of Qingxiang 頃襄王 (r. 298–263 BCE), was enthroned. He appointed his younger brother, Zilan, as his prime minister, though the Chu people all blamed Zilan for persuading King Huai to go to Qin and never returning.

Qu Yuan hated Zi Lan. Although he was exiled, he still missed Chu, worried about King Huai, and never gave up the idea of returning. He hoped that the king would wake up and the customs of Chu would change. He wanted to protect his lord, rejuvenate the state, and reverse the situation in Chu. All these are expressed repeatedly in one writing. However, in the end, he could do nothing, not even return to his home state. This shows that King Huai of Chu never did wake up.

No matter if a monarch is stupid or smart, worthy or unworthy, he always wants to find loyal vassals to serve him and promotes talented people to assist him. However, the demise of a state and the ruin of a family have occurred one after another, and a state being regulated by a sage king was rarely seen from generation to generation. The reason is that the so-called loyal vassals were in fact unfaithful, and the so-called worthy subjects were in fact not worthy.

Since King Huai of Chu was unclear about the qualities and duties of loyal vassals, he was snarled by Zheng Xiu in the inner palace and deceived by Zhang Yi outside of it; he alienated Qu Ping and trusted the Grand Master Shangguan and the Prime Minister Zilan. As a result, his army was defeated, and land was ceded; he lost six commanderies, he himself died as a guest in Qin and was laughed at by all people in the world. This is a disaster caused by not knowing how to distinguish people.

The Classic of Changes says, "If nobody drinks the water after the digging of a well, it makes me sad because well water is for people to drink. If the king is clear-sighted, his subjects will benefit from him." If a king is not clear-sighted, how could people benefit from it?

Hearing that Qu Yuan hated him, the prime minister Zilan was enraged and asked Grand Master Shangguan to defame Qu Yuan in front of King Qingxiang. King Qingxiang was angry and banished Qu Yuan to a remote place.

Qu Yuan reached the coast of the river, roamed along the water while chanting poems, with his disheveled hair spreading over his shoulders. His appearance was wan and sallow and his figure skinny. When a fisherman saw him, he asked, "Aren't you the Grand Master of the Three Wards?[31] Why did you come here?"

Qu Yuan replied, "The whole world is muddy, only I myself is pure; everyone is intoxicated, but I'm the one who is sober. For this reason was I exiled."

The fisherman said, "A sage should not be attached to things; instead, he should move along with [the trend of] the world. If the whole world is turbid, why don't you follow the worldly flow and be jostled by the waves? If the people are all intoxicated, why don't you taste some dregs and drink some wine? Why do you keep your purity like you are holding on to jade, and thus cause yourself to be banished?"

Qu Yuan replied, "I heard that people who have just washed their heads must dust their hat, and people who have just bathed must shake their clothes. Who would willingly allow his clean body to be stained by the filthy thing? I would rather plunge into the constantly flowing river and bury my body into the belly of the river fish. How can I allow my snow-white purity to be stained by the worldly dirt?"

Thus he composed the rhapsody, "Embracing the Sand" (Huai sha), and threw himself into the Miluo River and died.

(Sima Qian, *Shiji*, Chapter 84)

Notes

1　D. C. Lau, trans., *Mencius* (London: Penguin Books, 1970), p. 102.

2　See Dong Zhongshu 董仲舒 (179–104 BCE), Chunqiu fanlu 春秋繁露, in *Shanghai guji chubanshe, Ershi'er zi* 二十二子 (Shanghai: Shanghai guji chubanshe, 1986), p. 797.

3　Both Boyi伯夷 and Shuqi叔齊 are famous recluses in the early history of China.

4　Guzhu 孤竹 was a state located near modern Lulong County in Hebei and Chaoyang County in Liaoning.

5　Jichang 姬昌 is the name of King Wen (1152–1056 BCE) of Western Zhou (c. 1045–771 BCE).

6　Both King Wen 文 and King Wu 武 are depicted as sage kings in Confucian classics.

7 Taigong [Grand-Duke] Jiang 姜太公 (c. 1156–1017 BCE), whose given name was Shang 尚 and courtesy name was 子牙, was a noted politician and strategist who assisted King Wu of Zhou in defeating the Shang troops and establishing the Western Zhou dynasty.

8 Shouyang 首陽 Mountain is located southwest of Yongji 永濟 city in Shanxi.

9 Shennong 神農 and Yü Shun 虞舜 are part of the legendary Three Sovereigns and Five Emperors; Xia refers to the Xia dynasty (founded by Yü 禹 before the Shang dynasty).

10 Biga n比干 (c. 1110–1047 BCE) was the uncle and a loyal vassal of King Zhow of Yin Shang殷商. He was known for his brave remonstration with King Zhow but in the end was killed by him.

11 The last and notorious king of Yin Shang, who is known for being licentious and brutal.

12 Daji 妲己 was the favorite consort of King Zhou. She is considered by historians as the one who ruined the Shang dynasty.

13 Lutai 鹿臺, or the "Deer Terrace," was located by the capital of Shang, Chaoge 朝歌, in modern Qi 淇 County in Henan.

14 Jiu hou 九侯 appears as Gui hou 鬼侯 in another version.

15 Youli 羑里 was located four kilometers north of modern Tangyin County in Henan.

16 Mengjin 盟津 is located in modern Mengjinin Henan.

17 Weizi 微子, or the "Viscount of Wei," was an older half brother of King Zhou and the founder of the State of Song 宋. For his biography, see Zhenjun Zhang, trans., *The Viscount of Wei and [the Prince of] Sung: Hereditary House 8*, in *The Grand Scribe's Records*, Vol. 5. 1. William H. Nienhauser, Jr. ed. (Bloomington: Indiana University Press, 2006), pp. 267–295.

18 Quoted from *Kuodizhi* 括地志 in *Shiji zhengyi* 史記正義.

19 Jizi 箕子, or the "Viscount of Ji," was the uncle of King Zhou.

20 The first day in the ancient Chinese calendar where heavenly stems are matched with earthly branches.

21 Chong'er 重耳 was the oldest younger brother of Shensheng 申生, though they were not born by the same mother. He fled from Jin for 19 years but later came back and became the ruler of the state; he was known as Duke Wen of Jin 晉文公 (671–628 BCE).

22 James Legge, trans., *The Chinese Classics IV: The She King or Book of Poetry* (Hong Kong: Hong Kong University Press, 1960), p. 346.

23 One of the Five [legendary] Emperors in the early history of China.

24 One of the five hegemons during the Spring and Autumn period (770–476 BCE).

25 The founder of Shang dynasty (c. 1554–1045 BCE).

26 The Dan 丹 River originates in northwest of Shangzhou city in Shaanxi 陝西 and flows southeast to Henan. The Xi 淅 River originates in South Lushi 盧氏 County and flows south into Dan River.

27 This is in the northwestern part of modern Hubei province.

28 A county with its seat west of modern Lantian 藍田 county in Shaanxi.

29 Around modern Dengzhou 鄧州 city in Henan.

30 Wuguan 武關 was the southern pass in the State of Qin.

31 San Lü dafu 三閭大夫: The Grand Master of the Three Wards, in charge of the affairs of the three villages where lived the three clans, Zhao 昭, Qu 屈, and Jing 景.

Further Readings

Higgins, Kathleen M. "Loyalty from a Confucian Perspective." *Nomos* 54 (Loyalty) (2013): 22–38.

2   Filial Sons

Father-son is the second relationship in the Five Confucian relationships. "The father is kind while the son is filial" (*fuci zixiao* 父慈子孝) is found in an early Confucian text (the "Li yun" chapter in *Liji* 禮記). After the Three Cardinal Guides theory was gradually developed and inserted into the five relations from the Warring States period to the Han dynasty, the love between father and son became unidirectional – son to father. *The Classic of Filial Piety* (*Xiaojing* 孝經), assembled around the third or second century BCE, is the most comprehensive interpretation of filial piety (*xiao*), and *The Twenty-four Filial Children* (*Ershisi xiao* 二十四孝), compiled by Guo Jujing 郭居敬 (ca. 1295–1321), is the most popular biographical work on the subject.

Filial piety is so important in Chinese culture that Qian Mu 錢穆 (1895–1990) even described Chinese culture as "the culture of filiality" (*xiao de wenhua* 孝的文化).[1] Donald Holzman also says in "The Place of Filial Piety in Ancient China," "Filial piety in China came to be seen as having absolute value and that the worship of one's parents (that is, one's creators) can be compared to the worship of God in the West."[2]

Generally speaking, as the most important virtue in Confucian culture, filial piety requires children, especially sons, to respect their parents, support them financially, take care of them in person – especially when they are ill and aged, bring glory to them by achieving success, help them avoid mistakes by offering advice, protect them when needed – even if they have behaved improperly, avenge them if they are wronged, bury them with a befitting funeral, show sufficient grief during the mourning period as well as offer them sacrifices after their death, and ensure continual sacrificial offerings by begetting heirs. Each of the stories in this section shows at least one of the aforementioned features.

Dong Yong Sells Himself to Bury His Father

Dong Yong 董永 of the Han dynasty (206 BCE–220) was a native of Qiansheng.[3] He lost his mother when he was a child and lived with his father. He worked very hard as a farmer in the fields. While going out, Yong would carry his father on a small cart and follow behind it on foot.

DOI: 10.4324/9781003490821-3

When his father died, Yong had no money to bury him. So he sold himself as a slave to pay the funeral expense. Knowing that he was virtuous, his master gave him ten thousand coins and allowed him to leave.

Having finished observing the three-year mourning, Yong wanted to go back to his master's home and work as a slave for his debt. On his way, he met a woman who said to him, "I want to be your wife." Thus, together with her, Yong went to his master's home.

"I gave the money to you as a gift," his master told him.

Yong replied, "Thanks to your kind help, I was able to bury my father. Though I am a humble man, I would certainly work diligently for you to repay your kindness."

His master asked, "What is your wife good at?"

"She is good at weaving," Yong replied.

"If you insist on repaying me," his master said, "then just ask your wife to weave me a hundred bolts of fine silk."

Thus Yong's wife started weaving silk for his master and finished within ten days.

When the woman walked out of the door, she said to Yong, "I am one of the weaving maids in heaven. Because of your sincerest filiality, the Emperor of Heaven ordered me to help you repay your debt."

Having said this, she flew into the air and disappeared.

(From Gan Bao 干寶 [fl. 335–349], *Soushen ji* 搜神記, Chapter 1)

The Filial Son Wu Meng[4]

Attendant Wu, whose name was Meng and style name was Shiyun, was a native of Shu (modern Sichuan). He was extremely filial by nature.

When he was a child, he once lay by his parents. It was summer, and there were numerous mosquitoes and gadflies. But he never drove them away with his fan. The boy who slept together with him became aware of this and asked him why. Wu Meng replied, "I am just afraid that when the mosquitos and gadflies leave me, they will sting my parents."

After his parents died, Wu Meng stayed by the side of their tomb for the length of the mourning period.

The rebels of Shu were violent and out of control. They burned down houses in the town and dug open tombs in the wild fields. Thus everyone fled.

Instead of fleeing, Wu Meng remained by the side of his parents' tomb, crying loudly in deep grief.

Moved by him, the rebels felt sorrow, so they didn't encroach upon him.

(From Tao Qian 陶潛 (365–427), *Soushen houji* 搜神後記, Chapter 2)

Wang Shiming Avenges His Father

The scholar Wang Shiming was a native of Wuyi.[5] His father, Wang Liang, was beaten to death by Wang Jun, one of his cousins in the same clan. Having brought a lawsuit against Jun, Shiming was distressed at exposing and damaging his father's corpse and thus withdrew the accusation. Adopting the proposal by the respectable ones in the clan, his cousin Jun made an apology by offering Shiming a few acres of land. Shiming accepted it, but each year he would secure an amount of money the land was worth with a record and hide it somewhere. Nobody knew this. When his rival came with kindness, he would respond with kindness, merely for the sake of courtesy.

Not long afterward, Shiming secretly cast a sword. He engraved the word "revenge" on the sword and often wore it. He portrayed his father and a man wearing a sword by his side. When someone asked him why, he said, "In ancient times, nobody failed to wear a sword while going out."

Four or five years later, he obtained the title of *Youpan* 游泮 by passing the local civil service *keju* examination and also had a son. Then he told his wife, Yu, saying, "Patting this bawling baby, the ancestors of the Wang clan will not be hungry in the netherworld. The reason I have waited until this moment is that there is a need. Today is definitely the day of death [for my enemy]. Having a mother above and an infant below, you are the most valuable one in this family."

Holding a sword, he walked out of home and cut off his enemy's head at the foot of Mount Butterfly. Then he returned home and knelt down in front of his mother, saying, "Your son is dying to avenge his father, he will not be able to take care of you anymore." He took out all the money he secured and the sword, and with them he went to the county authority to request a death penalty.

On that day, all the commoners of the town felt angry. Distressed at his actions, Magistrate Chen asked him to get in an empty room, so he could inform various high-ranking officials. The high-ranking officials sent him to the Magistrate Wang of Jinhua to be judged.

Hearing of the details of his case, Wang Junlian felt more wounded, saying, "According to the law, we have to examine your father's corpse. The more serious the wound is, the lighter is his son's crime." Presumably he was trying to save his life.

The young man said, "At the beginning, it was only because I could not bear to expose and damage my father's corpse that I chose to die; otherwise, my enemy would have already died. How could one abandon his original will after committing a mortal sin to fulfill that will? How stupid that would be! I should have committed suicide. By coming to the court, I just wanted to receive punishment and that is all. But I still worry about my mother, so I will return briefly to bid her farewell."

Magistrate Wang allowed him to leave, but followed him, intending to still enforce the law as he had proposed. Shiming's friends and the several hundred scholars of the two towns all urged him, saying, "You must accept the proposal!" Yet the scholar had stopped eating. He struck the stairs with his head and died. Both of the magistrates shed tears for him, and the scholars all cried loudly.

When the scholar hid his hatred in laughing yet pledged to die, none but Yu knew it. She said to him, "If you can be a filial son, I will be able to be a chaste woman." The scholar said, "How could chastity be spoken of so easily?" The woman said, "Why cannot a woman behave like a man?" The scholar said, "I have entrusted you with my mother and son. How could you die?" She said, "I can endure it for three years. After that, none can stop me."

Three years later, his wife indeed went on a hunger strike and died.

Previously, his family intended to put the scholar's coffin in a grave, but his wife did not allow them to do so. Now they pushed out the two coffins and buried them together. When Mr. Ma reported this to the court, the court conferred imperial honor "Filial and Unyielding" upon their family.

Nobody but Yu knew the secret, indicating that she must be the one who can keep a secret. Yu was aware but did not stop her husband, meaning that she understood the grand righteousness instead of being cumbered by her feelings. The husband tolerated things for five years and then died for filiality, and the wife endured for three years and then died for chastity. How amazing!

(From Feng Menglong 馮夢龍 (1574–1646), *Qingshi* 情史, Chapter 1)

A Filial Son

In the eastern part of the Qingzhou[6] prefecture was a village at the foot of Xiang-shan Mountain.[7] There lived a man named Zhou Shunting, who served his mother with extreme filiality. Once, a big sore emerged on his mother's thigh. The pain was unbearable, causing her to frown and moan day and night. So preoccupied with scrubbing her skin and applying ointment, Zhou Shunting even forgot to eat and sleep. However, several months later, she still did not recover. Zhou Shunting worried and suffered but found no means to deal with it.

One night, he dreamed of his father who told him this, "The cure to your mother's illness all depends on your filial love. This sore cannot be cured unless it is smeared with human flesh ointment. Otherwise you worry and are grieved in vain."

After waking, he felt strange. Then he got up, cut off the flesh from his ribs under the armpit with a sharp knife. The flesh dropped off, but he did not feel much pain. He immediately wrapped his waist with a piece of cloth, and no blood poured out. Thus he boiled the meat, held the ointment, and smeared it onto the sore. The pain suddenly stopped.

His mother was delighted and asked, "What medicine it is? Why it is so effective?"

Zhou Shunting didn't tell her the truth. But his mother's sore was healed very soon.

Zhou always covered his wound with something. Even his wife did not know it. When the wound was healed, there was a huge scar as big as a palm. Upon inquiring him repeatedly, his wife learned the details of the story.

Commentary: Cutting flesh from one's thigh to cure illness is a kind of self-mutilation, and a gentleman would not value it. But how could commoners know that it is considered unfilial [because one's hair and flesh are given by one's parents]? What they have done is something they cannot help but do and that is all. Since there is such a man (Zhou Shunting), I know filial sons truly exist in this world.

(From Pu Songling 蒲松齡(1640–1715),
Liaozhai zhiyi 聊齋志異, Chapter 5)

Notes

1 See Liang Shuming 梁漱溟, *Zhongguo wenhua yaoyi* 中國文化要義 (Hong Kong: San-lian Shudian, 1987), pp. 20–21.
2 *Journal of the American Oriental Society* 118, no. 2 (1998): 185.
3 Qiansheng 千乘 was a county with its seat was in modern Gaoqing County in Shandong province.
4 Wu Meng 吳猛, a native of Fenning (modern Puyang in Henan) and a noted Daoist magician of the Jin 晉 (265–420), also known as one of the 24 filial sons.
5 Wuyi 武義 County is part of modern Jinhua city in Zhejiang.
6 A prefecture of the Qing dynasty (1644–1911). Its seat was in modern Qingzhou 青州city, under the administration of Weifang city, in Shandong.
7 22 kilometers east of modern Qingzhou city in Shandong.

Further Readings

Holzman, Donald. "The Place of Filial Piety in Ancient China." *Journal of the American Oriental Society* 118 (2) (Apr. – Jun., 1998): 185–99.
Knapp, Keith. *Selfless Offspring: Filial Children and Social Order in Medieval China.* Honolulu, HI: University of Hawai'i Press, 2005.

3 Chaste Wives

The husband-wife relationship is the third of the Five Confucian Relationships. The idea regarding the relationship between husband and wife is articulated artfully and naturally in the Chinese classics. The *Classic of Changes* says,

> Only after there were Heaven and Earth were there the myriad things. Only after there were the myriad things, were there male and female. Only after there were male and female were there husband and wife. Only after there were husband and wife were there father and child. Only after there were father and child were there sovereign and minister. Only after there were sovereign and minister were there superiors and subordinates. Only after there were superiors and subordinates did propriety and righteousness have a medium in which to operate.[1]

It appears so natural and harmonious that Heaven gives birth to the myriad things, the myriad things give birth to men and women, husband and wife, father and son, lord and subject, etc. But precisely through this kind of "natural" deduction, man and woman are likened to father and son and lord and subject, and the equal relationship between man and woman or husband and wife became instead the relationship between lord and subject or superior and inferior.

Although early Confucian texts (such as the "Liyun" chapter of *Liji*) mention a "distinction between husband and wife" (*fu youbie* 夫婦有別) and that a "husband is dutiful while wife is obedient" (*fuyi futing* 夫義婦聽),[2] the point from the *Classic of Changes* is echoed by two sentences found in the "Mourning Apparel" (*sangfu*) chapter of *Ceremonial Etiquette* (*Yili*): "The father is Heaven of the son, and the husband is Heaven of the wife."[3] The "Loyalty and Filiality" (*zhongxiao* 忠孝) chapter of *Hanfei zi*, too, addresses only the duty of the wife, "Subject serves ruler, son serves father, and wife serves husband" 臣事君，子事父，妻事夫,[4] signaling the Han dynasty interpretation – "The husband is the cardinal guide of the wife."

How should a wife serve her husband? Of the numerous instructions, including the noted "Three Obediences" (*san cong* 三从) and "Four Virtues" (*si de* 四德),[5] the most essential one is found in the "Hexagram 32: Heng (Perseverance)" of the *Classic of Changes*, "For the woman to practice constancy here means good

DOI: 10.4324/9781003490821-4

fortune, for to the end she should only follow one man."[6] *Liji* also says that "a woman would never marry two men" (一女不更二夫). In Liu Xiang's (79–8 BCE) *Biographies of Exemplary Women* (*Lienü zhuan*), the chapters of "The Chaste and Compliant" (*zhenshun* 貞順) and "The Principled and Righteous" (*jieyi* 節義) best represent the development of the concept of chastity in the Han dynasty. Since the Song dynasty (960–1279), along with the rise of Neo Confucianism, the concept of chastity was greatly enhanced. Cheng Yi 程颐 (1033–1107) insisted that "being starved to death is a trivial matter while losing chastity is a big one" (餓死事極小, 失節事極大). This became the most important rule for women, lasting for nearly 1,000 years.

The following stories are about exemplary chaste women of traditional China.

Lofty-Conduct, the Liang State Widow

Lofty-Conduct[7] was a widow in the State of Liang.[8] She was beautiful, and her conduct was renowned. When her husband died young, she became a widow and determined not to remarry. The nobles of Liang all desired to take her as a wife, yet none could have her.

Hearing of this, the King of Liang sent his prime minister to send her betrothal gifts.

Lofty-Conduct said, "Unfortunately, my husband died young and filled the ditch before the dogs and horses. It is fitting for me to offer my body to his coffin, yet in order to protect and nurture his young orphan, I could not be single-minded. Many nobles proposed to me, luckily all were avoided. Now Your Majesty proposes again. I heard that 'the righteousness of a woman means once she goes she can never make a change, thereby keeping the integrity of chastity and trust.' Now, avoiding death for life is not trustworthy, forgetting the humble after seeing the noble is against integrity, and abandoning righteousness in order to seek profit is not the way to be a human."

Thus, holding a mirror, she cut off her nose with a knife, saying, "I have been mutilated now. I did not commit suicide because I cannot bear to let the young orphan live without both parents. The reason why Your Majesty proposed to marry me was because of my beauty. Now I have become disfigured, I suppose you may let me go."

The prime minister reported this event to the king. The king praised her righteousness, highly valued her conduct, restored her position, and granted to her a title, Lofty-Conduct.

The gentleman said that Lofty-Conduct had dedicated herself to the principle of chastity. The *Book of Odes* says, "If you do not believe my words, I swear my heart is like the bright sun."[9] It is referring to this.

The hymn reads, "Staying in Liang, Lofty-Conduct dedicated herself to chastity. Seeking never to honor her own conduct, she endeavored to achieve trust. To refuse the betrothal gifts of Liang, she mutilated her own nose. Speaking highly of her, the gentleman shows her story to later generations."

(From Liu Xiang, *Lienü zhuan* 列女傳, Chapter 4)

Lady Xuan

Lady Xuan was the wife of Zhang Shutian of Jiading [County].[10] Her husband had long been wild and eccentric and was not getting along well with Lady Xuan. When her husband was ill, she served him from morning to night. When he died, she pledged to be buried alive with him.

At that time one of Shutian's friends also died. So his wife, Sun, and Lady Xuan agreed to die together. Each of them procured a foot of silk.

After Sun hanged herself, someone dissuaded Xuan, "She and her husband loved each other, and therefore she repaid her husband with death. Why should you imitate her?"

Xuan sighed, saying, "I just know how to fulfill the duty of a woman and that is all. Why should I mind whether my husband was virtuous or not?"

She then hanged herself.

(From Zhang Tingyu 張挺玉 (1672–1755), *Ming Shi* 明史, Chapter 301)

Lady Guo of Tiantai

Lady Guo, a native of Tiantai,[11] married a certain soldier. She was extremely beautiful and thus was coveted by Battalion Commander Li. While the soldier was away on guard duty, Li went to the soldier's home daily, assailing her with obscenities in various ways. But Lady Guo resolutely remained inviolate. When her husband returned home, she told him everything.

One day, when Li was passing by his home, the soldier thought of the previous event and betrayed his anger. Holding a dagger, he dashed out of his home. But Li had already fled. He then launched a lawsuit against the soldier in the county court.

The case was concluded that, for brandishing a knife to kill an official in the same army, his crime deserved the death penalty. He was imprisoned. Lady Guo personally delivered meals to him, and by weaving at home, she paid for his clothing and food.

This lasted for quite some time, during which the prison warden Ye grew fond of Lady Guo. So he took good care of the soldier with food and drink every day, as if they were brothers. The soldier was extremely grateful to him.

Once there was a rumor, saying that an official from the Five Chief Military Commissions had arrived, likely to execute the imprisoned criminal. Ye told the soldier, and the soldier said to Lady Guo, "I will die soon. Prison Warden Ye does not have a wife. You can marry him."

Lady Guo replied, "Your death is caused by my beauty. How can I remarry in order to keep my life?"

Returning home, she held her two young children and wept in grief, bewailing, "Your father is going to die, and your mother is also going to die soon. With nobody to rely on, my children will die of hunger and freeze to death in the end. Now I will sell you to keep you alive. When you live in the home of others, it is not the same as with your parents. You should not still behave as over-pampered children."

Her son and daughter were fairly intelligent, so they understood her mother's intention. Embracing their mother, they cried loudly and were reluctant to release her by clutching her lapels.

Consequently, carrying her two children, she walked out of her home and sought for people to entrust her children. Travelers all shed tears for them.

Pitying her, a rich man accepted her son and daughter and gave her 30 strings of coins. Lady Guo purchased wine and meat dishes with half of the cash and carried them to the gate of the prison, hoping to see her husband once more. Ye let her in.

Choking with sobs, Lady Guo could say nothing. Later, she said to her husband, "You troubled Prison Ward Ye so much, now you can repay him a bit with these dishes and wine. There is still some money here that you can keep for yourself. I will go to work in a wealthy family, so I'm afraid I cannot see you for around ten days." Then she bid him farewell, weeping.

Lady Guo reached the Ferry of Immortals, seated with her back straight in the water, and died. The torrent in the river was violent, but she had not fallen. Someone witnessed this and reported it to the county government. The officials of the county went there to verify the fact. All of them were startled and terrified. They got a coffin, buried her, and conferred an honor to her tomb, which read, "Chaste and unyielding."

Hearing about this, Pacification Commissioner Lian traced back why the soldier tried to kill the military official and released him. Then the wealthy family sent his son and daughter back to him. The soldier also pledged that he would never take a wife again.

(Feng Menglong, Qingshi, Chapter 1)

The Tale of Li Miaohui

Li Miaohui, a girl of Yangzhou, married Mr. Lu, a "Recommended Man"[12] from the same town. After failing the imperial examination, Lu made a firm resolution. He dedicated himself to study in a Buddhist monastery in the west mountain, cut off his connections with the outside world, and ceased communication with his family for a long time.

During the twelfth year of Chenghua reign (1465–1487), a man with the same name died at the capital. Lu's townsmen erroneously passed on the news that he had died, and his parents believed that it was true.

Not long afterward, there was a famine. The families north of Weiyang[13] could hardly support themselves. Sympathizing with Li for being widowed and poor, Lu's parents urged her to remarry, yet she would not listen.

Hearing of her beauty and virtue, Xie Qi, the son of a salt merchant of Linchuan also called Xie Nengbo, proposed marriage by sending betrothal gifts to her family. Li tried to commit suicide several times. Her parents-in-law were beside themselves.

At that time, Li's father was disciplining local schools in another commandery. Her mother, together with a neighboring old lady, persuaded her attentively and were always on guard. Li wept sadly day and night. Those who heard her crying all shed tears for her. Knowing that there was no other solution, she reluctantly resigned herself. She sent a letter to bid her father farewell, in which the words were extremely sorrowful.

After being married off to the Xie family, her will to resist became even stronger. Xie's stepmother was also a native of Yangzhou and had certain connections with Li. Li knelt down in front of her to request to be her life-long servant. Li insisted on serving by the side of her mother-in-law without leaving for a moment. Xie had many maids and concubines, so he did not force Li to sleep with him.

After living in Xie's home for several days, Li earnestly requested to become a Buddhist nun. Her mother-in-law only responded with "Yes." Xie thought that if they moved back to his hometown, Li would not be able to go back to Yangzhou. Thus he set forth in a boat himself, with his mother and Li in tow.

When they arrived at Jingkou,[14] they moored their boats at the Mount Jinshan Monastery. Li's mother-in-law brought her to the monastery to express gratitude for her new marriage. In the Buddhist abbot's room there were brushes and ink-stones. Li grabbed a brush and wrote on the wall:

Since the year when husband and wife were separated,
No message has been received from each other.
I won't be the wife of this official until I die,
In the underworld I would still follow the man who plucked
    osmanthus flowers.
In the morning mist I dream of returning home,
Night rain on the Xiao and Xiang Rivers broke my heart.
A new verse is written at Jinshan Monastery,
Listing sails, I pass Yuzhang Commandery.[15]

Underneath the poem she wrote: by Lady Li, the wife of Mr. Lu from Yangzhou.

Later, Lu ascended the top list in the court imperial examination. When the good news reached Yangzhou, his parents realized that their son was still alive. Yet it was too late.

During the first year of Hongzhi reign (1488–1505), the court initiated the compilation of the *Records of Xianzong Reign* (1465–1487) and sent Du Zikai, the advanced scholar of Gusu,[16] to gather materials. Since Du did not report back to the court, Lu was sent to hasten him. When Lu passed by his home, he knew that his wife had already remarried. Afraid to hurt his parents, he dared not say anything, yet he also could not bear another marriage proposal, so he left.

When Lu left Zhenjiang and climbed up to Mount Jinshan, he saw the poem on the wall of the monastery and was choked with anger. He inquired with the monks, the reply was, "Previously when a woman with her mother-in-law passed here, she wrote the poem on the wall and left." Lu copied the poem and left.

Having reached the area west of the Yangzi River, Lu secretly plotted with Xu Fangbo. Fangbo said, "The boats here number more than a thousand. Which one should you follow to search? Even if you finally find her by looking on all the boats, it would still be a disgrace. Why don't you find her with a better strategy?"

Thus, they chose the smartest servant, told him the circumstances, and asked him to recite the poem thoroughly while riding on a small boat, passing through the salt boats while singing the song.

Three days later, the servant suddenly heard the voice of a woman, who opened the window of a boat and asked loudly, "Where did you get this poem?"

The servant approached her to pass on the message from his master.

Li was surprised, saying, "Mr. Yang, the Recommended Man Lu of Yangzhou died long ago. You are deceiving me!"

The servant told her what he was told from beginning to end. When she asked for the names of Lu's parents and wife, the servant responded exactly the same.

Covering her face with her sleeves, Li wept, saying, "Lu is my husband! I was suspicious when I first heard your song, yet it was a shame that I did not find an opportunity to ask you. By chance today the merchant went to a brothel and his mother also has gone to a neighboring boat, therefore I was able to ask you. After returning, please try your best to speak on behalf of me."

Thereupon she secretly made an appointment with him, waving her arm while saying, "Go, go!"

The servant returned and reported this to Lu. The very same night, a boat arrived on time as expected. Li was taken to Lu's residence, and they were reunited and as happy as before their separation.

When the merchant was about to go out, he entrusted his money to his mother, and his mother entrusted it to Li. When the merchant returned, he examined his money and found that it was all secured and recorded in proper order. He sighed, saying, "In the past, when Guan Yu fled back to Han, Lord Cao did not run after him; rather he said, 'Each serves his own master.' Li's leaving is also for her husband. She is a chaste woman. Just let her go."

This happened during the second year of Hongzhi reign (1488–1505).

Although he had determined to dedicate to study, Lu should not have to cut off communication with his family; his parents should have spent some time to inquire about their son's whereabouts instead of marrying his wife off so hurriedly; and there are numerous beauties in the world, thus the son of the businessman did not have to take the scholar's wife as his concubine. Relying solely on Lady Li's unswerving loyalty to her husband, a charming tale is created.

(Feng Menglong, *Qingshi*, Chapter 1)

Notes

1 Richard John Lynn, trans., *The Classic of Changes: A New Translation of the I Ching as Interpreted by Wang Bi* (New York: Columbia University Press, 1994), p. 106.

2 D. C. Lau, trans., *Mencius* (London: Penguin Books, 1970), p. 102.

3 *Yili zhushu,* in Ruan Yuan (1764–1849), ed., *Shisanjing zhushu* (Beijing: Zhonmghua shuju, 1980), p. 1106.

4 Chen Qiyou 陳奇猷, ed., *Hanfeizi jishi* 韓非子集釋, Vol. 1 (Daibei: He Luo tushu chubanshe, 1974), pp. 107–108.

5 The "Three obediences" include: "To obey her father before marriage, obey her husband after marriage, and obey her sons after her husband dies." The "Four Virtues" include womanly virtue (obedience and chastity), womanly words (appropriateness), womanly bearing (cleanness), and womanly work (diligence).

6 "Commentary on the Images:" *Furen zhenjie, congyi er zhong ye* 妇人贞吉，从一而终也. See "Hexagram 32: Heng恒 (Perseverance)," Richard John Lynn, trans., *The*

Classic of Changes: *A New Translation of the Yijing as Interpreted by Wang Bi*, Vol. 32 (New York: Columbia University Press, 1994), p. 339.

7 This is a translation of her title *gaoxing* 高行.
8 Liang 梁 was one of the states during the Spring and Autumn period located around the Longxi area of modern Gansu and was conquered by Duke Mu of Qin 秦穆公 (683?–621 BCE) in 641 BCE.
9 "Da ju" 大車 of Wangfeng 王風 in *Shijing* 詩經 (Book of Odds): "謂予不信，猶如曒日."
10 Modern Jiading 嘉定 district of Shanghai.
11 Moden Taitai 天臺 county in Zhejiang.
12 The original Chinese term is *juren* 舉人 and refers to those men who passed the imperial examination at the provincial level.
13 Another name of Yangzhou.
14 Jingkou 京口, modern Zhenjiang in Jiangsu.
15 Modern Nanchang in Jiangxi.
16 Gusu 姑蘇, old name of Suzhou.

Further Readings

Ebrey, Patricia B. "Women, Marriage, and Family in Chinese History." In Paul S. Ropp, ed. *Heritage of China: Contemporary Perspectives on Chinese Civilization*. Berkeley, CA: University of California Press, 1990, pp. 197–223.
Kinney, Anne Behnke. *Exemplary Women of Early China: The Lienü Zhuan of Liu Xiang*. New York, NY: Columbia University Press, 2014.
T'ien, Ju-k'ang. *Male Anxiety and Female Chastity: A Comparative Study of Chinese Ethical Value in Ming-Ch'ing Times*. Leiden: Brill, 1988.

4 Respectful Brothers

Older brother-younger brother is the fourth relation in the Five Confucian Relationships. The "Liyun" chapter of *Liji* mentions "the older brother should be kind while the younger brother should be respectful" (*xiongliang diti*兄良弟悌). The third year of Duke Yin in *Zuo zhuan* also says, "The older brother should love [the younger brother] and the younger brother should respect [the older brother]" (*xiong'ai dijing*兄愛弟敬). But in later times the duty of the younger brother was highlighted while that of the older brother was neglected. This was probably related to one of the Five Constants, the idea of "precedence of old over young" in *Mencius*.

The four stories here are all about love between brothers. We can see not only the respect of younger brothers for their older brothers, which is promoted in Confucian teachings, but also the love of older brothers for their younger brothers, the idea highlighted in earlier Confucian classics and historical texts.

Filial Zhao Saves His Brother

Filial Zhao, whose style name was Changping, was a native of Qi County in the State of Pei 沛.[1] During the reign of Wang Mang (r. 9–23), his father, Zhao Pu, was the General of Field and Crop, and Filial Zhao himself was appointed as a Court Gentleman Attendant. Whenever he was on leave and returned home, he would wear white, shoulder his luggage, and travel on foot.

Once, while returning home from Chang'an, Filial Zhao intended to stay the night at an official inn. The innkeeper heard that Filial Zhao would pass by. Anticipating the noble as a guest, he swept the yard, sprinkled it with water, and waited for Filial Zhao. When Filial Zhao arrived, he didn't mention his name. Reluctant to accept him, the innkeeper asked, "I heard that the son of the General of Fields and Crops will come from Chang'an, when will he arrive?" Filial Zhao replied, "He will arrive soon." Then he left.

When the world was in chaos, people ate each other. Filial Zhao's younger brother, Zhao Li, was caught by famished rebels. Hearing of this, Filial Zhao had himself tied up and went to the rebels, saying, "Li, my brother, has long been starved and thus is emaciated and thin, not as fat as me."

DOI: 10.4324/9781003490821-5

Astonished, the rebels released both his younger brother and himself, saying, "You can return home for the time being, but bring some rice or grain back." Filial Zhao sought rice and grain but could obtain neither. So he returned to the rebels and was willing to be boiled.

Considering him a wonder, the rebels did not harm him. His fellow villagers were all impressed by his righteousness.

(Fan Ye 范曄 (398–445) and Sima Biao 司馬彪 (?-306),

Hou Hanshu 後漢書, Chapter 39)

Brothers Wang

During the Taiyuan era (376–396), a Daoist master came from afar, but nobody knew where exactly he was from. He said, "When one's life should end, but a living person is willing to die in one's stead, then one can continue living. If one coerces another to die on his or her stead, it works for only a short while." When people heard this, all dismissed his words as false and absurd.

The two Wang brothers, Ziyou (d. 388) and Zijing (344–388), lived in great harmony.[2] When Zijing became terminally ill, Ziyou told the Daoist master, "My abilities are not as good as my younger brother's, so [the promotion of] my position is blocked. Please exchange my lifespan with my younger brother's."

The master replied, "The case in which a living person may replace the dying one is only if the living person's lifespan still has time left, so that the time can be added to the lifespan of the dead. Yet now when your worthy younger brother's life will come to an end, your lifespan will be exhausted as well. Then, what are you going to use to add to his lifespan?"

Ziyou previously had a carbuncle on his back. After Zijing became terminally ill, they were forbidden to visit each other. When Ziyou heard that his brother had passed away, he stroked his heart with his arms in deep sorrow. Thereupon the carbuncle on his back burst and broke, and he died without uttering a single sound.

Thinking over the words of the Daoist master, they seem convincing and grounded.

(From Liu Yiqing 劉義慶(403–444), *Youming lu*幽明錄)

A Villager Hacks a Python to Save His Brother

In order to harvest wood, the Hu brothers from Hutian Village walked into a deep valley, where they encountered a giant python. Being in the lead, the older brother was swallowed by the python.

Terrified, the younger brother intended to flee at first. Seeing that his brother was being swallowed, he became angry and hacked the head of the python with his ax.

Although its head was wounded, the python did not stop swallowing. Luckily, however, the older brother's shoulders were still exposed outside of the python's mouth, though his head had been sucked into it.

Not knowing what to do, the younger brother held the two feet of his older brother and vied with the python. Unexpectedly, he pulled his brother out of its mouth. Writhing in pain, the python fled.

Looking at his older brother, he found that both his nose and ears had melted, and only a weak breath escaped in his nose. Shouldering his older brother, the younger brother walked back home. He took more than ten rests on his way before arriving at home.

The older brother healed after six months of good care and treatment with medicine, but his face was still covered by scars and only has holes left in the places of his nose and ears.

Alas! Among the villagers there is such a younger brother who loved his older brother so much! Someone said, "The python did not harm him because it was moved by his morality." It is so true!

(From Pu Songling, Liaozhai zhiyi, Chapter 1)

Zhang Cheng and His Older Brother

Mr. Zhang of Yu was a descendant of Qi.[3] At the end of the Ming dynasty (1368–1644), warfare erupted in Qi, and Zhang's wife was seized and taken away by the Qing troops. Zhang frequently visited Yu and eventually settled down there. He married at Yu and begot a son named Na. Later his wife died, so he took another wife and begot a son named Cheng.

His new wife, Lady Niu, was ferocious and always hated Zhang Na. She treated him as a slave and fed him the worst food but forced him to cut two bundles of firewood every day. If he failed to fulfill the duty, he would be cursed at and beaten with a stick, living an unbearable life. On the contrary, Lady Niu often stealthily gave Zhang Cheng tasty food and also let him study with a private tutor.

As Zhang Cheng grew up, he was filial to his parents and respectful to his older brother. Seeing his brother overworked, he couldn't bear it and thus privately persuaded his mother to treat his brother with more kindness. But his mother would not listen.

One day, Zhang Na entered the mountain to cut firewood again. Before he finished his work, a storm came. He took shelter under a huge stone. After the rain stopped, it was dusk. He was famished as he returned home with the firewood on his shoulder. Seeing that the firewood was less than usual, Lady Niu became angry and refused to give him food to eat. Extremely hungry, Zhang Na went to his room and lied down stiff on his bed.

When Zhang Cheng returned from the private school and saw that his brother was depressed, he asked him, "Are you sick?"

The reply was, "Just hungry."

Zhang Cheng asked the reason. Zhang Na told him everything. Zhang Cheng felt very sad and soon left.

Quite a while later, he came back with pancakes hidden in his shirt for his older brother. His brother asked him where he got them. He said, "I secretly took the flour and asked a neighbor woman to cook them. Just eat them, but don't tell anyone."

Zhang Na ate the pancakes and told his brother, "Don't do it again in the future. When your mother discovers this, you will be in trouble. Moreover, I will not die of starvation if I eat one meal a day." Zhang Cheng said, "You are not physically strong, how can you cut that much firewood?"

After breakfast the next day, Zhang Cheng secretly entered the mountain and reached the place where his brother was cutting firewood. Seeing him, his older brother was startled, saying, "Who asked you to come here?" The reply was, "I came myself." His older brother said, "You are not yet able to cut firewood. Even if you are able to, still you are not allowed to do it." Then he urged him to return quickly. Ignoring him, Zhang Cheng broke firewood with his hands and feet to help his brother. He said further, "Tomorrow I'll bring an ax." His older brother walked over to stop him and found that his fingers were hurt and his shoes damaged. He became sad, saying, "If you don't return quickly, I will cut my throat with this ax." Zhang Cheng withdrew. His brother escorted him halfway and then returned to work.

Having finished cutting firewood and returning home, Zhang Na went to his brother's tutor and told him, "My brother is young. It is better to keep him in the classroom because in the mountain there are a lot of tigers and wolves."

"I am not sure where he went," the tutor said. "But I have punished him with a stick."

After returning, Zhang Na asked his brother, "By not listening to my advice, you have been punished with a stick, right?" Zhang Cheng replied with a smile, "Not really!"

The next day Zhang Cheng arrived again, with an ax in his waist. Startled, his brother said, "I told you not to come. Why did you come again?" Without answering, Zhang Cheng started to cut firewood quickly and refused to rest even though he started perspiring. When he had cut about a bundle of firewood, he left without even saying goodbye. When his tutor was about to punish him again, he told him the truth. His tutor sighed for his moral courage and no longer prohibited him. His brother tried to stop him frequently, but he would not listen.

One day, Zhang Cheng was cutting firewood together with several people when a tiger arrived. While everyone was in fear and prostrated themselves on the ground, the tiger held Zhang Cheng in its mouth and left unexpectedly. Weighed down by Cheng, the tiger ran slowly so that Zhang Na caught up with it. Zhang Na hacked at it with an ax and hit it on its hipbone. Driven by the sharp pain, the tiger ran madly. Nobody could follow it or find where it went. Zhang Na came back, weeping. He wept much more sadly when others tried to comfort him, saying, "My brother differs from the younger brother of others. Furthermore, he died for me. How can I live?" Then he cut his throat with an ax. The others rushed to save him, but the blade had already cut about an inch into the flesh. As blood poured from the wound, he fainted and his eyes closed. Startled, those present tore his clothes to stanch the bleeding and carried him home.

Zhang Cheng's mother wept and cursed, "You killed my son! Then you wanted to shirk your responsibility by cutting your throat?" Zhang Na replied with a groan, "Mother, don't worry! Since my brother died, I definitely won't live." He was placed on a bed but could not sleep due to the pain of the wound. Leaning against the wall, he cried day and night. Fearing that he would die, his father approached his bed to feed him. But his stepmother would blame and curse at him. Consequently, Zhang Na refused to eat anything and thus died three days later.

On his way, [the soul of] Zhang Na met a sorcerer of the village who frequently served in the netherworld and poured his grievance to him. Accordingly, he inquired about where his younger brother was. The sorcerer said that he had not heard anything about his brother, but he turned around and guided Zhang to go somewhere. Having arrived at a big city, they saw a man in black coming out from the city. The sorcerer stopped the man and inquired about the brother. The man in black took out the records from his bags and examined them, but among the more than one hundred names there was nobody surnamed Zhang. The sorcerer suspected that Zhang was on another record. The man in black said, "This district belongs to me. How could it be wrong?"

Zhang Na did not believe him, so he forced the sorcerer to enter the city with him. In the city old ghosts and new ghosts were coming and going. There were some they had been acquainted with. When they approached them and asked, however, nobody knew where Zhang Cheng was.

Suddenly, the ghosts shouted together, "The Bodhisattva has come!"

Lifting their heads, they saw in the cloud there was a tall man whose body was gloriously radiant, and the world suddenly became dazzlingly bright. The sorcerer congratulated him, saying, "You are so lucky! The Bodhisattva hasn't come to the netherworld to help people remove their suffering for several dozens of years. Now you meet him by chance." Then he pulled Zhang Na to kneel down on the ground.

Moving forward in a disorderly fashion, the ghostly prisoners all brought their palms together and chanted "Mercy." The sound of their praying for help shook heaven and earth. With willow branches in hands, the Bodhisattva sprinkled over them nectar droplets [that were] as fine as dust. In a short while, the fog scattered, the light died away, and the Bodhisattva suddenly disappeared.

Zhang Na felt that his neck was moistened by the nectar droplets, and the ax wound no longer hurt. The sorcerer then led him back home. When they saw the gate of the village, the sorcerer bid him farewell and left.

After being dead for two days, Zhang Na unexpectedly woke up all of a sudden. He told his family what he had experienced and said that Zhang Cheng was still alive. His stepmother thought that he fabricated the story and continued to curse at him. Zhang Na was wronged and had no way to explain, but when he felt his wound with his hands, he found that it was completely healed. Struggling to get up, Zhang Na knelt before his father, saying, "I will pierce the clouds and enter the sea to look for my younger brother. If I cannot find him, I will not return for the rest of my life. I wish you would just consider me dead." The old man brought him to a place where nobody was present and wept together with him, yet he dared not ask his son to stay.

Consequently, Zhang Na left home to search for the whereabouts of his younger brother, including large streets and small lanes. He soon ran out of money but continued his search through begging. More than a year later, he reached Jinling. Ragged, Zhang Na walked on the road, bending his back. Seeing more than ten horses passing, he hurried to the roadside to escape. Among the horsemen, one about 40 looked like an official, with strong soldiers on the back of galloping horses in front and behind him. A teenager on a smaller horse looked at Zhang Na several times.

Believing him to be the son of a high official, Zhang Na dared not lift his head to look at him. The teenager stopped his whip to take a short rest and suddenly dismounted his horse. He said in a loud voice, "Aren't you my older brother?" Zhang Na lifted his head to look at him. He found that he was Zhang Cheng. Holding his hands, Zhang Na wept in grief. Zhang Cheng also wept, asking, "How come you are wandering destitute away from home like this?" Zhang Na told him what had happened. Zhang Cheng became even more sorrowful. All the horsemen dismounted to ask what had happened and then reported to the official. The official ordered Zhang Na be given a horse to ride on, and they went back to his home together. Then Zhang Na asked for the details of what his brother had experienced.

Previously, the tiger carried Zhang Cheng away in its mouth. He did not know when he was left by the side of the road. He slept there for a night. By chance, Assistant Magistrate Zhang was leaving from the capital and passed by there. Seeing Zhang Cheng's gentle appearance, he took pity on him and stroked him. Thus Zhang Cheng slowly woke up. Cheng mentioned his native homeland and became aware that it was far away. Thereupon Assistant Magistrate Zhang put him on his cart and returned home. He applied medicine on his wound. Several days later, his wound healed. Assistant Magistrate Zhang had no sons, so he adopted Zhang Cheng as his son. While traveling with his stepfather, Zhang Cheng met his older brother by chance.

Immediately after Zhang Cheng told his brother the whole story, Assistant Magistrate Zhang entered the room. Zhang Na bowed to him repeatedly to show his gratitude. Zhang Cheng entered the inner room, took out a set of silk clothes, and gave them to his brother. Then he set up a feast and invited his brother to talk

Assistant Magistrate Zhang asked, "At Yu, how many men are in your clan?"

Zhang Cheng replied, "No one else. My father was a native of Qi, and he later moved to Yu."

"I am also a native of Qi," Assistant Magistrate Zhang said. "Where is your hometown?"

Zhang Na replied, "I heard from my father that it was under the administration of Dongchang."

Startled, Assistant Magistrate Zhang said, "We are fellow-townsmen! Why did your father move to Yu?"

Na replied, "At the end of the Ming dynasty, the Qing troops invaded Qi and took my former mother away. In the turmoil of war, my father lost his home and family. At first, he went to the west to do business, became familiar with the area, and thus he settled down there."

Assistant Magistrate Zhang asked further, "What is your father's name?"

When Zhang Na told him, Assistant Magistrate Zhang stared at him with wide eyes, then lowered his head, as if in disbelief. Hurriedly, he entered the inner room.

In a short while, Assistant Magistrate Zhang's mother came out. After the two young men bowed together around her to pay homage, the old lady asked Zhang Na, "Are you the grandson of Zhang Bingzhi?"

Na responded, "Yes!"

All of a sudden, the old lady cried loudly, saying to his son, "This is your younger brother."

While both Na and Cheng were puzzled, the old lady said, "Three years after marrying your father, I was forced to leave home and wandered about to the north. Half a year later when I belonged to Hei Gushan, I gave birth to your older brother. Another half-year later Hei died, and your older brother was added to the banner system and promoted to this position. Now he has resigned. Longing for our home-town all along, we dropped off the banner system and were back to our old clan. We sent someone to Qi several times but failed to find any information about your father. How could we know that he had moved westward!" Then she said to his son, "You took your younger brother as your son. How sinful it is!"

Assistant Magistrate Zhang said, "When I asked Cheng previously, he didn't say that he is a native of Qi. Probably he could not remember because he was too young at that time."

Then they rearranged their sequence according to their ages: Assistant Magistrate Zhang was 41, so he became the oldest brother; Zhang Cheng, 16, became the youngest brother; and Zhang Na, 22, became the second older brother.

After gaining two younger brothers, Assistant Magistrate Zhang was very happy. He stayed and slept together with them, hearing all the details about their separation, and was about to schedule their return home together. When his mother worried that he might not be accepted, Assistant Magistrate Zhang said, "If I am accepted, we would be together, otherwise we would part. How could there be a fatherless state in the world?" Thereupon they sold their house, prepared what was needed for the trip, and set the time for the journey west.

Having arrived at home, Cheng and Na ran to inform their father first. After Na left home, his stepmother had passed away, leaving his father, a lonely old man, at home alone. Seeing Na enter suddenly, his father was overcome with joy and aston-ishment, as if in a trance. Upon seeing Cheng, he was greatly delighted; silently, he could do nothing but shed tears. Furthermore, he was told that Assistant Magistrate Zhang and his mother came together. Stupefied, the old man could neither cry nor laugh, but stood dumbly.

In a short while, Assistant Magistrate Zhang entered. After he *kowtowed* to his father, his mother held the old man, and they wept face to face. Later, while seeing maidens and servants filled inside and outside the room, they felt embarrassed, not knowing what to do. Zhang Cheng didn't see his mother. When he asked, he knew that she had passed away. He cried loudly until his breathing stopped and did not awake until after the time it takes for a meal.

Assistant Magistrate Zhang built a house and hired a teacher to teach his two younger brothers. With horses jumping in their stables and people bustling in their rooms, the Zhangs became a prosperous clan.

Commentary: "While listening to this story from beginning to end, I shed tears several times. As a teenager, Cheng started to help his brother with an ax. I exclaimed, 'Does Wang Lan appear again?' Then the tears came. When the tiger carried Cheng away in its mouth, I shouted wildly, 'How could Heaven be so muddleheaded!' Then I cried again. When the brothers met suddenly, I shed tears for their happiness; when they gained an old brother, my sad tears fell for Assistant Magistrate Zhang; when the family was reunited, both happiness and astonishment occurred unexpectedly, my unbeckoned tears fell for the old man. I'm wondering if, in the future, there will be anyone who sheds tears as easily as I do?"

(From Pu Songling, *Liaozhai zhiyi*, Chapter 2)

Notes

1 Its capital was in Xiang 相 County in modern Huaibei City in Anhui.
2 Ziyou 子猷, named Huizhi 徽之, was the fifth son of Wang Xizhi 王羲之 (390–c. 365), the well-known calligrapher of Eastern Jin. He was known as an eccentric and undisciplined man. Zijing 子敬, named Xianzhi 獻之, was the seventh son of Wang Xizhi and a famous calligrapher. He was the *Zhongshu ling* 中書令, president of the Central Secretariat, before his death. For their biographies, see Fang Xuanling 房玄齡 (579–648) et al., ed., *Jin shu* 晉書 (Beijing: Zhonghua shuju, 1974), 80. 3103–3106.
3 State of Qi in the Warring States period (475–222 BCE), covering northern and eastern parts of modern Shandong and southeast of Hebei.

5   Trustworthy Friends

All but one of the Five Confucian Relationships is hierarchical in nature. The exception is the relationship between friends (*you* 友). In the Western Zhou period (ca. 1045–771 BCE), the meaning of *you* was one's kinsmen within a lineage, including ruler and subject, father and son, as well as brothers. Between the Spring and Autumn period (770–476 BCE) and the Warring States period (475–222 BCE), its meaning changed to only "friends" outside of one's kinsmen – that is, men with common aspirations.[1]

Mencius defines "trust," or "faith," as the ethical code for friends – "There is trust between friends" (*pengyou you xin* 朋友有信). Regarding the meaning of "trust," Arthur Waley noted [on its use in the *Analects*], "In early Chinese it almost always refers to keeping promises, fulfilling undertakings. It does not mean telling the truth; nor do all early peoples regard telling the truth as good in itself."[2] It seems no change occurred regarding this code during the subsequent 2,000 years. "Trust" is the major theme of numerous stories about friendship in later times. This shows that as an ethical code "trust" has been widely accepted by the Chinese people, and their faith in it persist even now.

Trust between friends is a complement to the four hierarchical human relations in Confucian culture, but friendship was also considered by some to have the potential to undermine the stability of the family. For example, "Pursuing friendship at the expense of their relationships with their siblings" (*bogurou er zhongjiaoyou* 薄骨肉而重交友) was a frequent complaint about the dangers of friendship during the Ming dynasty (1368–1644).[3] Nevertheless, stories about friendship have been and still are loved by numerous readers.

It is hard to say that "trust" promoted by Mencius is the only ethical code in the first three of the following stories about friendship. Reciprocity (*bao* 報), for example, is another theme that reflects the common Chinese maxim – "a man cognizant of a kindness must repay it" (*zhi'en bibao* 知恩必報).

Besides the trustworthy friends presented in the first three stories, another type of friend in Chinese culture is the well-known *zhiyin* 知音 – a bosom friend, literally "the one who knows the tone." A *zhiyin* is a true friend who knows the heart of his or her friend and is deeply solicitous. Because of this, the term has long been highly cherished and has even become a substitute term for "true friend" in Chinese culture. A common saying goes that "one thousand taels of gold are easy

DCI: 10.4324/9781003490821-6

to obtain, but a *zhiyin* is hard to come across" (*Qianjin yide, zhiyin nanfeng* 千金易得, 知音難逢).

The last two stories about bosom friends presented here depict Bao Shuya, a historical figure of the Spring and Autumn period, and Zhong Ziqi, a fictional figure in a Ming dynasty storyteller's script. Both of them highlight equality and knowing each other's heart/mind. Obviously, this goes beyond the idea of friendship in Confucianism.

Life and Death Friends

Fan Shi of the Han, courtesy name Juqing and also known as [Fan] Si, was a native of Jinxiang County in the Shanyang Commandery. He became close friends with Zhang Shao from Runan,[4] whose courtesy name was Yuanbo. They studied together in the Imperial Academy. Later, Fan Shi took a temporary leave. Before returning home, he told Yuanbo, "I should be returning in two years, at which time I will visit your parents and see your children." Then they set the reunion date.

When the appointed time was approaching, Yuanbo told his mother everything and asked her to cook a meal to wait for his friend. His mother said, "He has been gone for two years and is now a thousand *li* away, how can you take his promise so seriously?"

Yuanbo replied, "Juqing is a trustworthy man. He would surely not betray his promise."

His mother said, "If that is true, I will prepare wine for you."

On that day, Juqing arrived as expected. He ascended the hall to kowtow to Yuanbo's parents, and then they drank wine together. After they enjoyed themselves to the full, he bid them farewell and left.

Later, Yuanbo was confined to bed with an extremely serious illness. Zhi Junzhang and Yin Zizhi, both from his own commandery, took care of him day and night. Before his death, Yuanbo sighed, "It is a shame that I cannot see my life-and-death friend once more!"

Zizhi said, "Junzhang and I are taking care of you with all our hearts. If we are not your life-and-death friends, who is?"

Yuanbo said, "You two are my friends in this life. Fan Juqing of Shanyang is my friend even in death." A moment later, he died.

Fan Shi suddenly dreamed of Yuanbo, wearing a black cap with tassels and slippers, shouting, "Juqing! I died on such-and-such day and will be buried at such-and-such time, returning to the Yellow Spring forever. I know you have never forgotten me, but how can you reach the funeral spot?"

Fan Shi faintly awoke. He sighed and wept sadly. Wearing a mourning cloth for [the death of] his friend, he galloped to arrive in time for the funeral. But before his arrival, the funeral carriage had set off.

When the hearse arrived at the tomb and the coffin was about to be lowered into the ground, the coffin would not move forward. Zhang's mother stroked it and said, "Yuanbo, are you still expecting someone?" Thereupon they stopped moving the coffin.

Quite a while later, someone was coming in a white carriage drawn by a white horse, crying loudly. Seeing him, Zhang's mother said, "He must be Fan Juqing!"

When Juqing arrived, he kowtowed to the coffin and offered his condolences, saying, "Please go forward, Yuanbo! The dead and the living have different roads. Let's bid farewell forever!" Of the thousand people who attended the funeral, all shed tears for them.

Fan Shi held the rein to pull the coffin then moved forward. Thus Zhang Shao stayed by the side of the tomb, built the mound, planted trees around it, and then left.

(Gan Bao, *Soushen ji*, Chapter 11)

Xun Jubo Visits His Friend

Xun Jubo traveled a long distance to visit his friend who was critically ill. By chance, the Northern Barbarians were attacking that commandery.

"I'm going to die," his friend said to Jubo. "You should leave right away."

Jubo replied, "I came from afar to see you, but now you ask me to leave. Is violating righteousness to save his own life what Jubo would do?"

When the barbarians arrived, they said to Jubo, "Our great armies have arrived, and the whole commandery is empty now. What kind of man are you? How do you dare stay here alone?"

"My friend is ill," Jubo replied. "I cannot bear to leave him. Please take my life instead of his!"

The barbarians talked with each other, saying, "We are the men who have no righteousness but entered the State of righteousness!"

Thereupon they withdrew their troops and returned to their home country, and thus the whole commandery remained intact.

(From Liu Yiqing, *Shishuo xinyu* 世說新語, Chapter 1)

Wu Bao'an Ransoms His Friend

Wu Bao'an, whose style name is Yonggu, was a native of Hebei Circuit and the Guard of Fangyi County in Suizhou.[5] His fellow villager, Guo Zhongxiang, was a nephew of Guo Yuanzhen. Zhongxiang had both talent and learning, so that Yuanzhen intended to help him to gain fame and a position in the government.

It happened that the Southern barbarians staged an armed rebellion, and the Court appointed Li Meng as the commander-in-chief of Yaozhou to launch a punitive expedition to suppress the insurgency. Before setting off, Li Meng paid a farewell visit to Yuanzhen, who recommended Zhongxiang to him and said, "This is the only child of my little brother; he has not yet had a post in the court. For the time being, please let him go with you; if he can do a meritorious deed in this expedition, I will give him a hand in the court, allowing him to keep a humble salary." Li Meng accepted his recommendation. Since Zhongxiang was quite talented, Li Meng appointed him as an administrative assistant and entrusted him with military affairs.

When they arrived at Shu, Bao'an wrote a letter to Zhongxiang, which read,

Because of your fame and morals, I feel honored to be your fellow villager. Although I haven't paid a visit to you because of my absence of formality, I have always admired you. You are the nephew of the prime minister and a talented man in the headquarters of a military general. Because of your superb capabilities, you have truly been entrusted with an important task. General Li is versed in both literary and military matters, and he has been appointed with full power to lead the great army to suppress a minor rebellion. Because of General Li's bravery and your talent, your army will exterminate the rebels, and success will be achieved in no time.

I loved learning when I was young and specialized in Confucian classics after I grew up, but I'm not more talented than others and currently serve only as the guard of a county, which is beyond the Sword Gate Pass[6] and close to the residence of Southern barbarians. My hometown is several thousand *li* away, and the road is blocked by passes and rivers. Furthermore, the term of office for my position has already expired; the next term is unpredictable. I am an incapable man and also restricted by the process of official selection, how could I have any chance even if I expect only to keep a humble salary? I am going to return home to farm and leave my dead body in a ditch.

I have heard that you worry about those who are in trouble and never neglect your affection for your native place. If you take special care of me and allow me to hold your whip and bow to serve by your side, when the court records the minor merits later, I will benefit from it. By taking advantage of the triumphant return, if I can get a minor position, that would be a great favor that I will never forget. I dare not expect that it might actually happen, but I only intend to make a plan for myself. I hope you will understand my sincerity and forgive my impertinence. Encouraging myself, an incapable man, I look forward to your summon.

Having received the letter, Zhongxiang was deeply touched. Immediately he talked with General Li and summoned Bao'an to be the chief secretary. Before Bao'an had reached their army, however, the southern barbarians attacked. General Li battled and defeated the enemy at Yaozhou.[7] Following up the victory with a hot pursuit, they marched deep into the land of the barbarians but were crushed in an ambush. General Li was killed, his troops were annihilated, and Zhongxiang was captured. The southern barbarians coveted property, so they allowed each of the captives to contact their families to obtain a ransom of 30 bolts of silk.

Bao'an arrived at Yaozhou just as General Li's troops were annihilated. He stayed there and had not yet returned home when he received a letter from Zhongxiang. He wrote to him from the southern barbarian's land. After several transferences it finally reached Bao'an. It read,

Yonggu, I hope this letter finds you well. Our army had set out before I could reply to your letter; deep in the barbarian's land, we were soundly defeated.

General Li died in the battle; and I became a captive, dragging out a shameful existence at the far corner of the earth. My life is almost over yet my hometown is far away. I am not as talented as Zhongyi of Chu,[8] yet I was unexpectedly captured; I am not the Viscount of Ji,[9] but I have become a slave. My status resembles that of Su Wu,[10] yet how could I expect anyone in the court to request my release or anyone here to act like Li Ling (134–74 BCE)?[11]

Ever since I was captured by the barbarians, I have tasted all kinds of hardship and bitterness. My skin and flesh are lacerated and even cut off, and my blood and tears shed. I have experienced the most intolerant tortures in the world. As a man from a noble family, I have now become a desperate prisoner in a remote place. As time passes and season changes, whenever thinking of my beloved seniors in my hometown, or seeing pine trees similar to those at my ancestral graveyard, I became mad and saddened, weeping in grief and allowing tears to flow randomly. Seeing this, even travelers would take pity on me.

Although you and I haven't met in person, as a noted senior of my hometown, you are dear to me because we share the same pursuits. I have imagined your brilliant appearance and also frequently dreamed of you. Previously, when you sent me the letter, I found a chance and spoke on your behalf. General Li had heard of your talents and reputation, so you were appointed as the chief secretary. But you didn't arrive before our army marched a long distance. It was yourself who was left behind by the troops, instead of me who neglected the affection for my native place. Your family passed down the exuberance of happiness, and Heaven sent down blessings to the family which stores up goodness. As a result, when disaster occurred you were not present, therefore both your body and fame remain intact. If you served under General Li's banner and joined our headquarters earlier, you would have become a man at this remote place, exactly like me.

I am currently stranded and have exhausted both strength and plans. But the southern barbarian convention allows relatives and families of the captives to ransom them. Since I am the nephew of the prime minister, differing from others, they persistently force me to request a thousand rolls of silk from my relatives for my ransom. Even the cost of sending out this letter takes one roll of silk. I pray you will send my uncle a letter to report on my situation as soon as possible, so that he can come at a proper time to ransom me back. I am relying only on you to make my lost soul return home and my dead bones grow flesh again. Please spare no effort for this matter of mine today. In case my uncle has left the court and you find none to report to, I hope you yourself will save me just like Guan Yiwu[12] saving Shifu by pawning one of his horses, just like Song people who spent one hundred carriages and horses to ransom Yuan Hua, their General. It has been challenging even for the ancient people to redeem prisoners. Because you have kept lofty morals and prominent integrity, I beg you to save me without any sense of doubt. If you do not pity me and disregard my request as earthlings do, then I will be an imprisoned slave when I am alive and a barbarian ghost after

I die. What else can I expect? This is all I have to say. Mr. Wu, please don't forget my trust!

Receiving the letter, Bao'an was saddened. At that time, Zhongxiang's uncle had already died. In order to repay the favor of his friend, Bao'an promised to ransom Zhongxiang. He sold all the property his family had, but only got 200 bolts of silk. So he stayed in Xizhou to do business for ten years, without going back home even once. From the beginning to the end, he earned 700 bolts of silk in total, but that still did not reach the required number. Bao'an has long been poor, and his wife was still staying in Suizhou. In order to redeem Zhongxiang, he ceased communication with his family. Whenever he gained something from others, even a foot of cloth or a pint of rice, he would save it [to exchange for silk].

Later on, his wife could no longer support her family herself, and they suffered from hunger and coldness. Carrying her son and riding on the back of a donkey, she set out to Lun'an to look for her husband. On her way to Lu'nan, they ran out of food and water, but there were still several hundred *li* away. Being helpless, his wife could only sit by the road and cry. Travelers passing by were moved by her grief.

The governor of Yaozhou, Yang Anju, was just then riding off to assume his office along the post road. Seeing that Bao'an's wife was crying, he was curious and thus asked her for the reason. She answered, "My husband was the guard of Fangyi County in Suizhou. Because his friend was captured by the Southern barbarians and begged him to ransom him, my husband now lives in Yaozhou. He abandoned me and his son for ten years with no message. Now I am poor and miserable, so I am going to find my husband. We have run out of food and there is still a long way to go; this is why I am crying."

Yang Anju marveled at what she said, saying, "When I arrive at the next inn, I will wait for you and give you whatever you lack." When she reached the post house, Yang offered her several thousand coins and provided a horse to ride on for her trip.

After galloping to his official residence, the first thing Yang Anju did was look for Bao'an. Seeing him, Anju held his hands, ascended to the hall together, and said to him, "I have frequently read ancient books and have seen how ancient people behaved. Unexpectedly, today I witness you doing something as admirable as what the ancients did. Nevertheless, why do you consider friendship to be much dearer than the kinship between a man and his wife and son? In order to ransom your friend, you have to abandon your family and let things go like this? I have met your wife who came to look for you. Admiring your moral character, I am eager to see you in person. Since I have just arrived here and have no money to assist you, for the time being I borrowed four hundred bolts of silk from the governmental warehouse for your urgent need. After your friend is redeemed, I will manage to pay them back gradually."

Wu Bao'an was delighted. He picked up the silk and asked the messenger from the southern barbarian land to carry them back. Around 200 days later, Guo

Zhongxiang reached Yaozhou. He was thin and pallid and barely looked human. Meeting each other face to face, Zhongxiang and Bao'an talked and wept together.

Yang Anju had once served under Minister Guo Yuanzhen, so he had Zhongxiang bathed, offered him garments, held his hands to a banquet, and entertained him with music. Admiring what Wu Bao'an had done, Anju doted on him extremely. Thereupon Anju appointed Zhongxiang to be the proxy guard of a county under his administration.

Zhongxiang had stayed quite long among the southern barbarians and knew everything there, so he purchased ten slave girls from a tribe, all of them beautiful. When the girls arrived, Zhongxiang bid Anju farewell to return to the land north and offered the slave girls to Anju as a gift.

Yang Anju refused to accept them, saying, "I am not a vulgar man. How could I expect anything in return? I admire Scholar Wu's moral character as a friend, therefore relying on his devotion I helped to save you and that is all. Since you have aged parents in the north, you can use the money spent on purchasing these girls to support your parents."

Zhongxiang replied, "My returning from hell rested on your favor, and my life was due to your offering. Even after death I dare not forget your great favor. These slave girls are purchased especially for you, but now you decline them. I beg you to accept them at the risk of my life."

Yang Anju could not violate his will, so he showed him his youngest daughter, saying, "Since you persuade repeatedly, I dare not to decline your kind intention. This is my youngest daughter, whom I dote on very much. I accept one of your slave girls on her behalf." Accordingly, he declined the remaining nine girls.

Generously treated by Yang Anju, Wu Bao'an also returned home with a large sum of money and much grain.

When Guo Zhongxiang arrived home, it had been fifteen years since he parted with his family. After arriving at the capital, he was commissioned to be the administrative supervisor of Weizhou based on his merit. He took his parents to live with him. Two years later, he was promoted to the position of revenue administrator of Daizhou. When his official term expired, his mother passed away. After the funeral, he observed three years of mourning for his mother by her tomb. Then he said to himself, "Relying entirely on Mr. Wu, I was able to be redeemed. Because of this I could be appointed as an official and support my parents. Now that my mother has passed away and my mourning period ends, I can do something of my own will." Then he set out to look for Wu.

After service as the Guard of Fangyi County, Wu Bao'an was appointed as the assistant magistrate of Pengshan County in Meizhou.[13] So Guo went to the region of Shu to look for him. However, Bao'an was not able to return home when his term expired, and both he and his wife died and were buried temporarily inside a monastery. Hearing of this, Zhongxiang wept in grief. He made mourning clothes out of burlap; wearing a mourning hat and burlap belt and leaning on a funeral stick, he walked by foot all the way from the Shu Commandery to Pengshan, his crying never ceasing.

Having finished offering sacrifice and pouring wine onto the ground in a memorial ceremony, Zhongxiang dug out Wu's skeleton, marked a serial number on each of his bones with ink, and put them into a silk bag. Then he dug out Wu's wife's skeleton, also marked them with ink, and stored them in a bamboo basket. Carrying them on his shoulder, he walked barefoot for several thousand *li* to the Wei Commandery.

Wu Bao'an had a son. Zhongxiang treated him as his own younger brother. He spent all of his family assets – about 200,000 strings of cash – to rebury Bao'an with full honors, and also built a stone monument to eulogize him. Zhongxiang built a cottage by the side of his tomb to observe the three-year mourning period. Afterward, he was appointed as the administrator of Lanzhou,[14] and then added the position of grand master for closing court.[15] He brought Bao'an's son with him to assume his position, made arrangements for his marriage, and pampered and nurtured him in every way. His gratefulness towards Bao'an had never faded. In the twelfth year of Tianbao (754), Zhongxiang went to the court and requested for a transfer of his honor and title to Bao'an's son to repay his favor. Everyone at the time spoke highly of him for his gratitude.

Earlier, when Zhongxiang was first captured, he was presented to the chief of the southern tribe as a slave. The chief adored him and allowed him to eat the same food as he ate. After a year, however, Zhongxiang missed the northern land and tried to escape but was recaptured and sold to the head of a cave further south. That master was a cruel one and demanded that he do heavy physical labor. He frequently whipped Zhongxiang. Zhongxiang escaped but was caught again and sold to a cave further south, called "Pusa Man." After living there for a year, Zhangxiang managed to escape again, and when he was recaptured he was sold to another place, where the master said to him angrily, "You kept escaping. Do you think there is no way to stop you?" So he took out two planks, both several feet long, and ordered Guo to stand on them with his feet nailed down into the wood. Every time he labored, he had to move his feet along with the two planks. During nights the master imprisoned him in a dungeon and locked his two feet. The wounds on his feet were not healed until several years later. The torture with the wooden locks and spending nights in the dungeon lasted for seven years. Zhongxiang could almost no longer bear it. When the person sent by Bao'an went to redeem him, he found his first master, and after several rounds of searching, Zhongxiang was finally able to return.

(From Niu Su 牛肅 (fl. 804), *Jiwen* 紀聞)

Bao Shuya and Guan Zhong

Guan Zhong (d. 645 BCE),[16] named Yiwu, was from the area by the Ying River. When he was young, he often interacted with Bao Shuya 鮑叔牙 (d. 644 BCE), who knew that Guan was talented. Guan Zhong was poor, so he frequently took advantage of Bao Shuya. But Bao Shuya never cared about that and always treated him well.

Soon, Bao Shuya served the Price Xiaobai while Guan Zhong served Prince Jiu of the state of Qi. After Prince Xiaobai was enthroned as Duke Huan of Qi (r.685–643 BCE), Prince Jiu was killed,[17] and Guan Zhong was imprisoned. Bao Shuya recommended Guan Zhong to Duke Huan.

After Guan Zhong was appointed as the minister, he was in power in Qi. Relying on Guan Zhong, Duke Huan of Qi became the hegemon among the numerous states. He repeatedly gathered the feudal lords from different states as a leader and regulated the whole realm. This was due to the strategy of Guan Zhong.

Guan Zhong said, "When I was in poverty, I used to do business with Bao Shuya and I often took more profit. But Bao Shuya did not consider me greedy because he knew that I lived in poverty. I used to make plans for Bao Shuya, and they made his life worse, but Bao Shuya did not consider me stupid because he knew that the timing could be favorable or unfavorable.

"I have been an official many times and have also been dismissed by the monarch many times, but Bao Shuya did not think that I had no talent, knowing that I have not encountered a favorable opportunity. I have fought many times and also escaped many times, but Bao Shuya did not think me timid, knowing that I still had an old mother.

"When Prince Jiu failed to be enthroned, Zhaohu died for him while I was prisoned and humiliated, but Bao Shuya did not think that I was shameless, knowing that I would not be ashamed of minor things but would be ashamed that my name could not be known in the world. The people who gave me life are my parents, but the one who truly knows me is Master Bao."

Having recommended Guan Zhong, Bao Shuya chose to place himself under him. His sons and grandsons have enjoyed the emolument in the state of Qi for generations. They have had manor estates granted by the monarch for more than a dozen generations and have consistently been famous officials.

People in the world do not praise Guan Zhong's talents; rather, they praise Bao Shuya's capability of knowing his talented friend.

(From Sima Qian, *Shiji*, Chapter 62)

Yu Boya Smashes His Zither in Gratitude to An Appreciative Friend

Everyone speaks indiscreetly about how Guan and Bao divided their silver,
Who truly understands when Boya plays his zither?
Nowadays "friends" are like foxes and ghosts,
Causing the earnest heart of heroes to learn disappointment.

A common saying goes, "When one person is wealthy and the other is poor, their friendship is plain; when one person is noble and the other is humble, their friendship is plain." In terms of the closeness of friends, few since ancient times are comparable to Guan and Bao. Guan was Guan Zhong, and Bao was Bao Shuya. Both of them were businessmen, and whenever they had profit they divided it equally. From time to time, Guan Zhong took more than half of the profits. Shuya did not consider him covetous because he knew Guan was poor. Later, when Guan Zhong was jailed, Shuya saved him and recommended him to Duke Huan of Qi to be his Prime Minister. Only a friend like this is a true bosom friend.

There are different types of friends: those who are connected by favor and graciousness are friends who truly know each other, those who show utter devotion to each other are friends of the heart, and those who share the same interests and purpose are bosom friends of each other. All of them can be generally called friends. The next story is about friends who share the same interests and purpose. Truly:

> Speaking only to a bosom friend,
> Instead of anyone who wants to listen.

As the story goes, during the Spring and Autumn period of Zhou, there was a famous gentleman named Yu Rui, whose courtesy name was Boya. He was a native of the capital Ying of Chu, in present-day Jingzhou in Huguang. Although Yu Boya was a native of Chu, his career was destined to thrive in Jin, and his official title reached that of senior grand master. With an order from the ruler of Jin, he went to pay a friendly official visit to Chu. There were two reasons for Boya to request this task: first, he was talented and would not fail the work that his lord entrusted him; second, he could visit his hometown in passing, killing two birds with one stone.

He arrived in Chu by land, paid an audience to the lord of Chu, and sent him the message from the ruler of Jin. The king of Chu offered a feast and treated him with courtesy. The capital of Ying was his hometown, so he visited his ancestral tombs as well as met his friends and relatives. However, since he was bearing the order of the king, he could not stay there for too long.

After the official business was done, Boya went to have an audience with the king of Chu and bid him farewell. The king of Chu granted him gold, colored silk, and a tall carriage with horses. It had been 12 years since Boya had departed Chu to serve as an official in Jin. Thinking of the beauty of the rivers and mountains in his old state, he intended to return by boat in a big detour so as to enjoy the rivers to his heart's content. So he lied to the king of Chu: "Unfortunately, I have an illness so I cannot bear riding on a galloping horse or carriage. If Your Majesty could offer me a boat so that I could treat my illness, that would be a great favor."

The king of Chu approved his request and ordered the navy to give him two huge boats – one was the primary boat and the other was supplementary. The main boat was for the envoy from the state of Jin only, and the other boat was for his baggage and servants. Both boats were equipped with patterned oars made of fragrant wood, brocade canopies, and tall sails. They were extremely beautiful. A crowd of officials accompanied him to the side of the river before bidding him farewell. Truly:

> To enjoy the scenery and explore the wonders,
> He ignored the distance to the mountains and rivers.

As an unrestrained scholar, Boya found the beautiful scenery was just what he had expected to see. Setting the sail, he rode on the thousands of layers of blue waves, enjoying the endless green mountains in the distance and clear waters within his view.

No more than a few days had passed when he arrived at the river outlet of Hanyang.[18] It was the evening of the fifteenth day of the eighth month, the Mid-Autumn Festival. Suddenly, the wind blew wildly while waves surged high, and it was pouring rain. There was no way to go forward, so he mocred his boat at the foot of the cliff. A little while later, however, the wind calmed down, the waves became tranquil, the rain stopped, the clouds were dispelled, and the bright moon appeared in the sky. The moon after the rain was much brighter than usual.

Sitting alone in the cabin, Boya felt bored. So he told the servant boy, "Please light up some incense in the incense burner. I'll play some music on my zither to give vent to my feelings."

After putting incense into the incense burner, the boy placed the zither on the short table. Boya opened the bag, took the zither out, adjusted the strings, and started to play. Before the first piece was finished, a string broke with a "gar" sound. Startled, Boya ordered the boy to ask the head boatman, "What place is this?"

The head boatman answered, "Because of the storm, we have just moored at the foot of a hill. Though there are some trees, no people live here."

Boya was astonished, thinking, "This is a wild mountain! If we were in a city or village, someone who loves to learn might secretly listen to my playing, so when the sound of my zither changes suddenly a string may break. In such a wild mountain, who will listen to my playing? Alas! I know what has happened. It must be my enemy who sent someone to assassinate me. Otherwise, there could be robbers who will board to loot my property at midnight." Consequently, he called the people around him, "Please follow me to ascend the hill in search of robbers. If the robbers are not deep in the willow trees, they must be in the reeds."

When they were about to set a plank down to ascend the hill, suddenly they heard someone's response, "The official in the boat, please don't be suspect. I am not an evil robber or anything of that sort. I am merely a woodcutter. While returning home this evening, I encountered the storm. Since my straw rainwear could not protect me, I waited by the side of a rock. Hearing your elegant playing, I secretly listened. I hope you will pardon me."

Boya laughed loudly, saying, "How could a woodcutter from the mountains understand zither playing? Your words are doubtful, but I don't care. Let him go."

The man did not leave; instead, he cried loudly from the hill, "Gentleman, you are quite mistaken! Have you not heard that 'within a town of ten households, there must be a loyal and trustworthy man,' and 'when there is a gentleman inside the door, another gentleman would come from outside.' If you belittle people in the wild mountains and believe nobody here could listen and understand your zither playing, then there shouldn't be a traveler who plays the zither in this wild hill at midnight!"

Considering his words were not common and he might be a real zither listener, Boya ordered the people around to keep quiet. Approaching the cabin door, he ceased to be angry and began to smile, saying, "The gentleman on the hill, you stood for a long time to listen to my playing. Do you know what song I have just played?"

The man replied, "If I did not know, I would not have come to listen to it. What you have just played was 'Kong Zhongni [Confucius] Lamented on Yan Hui.' As music on the zither, it went: 'It is a shame that Yan Hui died young. Let me think of him while the hair on my temples became as white as frost. Just because he enjoys the simple meal at a shabby alley . . .' Your string broke when you played to this line, so you did not play the fourth line, which is, as I know, 'his worthy name will be spread for ten thousand years.'"

Hearing of this, Boya was greatly pleased, saying, "Indeed, you are no ordinary man! Separated by the hill, we are far away from each other and thus it is hard to talk." So he ordered his attendants to set the plank and railings, and invite the gentleman to board the boat to chat. After the plank was set, the man ascended the boat. He was truly a woodcutter, wearing a bamboo hat and a straw coat, holding a sharp pole, and with an ax in his waist and a pair of straw sandals on his feet.

The attendants did not know what they had talked about. Seeing that he was a woodcutter, they belittled him by saying, "You woodcutter! After entering the cabin to see our master, you should kowtow to him. When he asks you anything, you should answer him carefully. His is such an honorable official!"

The woodcutter was truly funny. He said, "You guys, no need to be so rude! Let me untie my clothes to meet him." He then removed his bamboo cap, and there was a green cloth kerchief on his head. Taking off the straw raincoat, he wore a blue shirt, with a long bag worn around his waist and a pair of blue pants below. Composedly, he placed his straw coat, bamboo cap, sharp pole, and ax outside of the cabin door, took off his straw sandals, shook off the mud and water on them, put them on his feet again, and then walked into the cabin.

In the cabin, the lights and candles shined brightly on the short table. Instead of kowtowing, the woodcutter bowed deeply with joined arms before his chest and said, "Greetings, Your Excellency!"

As an official of Jin, when did Boya even glance at a commoner wearing two-part clothes instead of a robe? It would be impolite to leave the seat to salute him or let him leave. With no other choice, Boya lifted one hand slightly, saying, "Please don't stand on ceremony!" Then he ordered the servant boy to set a seat for him. The boy brought a stool and placed it in the place for the least prominent seat. Without the courtesy to a guest, Boya pointed it with puckered lips and said, "You can sit down." By addressing him as "you," it was clear that Boya was acting as a poor host. Without even making any modest remarks, the woodcutter sat down brazenly.

Seeing that he sat down without saying thanks, Boya wanted to correct him. So he neither asked his name nor ordered his servants to offer him tea. Sitting in silence for quite long a while, he asked, "It was you who listened to my zither playing on the shore?" The woodcutter answered, "Yes." Boya said, "Let me ask you.

Since you came to listen to the music, you must know the origin of the zither. Who made this zither, and what advantages does it have when being played?"

At this time, the head boatman came to report, "The wind is favorable, and under the moon, it is as bright as daytime. We may set off." Boya told him, "Please wait!" The woodcutter said, "I'm indebted to you for your kind inquiry. But if I talk too much, I'm afraid you will miss the opportunity of sailing with the wind." Boya said with a smile, "My only worry is that you don't understand the zither. If your talk is meaningful, it is no big deal even if I won't be an official. Let alone if my boat is going faster!"

The woodcutter said, "If this is the case, I will venture to state what I know. The first zither was curved by Fuxi. He once saw the spirit of the five stars flying and finally falling onto a Chinese parasol tree and a phoenix descended onto the tree as well. The phoenix is the king of the birds. It eats nothing but bamboo seeds, perches on no trees but parasol trees, and drinks nothing but the water from the Sweet Spring. Fuxi knew that the parasol tree has the best timber out of all the trees. Since it gathers the essence of Heaven and earth, it can be used to produce the most elegant music. Then he ordered someone to cut it.

"The tree was three *zhang* and three feet tall, it was cut into three sections according to the number of thirty-three layers of Heaven. The tree sections represent Heaven, earth, and man – the three potencies. Fuxi picked the upper section up and knocked on it, but the sound was too light. So he discarded it. Then he picked the lower part and knocked on it, but the sound was too deep. So he discarded it too. Then he picked up the middle part and knocked on it, he found its sound was neither too light nor too deep. He immersed it in the ever-running stream for 72 days, matching the 72 divisions (*hou*) of a year. Then he took it out and let it dry without exposing it to sunlight. On a selected auspicious day, he ordered the best craftsman, Liu Ziqi, to cut it into a musical instrument. Because it produced music played only at Jade Lake, it was named the Jade Zither.

"The length of the zither was three feet six inches and one *fen*, matching the 361 degrees of the cosmic circumference. The width of its front was eight inches, matching the eight solar terms of a year; the width of the rear part was four inches, matching the four seasons; it was two inches thick, matching the two polarities of Heaven and earth. It had a golden boy head, a jade maiden waist, a fairy back, a dragon pond, a phoenix pool, jade tuning pegs, and gold frets. The frets numbered twelve, matching the twelve months. There was a middle fret, indicating the leap month. In the beginning, it had five strings, matching the five elements without – metal, wood, water, fire, and earth – and the five sounds within – *gong, shang, jiao, zhi*, and *yu*.

"While under the sage kings Yao and Shun, the five-string zither was played and the 'Southern Air' of the *Classic of Odes* was sung; the world was in great order. Later, King Wen of Zhou was imprisoned in Youli. To mourn his son Boyikao 伯邑考, he added one more string to his zither, which sounded pure and sad and thus was called Wen's String. Later, King Wu of Zhou launched an expedition against King Zhou of Yin. Between battles he was surrounded by singers and dancers, so he added another string to his zither, which sounded sonorous and resounding, and thus was named Wu's String. With the original five strings and the added two strings, the new zither was called Wen and Wu seven-string zither.

"To play the zither one has six conditions to avoid, seven cases in which one should not play, and eight extremes in its sound quality. What are the six conditions to avoid? The first is bitter cold, the second is burning heat, the third is a strong wind, the fourth is a heavy downpour, the fifth is sudden claps of thunder, and the sixth is a heavy snowfall.

"What are the seven cases in which one should not play? They include hearing of a death, being busy with a variety of tasks, being unbathed, wearing sloppy clothing, burning no incense, and not having appreciative ears present.

"What are the eight extremes in its sound quality? They include extremely pure, extremely unique, extremely tranquil, extremely elegant, extremely doleful, extremely grandiose, extremely leisurely, and extremely lingering. When the zither is played in the perfect state, roaring tigers hearing it will not roar, nor will crying apes cry. That would be the sublime state of playing such elegant music."

Seeing that the woodcutter answered his questions fluently, Boya was still worried that he had just memorized the answers. He said to himself, "Even if he has relied on memorization, doing so is not easy for him. But let me test him again."

Instead of calling him "you" as he previously did, he asked him, "Sir, you truly understand zither! When Confucius was playing the zither in his room, Yan Hui came in from outside. He heard a sound low and deep, seemingly indicating killing. He felt strange, so he asked him. Confucius said, 'When I was playing the zither, I saw a cat was about to catch a mouse. I was hoping that the cat would catch it but was also afraid it would fail. The idea of killing was exposed in the music.' Through this story, I realized that the understanding of music under the supervision of the sage has reached such a subtle status. If I think of something while playing the zither, can you figure out what I am thinking by listening to the music?"

The woodcutter replied, "*The Classic of Odes* says, 'What other men have on their minds I can measure by reflection.' You can play a piece of music, Sir. I will try my best to guess your thoughts. If I fail, please don't hold it against me."

Boya fixed the broken string, then became lost in thought. When he thought of a towering mountain, he played the zither. The woodcutter praised it, saying, "Splendid! How grandiose it is! You are thinking about a towering mountain, Sir."

Boya did not reply. He was lost in thought for another little while and then played the zither again while thinking of flowing water.

The woodcutter praised his playing again, saying, "Splendid! What a turbulent and surging flood! You are thinking about flowing water, Sir."

Because these two sentences correctly pointed out what he was thinking about, Boya was greatly astonished. He put aside the zither, stood up, and carried out the courtesy as a host. He repeatedly stated, "Excuse me! Excuse me for slighting you! A piece of beautiful jade is hidden in a stone. If people are judged solely by their appearance, how could the worthies in the world not be neglected? What is your esteemed name?"

The woodcutter raised slightly from his seat and answered, "I am surnamed Zhong and named Hui; my courtesy name is Ziqi."

Boya bowed with both hands folded in front of him, saying, "So you are Mr. Zhong Ziqi!"

Then Ziqi asked Boya for his name.

"I am a minor official named Yu Rui and serve in the state of Jin. I came to visit your honorable state."

Ziqi said, "It turns out that you are Mr. Yu Boya."

Boya had Ziqi sit in the guest's seat, while he assumed the host's. He ordered the servant boy to prepare some dishes.

After drinking tea, Boya ordered the boy to fetch wine to drink together with Ziqi, saying, "I am sorry I only have these humble accommodations in which to entertain you. Please forgive me for failing to host you properly!"

Ziqi replied, "Nonsense!"

After the servant boy took the zither away, the two men took their seats at a banquet table to drink wine. Boya asked Ziqi again, "Based on your accent, it seems that you are a native of Chu. Where is your honorable residence?"

"Not far from here," Ziqi replied. "The place called Village of Worthies in the Mount Saddle is where I call home."

"The Village of Worthies? What a great name!" Boya said while nodding his head. Then he asked further, "What is your career?"

Ziqi said, "I make a living only by cutting firewood."

Boya said with a smile, "Mr. Zhong Ziqi, I know I should not speak presumptuously. However, with such an aspiration, why don't you seek rank and fame, thereby earning a place for yourself in your ancestral temple and letting your name be handed down to later generations? Now, instead, you chose to retreat with your lofty will and live among woodcutters and herdsmen, becoming rotten together with grasses and trees. I personally disagree with this approach."

Ziqi said, "To be frank with you, I still have aged parents at home but with no brothers to assist me. By cutting firewood, I am supporting my parents for the rest of their lives. I cannot bear to replace one day of my nurturing my parents with the honor of the Three Excellencies."

Boya said, "What a grand filial son! You are truly an outstanding man."

The two men exchanged friendly toasts with wine cups for quite a while. Ziqi remained indifferent whether being favored or humiliated. Boya liked and respected him even more.

Boya asked Ziqi further, "How old are you?"

Ziqi replied, "I lived twenty-seven years in vain."

Boya said, "I am ten years older than you. If you do not consider me too far beneath you, I invite you to pledge to be brothers with me. In doing so, we would not blemish the name of bosom friends.

Ziqi said with a smile, "You are so wrong! You are a well-known official of an honorable state, but I am only a humble man from a poor village. How can I make friends with someone of higher social status? Isn't that a humiliation to you."

Boya said, "The people one knows are numerous, but how many of them are true friends of the heart? I have been busy with worldly affairs. To pledge friendship with you would truly be a great blessing in my life. If I belittle a friend because he is poor and humble, what kind of man I would be?"

Thereupon he ordered the servant boy to add firewood to the oven and boil tea again. Then, just in the boat, they prostrated themselves to carry out the ceremony through eight times of kowtowing to each other. Since Boya was older, he was the older brother; Ziqi was the younger brother. They vowed, "From now on, we call each other brother and will never betray each other regardless of if we are alive or dead."

After that, Boya ordered more wine be brought. Ziqi asked Boya to take the seat of honor, Boya followed his words. After changing cups and chopsticks, Ziqi took the least honorable seat. Addressing each other brothers, they had a heart-to-heart talk. Truly:

> A preferable guest comes, one will never tire of,
> To an appreciative friend, one's talk is endless.

As the two men enjoyed their animated conversation, they didn't realize that the moon had grown pale and the stars had faded – daybreak had arrived. The boatmen had all arisen to set up the canopy cord in preparation to set off.

Ziqi stood up to bid farewell. Boya passed a cup of wine to Ziqi, held his hands, and said with a deep sigh, "My dear brother, why did we meet so late and have to part so soon?"

Hearing of this, Ziqi's tears dropped into his wine cup. He downed it in one swallow and then poured a cup of wine for Boya in return. Both were reluctant to part.

"Your humble brother hasn't yet expressed all his feelings," Boya said. "I would like to invite you, my dear brother, to travel with me for a few days. Is that okay?"

"I would love to accompany you, my brother!" Ziqi replied. "But my parents are aged now. As Confucius says, 'While your parents are alive, you should not travel too far.'"

Boya said, "Since your parents are now at home, you can go back to tell them and then come to Jin to visit me. That would be exactly what Confucius instructed us, 'If you travel, your whereabouts should always be known.'"

Ziqi said, "Your little brother dares not promise easily then renege easily. If I promise my dear brother, I must keep my promise. If, when I tell my parents, they do not allow me to go, that would cause you to be eagerly awaiting my arrival thousands of miles away in vain. It would not be well for me."

Boya said, "My dear brother is indeed an honest gentleman! Forget it, next year I will come to see you."

Ziqi asked, "When will you arrive next year? I should be ready then to serve you."

Boya counted on his fingers and said, "Yesterday was Mid-autumn Festival, and today is the sixteenth day of the eighth month. Dear brother, I'll still come within the five or six days of mid-autumn. If I come after the twentieth, or not until the ninth month in late autumn, I will have broken my promise and will not be a gentleman." He told his servant boy, "Tell the secretary to write the address of my dear brother Zhong and the appointed meeting time in the notebook."

Ziqi said, "In that case, I will be waiting for you by the river within the five or six days of mid-autumn next year. I dare not make any mistake. Now daybreak has come. I must leave."

"Please wait!" Boya said. Then he ordered the servant boy to take out two gold bullions. Without wrapping them up, he offered Ziqi with both of his hands, saying, "My dear brother, this humble gift is a little living expense for your honorable parents. We are amicable brothers. Please accept it."

Not daring to refuse, Ziqi accepted the gift. He bowed twice to bid Boya farewell, then left the cabin in tears. He picked up his shoulder pole, put his straw coat and bamboo cap on both ends of the pole, inserted the ax into his waist belt around his waist, stepped on the plank while holding onto the railing, and went ashore. Boya saw him off to the boat-head, and then they parted in tears.

Let us now leave off talking of Ziqi's returning home and turn our attention to Boya. After drumming the drum and setting off, he was not in the mood to enjoy the scenery on his way back home. His mind was completely occupied by his friend. A few days later, he left the boat and went ashore. Knowing that he was a senior grand master of the Jin court, the people he met at the places he passed dared not fail to treat him with courtesy. They sent him with a horse-drawn carriage directly to the capital of Jin, where he reported his visit to his lord. I will say no more about this now.

Time flew swiftly! After the autumn and the winter had passed, the spring passed as well. Then summer arrived unnoticeably. Not one day passed by that Boya did not think about Ziqi. When the Mid-autumn Festival was approaching, he memorialized the lord of Jin to request days off to return home for a visit, which the lord of Jin approved. Boya had his baggage prepared and still traveled by boat in a big detour.

After getting off the boat, he told the boatmen, "Whenever we arrive at a harbor, please report the place name to me." By chance, exactly on the night of the fifteenth day of the eighth month, the boatmen reported, "Mount Saddle is not far from here." Boya recognized vaguely that it was the place where he met Ziqi last year, so he asked the boatmen to stop the boat, casting anchors to the bottom of the river and striking a pole into the earth by the shore to moor the boat.

That night, the sky was clear and bright. A moonbeam entered the vermilion curtain in the cabin. Boya asked the servant boy to lift the curtain. He then walked out of the gate of the cabin, stood on the head of the boat, and lifted his head to watch the stars. From the bottom of the river to the middle of heaven, 10,000 acres of endless space under the moonlight was as bright as daytime.

Meeting a bosom friend last year on a night with a bright moon in the sky immediately after a heavy rain, Boya thought, "When I come again today it is another pleasant night. He promised to wait for me by the side of the river, why has he vanished without a trace? Has he broken his promise? I will wait a little while longer, he thought. I understood now. Many boats are coming and going. The boat I am in now is not the one I was in last year. How can my brother recognize it? Last year I drew his attention by playing zither; tonight I will play another piece with my jade zither. Hearing it, my brother will certainly come."

Boya ordered the servant boy to take out the zither table, place it at the head of the boat, burn incense, and set up the seat. Boya opened the bag, took out the zither, and adjusted the strings. When he just started playing, there was a sound of grief in the *shang* string. Boya stopped playing, "Alas! The sound in the *shang* string is sorrowful, my brother must have lost one of his parents. Last year he mentioned that his parents were aged. If the one who died was not his father, then it must be his mother. Ziqi is a filial son, and in order of importance and urgency, he would rather break his promise to me instead of violating etiquette to his parents, therefore he did not come. Let me wait until tomorrow, then I will ascend the hill to visit him." Then he asked the servant boy to collect the jade zither, and he entered the cabin to sleep.

Boya did not sleep for a whole night. He waited and waited, but it seemed the dawn would never come. While the moon disappeared and the sun rose on the mountain, Boya got up. He combed his hair, washed his face, straightened his clothes, and asked his servant boy to accompany him with the zither on his shoulder. He also brought ten catties of gold, thinking, "If my brother is in his mourning period, this can be a funeral gift."

After going ashore, they walked on a pass for woodcutters. They walked more than ten *li* before reaching the mouth of the valley where Boya stopped. The boy asked, "Why don't you go, my master?" Boya said, "The mountain is divided into north and south, and the road is going to the east and west. Coming out of the valley, the road is going in both directions, but which one leads to the Worthy-Gathering Village? We have to wait to ask someone who knows the direction, and then we can continue to walk." So Boya sat on a rock to take a rest while the boy stood behind him.

Not long afterward, on the broad road on the left came an old man with a white beard and white hair, wearing a bamboo cap and the plain clothes of a villager. Holding a rattan walking stick in his left hand and a bamboo basket in his right hand, he came along slowly. Boya stood up, straightened his clothes, and went forward to greet him. The old man placed his bamboo basket leisurely on the ground, held his rattan walking stick with both of his hands to greet Boya in return, saying, "What can I do for you, Sir?"

"May I ask," Boya said, "of the two roads, which one leads to the Worthy-Gathering Village?"

"Both," the old man replied. "At the end of each road, there is a Worthy-Gathering Village. On the left is the Upper Worthy-Gathering Village, and on the right is the Lower Worthy-Gathering Village. The government-financed road is thirty *li* in all. Coming out of the mouth of the valley, you are in the middle. Going to the east it is fifteen *li*, and to the west is also fifteen *li*. Which village are you going to go, Sir?"

Boya kept silent, thinking to himself, "My brother is a smart man, why was he so muddleheaded when he told me his address? When we met, he clearly knew there are two Worthy-Gathering Villages here. He should have told me it was the upper village or lower village."

Since Boya was slow to answer, the old man said, "Since you are so hesitant, I'm sure that the person who told you his address just said Worthy-Gathering Village but failed to tell you if it is upper or lower, so you cannot tell, right?"

Boya said, "Exactly."

The old man said, "In both Worthy-Gathering Villages, there are ten to twenty households, mostly of recluses. I have lived in these mountains for several generations. It is exactly as the saying goes, 'Living locally for thirty years, there is nobody who is not dear to me.' Of the people here, if they are not my relatives, then they are my friends. Going to the Worthy-Gathering Village, you must be visiting a friend. What is the name of your friend? If you tell me, I will know where he lives."

Boya said, "I am visiting the Zhong Family."

Hearing "Zhong family," tears fell from the old man's dim-sighted eyes. He said, "It is fine if you visit anyone's family, Sir. But as for the Zhong family, there is no need to go."

Boya asked with a startle, "Why?"

The old man asked, "Whom are you going to visit, Sir?"

"Zhong Ziqi!" Boya answered.

Hearing this, the old man cried loudly, saying, "Ziqi, named Zhong Hui, happens to be my dear son! On the fifteenth day of the eighth month last year, on his way back home late at night, he met the senior grand master of the state of Jin, Mr. Yu Boya. During their discussion, they found they have the same interests and grew fond of each other. While parting he sent Ziqi two gold bullion, with which my son purchased books to read. This stupid man did not stop him. He cut firewood with a heavy load on his shoulders in the morning and read books diligently in the evening. Having exhausted his energy and strength, he contracted with tuberculosis, died after a few months."

As soon as heard of this, Boya felt as if his bowels had been cut through, and tears poured like a spring. With a loud cry, he fell to the ground. While old Zhong tried to support him with his arms, he looked back at the servant boy. "Who is this gentleman?" The boy whispered in his ear, "He is none other than Master Yu Boya."

Old Zhong said while crying, "You are truly my son's good friend?" When Boya awoke, the old man hurriedly helped him to stand up. Frothing at his mouth, Boya slapped his chest repeatedly and wept bitterly, saying, "My dear brother! Yesterday evening when I moored my boat, I still suspected that you broke your promise! How could I know that you had become a ghost under the Yellow Spring? You have only talent, not longevity. How very sorrowful!"

Old Zhong also cried aloud. After recovering his composure, Boya addressed Mr. Zhang again. Instead of calling him old man, he called him uncle, thereby showing the close relationship between the two families. Boya said, "Old Uncle, is your son's coffin still at home, or has it been buried outside the village?"

Old Zhong said, "It is a long story! Before the death of my son, I sat with my wife before his bed. My son left his last words, saying, 'One's lifespan is decided by Heaven. While being alive, I could not serve you as a filial son; after my death, however, I beg you to bury me by the side of the Mount Saddle. Because I promised to wait for Yu Boya, the senior grand master of Jin, so I intend to keep my promise.' I did not betray my son's deathbed words. The fresh mound on the right of the pass that you have just passed is the tomb of my son. Today is the one hundredth day of mourning. I am taking one hundred pieces of paper money to burn in front of his tomb. Unexpectedly, I met you here."

"In that case," Boya said, "I'll accompany you, my uncle, to mourn him in front of his tomb." He ordered his servant boy, "Take the bamboo basket for your grandfather."

Old Zhang led the way with his walking stick. Boya and the boy followed him. After entering the valley mouth again, they saw a fresh mound on the left of the pass. Straightening his clothes, Boya knelt in front of the tomb, saying, "My dear brother! As a man while being alive, you were smart; as a spirit after death, you will be numinous and responsive. This kowtowing of your older brother will indeed be our last farewell!"

Once he finished kowtowing, Boya cried aloud, which disturbed the people around the mountain. Hearing that the senior official of the state of Jin came to mourn Zhong Ziqi, those folks, no matter traveler or resident, from afar or near, male or female, all came and encircled the tomb, jostling for a good position to watch.

However, Boya did not display any sacrifice. Being embarrassed, he asked his servant boy to fetch his zither and place it on the sacrifice stone. Shedding tears, he sat in front of the tomb with his legs crossed and played a piece on the zither. Hearing that the tone of the zither was sonorous, those onlookers all clapped their hands with laughter and scattered.

Boya asked, "My uncle! When I played zither to mourn my brother, I was so sad. Why did the crowd leave laughing?"

Mr. Zhong said, "The boorish villagers don't understand music. Hearing the zither, they thought it was for amusement, therefore they laughed."

Boya said, "I see. My uncle, do you know what song I have played?"

Mr. Zhong said, "I learned playing music when I was young, but now I am aged and half of my five organs have become useless. It has been a long time that I could not hear and understand things clearly."

Boya said, "It was just a short song to mourn your son, which was composed spontaneously. I'll read it aloud for you."

Mr. Zhong said, "I'd love to hear it."

Boya declaimed:

I remember, it was last spring,
By the river I met you.
Now I revisit this old place,
Where can I find my true friend?
A mound of earth is what I see,
It makes me broken-hearted.
Broken-hearted and broken-hearted,

I cannot help but shedding tears.
Happily I came, how sadly I leave,
Depressing clouds spread above the riverside.
Ziqi! Alas, Ziqi! The friendship of ours is worth a thousand pieces of gold,
Having wandered everywhere, nobody else is worth talking with.
After this song is finished, I will never play the zither again,
This three-foot jade zither will die for you!

Boya took out a dagger from his sleeves, cut off the strings, raised the zither with both of his hands, and hit it forcefully against the worshiping stone. He found the zither was broken into pieces and the jade tuning pegs and gold frets all scattered.

Astonished greatly, Mr. Zhong asked, "Why did you smash this zither, Sir?"

Boya said:

After the zither is smashed, the phoenix tail becomes cold,[19]
When Ziqi is gone, for whom should the zither be played?
With a smiling face, all call themselves friends,
But to find a bosom friend it is indeed too hard!

Mr. Zhong said, "I see! What a shame! What a shame!"

Boya said, "Is your honorable residence in the upper Worthy Gathering Village cr the lower Worthy Gathering Village?"

Mr. Zhong asked, "My humble residence is in the upper Worthy Gathering Village; it is the eighth house. Why do you ask?"

Boya said, "I am grieved, so I dare not follow you, my uncle, to ascend your main hall. I brought with me two catties of gold, half of it is the living expense for you on behalf of your dear son, and the other half can be used to buy a few acres of land for sacrificing – the expense for cleaning his tombs in the spring and autumn. When I return to my own court and submit a memorial to request retirement, I will come to the Worthy Gathering Village to pick up you and my aunt to go to my humble home to enjoy the rest of your life."

After finishing his words, Boya took out the gold, handed it himself to Mr. Zhong, and prostrated himself in front of him while weeping. Mr. Zhong bowed to him in return. After staying together for a long while, they parted.

This story is called "Yu Boya Smashes His Zither in Gratitude to a Bosom Friend." A poem by someone in later times praises it:

Snobbish relations mingle with snobbish hearts,
Among the gentlemen who cares about true friends?
Boya exists no more and Ziqi has gone,
After thousands of years, the smashed zither is still told.

(From Feng Menglong, *Jingshi tongyan* 警世通言)

Notes

1 This is reflected in the phrase *tongzhi yue you* 同志曰友 ("People with common aspiration are called friends"). See Zha Changguo 查昌國, "You yu lian Zhou junchen guanxi de yanbian 友與兩周君臣關係的演變," *Lishi yanjiu* 5 (1998): 94–109.
2 Arthur Waley, trans., *The Analects of Confucius* (George Allen & UNWIN LTD, 1938), p. 43.
3 Martin W. Huang, "Male Friendship in Ming China: An Introduction," *Nan Nü* 9 (2007): 14.
4 Modern Runan County in Henan.
5 A commandery with its seat at Fangyi 方義 County (modern Suining city in Sichuan).
6 Jianwai 劍外 refers to the area south of the Jianmen guan 劍門關 (Sword Gate Pass), an important pass to central Shu (Sichuan).
7 Its seat is located in modern Yao'an county in Yuannan.
8 Zhongyi 鍾儀 was a man of Chu during the Spring and Autumn period who was released after being captured by State of Zheng because of his proper wording.
9 A vassal of Yin who avoided calamity by pretending to be mad and dressed as a slave.
10 Su Wu 蘇武 (140–60 BCE) herded sheep in the barbarian land by the Northern Sea for 19 years when he visited the Huns as an envoy of Han in the year of 100 BCE.
11 Who bid farewell to Su Wu in a feast before Su returning home. See Ban Gu 班固, "Li Guang Su Jian zhuan 李廣蘇健傳," *Han shu* 漢書 44.
12 Should be Yan Ying.
13 Meizhou 眉州 was a prefecture with its seat in Tongyi 通義 county (modern Meishan City in Sichuan).
14 Lanzhou 嵐州 was a prefecture with its seat in Yifang 宜芳 county (modern Lan 嵐 county in Shanxi).
15 Hucker, p. 119.
16 Guan Zhong 管仲, a famous philosopher and politician of the Spring and Autumn period, served as the chief minister of the state of Qi and helped it become one of the most powerful states.
17 Prince Jiu was killed by the state of Lu.
18 Hanyang is located where present-day Wuhan is in Hubei.
19 "Phoenix tail" refers to the end of a zither, and thus it has been used as a reference to the zither.

Further Readings

Kutcher, Norman. "The Fifth Relationship: Dangerous Friendships in Confucian Context." *American Historical Review* 105 (5) (2000): 1, 615–29.
Lai, Whalen. "Friendship in Confucian China: Classical and Late Ming." In Oliver Leaman, ed. *Friendship East and West: Philosophical Perspectives*. Richmond: Cruzon, 1996, pp. 215–50.
Shields, Anna M. *One Who Knows Me: Friendship and Literary Culture in Mid-Tang China.* Cambridge, MA: Harvard University Asia Center, 2015.

6   Dutiful Individuals

Individuals in general are neither mentioned in the five human relations of Confucianism nor defined and discussed directly and thoroughly elsewhere in the Confucian classics, but the ethical code for individuals can be assumed and felt clearly throughout the Confucian classics and related texts. The *Analects*, for example, have a clear idea on the individual and his duties. The famous exchange between Confucius and Yan Yuan on *ren* 仁 in chapter 12 reads as follows:

> Yan Yuan asked about benevolence. The Master said, "To return to the observance of the rites through overcoming the self constitutes benevolence. If for a single day a man could return to the observance of the rites through overcoming himself, then the whole Empire would consider benevolence to be his. However, the practice of benevolence depends on oneself alone, and not on others."
>
> Yan Yuan said, "I should like you to list the items." The Master said, "do not look unless it is in accordance with the rites; do not listen unless it is in accordance with the rites; do not speak unless it is in accordance with the rites; do not move unless it is in accordance with the rites."[1]

One could argue that the standard of a gentleman (*junzi* 君子) has embodied in it – the ethical code for the individual.

Generally speaking, in Confucian culture each word and each move of a person are confined within the Confucian rites; individuals have to sacrifice their own benefits, happiness, and even lives, for the rites, namely, for the good of their parents, family, community, and country. If one plays such a role and is dedicated to his/her family and society, s/he would be considered "dutiful"; otherwise, s/he will be belittled or even abandoned by his/her parents, family, and society. There is in fact no room left for individuals in traditional China. Just as Robert Hegel remarks,

> It is no exaggeration to say that to a considerably greater extent than in the modern West, the real Chinese individual has been, and still is, identified by reference to the greater human context of his time . . . To the Chinese it has been the common features and not the uniqueness of an individual that draws attention . . . Deprived of social function, the individual becomes an

DOI: 10.4324/9781003490821-7

unknown, perhaps even meaningless, entity. In this regard, China's present demonstrates a high degree of continuation with China's past.[2]

The following two famous tales have been widely read and enjoyed as love stories, but an important value that has long been neglected is that both of them show vividly the place of an individual in his family and in the Confucian society as well. To read the stories from a Confucian perspective, Scholar Li in the first story, "Prince Huo's Daughter," is definitely not merely a faithless lover – as many would assume – but a dutiful man to his family, clan, and the society for which he gives up his true feeling, love. The dramatic change of status of the young scholar in the second tale, "The Courtesan Li Wa," witnesses his changing place in his family and the society – when he falls into dire straits, he's considered a disgrace to his family, is abandoned, and is even almost killed by his own father. But when he succeeds in the imperial examination and becomes an official in the government, he's viewed as bringing glory to his family and is accepted once again by his father and the community.

Prince Huo's Daughter

In the Dali period (766–779) of the Tang, there was a scholar from the area west of Long Mountain, named Li Yi,[3] who was picked out for the ranks by passing the imperial examination at the age of 20. In the following year an examination for the preeminent would be held,[4] so he waited for the test by the Ministry of Personnel. In the sixth month, in summer, he arrived at Chang'an and lodged in Xinchang Ward.

The scholar was from a lofty clan, with a genius for writing even since he was young. His fine verses and excellent lines were noted as matchless at the time; the accomplished elders praised and admired him unanimously. He was often proud of his unrestrained spirit and gifts and hoped to get a beautiful mate. He searched widely among the famous courtesans for a long time but found no suitable candidate.

In Chang'an there was a matchmaker surnamed Bao, her name Shihyi niang, the eleventh daughter of her parents. Formerly, she had been a bondservant-maid in the family of Commandant-escort Xue, but more than ten years ago she tore up the indenture and followed a good man. Flattering by nature and with a ready tongue, she came and went through all the rich and powerful families and the residences of the royal relatives. As for having a hand in romantic affairs and arranging matches, she was esteemed as a great leader. When she received the scholar's sincere trust and generous gifts, she felt very much indebted to him.

After several months had passed, just as Li was sitting leisurely in the south pavilion of his lodgings between *shen* and *wei* in the afternoon,[5] he suddenly heard someone announcing that she was Bao, very urgently knocking at the door. Lifting up his robe, he hurried to greet her and asked, "What brings you here unexpectedly today, Bao?"

Bao replied with a smile, "Haven't you, the bookworm,[6] been having good dreams yet? There is a fairy who has been banished down to this lower realm, and she does not seek wealth or property, but only longs for the gifted and unconventional. With such a character and appearance, she is really a match for you."

On hearing this, the scholar leapt for joy, feeling his spirit soaring and his body lighter. Grasping Bao's hands, he said to her with respectful bows and thanks: "I will be your servant for the rest of my life – I would even give my life for you." He took the opportunity to ask about the girl's name and dwelling. Bao said, "She is the youngest daughter of the former Prince Huo, styled Xiaoyu. The prince was extremely fond of her. Her mother was named Jingchi, a favorite servant-girl of the prince. Immediately after the prince's death, all Xiaoyu's half-brothers refused to accept her as a true sister because she was given birth by a humble concubine mother; accordingly, they gave her some property and money, and sent her to live elsewhere. She changed her family name to Zheng, and few know that she is the prince's daughter. But her appearance and gestures are so beautiful and charming, such as I have never seen in my life, and her refined tastes and elegant grace are beyond compare. She is well-versed, too, in music and the classics. Yesterday, she asked me to find a good young man who would match her in nature and style. I told her all about you. She also knew the name of Li Shilang, the Tenth Gentlemen, and was filled with joy. She lives in Old Temple Lane in the Shengye Quarter,[7] at the southern end; specifically the yard with a gate for carriages on the left is her residence.[8] I have made an appointment for you. Tomorrow at noon, just go to the entrance of the lane to look for a maid named Guizi, then you will find her."

Immediately after Bao's departure, the scholar began to prepare for the visit. He ordered the young servant Qiuhong to borrow a black charger with a gold bridle from his cousin Shang, who was adjutant-general of the capital. That evening, he washed his clothes, bathed, and shaved. The combination of joy and excitement kept him from falling asleep all night. At daybreak, he put on his kerchief, fetched a mirror and regarded his appearance in it, fearing only that he might fail. He paced back and forth until the noon hour. Then, ordering the charger harnessed, he galloped directly to the Shengye Quarter.

Having arrived at the appointed place, he saw a maid standing there, waiting as expected. She stepped forward and asked, "You are Li the Tenth, aren't you?" Li dismounted at once and ordered the maid to lead the horse to the rear of the house. She locked the door hurriedly. Li found, as expected, Bao coming out from inside. She smiled and quipped from a distance, "What kind of young fellow has broken into the house unannounced?" Bantering with him, she led the scholar through an inner gate. In the courtyard there were four cherry trees, and a parrot cage hung at the northwest corner. On seeing the scholar entering, the parrot cried: "Someone has come in, lower the curtains at once!"

Naturally bashful, Li still felt somewhat apprehensive. When he suddenly heard the words of the bird, he was stunned and dared not to enter. While he was hesitating, Bao led Jingchi down the steps to welcome him. They invited him inside and had him sit opposite them. Jingchi was a little more than 40, and she was graceful, charming, and seductive as she talked and smiled. She said to the young man, "I heard all along that you are gifted and unconventional, now I see that you are handsome and elegant, too. Your fame is really deserved. I have a daughter who, though lacking in proper instructions, is at least not ugly. It should be suitable if she could make a match with you. I heard your intention from Bao many times, and today I would like to offer my daughter to serve you with dustpan and broom." The scholar replied gratefully, "Clumsy and mediocre as I am, it is unexpected for me to receive your favor. If I am really chosen as a match for her, I should take it as an honor for the rest of my life."

Then she ordered wine and dishes to be served and asked Xiaoyu to come out from a chamber east of the hall. The scholar immediately welcomed her with bows and felt as if the entire room was filled with a forest of gems and jade trees, which shone brilliantly over all sides. So bright were her eyes and so bewitching her glances! Xiaoyu sat down beside her mother, who said to her, "You once loved to recite the lines:

'When the curtain was opened and the wind stirred the bamboo,
I suspect that my old friend is coming.'

That is from a poem by Li the Tenth. You have been chanting his poem and thinking of him all day long, how was it comparing with seeing him in person?"

Xiaoyu looked down with a smile and whispered, "Seeing him is not as good as hearing his fame, how could a gifted scholar not be handsome?"

The scholar got up several times and said while bowing, "The young lady [you] loves talent while this humble fellow adores beauty. The two set off each other, then we will have both talent and beauty."

The mother and the daughter glanced at each other and laughed. Then they raised cups to drink. After several rounds, the scholar stood up and asked Xiaoyu to sing a song. At first, she was not willing to, but her mother persistently insisted. Her voice was clear and resonant; the melody exquisite and wonderful.

When they had drunk their fill, it was dusk. Bao led the young man to the west courtyard to rest. It was a quiet courtyard with secluded rooms, and the curtains and screens were luxurious. Bao ordered the maids Guizi and Huansha to take off the scholar's boots and untie his belt. In a short while Xiaoyu came. She talked to him tenderly, the tone of her speech agreeable and charming. At the moment when her silk clothes were removed, her appearance and posture were exceedingly enchanting. They lowered the curtain and drew close to each other on the pillows, enjoying pleasure to their hearts' content. The scholar thought to himself that even [encountering the goddess] on Mount Wu or by the River Luo could not have surpassed what he experienced.[9]

In the middle of the night, Xiaoyu suddenly wept. She looked at the scholar and said, "I am merely a courtesan, and I myself know that I am not a match for you. Now, I am loved merely for my beauty, and [relying on beauty] I entrust myself to a benevolent and worthy man. But I worry that, when my beauty fades, your favor will shift and your love change likewise; this will make me like the vine that has nothing to cling to and the autumn fan that is discarded.[10] Therefore at the zenith of my joy I cannot help grieving."

On hearing this, the scholar sighed with deep feeling. He then pillowed Xiaoyu's arm, and said to her gently, "My lifelong wish has been fulfilled today. I pledge not to leave you, though my bones be grounded to powder and my body smashed to pieces. Why did you, my lady, say these words? Please let me get a piece of white silk and write my oath on it."

Xiaoyu stopped shedding tears and ordered the maid Yingtao to lift the curtain up and hold the candle, while she gave the scholar a brush and ink stone. In her spare time from playing the pipes and plucking the strings, Xiaoyu was fond of poetry and calligraphy. Her book cases, brushes, and ink stone were all old ones from the royal household. She then brought out an embroidered bag, from which she took out three feet of white silk lined with black, which was weaved by the belles of the Yüe,[11] and handed it to him.

Being a literary genius, the scholar grasped the brush and finished his writing in no time. In this, he compared his love to the mountains and the rivers, and his fidelity to the sun and the moon. Every line was so sincere that anyone who might read it would be moved. After he finished, Xiaoyu ordered the maid to put it in her jewelry box. From then on, they loved each other in harmony, just like a pair of kingfishers flying freely in the clouds. They lived this way for two years, together day and night.

In the spring of the next year, the scholar ascended the [selection] subject by passing "The Preeminent" examination of written judgments and was appointed Assistant Magistrate of Zheng County.[12] In the fourth month, he was about to leave for his post and, then, to visit his parents in East Luo.[13] Most of his relatives in Chang'an attended the farewell party for him. It was at the time in a year when the spring prospects still remained and the summer scene began to show its beauty. After the feast ended and the guests scattered, the sorrow of approaching separation occupied Xiaoyu's mind. She said to the scholar, "With your endowment, family, and fame, you are admired by most people. Of course there will be many people who want to be related to you through marriage. Furthermore, you still have parents at home, but have no daughter-in-law yet in your family. Once you leave this time, you are certainly going to make a good match. The words in your pledge are but empty ones. However, I have a small wish that I want to tell you right now, and hope that you will keep it in mind forever. Would you still be willing to listen?"

The scholar was startled, pleading, "What fault have I committed, that you say these words unexpectedly? Please tell me what you want to say, I will certainly respectfully follow it."

Xiaoyu said, "I am just eighteen years old, you are merely twenty-two; there are still eight years before you reach the prime of your life. I hope to complete the joy and love of my life during this period. After that, it would still not be too late for you to select from a high-ranking family to harmonize the Qin and the Jin.[14] I will then abandon the affairs of this world, cut off my hair, and put on black clothes.[15] That would be enough for the long-cherished wish of my life."

The scholar was regretful and moved, he couldn't help but shed tears. He promised Xiaoyu, "I will fulfill the pledge I made by the bright sun, no matter whether I am alive or dead. Even if I live with you for the rest of my life, I would still fear that it is too short to satisfy my long-held wish. How dare I think otherwise? I wholeheartedly beg you not to doubt me. Just stay here calmly and wait until the eighth month, I will return to Huazhou and look for someone to welcome you.[16] The date of our reunion is not far." After another several days, the scholar bid farewell to Xiaoyu and left for the east.

About ten days after he arrived at his post, Li asked leave to visit his parents at the East Capital. Before his arrival home, his mother had discussed his marriage with his cousin, Ms. Lu, and the agreement had already been settled. His mother was always strict and firm. The scholar, though hesitant, dared not refuse. Thus he followed the confirmation rites, and then a close date was set for the wedding.[17] The Lu clan was also a magnificent one. When marrying a daughter to another clan, they must get a promise of a million cash for betrothal money. If the money offered was less than this amount, the marriage would, on principle, not be allowed to proceed. The scholar's family had always been poor, so for the marriage they had to ask for loans. He took false reasons as pretext to look up his relatives and friends far away, crossing the Yangzi River and the Huai River, traveling from autumn till the next summer. Aware that he had reneged on his pledge and greatly exceeded the promised time, the scholar remained silent and hidden from others, with the intent to make Xiaoyu give up her hope. From afar, he also entrusted his relatives and friends to not make a slip of the tongue.

Since the scholar exceeded the appointed time, Xiaoyu had inquired about his whereabouts many times. The false news and unreliable messages she received differed one from the other each day. Filled with sorrow and regret, she sought widely for the fortune tellers and consulted with diviners, and this went on for more than a year. Then, with emaciated body lying in the empty chamber, she fell into a severe and lingering illness. Even though the scholar's letters never came again, Xiaoyu's longing for him never altered. She sent gifts to her relatives and friends, hoping they would bring her news of him. Her inquiries were so urgent and sincere that her resources were exhausted time and again. She frequently sent her maid out secretly to sell dresses and playthings from her suitcase, and most of them were entrusted to Hou Jingxian's commission shop in the West Market to sell.

Once, she sent the maid Huansha with a purple jade hairpin to sell at the residence of Jingxian. On the way, Huansha encountered an old jade craftsman who once served in the court. Seeing what Huansha was holding, he came up to identify it and said, "I crafted this hairpin. Many years ago, when the youngest daughter of Prince Huo was about to have her hair pinned up,[18] the prince ordered me to make this pin, and he gave me 10,000 cash as reward. I have never forgotten it. Where did you get it?" Huansha replied, "My mistress is precisely the daughter of Prince Huo. Her family was impoverished, and she lost her chastity to a man. Her husband went to the East Capital last year, but there has been no word from him. Languishing in sorrow, she fell ill. It has been nearly two years. She asked me to sell this to bribe someone and ask him to seek news of her husband."

The jade craftsman shed tears in sadness, lamenting, "How could the high born sons and daughters of noblemen be so out of luck and in dire straits like this! My remaining days are nearly at an end, but I cannot bear the sorrow of seeing this fluctuation of fortune." He then led Huansha to the mansion of the Princess of Yanxian[19] and related to her the story in detail. The princess also sighed in sadness for a long while, and she gave the maid 120,000 cash for the hairpin.

At this time the girl of the Lu family, to whom the scholar was engaged, was in Chang'an. Having finished raising the necessary sum for the betrothal gifts, the scholar went back to Zheng County, and in the last month of the year, he again asked for leave to go to the capital for his wedding. He chose a secluded lodging in secret and let no one know. There was a *mingjing* named Cui Yunming,[20] who was the scholar's cousin. He was extremely honest and kind in nature. In the years past, he had often enjoyed time together with the scholar in Miss Zheng's house. They laughed and chatted over food and drink, and there had been no distance between them (i.e., they had been on intimate terms). Every time he received news of the scholar, he would relay the news to Xiaoyu candidly. Xiaoyu frequently helped Cui with firewood, provisions, and clothes. For that, Cui was extremely grateful to her. After the scholar arrived [in Chang'an], Cui faithfully told Xiaoyu all what he knew. Xiaoyu sighed in indignation, saying, "How could this kind of thing happen in the world!" She then asked all her relatives and friends to make [Li Yi] meet her by all means.

The scholar was aware that he had exceeded the appointed time and broken his pledge, and he also knew that Xiaoyu's illness was serious and lingering. Ashamed of himself, he reluctantly cut off his relation with her and refused to go. He would go out in the early morning and return only in the late evening, trying to avoid everyone. Xiaoyu wept day and night and completely forgot to sleep and eat. She wished to meet Li Yi just once but, unexpectedly, could not find a chance. While her resentment and indignation deepened, she was exhausted and was confined to her bed. From then on, this was gradually known by people in Chang'an. Men of sentiment were all moved by Xiaoyu's affection, while gallant men were all enraged at the scholar's frivolous conduct.

It was the third month of the year, and many people were going on spring outings. In the company of five or six of his friends, the scholar went to Chongjing Temple to enjoy the peonies in bloom. They strolled along the west corridor, taking turns composing verses [for the occasion]. A man of Jingzhao named Wei Xiaqing, who was a close friend of the scholar, was then also walking along with the party. He said to the scholar, "The scenery is so beautiful, and the grasses and trees are so luxuriant and glorious. What a pity that Miss Zheng should nurse a bitter sense of wrong in her empty chamber! You could really abandon her at last. You are indeed a hard-hearted man! But a real man's heart shouldn't be like this. You should think it over again."

As Wei was sighing and reproaching Li, there suddenly appeared a gallant wearing a yellow silk shirt and carrying a bow. He was handsome, full of vigor, splendidly dressed, and followed only by a boy of the northern tribe with short-cut hair. Following them secretly, he overheard what they were discussing. After a moment, he went forward and greeted the scholar with hands clasped, exclaiming, "Aren't you Li the Tenth? My family comes originally from Shandong, and we are related to the relatives of the emperor through marriage. Though I lack literary talent, I like to make friends with talented men. Having been admiring your splendid reputation, I have always longed to make your acquaintance. Today I am so lucky to meet you and have an opportunity to behold your exquisite appearance. My humble residence is not far from here, and there are also songs and music that are enough for entertainment. Besides, there are eight or nine bewitching girls and more than ten fine horses, all of which you can do with what you desire. I merely hope that you will come and have a visit."

The scholar's friends all carefully listened to these words, and each in turn sighed with admiration so that they rode along with the gallant. After winding through a few wards, they arrived at Shengye Ward. Because it was close to Xiaoyu's residence, the scholar did not want to go. He made an excuse and wanted to turn the head of his horse back, when the gallant said, "My humble residence is well within reach; how can you bear to discard me?" He took hold of the scholar's horse and pulled it along. Delaying in this way, they had reached the entrance of the lane where Miss Zheng lived. The scholar was distracted. Whipping his horse, he intended to turn back. The gallant hurriedly ordered a few servants to take hold of him and force him to go. Walking quickly, they pushed Li into the carriage gate; [the gallant] at once had it locked and announced, "Li the Tenth has arrived!" The whole household called out in happy astonishment, which could be heard even outside.

The previous night, Xiaoyu had dreamed that a man wearing a yellow shirt brought the scholar to her; when he reached the mat, he asked her to take off her shoes. When she woke with a start, she related the dream to her mother and interpreted it herself, "The word *xie* (shoe), being homophonous with the word *xie* (in harmony), refers to the reunion of a husband and his wife; the word *tuo* (take off) means 'to divide'. Being divided immediately after the reunion also means to be separated forever. Judging from this, I am sure that Li Yi and I will meet soon, and after we see each other, I shall die."

In the early morning she asked her mother to comb her hair and put on her makeup for her. Considering that she might be somewhat distraught because of her lingering illness, her mother didn't really believe her. Reluctantly she tried to do her makeup for her. No sooner had she finished the makeup than the scholar indeed arrived. Xiaoyu had been ill so long that she needed others' assistance to even turn over in bed. But when she suddenly heard that the scholar had arrived, she got up swiftly, changed her clothes, and emerged, as if some divine force were assisting her. She met the scholar and stared at him in indignation, saying nothing. Her body was so slim and frail that it seemed as if she could hardly bear it. From time to time, she covered her face with her sleeve and looked back at scholar Li. Moved by the heart-rending past events and taking pity on the lady, all those present were sobbing.

In a little while, several dozen dishes of food and wine were brought in from outside. All present were surprised to see the feast. They asked immediately where the food had come from and found that all of it had been ordered by the young gallant. Thus they laid out the food and wine and sat down side by side.

Xiaoyu turned away [from Li], and turned her face back, staring sideways at the scholar for a long time. She raised her cup of wine and poured it on the ground, saying, "As a woman, I am so misfortunate. You, as a man, are so heartless. Pretty and young as I am, I will die with a grievance in my heart. My kind mother is still alive at home, but I cannot look after her; [as for] silk dresses, pipes and strings, from now on I have to leave them forever. In suffering, I shall go to the Yellow Springs,[21] and all of this is caused by you. Mr. Li, Mr. Li! Now we shall say farewell forever! After my death, however, I shall certainly become an avenging ghost and cause your wife and concubines to never have peace!" Then she grasped Li's arm with her left hand and threw her cup to the ground. With several long and bitter cries, she passed away.

Her mother immediately lifted her body and placed it in the scholar's arms, asking him to call her. But she could not be revived. Attired in white mourning clothes for her, the scholar wept sorrowfully day and night.

The night before the burial, the scholar suddenly saw Xiaoyu within the funeral curtains, her appearance as beautiful as in life. She was wearing a pomegranate-red skirt, a purple tunic, and a red and green cape. Leaning against the curtain and holding the embroidered sash in hand, she looked back at the scholar and said, "I feel ashamed for your sending me [to the other world], and it seems that you still have some feelings for me. In the netherworld, how can I restrain my sigh!" As soon as she finished speaking, she disappeared. The next day, she was buried at the Yüsu Plain of Chang'an. The scholar went to the place of burial, expressed all his mourning [for the dead] by wailing, and then returned.

More than a month later, the scholar carried out the wedding ceremonies with Miss Lu. In grief and moved by the past events, he fell into melancholy.

In the fifth month of the year during summer, Li went back to Cheng County together with Miss Lu. About ten days after they arrived, the scholar was in bed with Miss Lu, when he heard a whispering sound outside the bed curtain. The scholar was startled and looked out and found that there was a man around 20 years old, with a handsome appearance and gentle gestures, concealing himself within the curtain and repeatedly beckoning to Miss Lu. With fear and panic, Li rose and chased him around the curtain a few times, but the man suddenly disappeared. From then on the scholar harbored suspicion and evil thoughts in his mind, doubt and distrust consuming him. Between husband and wife, there was no longer any peace. One of his relatives or friends persuaded and soothed him mildly and tactfully. The scholar's suspicions were relieved a little.

Ten days later, the scholar returned from outside just as Miss Lu was playing the zither on the couch; suddenly, they saw an engraved rhinoceros-horn box was thrown in from the gate. It was over an inch in size, a ribbon of light silk in a knot of one heart tied to the middle. It was thrown exactly into Miss Lu's lap. The scholar opened it and looked inside. He found two love seeds, a kowtow beetle, a passion pill, and a modicum of aphrodisiac made from the mouth of a newborn donkey. At that point the young man roared in rage, his voice like a jackal or tiger. He grasped the zither and hit his wife with it, closely questioning and commanding her to tell the truth. But even Miss Lu could not clear herself. Thereafter, he often beat her fiercely and treated her with all cruelties. At last he accused her in the court and sent her back [to her home].[22]

After Miss Lu was divorced, the scholar was always jealous and distrustful of the women, such as the maidens or concubines, with whom he had shared a pillow and mat with. There was even one whom he killed just because of his jealousy.

Once, the scholar visited Guangling[23] and obtained a famous courtesan called Ying the Eleventh. Her appearance was sleek and charming. The scholar was fond of her very much. Every time they sat face to face, he would tell her, "I once obtained such and such a concubine from such and such a place, she committed such and such a crime, and I killed her by such and such a way." He repeated it every day, intending to make her fear him, and through this to keep her boudoir clean.

When he went out, he covered Miss Ying on the bed with a wash tub, sealing it, making marks around it. After he returned, he checked it carefully and then opened it. Furthermore, he kept a dagger that was very sharp. He looked around at his maidens, warning, "This is [made of] Gexi steel from Xinzhou.[24] It will only be used to cut off the head of a woman who commits a crime!" All the women whom the scholar met always caused him to be jealous. He married three times, but each marriage ended up just like the first had.

(By Jiang Fang 蔣防 [792–835]; from Li Fang 李昉 [925–996], *Taiping guangji* 太平廣記, Chapter 487)

Note: This is a slightly revised version of my 2020 rendition in Victor Mair and Zhenjun Zhang, ed., *Anthology of Tang and Song Tales* (Singapore: World Scientific, 2020), pp. 133–50.

The Courtesan Li Wa

The Lady of Qian,[25] Li Wa, was originally a courtesan in Chang'an. Her character was noble, and her conduct particular, with points worthy of praise. Therefore Bai Xingjian (776–826), the investigating senior, wrote this biography about her.

During the Tianbao reign (742–756), the prefect of Changzhou, a gentleman of Xingyang whose real name is omitted here,[26] was highly renowned and had a household filled with numerous servants. At the age of 50, he had a son who was only 20 years old. His son had delicate features as well as literary talent, was clearly distinct from ordinary people, and therefore was deeply esteemed and admired by his peers. His father loved him dearly and regarded him highly, saying, "This is the winged steed of our family."

When the young man was recommended by the local prefecture to the Capital to participate in the imperial Civil Service Examination and was about to set out, his father prepared for him an ample supply of clothes, utensils, and a decorated horse-drawn carriage. The father had also calculated the living expenses his son would incur while living in the Capital, and he told him, "Based on my observation of your talent, you will place first on your first attempt. I have now prepared two years' worth of expenses for you, and it is an ample amount. This will help you realize your ambitions." The scholar was very conceited, and he regarded the effort it took to obtain a rank in the examinations to be as easy as counting his fingers. He set out from Piling, arriving in Chang'an a little over a month later. He took up residence at Buzheng Ward.

One day, he was returning from a ramble around the East Market and was entering through the Eastern Gate of Pingkang Ward to visit a friend in its southwest corner.[27] Having strolled to Mingke Lane, he noticed a residence with a courtyard. Its doorway was narrow, but the houses within were neat, deep, and tranquil. One panel of the double doors was closed. A young girl stood there, leaning against her servant maid with double bun-type hairdos, that is, coiled hair knots. The young girl possessed a charming grace and exquisite countenance, truly not of this world. Beholding her without warning, the scholar, distracted, stopped his horse unawares for quite a while, lingering, reluctant to leave. He then pretended that his hand had slipped, dropping the horsewhip onto the ground, and he waited for his servant to come up to him and ordered the whip to be retrieved. Taking advantage of the interim, he stole many glances at the girl. The girl also turned her gaze towards him and observed him, expressing a look of great adoration for him. In the end, however, the scholar did not dare exchange one word with her, and he simply left.

After that, the scholar looked distracted. Then he located friends familiar with Chang'an in order to inquire about her secretly. His friends informed him, "That is the house of a courtesan with the surname of Li."

He asked, "Is that girl available?"

His friends answered, "The Li family is very rich. Those who associated with her previously were all wealthy aristocrats, so she had made a lot of money. If your wealth does not exceed a million, don't expect to move her heart."

The scholar replied, "I only fear that I will not succeed – otherwise, even if I spend over a million, what is there to regret?"

A few days later, the scholar donned neat, immaculate clothes and brought along many guests to accompany him to the Li residence. After he knocked on the door, a servant girl came in no time to open it.

The scholar asked, "Whose esteemed residence is this?"

The servant girl did not answer but rather raced back at lightning speed while loudly yelling, "The young gentleman who dropped his horsewhip last time has come!"

Li Wa was ecstatic, telling her maid, "Ask him to please wait a few moments. I must fix myself up anew, change my clothes, and then come out to meet him."

The scholar was privately pleased upon hearing this. The servant girl thus led him to a screen, where he saw a white-haired hunch-backed old granny, who was Li Wa's mother. The scholar went up to her to kowtow and pay his respects, inquiring, "I have heard that there is a vacant unoccupied yard here, and I wish to rent it to live in – if it is true."

The old granny replied, "I just fear that it is too shabby and cramped, not deserving to be lived by a nobleman – how could I dare ask for rent?" She then ushered him into the drawing room, which had extremely resplendent furnishings.

The old granny sat opposite the scholar, then mentioned, "I have a daughter, petite, and not skilled, but who really enjoys meeting guests. I hope you can make her acquaintance." Upon saying this, she called Li Wa out. Li Wa had clear bright eyes and flawless white wrists; her every move was delicate and charming, simply enchanting.

Amazed, the scholar immediately stood up, not daring to lift up his head to look. After bowing to her in greeting, he paid his respects and offered correct social formalities.

Each of her movements was seductive and arousing, unlike anything he had ever seen before. They retook their seats and steeped the tea and poured the wine. The cups, plates, and utensils were immaculately clean.

After quite a while, the sky darkened and the sound of the drum announcing evening could be heard. The old granny asked the scholar if his residence was far. The scholar lied to her with an answer, "It is many *li* beyond the Yanping Gate," hoping she would ask him to stay the night because of the distance.

The old granny cautioned him, "The evening drum has already sounded. You should hurry back to avoid violating the curfew."

The scholar said, "I was lucky enough to have made the acquaintance of you all, so that, between chatting and laughing, I did not notice that it had already turned dark. The road is very far . . . and having no relatives in the city – what am I to do?"

Li Wa offered, "Since you don't mind the remoteness and simplicity of this place, and furthermore, are going to rent a house here, what does it matter if you stay here for a night?"

The scholar repeatedly glanced at the old granny, who consented, "Yes, okay."

So the scholar called his servant boy over and presented two bolts of fine silk to the women, asking them to accept it as payment for the night's dinner expenses. Li Wa, smiling, stopped him and said, "It does not work like this according to the etiquette between guest and host. For tonight's expenses, please allow my poor humble family to serve you with some casually-prepared simple fare. If you insist on being the host, let's wait until some other time." The scholar repeatedly refused her offer, but in the end Li Wa still disagreed with him.

Soon, everyone moved to the west hall to sit. The splendor of the bed curtains, bamboo drapery, and wooden couch drew everyone's gaze. The vanity box, coverlets, and pillows were also all luxurious and resplendent. They lit the candles and laid out the banquet, a lavish assortment of dishes and wine spread out before them.

After the meal, the old granny rose and left. It was following this that the scholar and Li Wa's conversation started to become more intimate, joking and teasing without reserve.

The scholar admitted, "Last time, passing your doorstep by chance, I saw you at that moment standing before the screen. Ever since then, you have occupied my thoughts constantly – even when eating or sleeping, I could not leave off [thinking about you] for a moment."

Li Wa replied, "My heart was likewise."

The scholar further revealed, "I came here today not only because I wished to rent a house, but more in the hope of realizing my entire life's desire. It is only that I don't know what my fate is . . . .?"

Before he could finish, the old granny walked in and asked them what they were discussing. The scholar told her everything.

Smiling, the old granny said, "It is natural that a desire for romance develops between a young man and woman. If they fall in love, there is no way to prevent it, even if their parents command it. It is just that my daughter's visage is ugly. How is she worthy to serve you!"

The scholar immediately walked down the steps, kowtowed to the old granny, and expressed his gratitude. He vowed, "I willingly become your servant."

The old granny thus regarded him as her son-in-law. They drank wine to their heart's content before dispersing.

The next day, the scholar moved all of his belongings and thus took up residence at the Li house. From that point on, he went into hiding, vanishing without a trace, no longer contacting his relatives and friends. He spent every day with courtesans, performers, and the like, eating, drinking, and making merry. When he had spent all the money he carried, he just sold his fine horses, then his servant boy. Over a year later, his money, servants, and horses were all gone. As a result, the old granny's attitude towards him gradually cooled. Yet Li Wa's affection for him deepened and became more sincere.

One day, Li Wa said to the scholar, "I have been together with you, in love, for a year now, but I still have not become pregnant. I frequently hear people speak of a Bamboo Forest God that is very effective. Let's prepare some food and wine to make a prayer, shall we?"

The scholar did not know that this was their ruse, so, thrilled, he went to the pawnshop and pawned his clothes. He took the money and spent it on preparing the Three Sacrifices and wine, then went together with Li Wa to pray in the temple. They stayed for two nights before returning, with the scholar riding on a donkey, following behind Li Wa's carriage.

Upon reaching the north gate of Pingkang Ward, Li Wa said to the scholar, "My aunt's home is in the lane that turns east from here. Let's go there to rest for a bit and, incidentally, pay her a visit, shall we?"

The scholar assented. After walking forward for less than one hundred steps, they indeed beheld a carriage gate. Peering in through the crack in the gate revealed a very spacious interior. The servant girl, from the back of the carriage, told him to stop, adding, "We're here."

The scholar dismounted from his donkey. Coincidently, a person walked out at that moment and asked, "Who is it?"

The scholar answered, "It's Li Wa."

The person withdrew inside to report this.

A short while later, an old lady approximately in her forties emerged. Facing the scholar, she walked towards him, asking, "So has my niece come?"

Li Wa descended from the carriage. The old lady stepped up to welcome her and reproached her, "Why haven't you visited me in so long?"

They looked at each other and started laughing.

Li Wa led the scholar to greet her aunt, then they entered together a side court-yard by the side of the western gate. Inside, there were imitation mountains and pavilions, verdant bamboo and trees, and a remarkably tranquil pond and waterside terrace.

The scholar asked Li Wa, "Is this your aunt's own house?"

Li Wa smiled but did not answer, changing the subject by speaking of other matters. A little while later, tea and fruit were offered, all of which were quite precious and exotic.

The time it takes to eat a meal passed. Suddenly, a person riding a swift Dayuan horse appeared.[28] He ran over, drenched in sweat, reporting, "The old granny has suddenly taken ill with an acute illness, very serious, and can barely recognize anyone. You should go back quickly."

Li Wa said to her aunt, "I am so distracted. I will ride back first, let the horse return, then you and he can come together."

The scholar wanted to return with Li Wa but saw her aunt whispering to the servant girl and waving the scholar over. Her aunt asked him to stop just outside the door and said, "I fear the old granny is dying. We should discuss how to manage the funeral affairs together to rescue Li Wa in her crisis – why are you in a hurry to go with her?"

The scholar had no choice but to remain behind to calculate the expenses for the funeral and memorial.

It was getting dark, but the horse still had not returned. Her aunt said, "There still hasn't been a word . . . I wonder why? Hurry over to see what's happening. I will be right behind you."

The scholar thus set off. When he reached his original residence, he only beheld tightly locked doors sealed with mud. The scholar was shocked, and so questioned a neighbor. The neighbor said, "The Li family had originally rented this house to live in. Now that the lease has reached its full term, the landlord has reclaimed the house. The granny moved away, two days ago now."

Upon asking "where did she move to," the reply was, "I don't know where."

The scholar wanted to rush to Xuanyang to question Li Wa's aunt, but it was already too late. Calculating the journey, he realized he could not possibly make it before the curfew. So he could only take off his clothes as guaranty in exchange for a meal and rent a bed to sleep in. The scholar was greatly irritated and furious, unable to close his eyes the entire night from dusk to dawn.

As soon as it was light, he went on his way astride his donkey. Upon reaching her aunt's house, he knocked on the door repeatedly, but a long time passed without anyone answering. The scholar shouted loudly many times before an official finally leisurely strolled out.

The scholar hastily asked him, "Is aunt here?"

The person replied, "There's no such person."

The scholar retorted, "She was still here last night at dusk. Why are you hiding her?" He then asked whose house it was.

The person answered, "This is Minister Cui's house. Yesterday, someone rented this courtyard supposedly to wait for some cousins who were traveling here from afar. The person left before it was dark."

Upon hearing this, the scholar was aghast and alarmed, frantic to the point of madness. He did not know what to do and so could only return to the old house in Buzheng Ward. The landlord pitied him and gave him food. The scholar's resentment and anger made him unable to eat anything for three days. He became severely ill. After some ten days, his illness worsened. The landlord was afraid he would die, so he moved him to a funeral parlor. The scholar's illness was critical and dragged on for quite a while. Everyone in the funeral parlor bewailed and sympathized with what he had experienced, and so together took care of him.

As time went on, his illness improved slightly, and he could move about propped up on crutches. From then on, the funeral parlor employed him daily, letting him hold the screen in the funeral hall so that he could earn some money to support himself. He gradually recovered his health after a few months. Every time he heard the strains of a dirge, he would sigh that he was worse off than the dead, frequently weeping and shedding tears, unable to control himself. Immediately after returning, he would try to imitate what he had heard, learning to sing the dirges. The scholar was a clever person, and before long, he sang quite wonderfully and movingly. Within the entire city of Chang'an, there could not be found anyone who was his match.

Earlier, there had been two competing funeral parlors in the business of renting funeral supplies. The carriage supplies of the eastern shop were novel and magnificent, to which the other shop simply could not compare, though their dirge performances were somewhat inferior. The shopkeeper of the eastern shop knew that the scholar sang laments extraordinarily well, so he gathered together 20,000 coins to hire him. The elders in the group together seriously discussed this and, combining their various specialties, secretly taught the scholar to sing new tunes, as well as helping him with vocal accompaniment on the side. For dozens of days, no one else knew of this.

One day, the shopkeepers of the two funeral parlors consulted with each other, saying, "We will each display our rental funeral supplies on Heavenly Gate Street, and compete to determine whose are superior and whose inferior. The loser will be fined 50,000 cash, to be used for the cost of hosting a feast – how about it?" Both houses agreed.

So they engaged a middleman, established a contract, signed it, and then held the exhibition.

When that day arrived, men and women all came to observe, resulting in a gathering of tens of thousands of people. As a result, the local officer reported the event to the head of the bureau of banditry, who in turn informed the governor of the capital. People from all directions went to participate. No shadow of a human figure was to be found even in the small lanes.

The exhibition began in the early morning; at noon, the two shops laid out the carriage and ritual items piece by piece to compare them. The western shop could not win any of these, and the foreman felt somewhat ashamed. Thus just at the street's southern corner he set up a double-layered couch, and a long-bearded man, large bell in hand, stepped forward, with a few guards beside him. Shaking his beard and raising his eyebrows, wringing his wrist in despair and nodding his head, he stepped onto the lofty bed and started singing the "White Horse Song." Relying on his continuous past success, he glanced left and right, and seemed to regard the spectators as if they weren't there. Everyone lauded him in unison. He thought himself unrivaled; for the moment, no one could surpass him.

After a while, the eastern parlor's shopkeeper placed a few couches side by side at the northern corner of the street. With five or six people beside him, there came a youth wearing a black headscarf and holding a large feather palm fan. He was none other than the scholar. Straightening his clothes, he acted leisurely and calmly. When he opened his throat to vocalize, it seemed that he could not bear it. He sang the song "Dew on the Scallions": the sound was clear and sonorous and even shook the trees.[29] Long before he finished the dirge, the spectators had already covered their faces in order to weep.

Mocked by the crowd, the shopkeeper of the western parlor felt even more ashamed, and he quietly placed the money he lost before the couch and then stealthily slipped away. People from all corners gazed in astonishment, not knowing exactly what had happened.

Just prior to this event, the emperor had issued an edict commanding all the officials from each prefecture throughout the country to go to the Capital annually. This was called "Entry for Auditing." At this moment, it just so happened that the scholar's father was also at the Capital. He and his colleagues had changed into civilian clothes and had secretly gone forth to observe.

An old servant – in fact the scholar's wet nurse's husband – marked that the singer's manner of movement and voice resembled that of the scholar's. The servant wanted to go up to identify him, yet did not dare; he was so distressed that tears began to flow. The scholar's father was startled and questioned him about why he was crying. The old servant then informed him, "This singer's appearance is strikingly similar to that of the deceased young master."

The gentleman of Xingyang replied, "My son was killed by robbers for his wealth because he possessed a lot of money. How would he end up in this state?" Upon saying this, he also started to cry.

After they went back, the old servant took the opportunity to rush over again, asking the scholar's companions, "Who was the singer just a moment ago? He sang so wonderfully."

Everyone all answered, "He was so and so's son."

Inquiring again after his name, he found it had already been changed. The old servant was shocked and slowly approached to carefully identify him.

On beholding the old servant, the scholar's face changed color; dodging and evading, he wanted to hide in the crowd.

The old servant grasped his sleeve with one hand and asked, "But aren't you my young master?" The two held hands and wept loudly. They rode the carriage back together.

When they arrived in his father's room, his father rebuked him, "Your character and conduct have degenerated to this state, and you have disgraced our family's reputation! What face do you have to appear before me again?" He led the scholar to go out by foot to a place west to the Crooked River and east to the Apricot Garden, and then stripped him of his clothes. Using the horsewhip, he fiercely whipped his son a few hundred times. The scholar could not bear such a vicious beating and died. The father left him there and walked away.

At the same time, one of the scholar's teachers had ordered a close companion to secretly follow him. The man returned and informed his associates of what had occurred. Everyone sighed in dejection. They sent two people with a reed mat to retrieve his body and bury him. When the pair got there, they discovered that the scholar's chest still had some faint warmth remaining. So they helped him up. After a long while, his breathing finally slightly eased. The two men carried him back together. They used a reed pipe to trickle soup to feed him. The night passed before he regained consciousness.

A little over a month later, the scholar still could not move his hands and feet. All the areas where he had been viciously beaten festered and oozed pus; it was quite foul. His companions also grew tired of it. One night, they discarded him by the side of the road. Passers-by all pitied him, frequently throwing him leftover scraps for him to eat. He relied on this to alleviate his hunger.

A hundred days passed before he was finally able to stand up by leaning on crutches. Draped over him was a cloth coat, mended a thousand times and patched a hundred, tattered beyond recognition. He held a broken bowl, begging for food along the streets to subsist. From autumn to winter, he would hide inside the caves for piling garbage at night, roving around the city streets begging by day.

One day, with the heavy snow swirling down, the scholar had to venture out in the snow, forced by hunger and cold. The sound of his begging was very wretched. There were none who heard him who did not feel sorrowful and pity him. At the time, the snow was just coming down fast and heavily, and the outer gates around people's houses were mostly closed. He walked to the eastern gate of Anyi Ward, and following along the walls, he roamed over seven or eight houses northwards. Only one household had the left panel of a door open. That was Li Wa's residence. The scholar did not know this and kept continuously shouting. Since he was so hungry and so cold, the forlorn and disconsolate voice was truly mournful and difficult to bear hearing.

Li Wa heard it in her room and exclaimed to the servant girl, "That must be the scholar! I recognize his voice!"

Upon saying this, she hurriedly rushed out with quick steps. She saw the scholar: his muscles thin as kindling, scabies sores over his entire body, seemingly not human at all. Li Wa was deeply moved, so she asked him, "Aren't you the young gentleman?"

On seeing her, the scholar fainted onto the ground out of anger; rendered speechless, he only nodded his head. Li Wa went forward and embraced his neck, wrapping an embroidered coat around him and helping him back to the west wing. She cried bitterly, her voice cracking, "It is my fault that you have fallen to this state!" She sobbed her heart out.

The old granny, quite astonished, ran over to ask, "Who is this?"

Li Wa replied, "It is that young gentleman."

The old granny hastily ordered, "We must drive him out! How could you let him come here?"

Hearing this, Li Wa's face turned solemn. She turned to look at the old granny and asserted, "We can't do this. He is descended from a respectable family! At the outset, he drove a lofty carriage and fine steed, and carrying money, came to our house. Yet within one year, he had spent it all. We also designed a scheme together to get rid of him – that just simply was not a human act. We finally made him fall into depravity, scorned by others. The affection between a father and son is innate, but this matter caused his father to break his affection and sever their relationship, beating him to death and simultaneously abandoning him. Now, he has become impoverished to this state – everyone knows he is thus because of me. The majority of the scholar's relatives are officials in the imperial court – one day when those who have power figure out clearly the ins and outs of this matter, then disasters will befall us. Besides, even ghosts and gods will not protect those who deceive Heaven and wrong others. Don't create further trouble for yourself! I have been your daughter for twenty years now. The money I have made you exceeds a thousand *liang* of gold. Now, you are over sixty years of age; I wish to calculate and repay twenty years' worth of living costs to buy back my freedom. I will rent another place to live in with this young gentleman. The house I rent won't be very far, so I will still be able to come to pay my respects in the mornings and evenings. This way, my wish will be satisfied."

The old granny concluded that her determination was not to be altered and so could only assent. After Li Wa paid the old granny to redeem herself, she had a hundred *liang* of gold remaining. So she rented an empty house in a place to the north, four or five houses over. She washed the scholar's hair, bathed him, and changed his clothes. She initially cooked porridge for him to ease his stomach into food, followed by cheese to moisturize his internal organs. After more than ten days, she finally gave him fish, meat, and the like to eat. For the scholar's scarf and hat, shoes and stockings, Li Wa picked the most luxurious and costly for him to wear. Within a few months, the scholar's body had filled out somewhat. After a year had passed, he had recovered to his original condition.

One day, Li Wa told him, "Your body has recovered and your energy is abundant. Think back carefully and calmly – can you still take up your former studies?"

The scholar thought about this and admitted, "I only recall two or three tenths of it." So Li Wa ordered the carriage be harnessed to go out. The scholar followed on horseback.

When they reached a bookshop selling classics, by the southern side gate of the market tower, she asked the scholar to pick out the ones he needed, for which she spent 100 teals of gold and had all of them transported back to their home. Then she told the scholar to cast aside all distracting thoughts and devote himself to studying wholeheartedly. Taking nights as days, he worked tirelessly. Li Wa frequently sat at his side to keep him company, retiring only when it was late into the night. Sometimes, when she saw that he was fatigued, she would tell him to compose poetry and rhapsodies.

Two years later, the scholar's knowledge had progressed profoundly. There were no books in the world he had not read. The scholar announced to Li Wa, "Now I can register to take the examination." Li Wa cautioned, "Not yet. You must study until you are even more proficient and skilled, so that you can deal with all kinds of exam questions." Another year passed. Li Wa finally said, "You can take the tests."

Then the scholar became an advanced scholar by passing the Type-A examination.[30] His renown resounded throughout the imperial Board of Rites. Even among the senior scholars, there were none who were not filled with deep respect and admiration for him after reading his essays, desirous to become friends with him but afraid that it was beyond their reach. However, Li Wa warned, "It's not time to celebrate yet. Scholars today presume that, by passing one imperial examination, they can get a high position in the royal court and their fame will spread throughout the world. Your past moral conduct is stained, your behavior not honorable, and thus your character cannot be compared to that of an ordinary scholar. You must continue to assiduously delve into your studies and try to succeed once more in another imperial examination. Only in this way can you then associate and interact with the multitude of scholars, contending with the giants to vie for supremacy." From then on, the scholar became even more diligent and hard-working, his reputation also rising ever higher and higher.

That year, it happened that the imperial court was holding the national examination. The emperor issued an edict recruiting talent from all four corners of the nation. The scholar registered for the exam on the subject "candid extreme admonishment," placed first, and was appointed the adjutant of Chengdu Prefecture. Everyone in the imperial court below the Three Dukes all became friends with him.

As he was about to take his post, Li Wa said to him, "Now that you have regained your former aspect, I no longer have anything to apologize to you for. I wish to use my remaining days to return to look after my old granny. You should marry a young lady from a noble family, for the convenience of managing your familial sacrifices. You must find one whose family is your equal in rank and unite in a happy marriage. Never again abase yourself. I hope you take care. From here on, I will leave you!"

The scholar sobbed, "If you abandon me, I will slit my throat in front of you."

Li Wa resolutely refused to go along with him to take up his new office. The scholar pleaded bitterly, with an even more sincere attitude. In the end, Li Wa conceded, "I will see you off across the river, but when we reach Jianmen you must let me return." The scholar agreed.

A little over a month later, they arrived at Jianmen. However, before he had a chance to set off, the emperor's imperial decree appointing the new official arrived. The scholar's father had been summoned to the capital from Changzhou prefecture and appointed the governor of Chengdu, as well as the investigation commissioner of Jiannan Circuit.[31] The scholar had no choice but to remain and wait.

Twelve days later, the scholar's father arrived. The scholar therefore went to the courier station to pay respects to his father, offering his name card. His father dared not claim to know him until he saw the scholar's paternal ancestors' official ranks and names, back to three generations. He was then stunned and asked his son up the stone steps. Gently stroking his son's back, he wept in pain and sorrow for a long time, saying, "Let us restore our father-son relationship as it was originally."

Accordingly, he proceeded to inquire about the course of events, and his son related the matter to him from beginning to end. Amazed, he asked where Li Wa was.

The scholar answered, "After seeing me off here, I was preparing to let her go back."

His father replied, "This will not do." The next day, he ordered the carriage so that he and the scholar could go to Chengdu first, leaving Li Wa in Jianmen. He had a house built for her to live in. The very next day after they arrived in Chengdu, he sent a matchmaker to go ask for Li Wa's hand in marriage, and completed the entire six wedding formalities to welcome her. Thus, the scholar and Li Wa became husband and wife in the manner of a formal marriage.

After Li Wa became, through the full marriage rites, the daughter-in-law of the gentleman of Xingyang, every New Year's day and holiday, she would carefully and attentively fulfill her responsibilities as a wife and daughter-in-law. She managed her household strictly and was deeply beloved and respected by their relatives.

After a few years, the scholar's father and mother both died. She handled the funeral arrangements very considerately. A *Ganoderma lucidum* started to grow beside the straw hut where she observed mourning, with one branch growing three ears. The local officials informed the emperor of these occurrences. Additionally, tens of white swallows built nests on the roof beams of her home. The emperor thought these incidents extraordinary and consequently placed his particular confidence in the scholar and rewarded him especially. Following the period of mourning, the scholar thus repeatedly rose to hold important positions. Within ten years' time, he had been governor of several regions. Upon Li Wa was conferred the title "Lady of Qian." They had four sons, all of whom became high-ranking officials. Amongst these, even the lowest office held was the governor of Tianyuan. The brothers all married ladies of distinguished and prominent families. Inside and out, they had impressive power and influence. No one could compare to them.

Ah, a courtesan from a brothel, yet one whose integrity and conduct are like this – such that not even an ancient female martyr could surpass! How can I not sigh in admiration of her?

My granduncle had been prefect of Jinzhou, then was transferred to the Ministry of Revenue, and also once held the position of Water and Land Transport Commissioner. These three posts were all assumed to replace the scholar, so my granduncle was familiar with his story. During the Zhenyuan reign (785–805), I was discussing the noble character of women with Li Gongzuo (778–848),[32] a native of Longxi, and so spoke of Lady Qian's deeds. Having listened to it attentively while clapping his hands, Li Gongzuo asked me to write a biography. I grabbed a brush, dipped it in ink, and so recorded these matters in detail.

It is now the eighth month in the autumn of the *yihai* year (795). The cited example is recorded by Bai Xingjian, a native of Taiyuan.

(By Bai Xingjian 白行簡 (776–826); From Li Fang,
Taiping guangji, Chapter 484)

Note: This is a slightly revised version of my 2020 rendition in Victor Mair and Zhenjun Zhang, ed., *Anthology of Tang and Song Tales* (Singapore: World Scientific, 2020), pp. 210–28.

Notes

1 顏淵問「仁」。子曰：「克己復禮爲仁。一日克己復禮，天下歸仁焉，爲仁由己，而由人乎哉？」顏淵曰："請問其目。"子曰："非禮勿視，非禮勿聽，非禮勿言，非禮勿動 The translation is from Dim Cheuk Lau, trans., *The Analects*, Vol. XII (London: Penguin Books, 1979), p. 112.

2 Robert E. Hegel and Richard C. Hessney, *Expressions of Self in Chinese Literature* (New York: Columbia University Press, 1985), pp. 6–7.

3 Li Yi 李益 (748–827), styled Junyu 君虞, belonged to the clan of Li Kuei 李揆, who was the chief minister during the reign of Emperor Suzong 肅宗 (r. 756–762). He passed the *jinshi* examination in the fourth year of the Dali reign (769), and he was also a famous poet. He and Li He 李賀 (790–816) enjoyed equal fame at the end of the Zhenyuan 貞元 (785–805) period. Every time he finished a poem, the court musicians got it through bribery and took it as the lyrics of a song to sing for the emperor. However, he had a suspicious nature and was jealous of his wife and concubines, a tendency that was called "Li Yi's disease" during his time. He ended his official career as a Minister of the Board of Rites.

4 One of the two imperial examinations for selecting officials beyond the normal selection in the Tang dynasty. People who pass either of the examinations would be offered an official position immediately.

5 Around three o'clock in the afternoon. *Shen* 申 refers to the period from three to five o'clock, while *wei* 未 is from one to three o'clock in the afternoon.

6 The meaning of *suguzi* 蘇姑子 is unknown. Wang Meng'ou says that it may be equivalent to *sao guzi* 騷姑子 (coquette). Another view is that it is homophone of *shu guanzi* 書罐子 (bookworm), a kind of mocking name for the scholars. See Tan Fengliang 譚鳳梁, ed., *Lidai wenyen xiaoshuo jianshang cidian* 歷代文言小說鑒賞詞典 (Nanjing: Jiangsu wenyi, 1991), p. 367.

7 The Shengye 勝業 Quarter was located north of the Eastern Market and west of the Xingqing 興慶 Palace in the northeastern part of Chang'an. See the map of Chang'an (Wang Meng'ou, A, front matters).

8 The phrase *fu shang che men zhai* 甫上車門宅 has puzzled many scholars. Uchiyama Chinari 内山知也 suspects *fu shang* 甫上 is *pu shang* 浦上 (*Tangdai xiaoshuo xuanzhu* 唐代小說選注, Tokyo: Mokujisha, 1973), Dai Wangshu 戴望舒 suspects it is *jiao shang* 角上 (*Xiaoshuo xiqu lunji* 小說戲曲論集, Beijing: Zuojia chubanshe, 1958, p. 40), Wang Meng'ou considers it *pushang* 铺上 (*Tangren xiaoshuo jiaoshi* [A], Taibei: Zhongzheng shuju, 1983, p. 203–204). But all are obscure. Personally I think the *nan shang chemen zhai* 南上車門宅 in *Jiu Xiaoshuo* 舊小說 (2.117) is the best, because *nan* 南 makes much more sense than *fu* and *jiao*.

9 Wu shan 巫山 (Mount Wu) and Luo Pu 洛浦 (the bank of Luo River): reference of King Xiang 襄 of Chu 楚 encountering the goddess of mount Wu (see Song Yu 宋玉, Gaotang fu 高唐賦, in *Wenxuan* 文選, Vol. 19 (Hong Kong: Shangwu yinshuguan, 1936), pp. 393–397. and Cao Zhi 曹植 encountering the goddess of 洛 River (see Cao's "Lo shen fu" 洛神賦, *Wenxuan*, Vol. 19, pp. 401–405).

10 Nüluo 女萝, a kind of parasitic vine, can also be called *tusi* 菟絲. "Gushi" 古詩 (Old poems): 與君為新婚，菟絲附女萝 (I am newly married to you, just like the vine clings to the vine). See Shen Deqian 沈德潛, ed., *Gushi yuan* 古詩源 (Taipei: Taiwan shangwu yinshuguan, 1966), p. 54. The vine that has nothing to cling is a metaphor for a woman who has lost favor of a man she relies on. Qiushan jianjuan 秋扇見捐 (the autumn fan is

thrown away) is another metaphor. See Ban Jieyu班婕妤, *Yuan ge xing* 怨 歌行, Vol. 27 (*Wenxuan*), p. 598.

11 *Yue* 越 is the name of a nationality. In ancient China, the area of Jiangxi, Zhejiang, Guangdong, and Fujian Province, occupied by the *Yue* people, was called *bai Yue* 百越 or baiyue 百粤 (Hundred *Yue*).

12 Modern Hua County, Shanxi.

13 Dong Lo東洛 here refers to the Eastern Capital, Loyang 洛陽.

14 Xie Qin Jin 諧秦晋 (harmonize the Qin and the Jin) means to get married. This idiom originated from the generations-long intermarriage for generations between the two states in the Spring and Autumn period.

15 Pizi 披緇 (put on black clothes) means to renounce the family and become a nun. *Zi* is the gray-black colored clothes worn by nuns.

16 Huazhou 華州, modern Hua County in Shanxi Province. Zheng County belonged to Huazhou in the Tang dynasty.

17 Since the Spring and Autumn period, *Liu li* 六禮, six rites, became the fixed rites for marriage, which lasted in China for 2,000 years. They are *nacai* 納彩, sending first gift, normally a chicken or a goose, to the girl's home to request discussing and processing the marriage; *wenming* 問名, asking the girl's family background and birth date; *naji* 納吉, divining in the boy's ancestral temple to consult his ancestors if the marriage would be auspicious; *nazheng* 納徵, sending betrothal gifts to the girl's family, and this shows the marriage is formally effective if the girl's family accepted the gifts; *qingqi* 請期, setting the wedding date through consultation with the girl's parents; *and qinying* 親迎, the bridegroom, acting on the order of his father, goes to the bride's home to welcome her. See Sun Xidan 孫希旦, Hunyi 婚儀, in *Liji jijie* 禮記集解 (Beijing: Zhunghua shuju, 1989), pp. 1416–1423. Here Li Yi's mother had completed all the first three rites, and Li Yi himself just went to send the betrothal gifts to confirm the marriage. After that a close date for wedding was set.

18 In ancient China, a girl had her hair pinned up with a hairpin at the age of 15.

19 The Princess *Yanxian* should be *Yanguang*, the seventh daughter of Emperor Suzong.

20 *Mingjing* 明經 was a type of imperial examination in the Tang Dynasty. The exam consisted not of writing poems and rhapsodies, as required in the *jinshi* exam, but explaining the meaning of the classics. It was easier to pass the *mingjing* exam compared to taking the *jinshi* exam, but those who passed the *mingjing* exam were still commoners and couldn't get an official position.

21 *Huang quan* 黃泉, Yellow Springs, refers to the netherworld.

22 *Qianzhi* 遣之, discard her. We also can say *chuzhi* 出之 or *quzhi* 去之. In ancient China a husband could abandon his wife for various unreasonable excuses. "Benming" 本命, *Da dai li* 大戴礼, "婦有七去：不順父母，去；无子，去；淫，去；妒，去；有惡疾，去；多言，去；盜竊，去。" (There are seven kinds of situation in which a woman should be discarded. If she does not obey her parent-in-law, she should be discarded; if she cannot give birth to a son, she should be discarded; if she is promiscuous, she should be discarded; if she is jealous of other women of her husband, she should be discarded; if she has serious disease, she should be discarded; if she is gossipy, she should be discarded; if she steals things, she should be discarded). See Gao Ming 高明, *Da dai li jinzhu jinyi* 大戴禮今注今譯 (Taibei: Taiwan shangwu yinshuguan, 1975), p. 469.

23 Guangling 廣陵, modern Yangzhou in Jiangsu Province.

24 Xinzhou 信州, northwest of modern Shangrao 上饒 in Jiangxi Province. The steel produced there is the best for making swords.

25 Qian 汧 refers to Qianyang 汧陽 commandery, centered around modern Long County in Shanxi.

26 Xingyang 滎陽 commandery, modern Xingyang County in Henan, was the hometown of the noted Zheng clan, one of the seven noble clans during the Tang dynasty.

27 Pingkang Ward 平康里 was famous as a residence of courtesans.

28 Dayuan 大宛 was a state located west of the Pamir Range, covering the middle and lower course of the River Syr Darya and the Ferghana Basin. It is famous for its so-called "blood-sweating" horses.

29 "Xielu," Dew on the Scallions, was a famous dirge since the Warring States period.

30 *Jiake* 甲科, Type A exam, was one of the imperial exams during the Tang dynasty; the other one was *yike* 乙科, Type B exam, which was taken more frequently.

31 Its seat was modern Chengdu, Sichuan.

32 Li Gongzuo 李公佐, a famous tale writer of the Tang and the author of "Governor of the Southern Tributary Branch."

Further Readings

Hsia, C. T. "Society and Self in the Chinese Short Story." In *The Classic Chinese Novel: A Critical Introduction*. New York: Columbia University Press, 1968, pp. 299–321.

Hegel, Robert E. and Richard C. Hessney. *Expressions of Self in Chinese Literature*. New York: Columbia University Press, 1985.

Part II

Daoist Culture

Daoism (*Dao jia* 道家), also spelled Taoism, was established by Laozi (fl. 6th BCE) and developed by Liezi 列子 (c.450–c.375BCE) and Zhuangzi (c. 369–286 BCE). It is one of the major schools of Chinese philosophy and a system of speculative thought as a "complement to Confucianism."

The major teachings of Daoism are found in the two Daoist classics, the *Classic of the Way and Its Power* (*Dao de jing* 道德經), a long philosophical poem written in the 3rd century BCE, and the *Zhuangzi* (written between 4th–2nd century BCE), a collection of anecdotes and tales rather than a philosophical work, and full of wisdom, imagination, wit, and humor. Both discuss the nature of the Dao (Way) and essential related concepts; both are among the favorite books of Chinese readers throughout history. The *Dao de jing* is also the most translated book among all Chinese works.

Contrary to Confucianism, Daoism is centered on the individual and is pessimistic about society, seeking nature as a refuge from the artificial human world. It believes that man is not the center of all creatures, but one among them. Man cannot change the order of the universe; what man can do is merely adjust to or follow the Way of nature, the Dao. This understanding of the term differs from the Dao in Confucian texts, which is moral guidance or a code of behavior. The Dao in *Dao de jing* is nameless, ineffable, born before Heaven and earth, a mysterious entity, the genesis of the universe, and the Way of nature that everything follows.

Daoism (especially Laozi) promotes the idea of non-action (*wuwei* 無為), which is to be supple, humble, modest, and yielding. Non-action does not mean doing nothing; it means doing nothing against the Way of nature. By following the Way, even though there is nothing that needs to be done, yet nothing remains undone. Thus, the best ruler is one whom people know is there but who is not always in the limelight (by doing nothing).

Daoism considers Confucian morality useless "artificial devices," which are the source of trouble in the world by causing contention for profit and fame, creating more harm than benefit, and thus ruining the innate characteristics of things and their harmonious relationship with the Dao.

Now, the more taboos under heaven,
the poorer the people;

DOI: 10.4324/9781003490821-8

The more clever devices people have,
the more confused the state and ruling house;
The more knowledge people have,
the more strange things spring up;
The more legal affairs are given prominence,
the more numerous bandits and thieves.

For this reason, the sage has a saying:

"I take no action,
yet the people transform themselves;
I am fond of stillness,
yet the people correct themselves;
I do not interfere in affairs,
yet the people enrich themselves;
I desire not to desire, yet the people of themselves become simple as unhewn
logs."[1]

The ideal society in Laozi's eyes goes back to a more remote time:

Let there be a small state with few people,
Where military devices find no use;
Let the people look solemnly upon death,
And banish the thought of moving elsewhere.
They may have carts and boats,
But there is no reason to ride them;
They may have armor and weapons,
But they have no reason to display them.
Let the people go back to tying knots to keep records
Let their food be savory, their clothes beautiful, their customs pleasurable,
    [and] their dwellings secure.
Though they may gaze across at a neighboring state,
And hear the sounds of its dogs and chickens,
The people will never travel back and forth,
Till they die of old age.[2]

Daoism (especially Zhuangzi) also promotes the ideas of the equality of all things, the identity of life and death, and spiritual freedom (i.e., no self, no accomplishments, no fame, relying on nothing external), spontaneity, and being one with the Dao.

From the second to the fifth century CE, Daoism developed into a religion (*Dao jiao* 道教), based on a mixture of philosophical Daoism, Shamanism, and the practice of seeking immortality. It offered "emotional religious satisfaction to those who found the largely ethical system of Confucianism inadequate" (Encyclopedia Britannica).

The two major schools of religious Daoism are the Heavenly Master (*Tianshi* 天師), founded by Zhang Daoling 張道陵 (34–156), that emphasizes using talismans (*fulu* 符籙) to avoid calamity and heal disease; and the Total Perfection (*quanzhen* 全真), founded by Wang Chongyang 王重陽 (fl. 1167), that emphasizes alchemy (*danding* 丹鼎) to prolong life or achieve immortality.

As a salvation religion, Daoism has a complete system of deities headed by the Jade Emperor or the Daoist Trinity. The belief in immortality and the practice of seeking to achieve transcendence played an important role in the practice of Daoism.

The legends and tales selected here vividly touch on many aspects of Daoism with details that are difficult to acquire from scholarly monographs or conventional textbooks.

Notes

1 Victor Mair, trans., *Tao Te Ching: The Classic Book of Integrity and the Way* (New York: Bantam Books, 1990), p. 26.
2 Victor Mair, trans., *Tao Te Ching: The Classic Book of Integrity and the Way*, p. 39.

Further Readings

Hansen, Chad. *A Daoist Theory of Chinese Thought*. New York, NY: Oxford University Press, 1992.
Robinet, Isabelle. *Taoism: Growth of a Religion*. Stanford, CA: Stanford University Press, 1997.

7   Carefree Wanderers

As an individual-centered philosophy, Daoism values the self by promoting the idea of spiritual freedom. This is contrary to Confucian efforts in regulating the world by promoting a moral code centered upon the Three Immortalities: establishing virtue, establishing meritorious deeds, and establishing words. Daoism promotes a non-action alternative: no self, no accomplishments, and no fame; specifically, this includes clinging to nothing, being spontaneous, and wandering carefreely.

The carefree wanderers depicted in the following tales are all free from the constraints of Confucian ritual, duties, and mundane concerns, vividly illustrating the essence of Daoism.

Residents of the Huaxu Kingdom

Once, when the Yellow Emperor was sleeping during the daytime,[1] he dreamed that he was roaming in the Kingdom of Huaxu.[2] The kingdom is located west of Yanzhou and north of Taizhou,[3] and who knows how many millions of *li* from the state of Qi.[4] It was probably beyond the reach of boat, carriage, or any mortal foot. It was only a journey of his soul and that is all.

The kingdom had no monarch or leaders; it simply went on by itself. Its people had no hobbies or desires; they simply followed their instincts. They neither felt life enjoyable nor death abhorrent, thus there were no early ends. They neither favored themselves nor alienated others, thus there were no emotions for love or hate. They knew neither betrayal nor obedience, therefore no benefit or harm existed. They had nothing to cherish, and they had nothing to fear or avoid, either.

Submerged in water, they would never drown; leaping into fire, they would never feel hot. Cut or flogged, they suffered neither wound nor pain; scratching and tickling would cause them neither pain nor itch. They walked on the air as though walking on solid earth, and they cradled in the void as if resting in a bed. Cloud and mist could not hinder their sight, and thunder could not disturb their hearing; beauties would not disturb their mind, and valleys would not obstruct their steps. It was only a journey of his soul, nothing else.

(From *Liezi* 列子)

DOI: 10.4324/9781003490821-9

Zhuang Zhou

Zhuang Zhou 莊周 was a native of Meng in the state of Song.[5] When he was young, he studied the *Laozi* 老子[6] and served as the superintendent of the Lacquer Garden in Meng County. Then he shunned society, lived in solitude, and refused to be an official in the government. Of the princes and nobles, nobody could recruit him and let him serve in an important position.

Once, King Wei 威 of Chu (d. 329 BCE) sent a senior official, bearing 100 catties of gold, to hire Zhuang Zhou. Zhuang Zhou happened to be fishing on the Pu River.[7] With a fishing pole in hand and without even turning his head to look, he said, "I heard that there is a divine turtle in Chu which died two thousand years ago and is now held in a box covered with cloth and housed in the temple. Would this turtle be willing to become noble by having its bones kept [in the temple] rather than dragging its tail in the mud alive?" The senior official replied, "It would rather drag its tail in the mud." Zhuang Zhou said, "Then please go back! I'm just dragging my tail in the mud."

With 1,000 pieces of gold, someone again tried to persuade Zhuang Zhou to be the prime minister. Zhuang Zhou said, "Do you not see the ox prepped for sacrifice? It wears patterned silk and is fed with grass and beans. But when it is taken into the imperial temple [to be slaughtered], even if it wants to be a little pig [to be alive], how could it?" Thus, he never served as an official in the government.

(From Huangfu Mi's 皇甫謐 (215–282) *Gaoshi zhuan* 高士傳)

Master Chen Zhong

Master Chen Zhong was a native of the state of Qi.[8] His older brother, Chen Dai, was a minister of Qi, enjoying a salary of 10,000 bushels of grains. Chen Zhong considered him to be unrighteous. He moved to Chu with his wife and sons and lived at Ling, calling himself Master Zhong of Ling. Being in poverty, he never sought help improperly and never ate any ill-gotten food.

Once, during a famine, Chen Zhong had been out of food for three days. Crawling on the ground, he ate the moth-eaten plums on the well. After three mouthfuls, his eyes could see his body again. He weaved sandals from the hemp thread that his wife made to trade for clothes and food.

Hearing that Chen Zhong was worthy, the King of Chu intended to make him his prime minister, so he sent an envoy, bearing 100 pieces of gold, to Ling to announce his appointment.

Master Chen Zhong returned home and said to his wife, "The King of Chu intends to make me his prime minister. If I become the prime minister today, tomorrow the streets around our home will be filled with four-horse carriages and numerous horsemen, and a yard-long square dining table with a variety of delicacies will be laid before us. Do you think this is acceptable?"

His wife replied, "Master, you are already happy with just a zither on your left and books on your right. Among the four-horse carriages and numerous horsemen, what you sit on is but a small space for your knees; with a yard-long dining table with a variety of delicacies before you, what you enjoy is but one piece of meat. Now, for peace in a small space and enjoyment of one piece of meat, you have to bear the worry of the whole state of Chu. In these troubled times, calamities are numerous. I'm afraid you will not be able to keep your head intact."

Thereupon Chen Zhong went out and refused the envoy's invitation. He fled with his wife and made a living by watering someone's garden.

(From Huangfu Mi's *Gaoshi zhuan*)

Notes

1 The Yellow Emperor (Huangdi 黃帝) is a legendary figure and is considered the ancestor of Chinese people.
2 The Kingdom of Huaxu 華胥 first appears in the Yellow Emperor's dream recorded in *Liezi*. It became a substitute term for dreaming, although many scholars have tried to find its location. Some speculations include Shaanxi, Shanxi, Shandong, and Zhejiang provinces.
3 Yanzhou 弇州 is in modern Yanzhou 兗州 in Shandong. The *tai* 台 in Taizhou 台州 is likely 邰, which is in modern Zhangqiu 章丘, Shandong.
4 One of the states during the Spring and Autumn period.
5 Zhuang Zhou is the name of Zhuangzi 莊子 (Master Zhuang), the famous Daoist philosopher.
6 The *Dao de jing* 道德經 (Classic of Dao and De) by Laozi, the founder of Daoism.
7 An old river flowing through modern Puyang City in Henan.
8 Zhen Zhongzi 陳仲子, Master Chen Zhong, was a man of the Warring State period (475–222 BCE).

Further Reading

Mair, Victor H. *Wondering on the Way: Early Taoist Tales and Parables of Chuang Tzu.* University of Hawaii Press; Revised edition, 2000.

8　Seekers of the Dao

In religious Daoism, the main goal of achieving the Dao is not the carefree wandering of the seekers; instead, it is achieving immortality, ascending to heaven, and becoming an immortal.

To become an immortal, or to transubstantiate one's physical being, one needs first to cut off relationships with the mortal world, renouncing the filial duty to one's parents as well as mortal cravings; one also needs the "secret" stolen from the heaven and earth – alchemy, which is divided into two types: outer alchemy, or cinnabar (*dan*) making; and inner alchemy, a variation on embryonic respiration through conscious imitation of the life of a fetus in the mother's womb.

The two legends presented here, both from Ge Hong's 葛洪 (284–344) *Shenxian zhuan* 神仙傳 (Traditions of Divine Transcendents), are about the two famous historical Daoist masters, Zhang Daoling 張道陵 (34–156) and Wei Boyang (151–221): their pursuit of, courage in, and dedication to achieving immortality. The two tales following them, one by Niu Sengru (779–848) of the Tang and the other by Pu Songling (1640–1715) of the Qing, reflect the different ways of achieving immortality that circulated widely among laymen and commoners.

Zhang Daoling

Zhang Daoling, a native of the Pei Commandery,[1] was originally a student at the Imperial Academy and well versed in all of the Five Confucian Classics.[2] In his later years, he lamented, "All of these are not beneficial to longevity!" Then he began to study the way to achieve immortality. When he obtained the Yellow Emperor's Nine Cauldron method of elixir making, he intended to follow the method to develop a pill. But all the ingredients were extremely expensive, and Daoling's family had always been poor. He intended to make a living by farming and animal husbandry, but he was not good at either of these. Thus he simply gave up the idea of making an elixir.

Hearing that the people of Shu were pure, honest, and easily taught, and that there were numerous famous mountains, Zhang Daoling entered Shu with his disciples. He lived in Mount Huming[3] and wrote a Daoist book of 24 chapters. He then devoted himself to purifying his will by serious contemplation.

DOI: 10.4324/9781003490821-10

One day, numerous immortals suddenly descended from the sky; there were hundreds of thousands of them riding on feather-covered golden chariots drawn by dragons and tigers. Among them, someone called himself an archivist and someone claimed to be the Little Boy of the Eastern Sea. Thus, they taught Zhang Daoling the newly developed Way of the Covenant of Correct Unity. Zhang Daoling learned it and was then able to cure illness. So people flocked to him, served him as their mentor; his disciples numbered in the tens of thousands.

So Zhang Daoling created the position of libationer (*jijiu*), who led the disciples separately, as did the officials in the government. Further, regulations were established: his disciples are asked in turn to provide rice, silk, utensils, paper and brushes, firewood, and other things according to their needs, guiding people to repair roads; those who did not help with the repairs he would make sick. The county had some bridges and roads that needed repair, so people cut the weeds from trails and dredged the rivers, doing everything that needed to be done – all under Zhang's will. But some ignorant people did not realize that the regulation was created by Zhang Daoling and thought that the text was sent down from heaven.

Daoling also intended to regulate people by using their sense of shame because he disliked using legal punishments. So he set forth a rule, telling all those who were ill to write down the sins they had committed in their lives on paper and then throw the paper into a river, swearing to the god that they would never commit them again on the penalty of death. Thus, people thought in this way: when they confronted illness, they should confess their sins for two reasons. First, their illness would be cured; second, the sins they had committed would make them feel ashamed, so they dare not commit them again. Furthermore, they will grow in awe of heaven and earth. After that, all who had sinned actually changed from evil to good.

At this point, Daoling had amassed much money and property with which he purchased the cinnabar and developed the golden elixir. When the elixir was done, he took only half of it, because he did not want to ascend heaven right away. The result was he could then split his body into several dozen copies. Daoling often rode in a boat in the pond in front of his residence and played games on the boat. The coming and going Daoists and guests filled the front courtyard and the lanes. On the seat in the hall, there was always a Daoling, talking, eating, and drinking together with the guests, but the real Daoling was in the pond. In his affairs of curing illness, he adopted only the theory about exchanging of black (*yin*) and white (*yang*);[4] he might make certain changes to its major part or switch its head and tail, but the general method was always the same. As for adjusting breathing and taking cinnabar, he regarded these as the way to immortality, which could not be replaced with anything else.

Therefore, Daoling told the people around him, "You have mostly yet to overcome your earthly nature and cannot doff the cravings of this world, so can just learn my breathing techniques, methods of stretching, and the art of the bedchamber;[5] some of you may get the prescription for living several hundred years by taking herbs." He had the Nine Cauldron Grand Prescription given only to the king of the world. [He said that] later there will be a man who comes from the east who should obtain it. This man must arrive at noon on the seventh day of the seventh month. He also mentioned his height and appearance. On that day, a man called Zhao Sheng came, though not from the east. Daoling had never seen him, but his appearance was exactly the same as Daoling described. Then Daoling tested Zhao Sheng seven times, and Zhao passed all of them. Thus Daoling taught Zhao Sheng the *Classic of Elixir*.

What were the seven tests?

The first test was that when Zhao Sheng came to Zhang's residence, the door-keeper did not inform Zhang; moreover, Zhang sent someone to curse and insult him. But Zhao Sheng slept outside under the dew and refused to leave for more than 40 days. Then Zhang Daoling allowed him to enter.

The second test was to let Zhao Sheng guard the broomcorn millet and drive the beasts away. At night, Zhang sent an extremely beautiful woman pretending to be a traveler from afar, to ask for lodging and sleep next to his bed. The next day, pretending to have a pain in her feet, the woman refused to leave and thus stayed for several days. She also tried to seduce him, but Zhao Sheng never overstepped the bounds of propriety.

The third test was that, when Zhao Sheng was walking along the road, he suddenly saw 30 jars filled with gold, but he continued to walk, neglecting the gold.

The fourth test was to let Zhao Sheng cut firewood deep in the mountain where three tigers appeared before him and bit his clothes, yet they did not hurt his body. Zhao Sheng was not scared, and his look did not change. He said to the tiger, "I am a Daoist, and I have never done anything wrong since I was a child. I came from afar to serve the divine master, seeking the way to immortality. Why are you treating me like this? Did the mountain god send you to test me?" A moment later, the tigers left.

The fifth test was that when Zhao Sheng purchased more than a dozen bolts of silk at the market, after Zhang paid for them the seller falsely accused him of not paying. Zhao Sheng thus took off his clothes and sold them to pay the seller, and his face showed no trace of begrudging.

The sixth test was to let Zhao Sheng guard the granary. A man went and kow-towed in front of him begging for food. He was ragged, his face was dirty, his body covered in abscesses, exuding a stinky odor. Zhao Sheng became sorrowful and his countenance changed. He removed his own clothes and put them on the man, cooked food using his own grain for him, and also gave him his own rice.

On the seventh test, Zhang Daoling ascended a cliff with his disciples, where an arm-like peach tree grew on the stone wall overlooking the unfathomable abyss. It was densely ladened with large peaches. Zhang Daoling said to his disciples, "Whoever can obtain a peach, I will tell him the essence of achieving the Dao." At that time, more than 300 people knelt on the edge of the cliff to peer at the peach tree. Shaking and sweating, none dared to approach the cliff and look at the peach tree. Instead, they all withdrew and apologized that they could not pick a peach.

Only Zhao Sheng said, "We are protected by gods, so what is the danger? Our divine master is here, and he would not let us fall to die in the valley. The reason our master asked us to pick peaches is that there must be a way to get them." Then Zhao Sheng threw himself from the cliff onto the peach tree. Standing steadily, he picked up a handful of peaches. But the stone wall was so steep and there was nothing he could use to climb so that he could not return to the cliff. Instead, he tossed the peaches up one by one, a total of 202. Zhang Daoling gave a peach to each of his disciples, ate one himself, left one for Zhao Sheng, and waited for him. Then, Zhang Daoling pulled Zhao Sheng with his arm. Everyone saw that Zhang Daoling's arm lengthened two or three *zhang* to pull up Zhao Sheng. Suddenly Zhao Sheng was back on top of the cliff. Zhang Daoling then gave him the peach that he had left for him.

After Zhao Sheng finished eating the peach, Zhang Daoling approached the cliff and said with a smile, "Zhao Sheng's mind is upright, so he could stand steadily after throwing himself onto the tree. Now I want to try it myself. I should be able to pick a big peach." All of his disciples advised him not to jump. Only Wang Chang and Zhao Sheng kept silent. Then Zhang Daoling threw himself down but did not fall onto the peach tree, and instead, he disappeared. Seeing that around them there were only high mountains with their tips touching the sky surrounding them, with the unfathomable abyss below. There was no road either. The disciples all yelled in panic and cried.

Only Zhao Sheng and Wang Chang did not cry. After a long while, they spoke to each other, "Our master is like our father. Now he has fallen into the unfathomable abyss, how could we stay at ease ourselves?" Thus both of them jumped off the cliff and fell immediately in front of Zhang Daoling, and they saw he was sitting cross-legged on a bed covered with a curtain. Seeing Zhao Sheng and Wang Chang, he said with a smile, "I knew you two would come." Then he taught them the secrets of the Way.

Three days later, they returned to their old residence. His disciples were all astonished. Later, the three people, Zhang Daoling, Zhao Sheng, and Wang Chang, left by soaring into the sky. Looking up, the disciples saw that they flew slowly into the clouds then finally vanished.

At first, Zhang Daoling entered the Mountain of Shu, and there he developed the elixir and took half of it. Although he did not ascend to heaven, he was already an earthly immortal. In order to transform Zhao Sheng, he intentionally tested Zhao seven times and then fulfilled his ambition.

(From Ge Hong, *Shenxian zhuan*, Chapter 5)

Wei Boyang

Wei Boyang 魏伯陽 (ca. 151–221), a native of Wu,[6] was originally the son of a noble family. But he was by nature fond of the arts of the Way, so he was reluctant to be an official in the government. He lived leisurely to nourish his nature, and thus nobody knew him.

Later, he entered a mountain with his three disciples to make a divine elixir. When the elixir was completed, his disciples were not completely convinced. Thus he tested them, saying, "Even though this elixir is done, we should try it first. Now I'll give it to a dog. If the dog flies up immediately, we can ingest it; if the dog dies, then we cannot take it."

Then he fed the dog, and the dog died immediately.

Boyang told his disciples, "When I was making the elixir, I was only afraid that it could not be created. Now, it is created but the dog died after taking it. I'm afraid that this is against the will of the spirits, and if we drink it we will likely die like the dog. What can we do?"

His disciples asked, "Master, are you going to drink it?"

Boyang replied, "Being against the worldly ways, I left my home to enter the mountain. If I cannot achieve the Dao, I would be ashamed to return home. No matter if I die or live, I should drink it." Then he drank the elixir and died as soon as he put the substance into his mouth.

His disciples stared at each other and said, "The purpose of making the elixir was to seek longevity. Now he has died after drinking it. What can we do?"

One of the disciples said, "Our master is not an ordinary man. Since he died after drinking the elixir, does not that mean something?" Then he swallowed some of the elixir and died, too.

The remaining two disciples said to each other, "The reason we want to have the elixir is to attain longevity. But whoever takes it dies immediately. What use is this stuff? Without drinking this elixir, we will be able to live in this world for several dozens of years." Thus they did not drink the elixir. Instead, they left the mountain, intending to buy coffins for Boyang and his dead disciple.

Immediately after the two disciples left, Boyang stood up. He poured the elixir he drank into the mouths of his dead disciple and the dog. Both woke up as well. Along with his disciple, surnamed Yu, he ascended up to become an immortal. On their way, they met a woodcutter. They wrote letters to their fellow villagers to bid farewell and gave them to the woodcutter. Upon receiving them, the two disciples began feeling regret.

(From Ge Hong, *Shenxian zhuan*, Chapter 2)

Du Zichun

Du Zichun 杜子春 was a man who lived sometime between the Northern Zhou (557–581) and the Sui Dynasty (581–618). When he was a teenager, he was a loafer and did not care about managing his family's wealth. Rather, he did as he pleased and was given to drinking and frequenting brothels. After having squandered it all, he went to his relatives and friends seeking help. But they all believed that he was useless and thus refused to help him.

It was a cold winter. Zichun walked along the streets of Chang'an in rags and with an empty stomach. It was dark, and he still had not eaten yet. Pacing back and forth by the west gate of the East Market, he did not know where to go. He looked so hungry and cold. Lifting his head, he heaved a deep sigh toward the sky.

"Why did you sigh, sir?" An old man walked toward him with a cane in hand.

Zichun unbosomed himself to the old man. His resentment of the alienation and fickleness of his relatives, as well as his irritation, could be seen on his face.

"How many strings of coins will be enough for you?" The old man asked him.

Zichun said, "If I have thirty or fifty thousand strings, I would be able to survive."

The old man said. "Not enough, you can ask me for more!"

"One hundred thousand strings!" said Zichun.

"It's still not enough."

Zichun said, "Okay, one million strings!"

"Not enough," the old man said again.

Zichun said, "Then three million!"

Then the old man said, "That is good." Immediately, he took out a string of coins from his sleeve and said, "I will first give you this tonight. At noon tomorrow, I will be waiting for you at the Persian House in the West Market. Please make sure to not be late."

At the appointed time, Zichun went there. The old man gave him three million strings of cash and left without even telling him his name.

When Zichun became rich, his craving for reckless spending was reanimated, and he thought that he would never wander destitute for the rest of his life. He rode on fat steeds, wore silk clothes, gathered drunkards, and solicited singers and dancers to revel in the brothels, completely ignoring his future livelihood. Within a couple of years, his wealth was all but squandered. He had to replace his fine clothing, carriage, and horse with cheaper ones. First, he replaced his horse with a donkey, and then he started walking on foot instead of riding the donkey. In the twinkling of an eye, he became as poor as before.

Soon, he became helpless again and sighed by the gate of the market. As soon as his long sigh was uttered, the old man appeared in front of him. Holding his hand, he said, "How did you create such an incredible dilemma again, sir? Yet I will still help you. How much do you need?"

Zichun was too ashamed to reply. Then the old man urged him. Zichun felt so regretful that he could do nothing but refuse him.

The old man said, "At noon tomorrow, go to the place where I met you before."

Enduring the humiliation, Zichun went there the next day and received 10 million strings of cash.

Before receiving the money, Zichun determined that this time he would make a living himself and finally become wealthy so that the ancient rich men such as Shi Chong (249–300)[7] and Yi Dun[8] would be only a petty man compared with him. After receiving the money, however, Zichun's heart completely changed. He reverted to spending money as he pleased. In less than three or four years, he became poorer than ever before.

While seeing the old man in the place where they met in the past, Zichun was so ashamed that he started to run away, covering his face with his sleeve. The old man grabbed the back lapel of his clothes and said, "Alas! How stupid you are!" Then he gave Zichun 30 million, saying, "If you cannot turn yourself around this time, you will be incurable."

Zichun thought, "When I was wandering about downhearted and had exhausted all means of livelihood, none of my relatives and the noble families cared about me. Only this old man repeatedly gave me large sums of money. What should I do to repay him?" Thereupon he promised the old man, "With this money, I will be able to set up anything in this world; orphans and widows could have enough clothes and food, and the sage's desire for moral education could also be realized. I am grateful to you for your great kindness. After I finish what I would like to do, I'll do whatever you want me to do."

The old man said, "That is exactly what I had hoped for! After you have finished your business, on the Zhongyuan Festival next year,⁵ please wait for me under the twain cypress trees in front of the Temple of Lord Lao."

Since most of the orphans and widows lived in the area south of the Huai River, Zichun transferred his investment to Yangzhou, where he bought ten thousand acres of fine farmland, built residential houses in the city, and more than 100 guestrooms at important intersections. He then gathered all of the orphans and widows in the city to live in the houses, paid for the weddings of his own nieces and nephews, and transferred the tombs of his clansmen to the area. For those who had been gracious to him, he rewarded them; for those who had maltreated him, he retaliated against them.

After completing what he desired to do, Zichun went to attend the appointed meeting. When he arrived at the temple, the old man was yodeling under the two cypress trees. They immediately started climbing the Yuntai Peak of Mount Hua.

After walking into the mountain for more than 40 *li*, Zichun saw a place with a clean and solemn house, which seemed like it was not for ordinary people. While colorful clouds were lingering above it, simurghs and cranes flew over the roof. In the middle of the main hall, there was a drug stove about nine feet high. The purple light in the furnace was brilliant, illuminating the windows and doors. Nine jade girls were standing around the stove, and a black dragon and a white tiger on guard in front and behind.

It was about sunset. The old man in mortal clothes suddenly turned into a Daoist priest wearing a yellow cap and a crimson cloak. He gave Zichun three white stone pills and a cup of wine and asked him to take them quickly. Then he took out a tiger pelt and put it on the ground of the inner room by the west wall. He sat down toward the east and warned Zichun, "Be careful not to utter any sound. The honorable spirits, evil demons, rakshasas, fierce beasts, visions of hell, your relatives tied and imprisoned, and all such pain and suffering are not real. Neither move nor speak, be at ease with no fear; you will suffer from nothing in the end. Please keep my words in mind!" After saying this, he left.

Zichun glanced around the hall. There was nothing but a huge earthen jar filled with water. Just as the Daoist priest left, he saw flags, spears, armored men, hundreds of carriages, and thousands of horsemen come from outside and fill the mountain and valley. The sound of shouting shook the sky and earth.

A man more than ten feet tall appeared claiming to be a general. Both he and his horse were covered with dazzling golden armor. Hundreds of his guards, all holding swords and bows, rushed to the front of the hall and shouted at him, "Who are you that you dare not hide from the general?" Some approached him with swords and forced him to report his name and what he was doing. He did not respond. Enraged, those questioners rushed forward trying to slash him or shoot him. The raucous was like thunder. But Zichun still did not respond. So the general left angrily.

In a short while, fierce tigers, venomous dragons, lions, and thousands of serpents roared and rushed toward Zichun, vying to strike and swallow him, or jumping over him. Zichun's expression did not change, so not long afterward they vanished too.

Soon, the sky suddenly became dark, and heavy rain poured down with thunder and lightning. Fire wheels were rolling on his left and right, while lightning struck before and behind him so that he could not open his eyes. In a moment, the water in the hall surged to more than ten feet high, and the bright lightning and booming thunder struck with the power sufficient to carve a mountain or break a dike. It was impossible to stop. In the blink of an eye, the wave rushed under his seat. Zichun sat there properly, not even blinking. Soon afterward, the storm dispersed.

Then the general came back again, leading ox-head prison guards, demons, and spirits with strange faces. They placed a huge cauldron filled with boiling water in front of Zichun, encircled him with spears, knives, and forks in hand, and passed down the order of the general, "Tell us your name and we will let you go; otherwise, we will stab your heart with a fork and put you in the pot!" Zichun did not respond.

So the ghosts brought forth his wife. Pulling her to the stairs, they pointed to her and urged Zichun, "Say her name and we will release her." Du Zichun still kept silent. So the ghosts whipped his wife, slashed her with a knife, shot her with an arrow, put her in boiling water, and burned her with fire; the pain was intolerable.

His wife pleaded with Zichun through tears, "I am indeed ugly and stupid, and I am not worthy of you. But I have served you as your wife for more than ten years. Now I am being tortured by ghosts. I cannot bear the suffering. Although I dare not expect you to prostrate yourself to plead with them, if you just say one word, my life will be spared. As a human being, who can be emotionless? How can you, my husband, not be willing to say even a single word?"

While his wife wept in the hall, shouting and cursing, Zichun steadfastly ignored her. The general said, "Do you think I have no more sinister means to torture your wife?" Then he ordered a rasp taken out to grind his wife from her feet inch by inch. His wife was crying louder and louder, but Zichun did not even look at it. The general said, "This bandit has already completed the black arts. We cannot let him stay in this world for long!" So he ordered his attendants to execute Zichun.

After Zichun was executed, his soul was led to see King Yama. The king asked, "Is not this the demon of Yuntai Peak? Put him in jail!" So Zichun experienced the melted bronze pillar, the iron stick, the hammer, stone mills, fire pits, boiling water pots, knife mountain, sword forest, and many other kinds of torture. However, since he kept the Daoist priest's words in mind, it seemed that he could endure all of them without screaming.

When the guards of hell reported to the king that all the punishments had been applied, the king said, "This man is insidious and malicious, so he should not be a man; it is proper to have him be a woman in his next life!" So Zichun was assigned to be the daughter of Wang Qin, the deputy magistrate of Shanfu County in Songzhou. Zichun contracted a variety of illnesses after she was born. She was constantly taking medicine and having acupuncture. She had also fallen into the fire and off her bed, suffering helplessly but never uttering a sound.

Soon, Zichun grew into a woman of matchless beauty, but she had no voice. Considering her a dumb woman, her family and relatives insulted her in different ways. Zichun could not say anything.

In the same town, there was an Advanced Scholar named Lu Gui who heard of her beauty, admired her, and proposed marriage through a matchmaker. Her family refused with the excuse that she was dumb. Lu said, "If she is a virtuous wife, why does she have to speak? She can also serve as a warning to women who gossip." Thus her family agreed to the marriage. Lu carried out all of the six rites for marriage and welcomed her in person as his wife.

In the several years after their marriage, they loved each other deeply. Zichun also gave birth to a boy. The boy was two years old and incredibly smart. Lu held the boy and talked to his wife, but she did not respond. Lu tried many ways to get her to speak, but she never uttered a single word.

Lu became enraged, saying, "In ancient times, Master Jia's wife looked down upon her husband so she never smiled, but later when she saw that Jia shot a pheasant, she smiled so that his regret was erased. Now I am not uglier than Jia and my talents are not merely shooting a pheasant, but you do not bother to talk to me! If a husband is looked down upon by his wife, what is the use of her son?" Then he grabbed the boy's legs, hit his head onto a piece of stone. It split in two instantly, as blood splashed a few steps away.

Motherly love swelled up in Zichun's heart so that he forgot the Daoist priest's words and out slipped "Ahhhh!" Before the sound was over, he found himself sitting in the original place. The Daoist was also in front of him. It was dawn. Suddenly he saw the purple flame slam into the beam and spread all over the hall; in the blink of an eye, the house was burned.

"You down-at-the-heels pedant!" lamented the Daoist priest. "You have disappointed me!" He then grabbed Zichun by the hair and threw him into the jar. The fire was immediately extinguished.

Approaching him, the Daoist priest said, "In your heart, Sir, joy, anger, sorrow, fear, hate, and desire are all forgotten. The only thing you still have not yet overcome is love. If you had not uttered the sound 'Ahhhh,' my elixir would have been made and you would have also become a heavenly immortal. Alas! It is so hard to find one who is endowed to become an immortal. My elixir can be refined again, but you still belong to this mortal world. You are on your own!" Then he pointed the way he was to return.

When Zichun insisted on ascending the terrace to have a final look, he found the alchemy furnace was broken. Inside it was an iron pillar as thick as an arm and several feet long; the Daoist priest was cutting it with a knife without clothes on.

After Zichun returned home, he was very remorseful he had proven unworthy of the favor he received. He pledged to serve the priest again to make up for his disobedience. Yet when he went to the Yuntai Peak again, he found no trace of the man. He returned home with a deep sigh of regret.

(From Niu Sengru 牛僧孺 (779–848), *Xuanguai lu* 續玄怪錄)

Bai Yuyu

Wu Jun, whose courtesy name was Qing'an, was well-known for his talents when he was a teenager. The Grand Scribe Ge read his writings and spoke highly of him. Through his good friend, he invited Wu to his home to personally experience the literary grace of his speech. He said, "How could a man as talented as Scholar Wu stay lowly in poverty for long?" He also asked his neighbor to tell Wu, "If you work hard and achieve your aspirations, I will let my daughter marry you." At the time, the Grand Scribe was known for having an extremely beautiful daughter. Hearing this, Wu fell into ecstasy and became more confident.

Not long afterward, however, Wu failed the imperial autumn prefectural exam. He asked someone to tell the Grand Scribe, "I'll surely become rich and noble. But I do not know if it will come sooner or later. Please wait for three years. If I still fail to pass the imperial exam, then you can marry off your daughter to another man." Thereafter, he set his will resolutely on studying and being more diligent.

One evening, a young scholar (*xiucai*) called on him under the moonlight. He was fair-skinned, with a short beard, a thin waist, and long arms. When asked who he was, he said he was surnamed Bai, and his courtesy name was Yuyu. After having a brief heart-to-heart conversation with him, Wu suddenly felt himself become more open-minded. Wu liked him and put him up for the night. The next morning, when Bai was about to leave, Wu urged him to drop by as frequently as possible. Being grateful to Wu for his kindness, Bai was eager to lodge himself in Wu's house immediately. Having arranged the move-in date, they parted with each other.

On that day, a servant arrived first with some cooking utensils. A short while later, Bai arrived on the back of a horse, which was as energetic as a lively dragon. Wu arranged a room for him. Bai asked his servant to lead the horse away. From then on, they stayed together happily day and night.

Wu saw the books Bai read, which were rarely seen and also had nothing to do with the popular arts of the time.[10] Surprised, Wu asked him. Bai replied with a smile, "Everyone has his own ambition. I am not among those who are keen on rank and fame."

At night, he often invited Wu to drink, and once he took out a book and gave it to Wu. The content was all about the Daoist technique of inhaling and exhaling air, but Wu could not understand much. So Wu considered it impractical and put it aside.

On another day, Bai said to Wu, "The book I gave you that one day is about the essential way of the 'Classic of the Yellow Court,' the ladder to becoming immortal."[11]

Wu replied with a smile, "This is not what I am interested in. Furthermore, those who seek immortality must sever their love and eliminate all kinds of distractions. I cannot do that."

Bai asked him why. Wu said that he worried about having an heir for his family.

Bai asked, "Why have you not taken a wife?"

Wu smiled and replied, "I am a helpless lover of beauty."

Bai also smiled and said, "Your Majesty, please do not love the lesser beauty. How good is the one you love?

Wu told him the entire truth. Bai suspected that she may not be really beautiful. Wu said, "Her beauty is known far and near. I have good taste." With a subtle smile on his face, Bai kept silent.

The next day, Bai suddenly readied himself to bid farewell. Wu was saddened, talking with him incessantly. Bai asked his servant boy to leave first with his baggage on his shoulder. When the two men were reluctant to say goodbye, a green cicada suddenly fell onto the table. Bai said, "My carriage has arrived. It is time to bid farewell for now. If you miss me, stroke my couch and lie on it." Wu wanted to ask more questions, but Bai suddenly shrank as tiny as a finger, lightly jumped onto the back of the cicada, which flew into the clouds with a chirp. Wu knew then that Bai was not a mortal. He was both astonished and despondent for a long time.

A few days later, it was drizzling. Wu's longing for Bai became unbearable. Looking at the bed Bai had slept on, there were numerous mouse prints on it. Slightly perturbed, he cleaned it, placed down a mat, and slept on it. Not long afterward, Bai's servant boy came to summon him. Wu was delighted to follow.

In a moment, a phoenix was perched before them. The servant boy grabbed it and said to Wu, "The road is hard to navigate at night. Please ride this instead." Wu worried it was too small to carry him. The boy said, "Just try it!" When Wu mounted the bird, he felt there was more than enough space with the servant also sitting on the phoenix's tail. The phoenix flew into the air with a loud "caw."

After a short while, Wu saw a red gate. The servant boy jumped off first and then helped Wu get off by holding his arm. Wu asked, "What is this place?" The servant replied, "This is the gate of Heaven."

A huge tiger was squatting by the gate, scaring Wu. The servant blocked the tiger with his body. Wu discovered that the scenery there was very different from what was in the human world.

The servant boy led him to the Palace of Eternal Coldness,[12] where the steps were all made of crystal and people seemed to walk in the mirror. Two laurel trees stood towering and thick – the trunk of one could fill one's two arms. A rich floral fragrance drifted everywhere in the wind. The pavilions and houses were all equipped with red windows, and from time to time beautiful women strolled in and out, all with coquettish looks and graceful bones unmatched in the human world.

The servant boy said, "The ladies in the Queen Mother of the West's Palace[13] are even more beautiful." However, because he was afraid that his lord would be waiting too long, they did not have time to linger there, so he ushered Wu out in a hurry.

After a long while, they saw Bai was waiting in front of the gate. Having entered the gate hand in hand, the two men beheld clear springs slowly flowing on the white sands beyond the eaves. There were jade steps and carved railings. Wu suspected it was the moon palace.

Immediately after they had just sat down, a seductive young girl about 16 years old came to offer fragrant tea. After a short while, Bai ordered wine. Four beautiful women, lifting the lapels of their clothes and wearing tinkling bells, came to serve them on their left and right. Just as Wu felt an itch on his back, one of them stretched her slender fingers and long fingernails into his clothes and gently scratched it. Wu felt ill at ease. He became half-drunk and gradually lost control. He looked back at the beautiful women and smiled. Then he tried to strike up a conversation with them. They all laughed and avoided him.

Bai ordered them to sing songs to go along with the drinks. A girl in a crimson silk dress, holding a cup and facing the guest, sang a sweet and agreeable a cappella song at the feast. Then the other girls played music or sang to accompany the music. After that, a girl in green trousers sang while drinking. There were also a girl in purple and another girl in a light white soft silk dress, both of whom laughed sheepishly and were reluctant to go forward, each trying to get the other to go first. Bai ordered one to drink and the other one to sing. Then the girl in purple came to toast Wu. Feigning as if to pick up the cup, Wu teasingly scratched her slender wrist. The girl laughed and accidentally dropped the glass onto the ground. Bai scolded her for being careless. She smiled, picked up the broken cup, lowered her head, and whispered, "It's as cold as a ghost hand, but it tried to catch my arm by force." Bai laughed loudly and ordered her to sing and dance at the same time. After she finished dancing, the one in white clothes toasted Wu with another large cup. Wu excused himself, saying he could not drink anymore. Holding a glass of wine and standing in front of him, the girl looked ashamed. So Wu forced himself to drink it.

Examining the four girls carefully, Wu found that they all possessed unique but stunning features and were incomparably beautiful. He then said to the host without thinking, "Of the femme fatales in this world, I want only one, but it is so hard to choose. You gathered a variety of beauties. Can you truly allow me to enjoy a romantic moment today?"

Bai said with a smile, "Is not there a true love in your mind? How could these girls be even worth glancing at with your high tastes?"

Wu said, "Today I realized that I am only a frog at the bottom of a well."

Bai thus called all of the girls to the front and asked him to choose. Wu tried to pick and choose but could not make a decision. Because the arm of the girl in purple had been scratched by Wu, Bai ordered her to unfold a quilt to serve the guest. Thus, between the quilt and pillow, Wu enjoyed to the utmost an incomparable time with the girl. Then Wu asked the girl for a commemorative token, so she removed the golden bracelet on her wrist and gave it to him.

Suddenly, the servant boy entered and said, "The immortal and mortal go different ways. You had better leave right now." The girl quietly got up and fled. Wu asked where the host was. The servant boy replied, "He has gone to court, and he instructed me to see you off when he left."

Disappointed, Wu followed him to look for the road by which they came. When he was about to reach the gate, he looked back and discovered the servant boy had left. Suddenly, the tiger started roaring. Wu was startled and fled. Before noticing the unfathomable valley in front of him, his feet stepped out on the air and he fell. With a startle, he awoke from a dream. The red morning sun had already risen high in the sky.

When he was about to straighten his clothes, something smooth dropped onto the quilt. Looking at it, he realized it was the gold bracelet. He felt what had happened was even more strange and uncanny. Since then, he swept away all previous desires in the mortal world, and he only sought to become an immortal, though he still worried about being without an heir.

More than ten months later, once when Wu was taking a nap during the day, he dreamed of the girl in purple coming from outside with an infant wrapped in her breast, saying, "This is your flesh and blood. He cannot stay in the sky, so I respectfully bring him to you." Placing the baby onto the bed and covering him with clothes, the girl intended to leave hurriedly. Wu made love to her by force. Then she said, "The last time was for our marriage, and this time it is a farewell for good. Our marriage of a hundred years is over now. If you have aspirations to engage in self-cultivation, we may still possibly meet again." Wu woke up and saw the baby sleeping on the bedding. He wrapped him up and told his mother. His mother was pleased. She hired a wet nurse for him and named him Dream Fairy.

Wu thus asked someone to tell the Grand Scribe Ge that he would be a recluse and asked him to select another man for his daughter. The Grand Scribe did not consent, but Wu was determined. The Grand Scribe informed his daughter. His daughter said, "Everyone here knows that I am engaged to Scholar Wu, but now he has changed his mind. Does that not mean that I will have to remarry?" The Grand Scribe told Wu what his daughter thought.

Wu said, "Now I not only have no intention to seek rank but have also rid myself of the feelings between men and women. The only reason why I have not gone into the mountains is that my old mother is still alive."

The Grand Scribe spoke with his daughter again, and she said, "Scholar Wu is poor, I will take tasty food from wild grass; when he is away from home, I will take care of his mother. I will never marry another man."

The Grand Scribe Ge sent people back and forth three or four times, but things were still undecided. So one day he prepared the carriage, horses, as well as a dowry, and sent his daughter to Wu's home. Wu was deeply touched by the virtues of Ge's daughter, so he respected her very much.

Ge's daughter took care of her mother-in-law with filiality. She tried her best to obey and please her mother-in-law and did even better than the daughter of a poor family. After two years, Wu's mother passed away. Ge's daughter pawned her dowry to buy a coffin and did everything in accordance with the funeral rites.

Wu said to his wife, "I have a wife like you, what else need I worry about!? However, if one achieves the Dao of immortality, he will leave his residence to ascend to heaven, so I will be going far away from home. Everything in my family will be entrusted to you." The woman was unperturbed and did not even try to stop him. Then Wu left.

The woman made a living outside the home while she instructed her fatherless son inside the home. Everything she put her hand to became well ordered.

Dream Fairy gradually grew up and was incredibly intelligent. At the age of 14, he passed the provincial level of the imperial exam. At the age of 15, he entered the Imperial Academy. Whenever the emperor awarded his parents with a title, he did not even know the surname of his mother, so only Lady Ge was awarded a title.

Once when there was a sacrificial ceremony, he asked Lady Ge where his father was. Lady Ge told him everything. He wanted to abandon his official title to search for his father. His stepmother said, "Your father has been away from home for more than ten years. Now he may have become an immortal. Where would you go to find him?"

Later, Dream Fairy was sent to go to the Southern Sacred Mountain to offer sacrifice and encountered a robber along the way. At a critical juncture, a Daoist priest suddenly appeared with a sword. All the robbers fled and the siege was ended. Dream Fairy thanked the priest and wanted to repay his kindness with gold.

The priest refused the gold. Taking out a letter, he said, "I have an old friend who is your fellow townsman. I'd like to trouble you to greet the person on my behalf."

Dream Fairy asked, "What is the name?"

The Daoist replied, "Wang Lin."

Dream Fairy recalled that there was no Wang Lin in the village. The Daoist said, "Nobles like you, of course, would not know the humble old villager." Before leaving, he took out a gold bracelet and said, "This is the stuff of women. I found it somewhere but it is not useful to me. So I am giving it to you." Glancing at it, Dream Fairy observed the bracelet was very beautifully carved. So he brought it home and gave it to Lady Ge. Lady Ge loved it and asked a skilled craftsman to duplicate it, but the results were never as fine as the original.

Dream Fairy asked everyone in the village but nobody knew a person named Wang Lin. Thus he secretly opened the letter, which read,

> You and I were husband and wife for three years, and then we separated.
> I have relied on you, my virtuous wife to bury my mother and instruct my son.
> To repay your kindness, I have nothing but a pill. Open it and ingest the
> contents, and you can become a fairy.

The letter ended with "Address to Lady Linnian, Your Ladyship."

After reading it, Dream Fairy still did not know to whom the letter was written. So he took it to his stepmother. Holding the letter, his stepmother cried and said, "This is your father's letter. 'Lin' is my nickname." All of a sudden, Dream Fairy realized that the two characters "Wang Lin" (王林) was a separation of the graph "Lin" (琳). He felt very sad to have not recognized his father.

Further, he took out the gold bracelet and showed his stepmother. His stepmother said, "This is an item left by your mother. Your father showed me before."

Then they looked at the pill, which was only the size of a soybean. Dream Fairy said happily, "My father is already an immortal. After eating this pill you will live forever."

His mother did not immediately take the pill but hid it. Just as Grand Scribe Ge came to see his grandson, the lady read the letter and also gave him the pill for his longevity. Grand Scribe Ge cut the pill into two, and each of them ate half. In no time, they became energetic. At that time, the Grand Scribe was 70 years old and was doddering. After taking the pill, he was immediately rejuvenated. His strength suddenly came back. Instead of riding the carriage, he walked quickly. All of his family tried to catch up and barely kept up.

A year later, a large fire broke out in the capital city. It burned for a full day before finally being put out. Everyone gathered in the courtyard and dared not sleep all night. Seeing that the raging fire was approaching their property, the whole family panicked but had no idea what to do.

Suddenly, with a "caw" sound, the golden bracelet on the lady's arm flew away. When they looked, they saw it was several acres big, covering their house like the halo of the moon. The turn of events was shocking, but still, everyone clearly saw that the opening of the gold bracelet was at the southeast corner. Soon, the fire moved to the west. When it burned to the edge of the aperture it turned east.

When the fire gradually died down, everyone assumed that there would be no way to get the gold bracelet back again. Suddenly, the red light ceased, and the bracelet fell onto the ground with a loud noise. Tens of thousands of houses in the capital burned into ashes. Only the residence of the Wu family was left safe and sound, though a small pavilion in the southeast corner of the yard was burned, which was left without being covered because of the opening of the bracelet.

Dream Fairy's mother was over 50 years old then. Some have seen her and found she looks like she is still in her twenties.

(From Pu Songling, *Liaozhai Zhiyi*, Chapter 3)

Notes

1 Its seat was in Xiang county (modern Huaibei city in Anhui).
2 Include the *Shijing* 詩經 (The Classic of Odds), *Shangshu* 尚書 (Book of Documents), *Yijing* 易經 (Classic of Changes), *Liji* 禮記 (Records of Rites), and *Chunqiu* 春秋 (Spring and Autumn Annals).
3 Mount Huming 鵠鳴 is located northwest of modern Chongqing County in Sichuan.
4 *Xuansu* 玄素, or "black and white," refers to a theory from the *Classic of Changes* which states that everything is in the process of constantly changing.
5 Fangzhong 房中, or "the art of bedchamber," is a Daoist sexual practice which emphasizes gathering the essence of *yin* energy from women to nurture the *yang* of men.
6 The area around modern Nanjing and Suzhou.
7 Shi Chong 石崇 was a notorious official and a rich man during the Western Jin dynasty.
8 Yi Dun 猗頓 was a famous businessman during the Spring and Autumn period.
9 Zhongyuan Festival, also known as the Ghost Festival, is on the fifteenth day of the Seventh month.
10 Shiyi 時藝, "popular arts of the time," refers to *Bagu wen* 八股文 or the eight-legged essay, a type of regulated essay to be written especially for the imperial examinations during the Ming and Qing dynasties.
11 *Huang Ting Jing* 黃庭經, the "Classic of the Yellow Court," is a famous religious Daoist text dedicated to inner alchemy (neidan 內丹), one of the two ways to achieving immortality.
12 This is also known as the moon palace.
13 The Queen Mother of the West is a mythical goddess in Chinese culture who is beautiful and known for her peaches of immortality which grow every 3,000 years.

Further Reading

Kohn, Livia. *The Taoist Experience: An Anthology*. New York, NY: SUNY Press, 1993.

9 Exemplary Immortals

While deathless beings can be traced back to the *Classic of Mountains and Seas* (*Shanhai jing* 山海經), the *xian*仙, those who are immortal or transcendent, are portrayed in Warring States texts as godlike beings living on an island of immortals in the sea. The concept of men ascending to heaven to become immortals first appeared during the Western Han. During the Eastern Han period, immortals were divided into three categories: heavenly immortals, earthly immortals, and immortals released from corpses (*shijie xian* 屍解仙).[1]

The features of the *xian* archetype were first depicted in *Zhuangzi*:

> On Mount Miaoguye, there lived a divine being, whose skin is as white as ice and snow and whose demeanor as elegant as a virgin girl. He does not eat the five grains but only exhales wind and drinks dew; he rides clouds and air and drives a flying dragon, traveling beyond the four seas.

Victor Mair summarizes them as follows:

> They are immune to heat and cold, untouched by the elements, and can fly, mounting upward with a fluttering motion. They dwell apart from the chaotic world of man, subsist on air and dew, are not anxious like ordinary people, and have the smooth skin and innocent faces of children. The transcendents live an effortless existence that is best described as spontaneous. They recall the ancient Indian ascetics and holy men known as *ṛṣi* who possessed similar traits.[2]

Robert Campany defines *xian* as "extraordinarily long-lived if not deathless beings to whom godlike powers and celestial status were attributed."[3]

The three legends included here, one from Liu Xiang's (77 BCE–6 BCE) *Biographies of Exemplary Immortals* (*Liexian zhuan*) and two from Ge Hong's *Traditions of Divine Transcendents*, are about three famous immortals.

Yuan Ke

Yuan Ke, a native of Jiyin,[4] was handsome and kind by nature. Many of his fellow townsmen proposed to marry him with their daughters, but he never accepted.

DOI: 10.4324/9781003490821-11

He often planted the five-colored fragrant grasses and ate their seeds for dozens of years.

One morning, some five-colored moths alighted or the top of his fragrant tree. Yuan Ke gathered and spread them out on a straw mattress, allowing them to bear silkworms.

When he started collecting the cocoons, there came a beautiful girl who called herself Yuan Ke's wife and talked with him about raising silkworms. Yuan Ke collected cocoons with her. They gathered 120, each the size of an earthen jar. It took 60 days to reel off the raw silk from one cocoon. When they finished all the work, both of them left, and nobody knew where they went.

Therefore, the people of Jiyin offer sacrifices to silkworms and built an altar for that purpose. Some also say that Yuan Ke was a native of Jiyang County in the Chenliu Commandery.[5]

> What a nice guy you are, Yuan Ke!
> Your young face is like the morning flower.
> Facing up, you inhale the mysterious essence,
> Lowering your head, you pick the five-colored flowers.
> How fragrant are the flowers,
> How brilliant are the silkworms!
> A fair maiden came down at night,
> Matching your virtue, you ascend to the immortal land.

(From Liu Xiang, *Liexian zhuan*)

Lord Mao

Lord Mao was a native of Youzhou,[6] but he studied the Dao in Qi. When he had mastered the Dao 20 years later, he returned home. However, his parents became very angry on seeing him, saying, "You are not a filial son! Instead of taking good care of us in person, you have wandered everywhere, seeking absurd things!"

When his parents intended to flog him, Lord Mao knelt in front of them, holding his body erect, and begged for forgiveness, "I received a mandate from Heaven, so I am destined to attain the Way. I had no way of doing these two things at the same time – taking care of you my parents and dedicating myself to the Dao. Though I've been far away from home and thus ignored my duty to support you, and you have not received any support from me in so many days, now I am capable of keeping our family peaceful and enabling both of you to enjoy longevity. I have already attained the Way, so you cannot disgrace me with your whip. However, if you do proceed to whip me, I'm afraid it won't be a minor incident."

Hearing this, Lord Mao's father was enraged, so he picked up his walking stick to hit him. However, as he was about to lift the walking stick, it broke into dozens of pieces and shot out in all directions, just like shooting arrows. The pieces penetrated the walls and damaged the house's columns. This caused Lord Mao's father to stop.

Lord Mao said, "This is the terrible incident I said might happen. I'm truly afraid someone will get hurt."

"You said you have attained the Dao," Lord Mao's father asked him. "Then can you resurrect the dead?"

Lord Mao replied, "The dead who have accumulated too many sins are not allowed to be resurrected. As for those who died from sudden accidents that unfairly affected their lifespan, I can resurrect them with no problem."

His father asked him to try. His ability was confirmed.

Lord Mao's younger brother was appointed as an official with a salary of 2,000 bushels of grain a year. When he was leaving to assume his post, thousands of local folks came to see him off. Lord Mao was also there. Lord Mao said, "Although I did not receive an official position with a salary of two thousand bushels of grain a year in the human world, I will be appointed an official position in Heaven, and on such-and-such a day I will go up to the immortal world to assume my post."

The guests all said, "In that case, we are willing to see you off then."

Lord Mao said, "If you are truly willing to bid me farewell, I'd like to thank you for your great kindness. However, you should come with empty hands. Do not spend your money to buy any gifts. I will have something to treat you all."

The guests all showed up on the appointed day, and Lord Mao held a splendid feast. All the tents were made of green brocade, with thick white carpet on the floor; a variety of rare fruits and delicacies displayed on the table, as fragrant as could be. While beautiful courtesans danced with the music, both golden bells and stone bells rang, shaking Heaven and earth, audible from a few miles away. The thousand or so people present were all drunk and full of food.

Later, the heavenly officials arrived to welcome Lord Mao. Among them were hundreds of civil officials all dressed in vermilion gowns with a white belt around their waists; the military officials were wearing suits of armors, holding flags, and displaying their shiny weapons under the sun. Their tents spread for several miles.

Lord Mao said goodbye to his parents and the local folks, then he ascended on a carriage with a feather canopy and left. The carriage was covered with flags blocking the sun and drawn by hornless dragons and white tigers; all types of flying birds and beasts were jumping and dancing on it, and pink clouds floated close and encircled it. The carriage disappeared a few miles away from Lord Mao's home.

The local folks, far and near, built a temple on behalf of Lord Mao and offered sacrifices to him. Lord Mao often had conversations with people behind a curtain. When coming and going, he sometimes appeared as a man on the back of a horse and sometimes changed into a white crane.

When those who were sick went to pray for blessing, they often boiled ten eggs to send to the tent. In a moment, each of the eggs would be thrown out. When the people took the eggs back home and broke them, if the color inside the egg was yellow, then the patient would heal. If there was mud inside the egg, then the illness would not be treatable.

Patients often relied on this method to predict their fortune.

(From Ge Hong, Shenxian zhuan, Chapter 5)

The Immortal Li Shaojun

Li Shaojun 李少君 was a native of Qi. When Emperor Wu of Han (r. 140–87 BCE) was recruiting masters of occult arts (*fangshi*), Li Shaojun obtained a secret alchemical recipe for refining elixir from Mr. Anqi.[7] However, his family was poor, so he could not afford the ingredients to make the elixir.

One day he told his disciples, "I am getting older but still lack money. Even if I work hard at farming, I cannot earn enough money to buy the ingredients. Now that the Emperor is fond of Daoist elixir practices, I intend to go and seek help from him to make the elixir. Hopefully, I will finally be able to fulfill my wish."

Thus he submitted the secret recipe to the Emperor and said, "The elixir can be made from cinnabar. Once the elixir is made and one ingests it, one will ascend to Heaven and become immortal. I have traveled across the seas and met Master Anqi, who ate jujubes as big as watermelons."

Emperor Wu was extremely respectful to him and bestowed numerous gifts upon him.

Once when Li Shaojun was drinking with the Marquis of Wu'an, among the seated there was an old man more than 90 years of age. Li Shaojun asked for the old man's name and then said that once he went on a night stroll and had fun with the old man's grandfather. He saw the old man then – a little boy at the time, and therefore knew the old man. Hearing this, those seated were all shocked.

On another day, Li Shaojun saw an ancient bronzeware piece belonging to Emperor Wu. He said to the emperor, "I have seen this bronzeware before. Duke Huan of Qi (r. 685–643 BCE) used to place it on his couch." On hearing this, Emperor Wu checked the inscription engraved on the bronzeware carefully and found the bronzeware was indeed an old relic from Qi. Thus the emperor realized that Li Shaojun was several hundred years old, even though he looked only around 50, with smooth cheeks, shiny skin, and good teeth as strong as a boy's.

Hearing that Li Shaojun was capable of enabling people to avoid death, the high-ranking officials and nobles all highly respected and admired him. The money they bestowed upon him accumulated into mountains.

Li Shaojun thus secretly tried making a divine elixir. When the elixir had been made, he told the Emperor, "Your majesty, if you cannot stop indulging in luxury and seeking excessive pleasure from amusement and sex, if you continue launching attacks and slipping often into temperamental moods, so that the wandering souls of the dead soldiers from ten thousand *li* away have no way to return home, and severe executions like decapitations are still performed at the market, then you will be unable to achieve the grand way of divine elixirs."

Li Shaojun gave the emperor his recipe for longevity and then left with the excuse that he was ill.

That night, the emperor dreamed of climbing the Songgao Mountain with Li Shaojun. Midway, a heavenly envoy descended from the clouds, riding on the back of a dragon and holding an official tally, saying that the Perfect Man of Grand Unity invites Li Shaojun to visit him. Thereupon the emperor woke up. He immediately sent others to enquire about Li's whereabouts. He also told his close cabinet ministers, "Last night, I dreamed that Li abandoned me and left."

At that time, Li Shaojun was suffering from a severe illness. The emperor went to visit him. He asked someone to write down the recipe for making elixirs. But Li died before it was finished. The emperor said, "Shaojun would not die. He has just transformed into an immortal!"

When Li Shaojun's corpse was about to be encoffined, it suddenly disappeared. His garment remained like a cicada shell, with no buttons unfastened. The emperor felt more regret for having not asked for the elixir recipe from Li sooner.

Earlier, Li Shaojun was on good terms with Dong Zhonggong, the Gentleman for Court Discussion. Dong had a long-term illness. He had an emaciated body and deficient vital energy. Li left Dong two sets of medicine and a prescription: grass grown in the year of *wusi*, grease produced locally, the roots of many flowers, Solomon's seal, fat from wild beasts, roots that withered earlier during autumn, and honey extracted from all spring flowers. Early in the tenth month, all the ingredients should be gathered in a bronzeware to stew; then ask a young boy to take a bath before adjusting the fire and making the stewed medicine into egg-sized pills. Each dose consists of three pills. After taking one dose, one's body will feel light; after three doses, one's old teeth will fall out and new teeth will grow; after five doses, one will live a long life without stooping or hunching.

Dong Zhongshu was an upright and outspoken man. He was well versed in the Five Confucian Classics but could not understand Daoist practices. He mocked those ingesting pellets and learning the Dao. Dong frequently submitted memorials to Emperor Wu, saying that one's lifespan is set by fate, aging is a natural process, and one's lifespan cannot be prolonged through the Daoist arts. He thought that even though there were exceptional examples, these were due to natural endowments, not the Daoist arts. So after receiving the medicine from Li Shaojun, Dong neither took it nor inquired into the way to make it.

Several months after Li Shaojun passed away, Dong's illness became worse. Frequently hearing Emperor Wu talking about the dream and how regretful he was, Dong Zhonggong remembered the medicine Li left and began to take it. Even before finishing half a dose, he felt his body was lighter and stronger. His illness was suddenly cured. After taking a whole dose, he felt as energetic as when he was young. This led him to believe a way to achieve longevity and immortality existed.

Then, Dong resigned from his official post, inquired with Daoist priests about the way to immortality. But he was unable to understand all of it. Zhonggong only kept his hair from turning white and was always full of energy, but he died in his eighties. Before he died, he exhorted his son Dong Daosheng, "I procured Li Shaojun's esoteric medicine when I was young. I did not believe it at first, but later I took it and recovered my strength and energy. I could not grasp the essence of it, so I can only carry this regret with me when I go under the Yellow Spring. You should seek for the Way in the occult arts, grasp its essence, and take the elixir frequently. Then you will certainly achieve immortality."

At that time, there was a general named Wen Cheng, who also acquired the occult arts of Li Shaojun. Wen Cheng served under Emperor Wu, but later the emperor sent an envoy to kill him. Wen Cheng said to the envoy, "Please ask the Emperor on my behalf: Why could you not wait for a few more days instead of coming now and ruining my great endeavor? If Your Majesty is still fond of searching for the way to immortality, thirty years hence please find me in the Chengshan Mountain. We can practice the way together without any resentment from me towards you."

After the envoy killed Wen Cheng and returned to pass Wen Cheng's words on to Emperor Wu, the emperor ordered Wen Cheng's coffin to be opened and examined. However, they found nothing but a bamboo tube inside the coffin. The emperor suspected that Wen Cheng's disciples had stolen and hidden the corpse, so he had people search for Wen Cheng's whereabouts but found nothing. Then he was very remorseful for killing Wen Cheng.

Later, Emperor Wu summoned the masters of occult arts again. Furthermore, he had sacrifices offered to the Perfect Man of Grand Unity at the Palace of Sweet Spring. In addition, he ordered another altar to be set up to present offerings to General Wen Cheng. The emperor himself conducted the ceremony.

(Ge Hong, Shenxian zhuan; from Taiping guangji, Chapter 9)

Notes

1 Cf. Li Fengmao 李豐楙, *Xianjing yu youli: shenxian shijie de xiangxiang* 仙境與游歷: 神仙世界的想象 (Beijing: Zhonghua shuju, 2010), pp. 21–46.
2 Victor H. Mair, trans., *Wandering on the Way: Early Taoist Tales and Parables of Chuang Tzu* (Honolulu: University of Hawai'i Press, 2000), p. 376.
3 Robert Campany, *Making Transcendents: Ascetics and Social Memory in Early Medieval China* (Honolulu: University of Hawai'i Press, 2009), p. xiii.
4 Jiyin was a commandery with its seat in Dingtao 定陶 (modern Dingtao district of Heze city) in Shandong.
5 The Chenliu Commandery was located in what is the present-day Chenliu district of Kaifeng city in Henan.
6 Youzhou was located in what is present-day Beijing during the Han Dynasty.
7 Anqi 安期, a famous immortal of the Qin and Han period, was also known as the Old Man of One Thousand Years.

Further Readings

Campany, Robert. *Making Transcendents: Ascetics and Social Memory in Early Medieval China*. University of Hawai'i Press, 2009.
DeWoskin, Kenneth. "Xian Descended: Narrating Xian among Mortals." *Taoist Resources* 2, no. 2 (1990): 70–86.
Kohn, Livia. "Transcending Personality: From Ordinary to Immortal Life." *Taoist Resources* 2, no. 2 (1990): 1–22.

10 Daoist Magicians

Religious Daoism can be divided into two major sects according to their primary practices. In addition to the alchemy sect (*danding* 丹鼎), which focuses on the practice of longevity and the pursuit of immortality, the other is the talisman sect (*fulu* 符籙), which focuses on removing calamities by expelling monsters and curing illness. Just as the immortals symbolize the ideal of the alchemy sect, the Daoist priests (*daoshi* 道士) represent the ideal of the talisman sect.

Monsters and goblins belong to the tradition of animistic phenomena. As Ge Hong (283–343) says in *The Master Who Embraces Simplicity* (*Baopu zi* 抱樸子), "As for all the old creatures, their spirits can change into the form of a person so as to dazzle and delude man's eyes." While records regarding monsters harming men are seen before the establishment of Daoism, stories about expelling monsters are found mainly in Daoist texts. The simple reason is that the Daoists intended to deify themselves and the religion. Thus, while creating the image of the Daoist priest, the Daoists also created numerous images of monsters; these images were sometimes significantly humanized under the pen of fiction writers – examples can be seen in the stories under the subtitle of "Spirit Maiden" in Part IV of this book.

The image of the Daoist priest in Chinese legends and tales features the following characteristics: being mighty, unyielding, upright, and awesome; possessing magical power that assures victories against monsters; and transcending worldliness while possessing an elegant bearing.[1] All of these features can be seen in the following stories.

The Old Immortal Ge

Ge Xuan 葛玄, courtesy name Xiaoxian, studied the *Immortal Classic of Nine Cinnabar Liquids* under Zuo Yuanfang.[2] Once when he was dining with his guest, he talked about magic transformation. The guest asked, "After you finish talking, could you demonstrate something special?" Xuan said, "Do you want to see something right now?" Then he spat out the food from his mouth, which turned into hundreds of big wasps, which all landed on the body of his guest, although they did not sting him. A while later, Xuan opened his mouth, and the wasps all flew in. Xuan chewed and swallowed them, or rather the original food.

DOI: 10.4324/9781003490821-12

Furthermore, by pointing with his fingers to shrimp, frogs, other crawling reptiles, as well as sparrows and the like, Xuan could get them to dance to the rhythm cf the music as humans do. In the winter, he set up fresh watermelon and dates for his guests, and in the summer he got ice and snow. He also asked people to cast dozens of coins separately into wells, then he used an apparatus above the water to suck them up, causing the coins to fly up out of the well one by one. When he set up wine for his guests, no one passed the cups, yet the cups reached the guests on their own. If there was anyone who did not drink all of the wine, the cup would not leave.

Once Ge Xuan sat together with the Emperor of Wu on a terrace. They saw the local people praying for rain. The emperor said, "The commoners desperately desire rain. Can they get some?" Xuan replied, "That is easy!" Then he wrote some magic figures and put them inside the shrine. In a moment, darkness filled the space between the sky and earth, and it began pouring rain. The emperor asked, "Are there fish in the water?" Xuan wrote some magic figures again and threw them into the water. In a moment, hundreds of big fish appeared in the water. Then the emperor asked his attendants to catch them.

(From Gan Bao, *Soushen ji*, Chapter 1)

Mr. Gourd

Mr. Gourd's name is unknown. Both the "Charm for Summoning the Spirit Army" and the "Jade Palace Charm for summoning ghosts and spirits to cure illnesses" that exist today were written by Mr. Gourd and total more than 20 volumes. Therefore, they were collectively named "Mr. Gourd's Charms."

At the time, Fei Changfang, a native of Runan, was the market supervisor. Once he saw Mr. Gourd coming from afar to sell medicine in the market. Nobody knew him. When he sold his medicine he never allowed counteroffers or petty bargaining because his medicine could cure any disease. When selling the medicine he always told the buyer, "After taking the medicine, you will surely spit such-and-such thing out, and on such-and-such a day the disease will be cured." Everything he said would always come true. The cash he received each day reached in the tens of thousands. He would give the money to those who were poor, cold, and hungry in the market, leaving himself a mere thirty to fifty coins.

He often hung an empty gourd on the roof of his house. After sunset, he would jump into the gourd, and nobody could see him. He could only be seen by Fei Changfang upstairs, thus Changfang knew that he was not an ordinary mortal. Every day, Fei Changfang swept the ground in front of his house, and when he offered food, Mr. Gourd never declined. This went on for quite a long time. Fei Changfang had never been lazy, but he also dared not request anything from him.

Knowing that Fei Changfang was an honest man, he once told Fei Changfang, "When it is dark and there is no one around, come here to see me again." Following his instructions, Fei Changfang went there. Mr. Gourd told him, "When you see me jump into the gourd, jump in the same way that I do and you will be able to enter."

Fei Changfang jumped as he was told, and sure enough, he was in the gourd before he knew it. Only when he was inside the gourd did he realize that it was no gourd at all, but a celestial world. There were only multi-storied buildings, with double gates and a plank path, as well as scores of attendants around Mr. Gourd. Mr. Gourd said to Fei Changfang, "I am an immortal and previously lived in Heaven. But because I was not diligent enough in dealing with my official duties, I was punished and demoted to the mortal world. You have the potential for instruction, thus your path crossed mine."

Fei Changfang immediately left his seat, kowtowed, and said, "I am a very ignorant mortal who has committed many sins. Fortunately, I have received your mercy and pity. It is like opening a coffin and blowing the air of immortality into the corpse, making withered and dead bones return to life. I fear only that I am slow and stubborn and so cannot serve you well. If you still choose to take pity on me, it would be a great fortune in my life." Mr. Gourd said, "I see that you are a great man, but do not reveal your secret to anyone."

Sometime later, Mr. Gourd went to see Changfang upstairs and told him, "I have some wine here. Let's have a few drinks together." The wine was in a jug on the floor below. Changfang sent someone to get the jug, but he could not lift it; when a score of people had gathered to try, they still could not lift it. Then they had to tell Mr. Gourd. Mr. Gourd came downstairs and with one finger lifted the jug. He took it upstairs to drink with Changfang. The jug was only the size of a fist, but the two drank all day until it was dark, yet the wine was still not gone.

Mr. Gourd told Fei Changfang, "I will return to the celestial world one day. Are you willing to come with me?"

Fei Changfang replied, "Of course I am. However, I do not want my family to know that I am leaving. Can this be arranged?"

Mr. Gourd said, "Yes, quite simply!" Then he gave Fang a green bamboo stick, telling him, "Take this bamboo stick home and tell your family that you are ill; then put the stick on your bed and come to me quietly."

Fei Changfang did as he was told. After he left home, his family saw that he was already dead. His corpse was there on his bed. In reality, the body was the bamboo stick. After crying and grieving, the family buried Fei.

Fei Changfang visited Mr. Gourd, and suddenly he did not know where he was. Mr. Gourd had intentionally placed him amongst a pack of tigers. The tigers bore their teeth and slashed their claws at Fei Changfang, intending to eat him. Fei Changfang felt no fear.

The next day, Mr. Gourd shut Fei Changfang in a cave. A large flat stone was hung from the ceiling by a thin rope just above Fei Changfang's head, and further, a few snakes approached the rope to bite through it. The rope was about to snap. Below the stone, Fei Changfang maintained perfect composure. When Mr. Gourd came into the cave, he patted Fei Changfang on the shoulder and said, "You can be taught."

After that, Mr. Gourd offered Fei Changfang feces to eat. The smelly and filthy feces was lined with more than an inch of dirty maggots. It was too much for Fei to take.

With a long sigh, Mr. Gourd sent him back and said, "It seems as though you still cannot achieve the Dao of immortality. I will make you the lord of the human world. You will be able to live for hundreds of years." Then he gave Fei Changfang a sealed charm and said, "Take this with you, you can be the lord of ghosts and spirits and the envoy to the gods, and thereby to cure disease and remove calamities."

Fei Changfang worried that he could not get home. Mr. Gourd gave him a bamboo stick and said, "You can go home by riding it." Fei Changfang mounted the bamboo stick, bid him farewell, and left. Suddenly, as if waking from a dream, he found he had already arrived home. His family thought that he was a ghost. He told his family everything in great detail, convincing them to open the coffin. They found there was only a bamboo stick inside. Thus they believed him. Fei Changfang threw the bamboo stick that he had ridden into the Ge Lake.[3] Looking at it again, he saw that it was a green dragon. Fei Changfang thought that it had only been one day since he left home. After asking his family, however, he realized that he had been gone for an entire year.

So Fei Changfang used the charm, summoning a ghost to cure diseases. No illness was not curable. While sitting down with people, he often yelled angrily. When others asked him what was going on, he would reply, "I was just yelling at a ghost."

At that time there was a demon in Runan, who visited the commandery a few times each year. When he came, the horsemen that followed him resembled those of a governor. When he entered the government office, he would order the drums to sound and would walk around inside and outside. Then he would leave. Everyone in the commandery worried about his visits.

One day, Fei Changfang called on the local office. It happened that the demon returned as well. The governor ran inside when the demon arrived in front of the office. Only Fei Changfang was left in the grand hall. The demon sensed Fei Changfang's presence, so he did not dare move forward. Fei Changfang shouted, "Catch the ghost right away!" The demon got off from the chariot and knelt in front of the hall, kowtowing and begging, "Please allow me to correct my wrongdoings!"

Fei Changfang harangued him, "You miserable old ghost! How dare you disregard honesty and unreasonably offend the government with your followers! Do you know that you should die? Show your true form right now!"

The demon suddenly turned into a softshell turtle with a cartwheel-sized body and a head that was tens of feet long. Fei Changfang changed the demon into its human form, gave him a talisman, and demanded that he deliver it to the Lord of Ge Lake. The demon kowtowed, wept, and left with the talisman in hand. Fei Changfang sent someone after him to make sure it went. However, they found the talisman lying by the side of the river. The demon had wrapped its neck around a tree and died.

Fei Changfang later went to Donghai, a commandery that had been in drought for three years. Fei Changfang told the people who were praying for rain, "The divine Lord of Donghai came to rape the Lady of Ge Lake, and I detained him. I did not inspect the confession that he had made before I had dismissed the incident from my mind; as a result, there has been a long drought here. I will now release him and let him spread rain." It then started to rain heavily.

Fei Changfang had the divine power to shrink land into just one small piece. This means a scene of a thousand *li* would be right before one's eyes. When he released it, it would expand to its original state.

(Ge Hong, Shenxian zhuan; from Taiping guangji, Chapter 12)

The Perfected Lord Xu

The Perfected Lord Xu 許, named Xun 遜 and styled Jingzhi, was a native of Runan.[4] Both his grandfather and father admired the perfect Way their whole lives. At the age of 20, Jingzhi studied with Wu Meng, the Perfected Lord of the Grand Grotto, who taught him the method of the Three Purities.

Lord Xu had been recommended as one "filial and incorrupt" (*xiaolian* 孝廉) and appointed as magistrate of Jingyang of Shu. Due to the chaos during the Jin, he resigned from the position and traveled to the south of the Yangzi River with Lord Wu.[5] At that time, Wang Dun was just starting a rebellion. Using casting charms and spells as a pretext, the two lords visited Wang Dun, intending to stop him to save the Jin.

One day, the two Lords and Guo Pu waited for Wang Dun. Dun showed up angry. "Last night I dreamed I was holding a piece of wood that pierced through the sky. Does this mean that it will be safe for me to be enthroned? Please interpret my dream." Lord Xu said, "This dream is not auspicious." Lord Wu said, "A piece of wood piercing the sky is the character *wei* (未), 'not yet,' you should not move rashly." Dun asked Guo Pu to divine for him using stalks. Guo said, "Your efforts will not be successful." Dun then asked about his lifespan. Guo replied, "If you rebel, disaster will befall you in no time. If you live in Wuchang, your lifespan is unfathomable." Dun asked angrily, "How long can you still live?" Guo replied, "My life will end today." Dun ordered his soldiers to seize Guo Pu and execute him outside. While drinking with Wang Dun, the two lords left through the technique of invisibility.

Having arrived at the mouth of Lu River, the two lords summoned a boat to cross Zhongling. The boatman declined, saying that there was no laborer to row the boat. The two lords replied, "Just let us aboard. We will drive the boat ourselves." Then they told the boatman, "Close your eyes tightly. When you can faintly hear the sound of the boat moving, be careful not to secretly peek!" Then they boarded the boat. In a short while, the boatman heard the sound of the boat shaking and leaves falling. Then he opened his eyes ever so slightly and saw that two dragons pulling the boat on top of the purple hills. The dragons noticed that he was peeking, so they abandoned the boat and left. The two lords said, "You disobeyed our instruction and this is the result. What can we do?" Thereupon they urged the boatman to become a hermit on top of the hill, let him ingest a grass elixir (*lingcao*), and taught him the technique of immortality. The remains of the boat still exist today.

Later on, at Yuzhang, Lord Xu met a young man who appeared clean and tidy, who called himself Shenlang. While conversing with him, Lord Xu knew that he was not human. After he left, Xu told his disciple, "The young boy is a flood dragon spirit. Since Jiangxi has been flooded several times, it will escape if I do not remove it." Then he looked around with his Daoist divine eyes[6] and found the flood dragon spirit had become a yellow bull on the sandy beach. Xu told his disciple Shi Taiyu, "He is the yellow bull. I will turn into a black bull and fight him with a white cloth tied to my head. When you see us, you should cut him with your sword." In a short while, two bulls ran one after the other. Taiyu cut the leg of the yellow bull with his sword, causing it to fall into a well west of the town. The black bull also entered the well, but the flood dragon spirit escaped in the end.

Previously, the flood dragon spirit had transformed into a smart young boy with a lot of treasure, who took the daughter of the governor Jia Yu as his wife and traveled frequently over the rivers and lakes, returning with a lot of precious goods each time. This time he returned with nothing on him and said that he was hurt by robbers. In a short while, the custodian of foreign visitors (office of receptions) reported, "Xu Jingzhi, a Daoist, is paying a visit to you." Governor Jia went out to welcome Xu and offer him a seat. Lord Xu said, "I heard that you have had a good son-in-law. I'd like to see him briefly." Shenlang refused to come out on the pretext that he was ill. Xu shouted with a growl, "Flood dragon spirit, you old demon! How dare you hide your true form!" Then the flood dragon changed back into its original form and arrived at the front of the hall. Xu summoned the spirit in the air and killed it. Furthermore, he ordered their two sons to be brought. When Xu spat water onto them, they became small flood dragons. The wife, Lady Jia, was about to change her form, but she stopped when her parents pleaded Xu. Xu ordered them to dig more than ten feet under the house, and they found it was the border of a river. He ordered them to move immediately. In a short while, the official residence sank and became a pool, which is still there.

Afterward, on the first day of the eighth month in the second year of the Taikang reign of the Jin, Xu and his whole family ascended into the sky during the day from the western maintain in Hongzhou.[7]

(From Liu Fu 劉斧 [fl. 1073], *Qingsuo gaoyi* 青瑣高議, Chapter 1)

Liu Haishi

Liu Haishi, a native of Putai,[8] once found shelter at Binzhou[9] to escape turmoil. He was then 14 years old. He studied together with Liu Cangke, a young native of Binzhou, at the same private school. They became good friends and pledged to be brothers for the rest of their lives. Shortly afterward, however, both of Liu Haishi's parents died. Escorting his parents' coffin back to his home, no news of Haishi was received after he left.

Liu Cangke's family was fairly wealthy. He had two sons when he was 40. The eldest son, Liu Ji, was 17 and became well-known locally. The second son was also smart. Further, Liu Cangke took a girl from the Ni family in the town as his concubine and was very fond of her. A half year later, however, the eldest son began suffering from headaches and died. Cangke and his wife were dismayed. Soon, Liu's wife became sick and died; a few months later, the wife of their oldest son also died. Furthermore, their maids and servants died one after another. Grieving over the dead, Cangke felt it was almost unbearable.

One day, when he was sitting alone with his worries, the doorkeeper suddenly informed him that Liu Haishi had come. Cangke was delighted and rushed out to welcome him. Before exchanging greetings, Liu Haishi was suddenly startled, saying, "Brother, you are experiencing a disaster that will destroy your entire family. Do you know this?" Cangke was stunned and did not understand what he was saying. Liu Haishi said, "We have not heard from each other for a long time. I suppose your recent situation is not very good!" Cangke could not help but shed tears. He told him what had happened in his family. Liu Haishi was saddened and in tears, but then he said with a smile, "This disaster is not over yet. I lamented your fate at the beginning; fortunately, however, you now have me here, so please allow me to say congratulations to you." Liu said, "We have not seen each other for a long time. Have you mastered the medical technique of the state of Yue?" Liu Haishi replied, "No, that is not my specialty. What I'm good at is geomancy and face-reading." Liu Cangke was very happy and asked him to look around and examine his house.

Entering the house, Haishi inspected it from the inside out. After that, he requested to see all the members of the family. Following his instructions, Liu Cangke gathered his son, daughter-in-law, and servants and maids into the hall and introduced them to Haishi one by one. When it was Lady Ni's turn, Liu Haishi looked skyward and let out a long laugh.

To everyone's amazement, they saw that Lady Ni tremble and her face turned pale. Her whole body suddenly shrank to merely a little more than two feet long. Liu Haishi tapped on the head of Lady Ni with a ruler, which made a sound like he was hitting a stone jar. Holding Lady Ni's hair, he carefully examined the back of her head and saw a few white hairs. When he was about to pull them out, the woman pulled back, kneeled on the floor, and cried, saying that she would leave immediately and only asked him not to pull them out. Liu Haishi became angry. "Do you still intend to harm people?!" Then he pulled the white hairs out. The woman turned into a black raccoon-like animal. While everyone was extremely scared, Liu Haishi grabbed the animal and put it in his sleeve.

Liu Haishi looked at Liu's daughter-in-law and said to him, "Your daughter-in-law has been severely poisoned. This means there must be something abnormal on her back. Please let me check it." The woman was shy and reluctant to expose her neck. Liu's son forced her to do so. They saw that the white hairs on her back were four fingers long. Liu Haishi picked them out with a needle, saying, "These hairs are old. You would not have lived past seven days." Then he examined Liu Cangke's son and found white hairs two fingers long. He said, "With hairs like these, you would have died after a month." He then examined Liu Cangke and his servants one by one and picked out the white hairs on them, saying, "If I did not arrive in time, none of your household would be alive."

Liu Cangke asked, "What is this?" Liu Haishi replied, "It belongs to a species of fox that leeches the essence of people to become a spirit. It is a most dangerous killer." Liu Cangke said, "We have not seen each other for so long. When did you come to possess such magical power? Are you an immortal?" Liu Haishi said with a smile, "I have just learned a little skill from my master, that's all. I am by no means an immortal." Cangke asked who his master was. Liu Haishi replied, "The Daoist of Mountain Stone. I am not capable of killing the creature that I have just caught, so I will bring it to my master to deal with."

After this exchange of words, he bid Cangke farewell. Suddenly, he felt that his sleeve was empty. He said with astonishment, "I forgot! There are still big hairs on its tail that have not been pulled out, and thus it has escaped." While everyone was terrified, Liu Haishi said, "The hairs on its neck have all been pulled out. It can only become a beast, instead of a human being, so it will not run too far away." Then he went through the house to examine the cats and went out to examine the dogs. But it was not either place. Opening the pigpen door, Liu Haishi said with a smile, "Here it is!" Liu Cangke looked at it and found there was an extra pig. Hearing Liu Haishi's laughter, the pig lay prone on the ground and dared not move. Liu Haishi grabbed it by its ear and saw that there was a white hair on the tail, which was as hard as a needle. When Haishi was about to pull it out, the pig flipped over and screamed in resistance. Liu Haishi said, "You have committed so much sin, but still you are reluctant to lose a hair?" So he held it and pulled the hair out. Immediately the pig turned into a raccoon again. Liu Haishi put it into his sleeve and intended to leave, but Liu Cangke urged him to stay just for a meal. Before leaving, Liu Cangke asked him when they would meet again. Liu Haishi said, "This is difficult to predict. But my master has great aspirations so he often lets us travel the world saving sentient beings, so there may be opportunities to meet again in the future."

After Haishi left, Liu Cangke thought about his name carefully and suddenly realized who he was, "Haishi is probably an immortal! The combination of 'mountain (山) stone (石)' is the word 'rock' (岩), which is the name of the immortal Lü Dongbin."

(From Pu Songling, *Liaozhai zhiyi*, Chapter 3)

Notes

1 Zhang Zhenjun 張振軍, "Lun Daojiao dui chuantong xiaoshuo zhi gongxian 論道教對傳統小説之貢獻 [On the Contributions of Daoism to Traditional Chinese Fiction]," *Daojia wenhua yanjiu* 道家文化研究 [*Daoist Culture Studies*] 9 (1996): 332–346; *Chuantong xiaoshuo yu Zhongguo wenhua* 傳統小説與中國文化 (Nanning: Guangxi daxue chubanshe, 1996), pp. 115–116.
2 Zuo Ci 左慈 (156?–289?), whose courtesy name was Yuanfang 元放, was a famous fangshi-magician of the Eastern Jin.
3 The lake is located north of present-day Xincai County, Henan.
4 This is called Runan 汝南 County in Henan province today.
5 This refers to Wu Meng, a magician of the Jin.
6 This is the translation of *dao yan* 道眼.
7 Hongzhou 洪州 should be modern Hui 輝 county, though Nanchang in Jiangxi also called Hongzhou in the ancient time.
8 An old county today belongs to Boxing county in Shandong.
9 In modern Shandong province.

Further Readings

DeWoskin, Kenneth. *Doctors, Diviners, and Magicians of Ancient China: Biographies of Fang-Shih*. New York, NY: Columbia University Press, 1983.
Kohn, Livia. "Magic Powers." In *The Taoist Experience* (Albany: State University of New York Press, 1993), pp. 290–99.

11 Descended Goddesses

The descended goddess is a popular motif in narratives from the Jin 晉 (265–420) to Tang (618–907) dynasties. Rooted in ancient shamanism, nurtured in Daoism and folktales, and aestheticized by literati writers (*wenren* 文人), this motif blossomed in the garden of popular Chinese literature as well as in Daoist literature into something quite beautiful.

Spiritual love interaction between goddesses and men first appeared in shamanism – this can be seen in the *Chuci* 楚辭 (Songs of the South), such as Qu Yuan's "Nine Songs." The earliest hierogamous encounter between a mortal and a goddess is found in the "Rhapsody on Gaotang" and "Rhapsody on the Goddess," both attributed to Song Yu 宋玉 (c. 290–c. 223 BCE). This motif was inherited in rhapsodies during the Jian'an period (196–219) of the Three Kingdoms and in narratives from the Jin to Tang.[1]

The basic structure of the motif is as follows: (1) a mortal young man lives alone and practices personal cultivation, (2) a goddess descends to the man's home and takes the initiative in their relationship, and (3) after living as husband and wife for a period of time, they end up reluctantly separating – a tragic ending.

This motif is obviously related to Daoism. Daoist traditions posit that through cultivation and taking an immortality pill made of cinnabar (*dan* 丹) one can achieve longevity and rejuvenation, even attracting a jade girl from Heaven to serve him (*yunü laiyü* 玉女來御). Daoist traditions also postulate that when a goddess violates the heavenly rules or has worldly desires, she is banished by the God of heaven to the mortal world; after experiencing love affairs or repaying debts from her previous lives, she finally returns to heaven. These are beyond doubt the religious basis of the descended goddess motif, though the stories featuring this motif were also nurtured by folktales and thus can be interpreted from different perspectives and approaches.

Presented next are four well-known stories of the descended goddess.

Du Lanxiang

During the Han dynasty, there was a girl named Du Lanxiang who called herself a native of Nankang.[2] In the spring of the fourth year of the Jianxing period (236), she visited Zhang Chuan several times. Chuan was then 17 years old when he first

DOI: 10.4324/9781003490821-13

saw her carriage outside his door. A maid said to him, "The mother sent her daughter to marry you. Dare you not respectfully obey?"

Chuan had changed his name to Shuo previously. Shuo thus asked the girl to meet him. He saw that the girl was about 16 or 17, yet what she talked about were things that had happened long ago. She had two maids. The older one was named Xuanzhi and the younger Songzhi. Their carriage was decorated with gold and filled with food and drink. The girl composed a poem, which read:

> My mother lives in the divine mountain,
> Frequently she visits the zenith of clouds.
> Numerous maidens serve me with feather banners,
> I have never gone out of the heavenly palace.
> Now the floating wheels sent me here,
> How could I still be ashamed of worldly affairs?
> Being together with me is being with blessings,
> A cold shoulder to me brings you calamities.

One day morning in the eighth month, she came again and composed another poem, which read as follows:

> Wandering leisurely amid the Milky Way,
> My breath spread in Mount Jiuyi.[3]
> Even though the Weak River is remote,[4]
> Seeking for you, I would not delay.

Then she took out three yams, each the size of an egg, and said, "By eating these, you will neither be afraid of wind and waves nor troubled by heat and cold." Zhang Shuo ate two and intended to leave one. Yet she asked him to eat all of them, saying, "I wanted to be your wife at first so that our feelings would not be estranged. However, because there is a discrepancy in our fortunes, we may have to part for a while. When the Yearstar (i.e., Jupiter) rises east in the early morning, I'll be back again for you."

When Lanxiang arrived again, Zhang Shuo asked her, "What do you think about prayer and sacrifice?" Lanxiang replied, "Expelling monsters can cure illness. Excessive sacrifice is not helpful." Lanxiang called medication "expelling monsters."

(From Gan Bao, *Soushen ji*, Chapter 1)

The Heavenly Jade Maiden

Xian Chao 弦超, whose courtesy name is Yiqi, served in the kingdom of Wei as the governor assistant of the Jibei Commandery.[5] One night, during the Jiaping period (249–256), while sleeping by himself, Xian Chao dreamed that a goddess came to keep him company. The goddess stated that she was the Heavenly Jade Maiden, a native of Dongjun 東郡, surnamed Cheng Gong 成公 and styled Zhiqiong 知琼.

She had lost her parents when young; the Heavenly Emperor, pitying her loneliness, had allowed her descent to marry a human husband. In the dream, Xian Chao was happy and exuberant; he was awed over the goddess's astounding beauty, incomparable to a normal person's countenance. After he woke, he kept thinking over the scenes of his dream – one moment feeling as if she must indeed exist, while the next thinking she was just a dream. This occurred for three or four nights in a row.

One morning, the goddess actually came, driving an exquisite carriage and attended by eight maidservants; the clothing she wore was made from splendid silks, and her countenance and demeanor were like that of an aerial immortal. She said she was already 70 years of age, but looked 15 or 16. There was a wine pot and wine cups in the carriage and five sets of luxurious green and white glassware. She invited Xian Chao to eat and drink with her; the wine, food, and wine utensils were all things rarely encountered in the human world.

The goddess said to Xian Chao, "I am the Heavenly Jade Maiden. The Heavenly Emperor permitted me to marry, so I have come to accompany you. I did not expect you to be virtuous, simply an inspiration from the fate of a previous life indicates that our becoming husband and wife is mutually suitable – even if it does not benefit you, neither will it harm you. Being with me, you can drive a swift carriage when coming and going, ride stout horses, frequently eat delicacies from far-off lands, and maintain an abundant supply of clothes and fabric. It is just that, being a celestial, I cannot bear you a child, nor is it in my nature to feel jealousy; our union would not interfere with you taking part in marriage in the human world." Thus, they became husband and wife.

The goddess presented Xian Chao with a poem. The poem read,

Leisurely I roamed over Bohai Sea and Mount Penglai,[6]
Listening to the music produced by patterned rocks.
The magic *lingzhi* grass does not need nurturing,
Perfect virtue will be expected with time flowing.
How could a goddess react with no reason?
Alongside fate, she comes to assist you.
Accepting me will glorify your five clans,
A refusal will bring you disasters.

This is the poem's general gist. Since the complete poem was over 200 characters long, it could not be recorded in its entirety. The goddess also annotated the *Classic of Changes*, totaling seven volumes, with hexagrams, images, as well as explanations. Therefore, her work is not only an interpretation of the classic, it can also be used for divination, just as Yang Xuan's *Great Subtlety* and Mr. Xue's *Zhongjing*. Xian Chao could understand its decrees, using it to judge things as auspicious or ominous.

They lived as husband and wife for seven or eight years. After Xian Chao's parents obtained a wife for him, his meal and sleeping times were staggered between his wife and the goddess. The goddess came at night, leaving in the morning, moving so quickly as if she were flying. Only Xian Chao could see her; no one else saw her. When they were in a quiet room, others could sometimes hear noise from within; they also frequently found traces of her, but in the end, never saw her form or appearance. As time went on, people found it strange, so they queried Xian Chao. Xian Chao unwittingly leaked the truth.

The goddess thus asked to leave, saying, "I am a celestial; even though I have associated with you, I do not wish strangers to know. But you have a careless disposition. Now that my whereabouts are revealed, I can no longer be with you. We have lived together for many years, and the gratitude we owe each other for having been husband and wife is not insignificant; upon parting, how can we help but feel sorrow and regret at the loss? But now, it cannot be otherwise – let us each strive to take care!"

Further, she instructed her servants to prepare a parting feast. She opened a rattan trunk, taking out two gowns that she had knit herself to leave to Xian Chao, and additionally presented him with a poem; then, she grasped his arm to take leave of him, unable to stop the tears that covered her entire face. With a respectful expression, she stepped into the ethereal carriage, which immediately sped off as if flying. Xian Chao was despondent for a long time, barely able to endure this change of circumstances.

Five years after the goddess had departed, Xian Chao, following the governor's orders, was traveling to Luoyang; having arrived at the foot of the Fish Mountain of Jibei, just as he was on the road traveling west, he saw in the distance at the end of a serpentine road, a carriage that appeared to be Zhiqiong's. He quickly drove up to it – and lo and behold, it was! Thus, Xian Chao lifted the carriage curtain to meet the goddess. Each was brimming with mixed feelings of joy and sorrow. He took control of the horse on the left, grabbed the rope to step into the carriage, and rode in the carriage with her to Luoyang. There, they lived together again as husband and wife, revisiting erstwhile affections of times past.

Even until 20 years later into the Taikang period they were still there, though they did not meet daily; every third day of the third month, the fifth day of the fifth month, the seventh day of the seventh month, the ninth day of the ninth month, as well as the first and fifteenth days, the goddess would descend to meet Xian Chao, staying for one night each time. The Jin dynasty writer Zhang Hua wrote the "Rhapsody on the Goddess" about this.

(From Gan Bao, *Soushen ji*, Chapter 1)

The Pure Maiden of White River

Xie Duan 谢端, a native of Houguan, the capital of the Jian'an commandery,[7] lost both mother and father when young; having no relatives, he was raised by neighbors. When he was around seventeen or eighteen years old, he had a humble, cautious disposition, was self-disciplined, and never did anything against the law. After reaching adulthood, he left his neighbor's house and lived by himself without a wife; his neighbors all greatly pitied him and urged him to get a wife, but he never had the chance.

Xie Duan went to bed very late and rose very early, diligently farming day and night. One day, when he was near town he picked up a large river snail that seemed as large as a pot that could hold three liters of water. He thought this was a rare object, so he brought it home, put it in the water vat, and raised it for some ten days. Every morning, Xie Duan went out to the fields; when he returned, he always found food, drink, hot water, and a warm stove at home, as if there was someone who was doing these things for him. He thought it was his neighbors helping him and looking after him. It was like this for many days in a row, so Xie Duan went to express his gratitude to his neighbors.

The neighbor said, "But I have never helped you do anything, how do I deserve your gratitude?" Xie Duan thought the neighbor did not understand his meaning; however, there was still a hot meal each day, so he went to ask his neighbor more directly.

The neighbor, laughing, said, "You already got a wife, secreted away in your home cooking for you every day, and you still say I cooked for you?" Xie Duan had no reply and felt even more puzzled, not knowing the reason.

The next day, he went out at the rooster's crow; stealthily returning at dawn, he hid outside the bamboo fence and peeked inside his house. He saw a young girl walk out from the water vat to light a fire beneath the stove. Xie Duan rushed in and stopped beside the water vat to look at the river snail – he only saw an empty snail shell. He turned around and walked over to the stove, asking, "From where does this bride come? Why do you want to help and cook for me?"

The girl, shocked and panicking, wanted to force her way back to the water vat, but Xie Duan was in the way, so she could not go back. She could only reply, "I am the Spiral Shell Goddess from the Milky Way. The Emperor of Heaven had pity on you since you were an orphan from a young age. Since you are humble and cautious and adhere to duty, he told me to temporarily watch over your home and cook for you. He further said within ten years you would become wealthy, get a wife, and I would return. Why did you peek in for no reason and suddenly charge in? Now that my true appearance has been exposed, I cannot remain here any longer but must go back. Even though I have to leave, your ensuing days will gradually improve. You must be thrifty, farm, catch fish, and cut firewood for a living. I will leave you this snail shell – use it to store millet and you will never lack millet year-round." Xie Duan entreated the river snail girl to stay, but in the end, she did not acquiesce. At this time, the wind suddenly started blowing and the rain falling. The girl floated away.

Xie Duan built a shrine for her. On festivals and holidays, he would always punctually offer sacrifices to this Spiral Shell Goddess. His days were bountiful, though he was not wealthy. A villager married his daughter to him. Later, Xie Duan became an official, rising to the position of magistrate. Today, one can still see the Spiral Shell Goddess temple.

(From Tao Qian, *Soushen houji*, Chapter 5)

Guo Han

While he was young, Guo Han of Taiyuan was unceremonious, lofty, and distinguished with a pure demeanor. He was handsome, eloquent, and accomplished in calligraphy – especially in the cursive and seal style. He lost his parents when he was a child and since then had lived alone.

It was midsummer. Taking advantage of the moonlight, he lay in the middle of his courtyard. A cool breeze came from time to time. He inhaled a fragrant smell, which became stronger and stronger. Guo Han felt very strange. Looking up, he saw someone descending slowly and arriving directly in front of him. She was a young girl of matchless beauty and dazzling glory. She wore a black silk shirt, a long white silk robe, a phoenix cap decorated with green feathers, and jade patterned shoes. Both of her maidens were beautiful and alluring.

Guo Han straightened his clothes and kerchief, got off the bed, and bowed to greet her, saying, "Beyond my expectations, an honorable goddess from afar descends into my humble home. I'd like to listen to your virtuous instruction."

The girl said with a smile, "I am the Weaving Maiden of Heaven. For a long time, I have not met my husband, and our tryst day has been blocked forever. An unnamable sorrow has filled my heart. God granted me a visit to this mortal world. I admire your pure demeanor and am willing to entrust myself to you, my congenial friend."

Guo Han said, "I dared not expect what has happened. Your words touch me deeply."

The Weaving Maiden commanded her maidservant to sweep the room, unfold the frosty fog red silk curtain, lay the crystal jade mat, and turn the wind-producing fan – it was as if it were a more cool autumn.

Then they ascended the main room hand in hand, undressed, and lay together. The Weaving Maiden's light red silk underwear was like a small sachet, which filled the entire room with fragrance. There was also a concentric dragon brain pillow, covered with a quilt with Mandarin duck patterns embroidered with double thread. The girl's soft skin, smooth body, deep affection, and intimate manner were all beautiful and unrivaled. At dawn, when the girl bid farewell before leaving, the makeup on her face was as it was the night before. Guo Han tried to wipe it off, but it turned out to be her true complexion. Guo Han accompanied her outside, and the girl soared into the clouds and disappeared.

After that, the girl came every night, and their love became stronger. Guo Han teased her, "Where is the Cowherd? How dare you go out alone?"

The girl replied, "The *yin* and *yang* keep changing all the time. What do our affairs have to do with him? Furthermore, we are blocked and separated by the Milky Way, so it is impossible for him to know. Even if he knows, it's still not worth worrying about." Thereupon she stroked the pit of Guo Han's stomach and said, "The people in this world cannot understand this clearly, that is all."

Guo Han added, "You have already entrusted your spirit to the constellation, could you tell me something about that?"

The girl replied, "When people look at the constellations, they only see that they are stars. But there are palaces and residences there, and the crowd of immortals is all roaming around inside. Of the spirits of all creatures, each has an image in the sky and a form on the earth. The changes of a person on the earth must be manifested in the sky. Now I have observed it, and I clearly understand it myself." Thereupon she told Guo Han the locations of the various stars and explained the constellation system to him in detail. For the phenomena that his contemporaries did not understand, Guo Han thoroughly understood.

Later, when the Double Seventh Eve was about to arrive, the girl did not come. After several nights, she appeared again.

Guo Han asked her, "Were you happy to meet him?"

The girl replied with a smile, "How could Heaven be better than this mortal world? I just feel that it is my fate to meet him like that. There is no other reason. You should not be jealous."

Guo Han asked her, "Why did it take you so long to come then?"

The girl replied, "Five days in this world equals only one night there."

Furthermore, the girl brought heavenly cuisine, none of which were foods of this world. Seeing that her clothes were all seamless, Guo Han asked her the reason. She said to Guo Han, "The clothes are not made using needlework." Each time the Weaving Maiden arrived, she always brought her own clothes.

One night after a year, the girl suddenly became sad, and tears poured down her face. Holding Guo Han's hand, she said, "God's command has a limit. Now it is time to bid farewell!" Then she could not help but sob.

Guo Han asked with surprise and regret, "How many days left?"

The girl replied, "Only tonight."

Thereupon they shed tears in sorrow and did not sleep the whole night. When it was dawn, they caressed and hugged each other to bid farewell. The girl left him a seven treasure bowl as a gift, saying that on such-and-such a day next year, there would be a letter to greet him. Guo Han gave her a pair of jade rings in return. Then the girl left by stepping onto the air. She turned her head back to look, waved her hands for a long while, and then vanished. Guo Han became ill from thinking of her. He never forgot her.

On the appointed day the next year, as expected, the Weaving Maiden sent a servant girl who had been there before to deliver a letter to Guo Han. Opening the letter, he found that she had used blue silk as paper. The words were written in red lead. The words were beautiful, with lingering affection. At the end of the letter were two poems. The first poem read,

> Though the Milky Way is broad,
> Still, there is an appointed date after three autumns.
> Now our relationship has come to an end,
> When will our next tryst day be?

Another poem read,

> A red tower stands by the pure Milky Way,
> The jade palace houses purple rooms.
> My longings for a tryst is still here,
> It gives me but a broken heart.

Guo Han replied to her letter with fragrant paper. The words were very earnest, and there were two poems in response. The first poem read,

> A human is involved with Heaven,
> Who could have expected this?

Who knew that once you visited me,
It would initiate our endless thinking of each other.

The other read,

The pillow you sent me still bears your fragrance,
My clothes are still stained with our tears.
Your beautiful face is now in Heaven,
Our souls go back and forth in vain.

From then on, their connection was cut.

That year, the Grand Astrologer submitted a memorial to the emperor, saying that Vega was dull. Missing the Weaving Maiden endlessly, Guo Han no longer paid any attention to beauty in the human world. Later, because of the need for progeny, the great righteousness that requires one to marry, he was forced to marry the daughter of the Cheng family. He was very dissatisfied with the marriage, and further, he and his wife fell out with each other without sons. Guo Han's official title reached the Attendant Censor before his death.

(Zhang Jian 張薦 [774–804], *Lingguai ji* 靈怪集)

Notes

1 Zhang Zhenjun, "Luelun Zhongguo gudai xiaoshuo zhong de renshenlian gushi 略論 中國古代小說中的人神戀故事 [Brief Remarks on the Love Stories between Man and Goddess in Ancient Chinese Fiction]." *Xinan shida xuebao* 西南師大學報 *Journal of Southwestern Normal University* 1 (1991): 94–99.
2 Nankang is located in present-day Nankang City in Jiangxi.
3 This mountain is located south of Ningyuan in Hunan.
4 The Weak River, or *ruoshui* 弱水, is the name of an old river in northwest China.
5 This commandery is located north of what is now Shanxi and Hebei.
6 Penglai is one of the three legendary immortal islands.
7 Its seat was in Houguan 侯官 county (modern Fuzhou in Fujian) during the Jin dynasty.

Further Reading

Zhang, Zhenjun. "Two Modes of Goddess Depictions in Early Medieval Chinese Literature." *Journal of Chinese Humanities* 3 (2017): 117–34.

12 Immortal Land Adventurers

Traveling to the land of the immortals has been an enduring motif since the late Han dynasty when the idea that immortals exist in the mountains and islands over the seas entered popular culture. The immortal lands include the three immortal islands (*Penglai, Fangzhang*, and *Yingzhou*), the Ten Islets, the Thirty-six Caves, and the Seventy-two Blessed Lands.

In early stories of immortal land adventures, protagonists find strange things rarely seen in the mortal world, watch chess games between immortals, and have immortal food (such as elixirs). In later stories, the adventurers experience love affairs with beautiful transcendent girls, or fairies. Besides the archetypal theme of "Fairy Encounters," the "otherness" such as a story's unique concept of time, in which one day in the immortal land is equivalent to a year in the human world, was probably an additional reason why these tales became so fascinating in later generations, especially to the literati.

Next are six stories of immortal land adventurers.

Hanzi

Hanzi claimed to be a native of Shu and liked to raise puppies. Once a dog walked into a mountain cave. He followed it. Having spent more than ten days walking over several hundred *li*, he got out of the cave and reached the top of the mountain where there was a palace with a terrace, lush green pine trees, as well as immortal officials and majestic guards. Hanzi saw his previous wife who was in charge of cleaning fish. She gave him a charm with a letter and some drugs, letting him return to give them to the magistrate of Chengdu, Sir Qiao.

Sir Qiao opened the letter. There were fish eggs in it. He placed them in the pool and raised them for a year. All the fish grew into the shape of dragons. Then Hanzi sent the charm back to the mountain and saw that the dog's color had turned even redder, and long-feather pheasants often followed him. Hanzi went up and down the mountain for more than 100 years before he remained on the mountain. From time to time though, he went down to shelter the people in his clan.

DOI: 10.4324/9781003490821-14

The Shu people built a temple for him by the entrance of the cave. The sound of drumming and music were frequently heard. Within thousands of *li* in the southwest, people are still offering sacrifices to him.

(From Liu Xiang, *Liexian zhuan*)

Wang Zhi

During the Jin dynasty, Wang Zhi 王質 entered Mount Stone Room in the Xin'an Commandery to cut firewood.[1] There he saw several young boys playing chess and singing. He stayed there, listening to the song. A boy gave Wang Zhi something like the pit of a jujube. Wang Zhi kept it in his mouth and did not feel hungry.

"Why do you not leave?" the boy asked him.

Wang Zhi stood up, and he discovered the handle of his ax had rotted. After returning home, he found he was no longer a man of the time.

(From Ren Fang 任昉 (460–508), *Shuyi ji*述異記)

Dragon Pearl

During the Han dynasty, there was a cave in the city of Luoyang. Its depth was unfathomable. A woman who harbored murderous intentions said to her husband, "I have never seen this cave." Even though it was against his inclinations, her husband accompanied her to see it. As soon as they arrived, the woman pushed him down into the cave, and after quite a while he reached the bottom. The woman later threw food into the cave, seemingly offering sacrifice to him.

While suddenly falling, the man was in a trance. After a long time, he regained consciousness. He got the food and ate it, so his strength returned a bit.

Flustered, he searched for a path out and found another cave. He crawled forward to go in it. The path in the cave was rugged and zigzagged. After walking several *li*, it became a bit brighter. Then the path turned into broad and flat ground.

After walking more than one hundred *li*, he felt that he was stepping on dust. He smelled the fragrance of round-grained nonglutinous rice. He ate the rice, which was fragrant and delicious, not merely killing his hunger. So he packed some of the rice as provisions and kept walking as he ate.

When the cave came to an end, he passed a path filled with a mud-like substance, the smell of which resembled the dust he encountered previously. Again he got some of it and left. He had covered a long distance, but how long exactly was difficult to determine. He kept walking in the direction that was bright and broad.

When he had eaten all that he had brought with him, he reached a big city. The city walls were built in good order; the palaces were magnificent; the terraces, pavilions, and residences were all decorated with gold foil. Though there was neither sun nor moon, they were brighter than the natural light from the three sources of light.[2] People there were all thirty feet tall. They wore silk garments and played unique music, which was never heard in this world.

Then the man begged for some food. A tall man told him to keep walking forward. Following his advice, he walked ahead and passed nine palaces which were exactly the same. When he arrived at the last palace, he was even hungrier.

The tall man pointed to a huge cypress tree, which was about 100 arm spans around, in the yard. Under the tree was a goat. He was asked to kneel down to stroke the goat's beard. He first obtained a pearl, which the tall man grabbed. The pearl he got when he stroked the goat's beard the second time was snatched away again by the tall man. When he got the third one, the tall man asked him to eat it himself. Then he was able to cure his hunger.

He asked the names of the nine palaces, pleading to stay there and not leave. The tall man replied, "Our ruler said that you cannot stay here. After returning home, you may ask Zhang Hua (232–300),[3] who should be familiar with this place." The man then continued walking along the cave, and consequently, he was able to come out in Jiaozhou.[4]

Six to seven years after his return, he came back to Luo. He visited Zhang Hua and showed him the two items he had obtained. Hua said, "The substance like dust was the saliva of the Yellow River dragon, the mud was mud from Kun Mountain,[5] and the immortal at the nine palaces is called the Grand Master of Nine Palaces. The goat was an infatuated dragon. The first pearl you got enables one to live as long as Heaven and earth if one eats it, the second can prolong one's life span, and the third one may be eaten just as food."

(From Liu Yiqing, *Youming lu*)

Liu Chen and Ruan Zhao[6]

In the fifth year of the Yongping reign period (58–75) under Emperor Ming of the [Eastern] Han Dynasty (25–220), Liu Chen and Ruan Zhao, natives of the Shan County (present-day Sheng County, Zhejiang), went together to the Tiantai Mountain to gather paper mulberry bark;[7] there, they got lost and could not return home. After 13 days, they exhausted all of their provisions and were starved almost to death.

From a distance they saw a peach tree bearing many fruit on top of the mountain, but the cliffs were steep, the stream deep, and they could never find a path leading up to the top. They climbed by grabbing the kudzu vines, and thus they were eventually able to get to the top. After they each ate several peaches, their hunger ceased, and their bodies were filled with energy.

They went back down the mountain and scooped up water with cups, intending to wash their faces and rinse their mouths, when they saw some turnip leaves, which were extremely fresh, being swept downstream from the mountain's interior. Then a cup which contained sesame seeds, mixed with yellow millet, drifted down as well.

"Judging from this, we know someone's residence is not far from here!" Liu and Ruan said to each other. Thus they dove together into the water, swam upstream two or three *li*, and were able to cross the mountain before climbing out of the large stream.

By the stream were two girls of wonderful natural endowment and matchless beauty. Upon seeing the two men wade ashore from the stream with the cup in hand, they smiled and exclaimed, "Mr. Liu and Mr. Ruan caught the cup that we set adrift!"

Liu Chen and Ruan Zhao did not know them, yet the two girls called them by their surnames, as if they were all old friends. Thus they were delighted to see each other.

"Why do you come so late?" The two girls asked. Then they invited the two men into their home.

Their house had a roof of bronze tiles. By the south and the east walls stood two large beds, both draped with crimson silk curtains. On each upper corner of the curtains, bells in gold or silver hung. By the head of each bed, ten servant maidens stood.

An order [from the two girls] was passed down [to the maids], saying, "Mr. Liu and Mr. Ruan have just scaled mountains and valleys. Although they have just eaten the carnelian fruits, they are still weak and tired. Hurry up and cook something for them!"

The foods they cooked were millets with sesame seeds, dried goat meat, and beef; all were delicious. When Liu and Ruan were finished eating, wine was laid out, and a crowd of girls approached. Each of them held three or five peaches in their hands, smiling and saying to the two girls, "Congratulations on the arrival of your bridegroom!"

Music was played while they drank to their hearts' content. Liu and Ruan were filled with both happiness and apprehension. Once it was dark, each of them was ordered to sleep on one of the curtained beds, and the two girls went to sleep together with them for the night. The voices of the girls were gentle and sweet, making both men forget their worries.

Ten days later, Liu and Ruan intended to go home, and made a request to do so. The two girls said, "You've already come here, and it was your fated fortune that led you here. Why do you still want to return?" Thus they remained there for half a year. When the climate, grass, and trees all indicated that it was the spring season, hundreds of birds were chirping and singing. This made the two men harbor even more sadness, and they earnestly pleaded to return. The girls replied, "If you are still tied to sinful, worldly cravings, then what can we do?" Consequently, they summoned 30 or 40 girls, who showed up previously, to gather and play music. Then all of them escorted Liu and Ruan together, showing them the way to return home.

By the time they came out, their relatives and old friends had all passed away, the town and their residences had been changed, and there was no one left who knew them. Making inquiries, they found their seventh-generation grandsons, who had heard that their ancestors once entered the mountain and became lost, unable to return. During the eighth year of Taiyuan reign (383) of the Jin dynasty (265–436), Liu and Ruan suddenly left again, and nobody knew where they had gone.

(From Liu Yiqing, *Youming lu*)

Huang Yuan Encounters Miaoyin

During the Han dynasty, Huang Yuan, a native of Taishan Commandery (modern Tai'an County, Shandong), once opened his door in the morning. Suddenly he saw a black dog sitting outside the door, guarding his home completely like a dog that he raised. Yuan tied the dog with a leash to hunt with his neighbors.

Around sunset, he saw a deer. Then he released the dog. The dog ran very slowly. Yuan ran after it with all his strength, yet could never reach it.

After running for several *li*, they reached a cave. After entering it for more than a hundred paces, Yuan suddenly saw a smooth thoroughfare where scholar trees and willows were planted on both sides and were surrounded by fences. Following the dog, Yuan entered the door where stood several dozen houses with windows, all filled with girls who were beautiful in appearance and wore colorful garments. While some of them were playing zithers, others were playing chess.

When he arrived at the northern attic, there were three rooms with tow maids on duty, and they looked as if expecting someone. After seeing Yuan, they smiled at each other, saying, "This is Miaoyin's husband who was led by the black dog." While one of them was staying, the other entered the attic.

A moment later, four maids came out, saying, "Lady Taizhen let us inform Mr. Huang: 'There is a girl who is not yet fifteen, the age a girl has her hair pined-up, but she is fated to be your wife."

When it was dark, they led Yuan into the inner quarter. Inside, there was a hall facing south. In front of the hall there was a pool. In the pool there was a terrace. At each of the four corners of the terrace there was a one-foot deep cave. Inside the cave, curtains and mats were illuminated by light. Miaoyin was gentle and attractive. Her maids were also beautiful. After the wedding was finished, they feasted and lived together like old friends.

After several days, Yuan intended to return home temporarily to inform his family what had happened. Miaoyin said, "The ways of human beings and the spirits are different. Intrinsically it could not last long for us to stay together."

The next day, she untied her jade pendant and gave it to him as a gift and parted with him. By the steps where they parted, she was in tears. "Since there might be no chance for us to meet again, my love and adoration became even deeper. If you still miss me, when the first day of the third month comes, you may fast, take a bath, and make sacrificial offerings to me."

The four maids sent Yuan out of the door and saw him off. In half a day he arrived at his home, yet it seemed that he was in a trance. Every time the appointed time arrived, he often saw a curtained carriage seemingly flying in the air.

(From Liu Yiqing, *Youming lu*)

The Gentlemen Yuan and Liu

During the early Yuanhe period (806–820), Yuan Zhe and Liu Shi lived in Mount Heng.[8] Both of them had an uncle who served as officials west of the Zhe River.[9] Involved in the rebellion of Li Qi, who was later demoted to a commoner, their uncles were exiled to Huanzhou and Aizhou respectively.[10] The two gentlemen prepared their baggage together and set off to visit their uncles.

When they arrived at Hepu County[11] in Lianzhou, they boarded a boat, intending to cross the sea and reach Cochin. The boat was anchored on the shore of Hepu. At night, folks of the village were offering sacrifice to the gods, drumming the drums and blowing the vertical flutes loudly. The boatman and the servants of the two gentlemen went together to watch.

It was about midnight when a hurricane suddenly burst forth. It broke the cable and pushed the boat out to sea. Nobody on the boat knew where it was drifting to. Sometimes, the ship bumped against the fin of a big whale; sometimes, it hit the back of a huge turtle. The surging waves resembled a snowy mountain, and the red sun emerged like a rolling fire wheel. When the boat touched a residence of a mermaid,[12] it was like it stuck a shuttle on the loom; when the boat hit the mirage, the mirage collapsed. The boat swayed and thumped on the water numerous times and was almost ready to tip over and sink. But in the end, it reached an island. The wind had stopped.

Pulling a long face, the two gentlemen boarded the island. They saw an idol of Heaven shining brightly by the hill. Apart from a golden incense burner filled with incense ashes, there was nothing else. While the two men were roaming around, suddenly they saw a giant beast in the sea. It looked around and around – as if detecting something. Its teeth were like swords and its eyes shined like lightning. After a long while, it disappeared.

In a moment, purple clouds emerged on the surface of the sea and stretched out for hundreds of steps. Among them, there was a five-colored lotus, which was more than one hundred feet tall with all petals open. Inside the petals there were curtains, intertwined like dazzling embroidered silk. Furthermore, they saw a rainbow bridge suddenly unfold and stretch straight to the island. In a short while, a maid with a pair of buns on her head, holding a jade box and a golden burner, came from the lotus to the place of the idol of heaven. She removed the incense ashes and lit some special incense.

Seeing the maid, the two gentlemen rushed forward to kowtow and beg piteously, asking her to help them return to the mortal world. The maid did not answer. The two men begged her again for a long time. Then the maid asked, "Who are you? How come you suddenly arrived here?"

The two gentlemen told the maid the truth in detail.

The maid said, "In a little while, the Honorable Master of the Jade Void will come to this island to date the Lady of Southern Sea. If you beg him persistently, your wish will be fulfilled."

After their conversation had finished, a Daoist priest riding on the back of a white deer and driving the pink clouds descended directly onto the island.

The two men kowtowed together and begged him in tears. The Honorable Master took pity on them, saying, "You can follow this maid to meet the Lady of Southern Sea. There should be a date of returning for you. Your return will be without incident."

The Honorable Master said to the maid with the unique hairdo, "I am here for cultivation. After I finish, I will go to visit her."

The two men accepted the instruction, arrived in front of the tent of the Lady of the Southern Sea, and kowtowed to her as visitors. They saw a young girl who had not yet reached the age to have her hair pinned up. She wore colorfully patterned clothes. Her skin was like white jade, smooth as congealed fat and beautiful as blossoms. Her look was as pure as the morning dew, and her air was as solemn as the blue ocean.

The two men told her their names. The lady teased them, saying, "In the past, there was a Liu Chen who visited Mount Tiantai, now there is a Liu Shi; in the past, there was a Ruan [Zhao], now there is a Yuan Che; in the past, there were Liu and Ruan, now there are Yuan and Liu. Is not this the God of Heaven's will?" Thus, two couches were set up for them to sit on.

After a short while, the Honorable Master arrived. The Lady of the Southern Sea went forward to salute him and then went back to her seat. Several fairies started playing panpipes and flutes. By the side of them, beautiful girls were singing and dancing to the rhythm of music. The two men were beside themselves, as if visiting heaven in a dream. Everything they saw and heard was rarely found in the human world.

Thereupon, the Lady of the Southern Sea ordered to play a drinkers' forfeit game by passing wine cups. Suddenly, a black crane came down from the air, with a letter in its mouth. The letter read, "Anqi Sheng[13] knew that you are going to the Southern Sea for a date. Would you be so kind to visit me?" The Honorable Master read the letter and said to the black crane, "I'll be there soon."

The Honorable Master said to the Lady of the Southern Sea, "I have not seen Anqi Sheng for more than a thousand years. If I had not been visiting the Southern Sea, I would have no chance to visit and talk with him."

Thereupon the lady urged the maidservant to serve the food. The jade containers were glistening and clean. The lady had dinner together with him, but the two gentlemen had no food to eat.

The Honorable Master said, "Although the two gentlemen should not eat together with us, we should find some human food for them." The lady agreed. Then they offered Liu and Yuan food that tasted like it was from the human world.

After finishing the dinner, the Honorable Master took out a book written in red seal script from his bosoms and gave it to the Lady of the Southern Sea. The lady bowed and accepted it. Then the Honorable Master bid her farewell and walked out.

Looking back at the two men, he said, "Both of you have an elegant bearing. It is not difficult to go back home; but since I met you inadvertently, I should give you a divine elixir as a gift. You are destined to have a mentor, so I will not make myself your mentor."

The two gentlemen kowtowed to him, and the Honorable Master left.

In a short while, there was a warrior on the sea who was several *zhang* tall and wore gold armor. Holding a sword, he approached them and said, "The heavenly soldier who was ordered to patrol was not careful on his watch. So he will be executed according to the law. Now he has been executed." Then he retreated quickly and vanished.

The Lady said to the maid wearing a purple cloth and a phoenix crown, "You can see the guests off. But what will they ride?"

The maid said, "There is a hundred-flower bridge that can carry them."

The two men bowed in gratitude and bid farewell. The lady gifted them a jade pot, which was more than a foot tall. The lady picked up a brush and wrote a poem on the pot:

When you came, you came out of a single boat,
While leaving, you leave in the hundred-flower Bridge.
If you knock on the jade pot after returning to the mortal world,
The Mandarin duck would understand the words clearly.

In an instant, a bridge appeared on the water. It was hundreds of steps long, with strange flowers and plants on its railings. The two men sneaked in the flowers to peek, seeing thousands of dragons and snakes entangled with each other to form the pillars of the bridge. They also saw the beast previously seen on the sea, which had been cut into two and floated on the waves.

The two men asked the envoy the reason. The envoy said, "This beast was killed because it did not know that you two were on the island."

The envoy added, "I would not see you off as an envoy, but since I have important things to entrust you with, I had no choice but come." So she untied an amber box from her sash, in which something was vaguely like a spider.

She said to the two men, "We are narcissus. The narcissus belongs to *yin*, so there is no male. I once met a young man of Panyu. We loved each other very much, and as a result, we had a son. The boy was not yet three years old and should have been thrown away, but the Lady of the Southern Sea asked him to be the son of the god of the Southern Sacred Mountain. It has been a long time. Once I heard that the envoy of the Goose-back Peak of the Southern Sacred Mountain came to discuss a matter at our water palace. When he was returning, I asked him to take my son a jade ring that he had played with, but he took it as his own. I am fairly resentful. I hope that you two will take this box to the back of the Geese-back Peak, find the envoy temple, and throw the box in. Then there should be some unique changes. If you find the jade ring, give it to my son. He will naturally repay you. Never open this box, please!"

The two men took the box and said to the envoy, "The Lady's poem says: 'If you knock the jade pot after returning the mortal world, the Mandarin duck would understand the clear words.' What does it mean?"

The envoy replied, "After you go back, if there is something urgent, just knock on the jade pot. There should be a pair of Mandarin ducks to respond to you, and everything will go well."

They asked further, "The Honorable Master of the Jade Void said that we will naturally have a teacher. Who is our teacher?"

The envoy said, "He is Mr. Taiji of the Southern Sacred Mountain. You will meet him yourself."

Thus Yuan and Liu bid the envoy farewell. The bridge ended where the ship was previously anchored at Hepu County. Looking back, the bridge had already vanished.

The two gentlemen inquired and found that 12 years had passed. The relatives in Huanzhou and Aizhou had already passed away. They inquired about the road returning to Mount Heng, and because of hunger, they knocked on the pot halfway. Then a Mandarin duck responded, "If you want to eat, just go forward and you will naturally encounter it."

In a short while, there were plates with sumptuous food on the left side of the road. After they had eaten, they do not want to eat anything for a few days. So they returned home much quicker. Their children were then in their twenties. The two men's wives had been dead for three days, and the family could not stand both the sadness and joy, saying, "Some said that you died at sea. After the three years of mourning, it's been an additional nine years."

The two men were tired of the mortal world because their minds were pure and empty. Seeing the funeral of their wives, they did not feel sad.

Consequently, they went together to the Geese-back Peak, found the envoy's temple, and threw the box in. Suddenly there was a black dragon, a few feet long, stirring up the wind, spitting lightning, breaking the trees, uncovering the house, and along with a loud sound, the temple was immediately destroyed. The two gentlemen were scared and dared not look at it. Someone in the air threw a jade ring down. The two men picked up the jade ring and sent it to the Temple of the Southern Sacred Mountain.

When they returned home, a boy in yellow, taking two gold boxes, went to each of their homes, saying, "My master asked me to bring this life-reviving cream to repay the two gentlemen. If there are people who have died at home, even if for sixty years, they can still be saved with this ointment smeared on their heads." After they accepted the ointment, the envoy disappeared.

Thereupon the two gentlemen revived their wives with the ointment. After that, they roamed about together looking for Mr. Taiji. But there was no news at all, and they went back unhappily. Because of the heavy snow, the two men saw an old man carrying firewood to sell. Sympathizing with the elderly's weakness and age, they treated the old man with a drink. Seeing that there was "Taiji" on the firewood, the two men kowtowed in front of him, formally became his disciples, and told him about the jade pot.

The old man said, "This is the very pot I used to hold wine. I lost it for several sixty-year cycles. I am extremely pleased to see it again."

The two gentlemen thus followed the old man to visit Zhu Rong Peak.[14] Since then, both have become immortals, and nobody has ever seen them again.

(From Pei Xing 裴鉶 (fl. 860), *Chuanqi* 傳奇)

Notes

1 Xin'an 信安 was a commandery with its seat in modern Quzhou 衢州 in Zhejiang. The Mount Stone Room, or Mount of the Rotten Ax, is ten kilometers east of Quzhou.
2 For ancient Chinese, the three sources of light were the sun, the moon, and the stars.
3 Zhang Hua 張華 was the Minister of Works of the Jin and the author of *Bowu zhi* 博物志 (A Treatise on Curiosities). He was considered the most knowledgeable of his time.
4 Jiaozhou was where Guangdong and Guangxi are today.
5 Kun 昆 Mountain refers to the Kunlun 崑崙 Mountain. Legend has it, the goddess of Kunlun is Queen Mother of the West.
6 Yet this piece is perhaps the most frequently quoted example among all the classical tales of the supernatural in the Six Dynasties. "Mr. Liu" 劉郎, "Mr. Ruan" 阮郎, and "Liu and Ruan" 劉阮 all became allusions that appear in numerous poems, dramas, and fiction in later times.
7 Tiantai 天台, the mountain noted for its relations with Daoism and Buddhism in modern Tiantai County, Zhejiang.
8 This is the noted Southern Sacred Mountain, one of the Five Sacred Mountains in China; around ten miles north west of Hengshan 衡山 County, Hunan.
9 The Zhe 浙 River is known as the Qiantang River in Zhejiang in modern times.
10 Both Huanzhou 驩州 and Aizhou 愛州 are in Vietnam today.
11 Modern Hepu 合浦 is in Guangxi.
12 *Jiaoren* 鮫人 is a legendary Chinese mermaid whose tears could become pearls.
13 A noted legendary immortal.
14 The highest peak of the Southern Sacred Mountain.

Further Reading

Smith, Thomas E. "Records of the Ten Continents." *Taoist Resources* 2 (2): 87–119.

Part III

Buddhist Culture

Buddhism was founded, according to tradition, by Gautama Buddha, who was also called Shakyamuni (c. 566–c. 486 BCE), or the "Sage of the Shakya," because he was the prince of the Shakya Kingdom in India. Since Buddhism was introduced to China during late Eastern Han (25–220), it spread widely and became one of the noted "Three Teachings" in Chinese culture.

The basic teachings of Buddhism are the Four Noble Truths: (1) the truth of suffering: suffering is an intrinsic part of life; (2) the truth of arising: thirst or craving gives rise to suffering, (3) the truth of cessation: when cravings are removed suffering ceases; and (4) the truth of the path: the eightfold path leads to the cessation of suffering and the transition from *samsara* (cycle of rebirth) to *nirvana*.[1] The second and third noble truths have correlations in Daoism.

Buddhism also promotes moral behavior, such as non-attachment, benevolence, and understanding. Based on Buddhist teachings, every act produces fruit. A good deed bears good fruit, while an evil deed bears evil fruit; and the moral deed, or *karma*, is the only law that determines the status of one's future life or next incarnation. This is called karmic retribution. Buddhist ethics also include the five precepts: refrain from killing, stealing, sexual immorality, lying, and taking intoxicants.

The major otherness that Buddhism brought to China is beyond doubt the idea of rebirth. The focus of both Confucianism and Daoism is only on one's current life. Confucianism is in fact a series of moral codes about people's life in this world. When a disciple asked Confucius about death and afterlife, he answered, "Without having first understood life, how can one understand death? (未知生, 焉知死). The Daoist practice of longevity and immortality is but an extension of one's current life. In Buddhism, however, betterment in the next life is the pursuit of most devotees (for details about the six realms of rebirth, see the first topic in this section). This became a new hope for people who were tired of Confucian ethics and felt Daoist immortality unreachable, and probably the reason why Buddhism was widely accepted in China.

It is worth mentioning that while Buddhism was introduced into China, its influence on Chinese culture has never been one-directional. The general dynamic of "how Chinese Buddhism became Chinese Buddhism" consists of two extremes that are represented by the positions outlined in the following titles: Kenneth Chen's *The Chinese Transformation of Buddhism*[2] and Eric Zürcher's *The Buddhist*

DOI: 10.4324/9781003490821-15

Conquest of China.[3] Paradoxically, although these works oppose each other, they complement each other as well, because each book represents one side of the same coin. The general development of Chinese Buddhism is stated as follows: Buddhism was "first imported from India and central Asia around the first century CE." Later, Buddhism in China became "an evolving hybrid of Chinese and foreign elements."[4] Chinese Buddhist history can be divided into four periods: (1) "preparation" (Eastern Han and early Six Dynasties), (2) "domestication" (Northern and Southern Dynasties), (3) "independent growth" (Sui and Tang Dynasties), and (4) "appropriation" (Five Dynasties to 1900).[5] It is clear that Chinese Buddhism differs in many ways from Indian Buddhism.

While Buddhism became sinicized, under the influence of Buddhism, many indigenous Chinese beliefs and practices changed as well, including retribution (*bao* 報), the concept of the netherworld, views on a savior, and even the organization of Daoism.

Indian Buddhism has two major schools, the Mahayana (Great Vehicle) and Hinayana (Small Vehicle). The former is so called because of its promotion of universal salvation – everyone can achieve Buddhahood. This greatly influenced Chinese culture.

The most popular schools of Buddhism in China are Chan (*chan* 禪) Buddhism and Pureland (*jingtu* 净土) Buddhism. Both became a shortcut to achieve enlightenment, the former by "sudden enlightenment" and the latter by merely chanting the name of Amitabha or other bodhisattvas, rather than long meditation and self-cultivation.

The tales selected in this section are about the multiple lives of people, traveling in the levels of hell, Buddhist saviors, current-life retribution, legendary monks, and dream adventures related to Buddhist ideas.

Notes

1 The Eightfold Path includes Wisdom: Right view and Right resolve; Morality: Right speech, Right action, and Right livelihood; and Meditation: Right effort, Right mindfulness, and Right meditation.
2 Kenneth Chen, *The Chinese Transformation of Buddhism* (Princeton: Princeton University Press, 1973).
3 Erik Zürcher, *The Buddhist Conquest of China: The Spread and Adaptation of Buddhism in Early Medieval China* (Leiden: E. J. M Brill, 1959).
4 Stephen F. Teiser, Buddhism: Buddhism in China, in *Encyclopedia of Religion,* Lindsay Jones, ed., 2nd ed. (Detroit: Macmillan Reference USA, 2005), p. 1160.
5 Cf. Arthur F. Wright, *Buddhism in Chinese History* (Stanford & London: Stanford University Press, 1959).

Further Readings

Keown, Damien. *Buddhism: A Very Short Introduction.* Oxford: Oxford University Press, 2nd edition, 2013.
Zhang, Zhenjun. *Buddhism and Tales of the Supernatural in Early Medieval China: A Study of Liu Yiqing's Youming Lu.* Leiden and Boston, MA: Brill, 2014.
Zürcher, Erik. *The Buddhist Conquest of China: The Spread and Adaptation of Buddhism in Early Medieval China.* Leiden: E. J. Brill, 1959.

13 People of Multiple Lives

Of the new ideas that Buddhism brought into China, reincarnation, or rebirth, is beyond doubt the most striking one.

Traditionally, the Chinese believe that "The dead cannot be revived, while the disconnected cannot be reattached."[1] Early Daoists insisted that everyone had only one life and could not be reborn after death.[2] But rebirth is at the core of Buddhism.

Based on Buddhist teachings, all creatures are part of the cyclic movement of rebirth known as *samsara* or endless wandering until they attain *nirvana*. The "Six Realms" of rebirth include the realms of gods [who have not yet achieved enlightenment], human beings, titians [a race of demonic warlike beings at the mercy of violent impulses], ghosts [unsatisfied hunger], animals, and hell [the most undesirable place]. In the process of rebirth, one's moral deed, or karma, is the only law that determines the status of one's next life.

The four tales here provide a vivid picture of karmic retribution through transmigration: one's current life is closely related to one's previous life, and one must repay what one owed in one's previous life.

The Prince of Anxi[3]

An Shigao, the marquis, was the prince of Anxi State (Parthia). He became a monk together with the son of a great patron and studied the way [of enlightenment] in a city in Shewei.[4] Every time a host refused to help them, the son of the great patron would become angry. Shigao always admonished him.

Having roamed for 28 years, Shigao said that he should go to Guangzhou. It happened that there was a revolt. A man met Shigao and drew his knife out smoothly saying, "I have really got you now!" Gao replied with a laugh, "I owed you a debt in a previous life; thus I came from afar to repay you." Then the man killed him.

A teenager said, "This stranger, who came from a state far away, could speak our language, and did not show any sign of reluctance. Could he be a deity?" The people all laughed in astonishment.

The soul of Shigao returned and was reborn in the State of Anxi, becoming the son of the prince again with the name of Gao. At the age of 20, the Marquis of Anxi

DOI: 10.4324/9781003490821-16

discarded the lordship again so as to learn the Way [of enlightenment]. Ten and some more years later, he said to those who studied together with him, "I shall go to Guiji Commandery to repay my debt."[5]

As he passed by Mount Lu,[6] he visited his friends, and then he passed by Guangzhou. Seeing that the teenager was still alive, he went to his home directly and talked about the events in the past with him. The young man was greatly delighted and then followed him to Guiiji.

While passing by the Monastery of Mount Ji, Shigao summoned the deity of the mountain and talked with him. The shape of the god of Mount Ji was like a python, his body was several dozen feet long, and he shed tears. Shigao spoke to him; the python then left. Shigao also returned to his boat. There was a young man who got onto the boat, kneeled down, and went forward to receive an incantation; then he disappeared. Shigao said, "The young man you saw a moment ago was the deity of the temple, and he is now able to get rid of his ugly form."

It was said that the deity of the temple was the son of the great patron. Later the temple attendant noticed a bad smell and saw a dead python. From then on the temple deity disappeared.

Shigao went forward to Guiji and entered the gate of a market. It happened that there were some people fighting each other, and someone hit Shigao's head by mistake. Thus he passed away.

Consequently the guest from Guangzhou worshiped Buddha more diligently.

(Liu Yiqing, *Youming lu*)

The Son of Gu Kuang

Gu Kuang had a son who died only a few years after he was born. Gu was saddened, and his grief lingered. He wrote a poem to mourn his son, which went as follows:

> This old man is mourning his beloved son,
> Thousands of lines of bloody tears flew until sunset.
> His heart is startled by apes' broken-hearted crying,
> His form is going to vanish with birds' flying.
> This old man is now over seventy,
> His separation with his son will not be long.

Although his son was dead, his soul often lingered around his home.[7] Each time when he heard his father's weeping, he would be touched. Therefore, he pledged to himself, "If I were to become a man again, I would like to be a son in the Gu family."

One day, it seemed that he was seized and brought to a place like a county government office. There he was judged and told that he would be born to the Gu family in his next incarnation. Then he lost his consciousness.

When he suddenly came back to his senses and opened his eyes, he recognized his old home and his brothers and beloved ones all around him. It was only that he could not speak. After he was born, he forgot everything.

When he was 7 years old, however, his older brother teasingly blamed him. Suddenly, he said, "I was your older brother. Why do you blame me?" All his family was amazed.

Then he narrated the events that occurred in his previous life. Not one detail was incorrect. He even knew the nicknames of all his brothers and sisters. He was Gu Feixiong.

(Duan Chengshi 段成式 [803–863], *Youyang zazu* 酉陽襍俎)

A Certain Gentleman

A certain gentleman from west of Shanxi, a Presented Scholar[8] of the *xinchou* year (1661),[9] was able to recall the events in his previous life. Once he said that he was a scholar in his last incarnation and died at his middle age. After death, he saw the king of the netherworld judging legal cases with boiling pots, just as rumor had it in the human world. In the east corner of the palace stood a few shelves on which skins of pigs, sheep, dogs, and horses were hung. The record keeper called people's names, and some were punished to reborn as horses while some were punished to be pigs. All of them were made naked, and the skins were selected and put onto them.

A short while later, it was the gentleman's turn. He heard the king of the netherworld say, "It is appropriate that this one be a sheep."

Then a ghost picked up a piece of white sheepskin to put on his body. Then a ghost official said, "This man saved a person's life from death."

The king picked up the record and double-checked it, saying, "Release him! Although his wrongdoings are many, this goodness can redeem them."

The ghost then tried to take back the furred skin but it was stuck to his body. One of the ghosts pulled his arms, and the other pushed on his chest, tearing it apart forcefully. The pain he experienced was beyond depiction. The sheepskin was ripped into pieces – there was no way to peel it off completely. After the skin was torn off, a small part the size of his hand was still stuck on his back close to his shoulders.

After the gentleman was reborn as a man, sheep fur grew on his back; it grew again after being cut with a pair of scissors.

(Pu Songling, *Liaozhai zhiyi*, Chapter 2)

Three Lives

A Recommended Man[10] surnamed Liu had the ability to recall events from his previous life. He said that he had been an official who had many wrongdoings and died at the age of 62. When he first met the king of the netherworld, he was treated with the courtesy due a retired official, being offered a seat and a cup of tea. Stealing a glance at the cup of the king of the netherworld, he noticed that the color of his tea was clear, but inside his own cup, the tea was as muddy as cream. Puzzled and suspicious, he said to himself, "This is probably the water of oblivion?" While the king did not pay attention, he poured his tea down the corner of the table, pretending that he had finished drinking it.

A moment later, the king of the netherworld traced the record of the evil things Liu had done in his previous life. Enraged, the king ordered the ghosts to take him away and punish him by making him be a horse in his next incarnation. Right then he was taken away by ferocious demons.

When they walked to a house with a high threshold, Liu could not pass over it. While he was hesitating, the demon flogged him forcefully, causing him so much pain that he fell down. When he looked around, he found himself inside a stable. He heard someone say, "The black horse has given birth to a pony, a colt." Everything was extremely clear in his mind, but he just could not speak. He felt very hungry, and there was no other choice, so he approached the mare to seek milk.

Four or five years later, he became tall and long. But he was extremely in fear of being flogged, and upon seeing a whip he would be terrified and flee. Whenever his master rode him, his master would make sure to add a saddle on his back and gently hold the reins to let him go slowly, so it was not unpleasant; as for the servants and horsemen, they always rode him without adding a saddle but often dug their heels into his sides, causing him unbearable pain. This made him furious. He refused to eat for three days and then died.

When he arrived again at the court in the netherworld, the king found that he had not yet finished the term of punishment. Blaming him for avoiding punishment, the king of the netherworld peeled his skin off and condemned him to be a dog. He was disappointed and reluctant to go, so the demons flogged him fiercely. It was so painful that he ran into the wild fields. Thinking that it would be better to die, he angrily dashed off the cliff and was unable to stand up. Looking around, he found himself prostrated in a kennel, with a female dog licking and feeding him. Then he knew that he had returned to the mortal world again.

When he had gotten a bit older, he knew the feces was dirty, though it smelled nice to him. He was determined not to eat any. After being a dog for a year, he often felt angry and wanted to die. Part of him feared being punished for evading punishment again, and his master wanted to raise him instead of killing him. Still, he bit his master and tore a piece of flesh off his thigh. His master became angry and killed him with a stick.

Examining his case, the king of the netherworld was enraged. He had him flogged hundreds of times then assigned him to become a snake. Jailed in a dark room that could not see the sky even during the daytime, he was extremely depressed. Climbing up along the wall, he dug a hole in the roof and got out of the room. Looking at himself, he found his body prostrate in the lush grass. He then pledged not to kill creatures and swallow only fruit and seeds of plants.

After a year, he thought of committing suicide and being killed by biting someone, but he knew neither was allowed; he intended to find a good way to die but could not. One day, he lay in the grass. Hearing a cart approaching, he dashed out to block the road. The cart passed on him and cut him into two parts.

While the king of the netherworld was astonished by his quick return, he prostrated down to explain what had happened. Because he was killed innocently, the king of the netherworld pardoned him, allowing him to be a human after his term was finished. Thus he became Mr. Liu, the gentleman.

Mr. Liu was able to speak immediately after he was born. He was able to memorize articles, books, and history after browsing at them. He passed the provincial level imperial exam in the *xinyou* year. He often exhorted people, while riding a horse you must add a thick saddle; the punishment of digging heels into its sides is much more painful than flogging.

Comments: Among the beasts with fur and horns, there are nobles and officials; it is so because among the nobles and officials, there are not necessarily no beasts with fur and horns. Therefore, the humble's doing good is like planting a tree for its flowers; the noble's doing good is like adding soil to the roots of a tree that has already blossomed. Planting a tree enables flowers to grow big, while adding soil to roots of the tree enables the flowers to live longer. Otherwise, one would have to draw a heavy salt cart and be bridled like a horse, to eat feces and be slaughtered and boiled as a dog, or to bear scales and be eaten by a crane or stork as a snake.

(Pu Songling, *Liaozhai zhiyi*, Chapter 1)

Notes

1 死者不可復生, 斷者不可復屬, in Ban Gu, *Han shu* (Beijing: Zhonghua shuju, 1962), Vol. 51, p. 2369.
2 人居天地間，人人得一生，不得重生也。and 人人各一生，不得再生也 See Wang Ming王明, *Taiping jing hejiao* 太平經合校, Vol. 72 (Beijing: Zhonghua shuju, 1960), p. 298, 90. 340.
3 This tale describes the three lives of the Prince of Anxi 安息. It was the earliest literary work in China that expresses the Buddhist idea of rebirth and transmigration. It also gave rise to a new yet popular motif in Chinese literature.
   An Shigao 安世高, also known as An Qing 安清 (fl. 148–171), was a productive Buddhist sutra translator and a great master of Buddhism in the late Han period. According to the conventional viewpoint, he was a crown prince of Parthia who abandoned his rights to the throne in order to devote himself to religious life.
4 Shewei 舍衛, an old state in India.
5 Guiji Commandery covered the modern southern part of Jiangsu and western part of Zhejiang in the Han dynasty.
6 Mount Lu 廬山, a noted mountain located south of Jiujiang, Jiangxi. It is also a famous Buddhist holy site.
7 In Chinese religion, a person has two souls, the *hun* soul, which is attached to one's vital energy, and the *po* soul, which is attached to one's body. When one of the souls departs, the host will be sick; when both of the souls depart, they will die. Differing from Indian Buddhism in which no soul is mentioned in the process of rebirth, Chinese Buddhism believe one's soul will transfer to his or her next life or incarnation.

8 Presented Scholar (*jinshi* 進士) refers to a man who has successfully passed the imperial examination at the national level, generally in the capital, and will most likely become an official in the government.

9 According to the Chinese Stem-Branch 干支 Cycle of dates system, each year is named by a pair of one of the 10 Heavenly Stems 天干 and one of the 12 Earthly Branches 地支. The *xinchou* 辛丑 year is the 38th year of the 60-year cycle of dates (e.g., 1961, 2021 etc.).

10 Juren 舉人, "Recommended Man," is someone who passed the imperial examination at the provincial level.

14 Travelers in Hells

The "Netherworld Adventure" was a popular motif in early medieval Chinese narratives. It likely originated from the curiosity of people about the afterlife, but the evolution of the depictions of the netherworld in the stories featuring this motif reflected the changing Chinese notions of netherworld in this period under the influence of Buddhism. From these stories we can see the Buddhist conquest of China in literature, as well as the critical conflict between Buddhism and Confucianism.

The most striking difference between Chinese indigenous concepts of a netherworld and the Buddhist hell is that the latter is a place for the dead to be judged through court trials.[1] "Zhao Tai Travels in Hell" presented here is among the earliest examples of netherworld court trials in Chinese literature: there everyone receives a court trial after death and, according to what they did when they were alive, receives different treatments.

Another striking feature of the Buddhist hell that differentiates it from indigenous Chinese concepts of a netherworld is that it involves physical torture. The earliest literary depictions of the multitude of physical tortures in Buddhist sutras are seen in "The Shaman Shu Li."

New images of the afterlife were also created in the tales. In "Zhao Tai Travels in Hell," for example, a passage describes the "city of receiving transformation" (*shou bianxing cheng*) where punishments are mainly based on the Five Precepts, showing a distinct Buddhist origin.[2]

In a remark on this tale, Qian Zhongshu points out that the Buddhist sutra, *Daban niepanjing*, "enumerates a few examples of 'people receiving animal bodies after coming out of hell'. Fiction and scripts of plays in our country have inherited these themes and are finely woven with details."[3] Through reading these stories, we can see how accurate Qian's observation is.

Shaman Shu Li[4]

In Baqiu County there was a shaman called Shu Li.[5] He died of an illness in the first year of the Yongchang reign (322–323) of the Jin. The local Earth God escorted him to Mount Tai.

The laymen usually addressed a shaman as Daoist. When they first passed by the "Houses of Good Fortune" in the netherworld,[6] the local Earth God asked the

DOI: 10.4324/9781003490821-17

official, "What kind of place is this?" The official replied, "The Houses of Daoists." The local Earth God said, "This man is a Daoist." Then he handed him over.

Li entered the gate. He saw hundreds and thousands of tiled-houses, all hung with bamboo curtains and naturally fitted with beds and couches. Men and women stayed separately. Some were chanting sutras, some were singing hymns, and some were eating leisurely. All of them were happy beyond expression.

Shu Li's document and name reached the gate of Mount Tai, yet he himself did not. The local Earth God was investigated and questioned.

The god said, "On the way here we saw several thousand tiled houses. I asked the official, who said that they were for Daoists, and thus I handed Li over."

Thereupon a spirit was sent to bring him again.

At that time Shu Li had not yet finished looking over all the places, when he saw a man with eight hands and four eyes. With gold pestles in hands the man ran toward Shu, intending to crash into him. Terrified, Shu ran back out of the gate. The spirit was already waiting for him by the gate, and he caught Shu and brought him to Mount Tai.

The governor of Mount Tai asked Shu, "When you were in the world of human beings, what did you do?"

Shu replied, "I served thirty-six thousand spirits, exorcised evil demons for people, and presided over temple sacrifices. Sometimes I slaughtered cows, calves, pigs, sheep, chickens, and ducks."

The governor said, "You flattered spirits by killing living creatures, so you are guilty of a crime for which you deserve to be put on a hot grill."[7]

The governor had an official lead Shu to the place featured hot grill. There he saw a creature with an ox head and a human body. The creature held an iron fork, pierced Shu with it, and placed him onto the iron grill. After tossing and turning on the grill, his body was scorched and mashed; he pleaded in vain for death. Being tortured for two days and one night, he experienced the most intolerable sufferings.

The governor asked the supervisor [of record keeping], "Should Shu Li's life be ended? Or did someone deprive him of the rest of his years?"

After checking the record, it turned out that eight years still remained in his lifespan. The governor said, "Bring him over here." The man with the ox head skewered Shu again with the iron fork and placed him by the side of the grill.

The governor said, "Now I will send you back to live out the rest of the years in your lifespan. Never again kill creatures and engage in licentious sacrifices!"

All of a sudden, Shu Li was revived, and subsequently he did not work as a shaman anymore.

(Liu Yiqing, *Youming lu*)

Shi Changhe

Shi Changhe died, yet four days later he revived, saying that when he first died he walked toward the southeast. He saw two people fixing the road ahead, who always kept 50 steps away from him; when Changhe walked faster, they walked faster as well so that the distance between them remained the same. On both sides of the road were shrubs with thorns, all of which were like falcon talons. He saw a crowd of people, old and young, walking in the thorn bushes, as if they were being pursued. Their bodies were wounded by the thorns, and congealed blood was seen on the ground.

Seeing that Changhe walked alone on the smooth road, the people in the thorn bushes sighed, saying, "Only the disciples of Buddha are happy – they can walk on the main road."

Walking forward, Changhe saw 70 or 80 tiled houses; among which there were more than ten attics with windows. A man with a face three feet square wide, wearing a long-sleeved black gown, was sitting by the window. Only the upper part of his gown could be seen.

Changhe then bowed to the man. The man said to him, "Worthy Shi, you have come? It has been more than twenty years since we parted."

Changhe replied, "Yes." Then, in his mind, it seemed that he recalled the moment of parting.

Meng Cheng, governor of Pingyi Commandery,[8] and his wife had died previously. The man in the attic asked, "The worthy man, did you know Cheng?"

Changhe replied, "I knew him."

The man in the attic said, "When he was alive, Meng Cheng did not make a great effort [in religious pursuits], now he is constantly doing the cleaning for me. His wife made a great effort, now she lives leisurely without being bothered by affairs of the government authority."

He lifted his hand and pointed to a house to the southwest, saying, "Now Meng Cheng's wife lives there."

Right then Meng Cheng's wife opened the window and saw Changhe. She asked, "Worthy Shi, when did you come?" Then she asked about each of his sons and daughters by name, old or young, and if they were doing well. Finally she said, "Before returning home, please drop in. I rely on you to bring a letter to them."

In a moment, Changhe saw Cheng coming from west of the attic with a broom and a manure basket in one hand and a walking stick in the other. He also asked about his family. The man in the attic said, "I heard that Yulongchao is making a great effort in his practice. Do you believe? What do you practice?"

Changhe replied, "I don't eat fish or meat, never drink wine, constantly practice chanting the honorable sutras, and save those who experience various illnesses and sufferings."

The man in the attic said, "It looks like what others have said about you is not false." Then he asked the Supervisor of Record Keeping,[9] "Is Worthy Shi's lifespan exhausted, or did someone absurdly deprive him of his life?"

The supervisor replied, "According to the record, there are still forty years left [in his lifespan]."

The man in the attic ordered the supervisor: "Please prepare one carriage, two horses, and two officials to escort Worthy Shi home."

Just a moment later, from the east the carriage, horses, and attendants came, and the number was exactly as dispatched. Changhe *kowtowed*, bid farewell, mounted the carriage, and started the trip home. By the side of the road he had previously passed, there were post houses, the beds, couches, and cooking and dining utensils used by the officials and commoners.

Abruptly, they arrived at his home. Walking forward, Changhe saw his parents sitting by the side of his corpse.

Seeing his corpse as big as an ox and smelling a bad odor from it, Changhe was reluctant to enter it anymore. He walked around the corpse three times and sighed. When he passed by the head of his dead body, he noticed his late elder sister pushing him from behind. He fell down onto the face of his dead body and, due to this, revived.

(from Liu Yiqing, *Youming lu*)

Zhao Tai Travels in Hells[10]

Zhao Tai, styled Wenhe, was a native of Beiqiu of Qinghe.[11] The government summoned him to take office, but he did not accept. He devoted himself to the study of books and documents and became famous in his village. At the age of 35, Zhao Tai suddenly felt a pain in his heart and died at the midnight of the thirteenth day of the seventh month in the fifth year of Taishi reign of the Jin (265–274).[12] His heart remained somewhat warm and his body flexible. After the corpse had been kept for ten days, a breath that sounded like thunder erupted from his throat. Opening his eyes, he asked for water to drink. Having finished drinking, he got up right away.

He said that when he first died, there were two men who rode yellow horses and were followed by two soldiers. They simply said, "Catch him and take him away." The two soldiers supported him under his arms from both sides and proceeded toward the east.

Not knowing how many miles had passed, he then saw a big city wall, which resembled tin and iron in color and was extremely tall. Entering from the western gate, he saw the official residence, which had a black double gate and included several dozen tile-roofed buildings. There were about 50 or 60 men and women. The major official, wearing black clothing, listed Zhao Tai's name as the thirtieth. After a moment he was taken in. The prefect sat facing westward, and double-checked his name and surname.

Then Zhao Tai was taken southward through a black gate. There was a man wearing scarlet clothing, sitting in a large room, calling out names in order, and asking the people what they had done during their lives: what crimes they had committed, what merits they had achieved, and what good deeds they had done. Each person replied differently.

The supervisor said, "Please make sure what you say is true. From the six ministries we always dispatch Emissaries of Record Keeping,[13] who reside permanently in the human world, recording the good and evil one has done, so as to verify it. There are three bad realms for the dead, and killing creatures or using them as sacrifices result in a rebirth in the worst realm.[14] Following Buddhist dharma, observing the Five Precepts and Ten Good Characteristics,[15] and distributing alms with a merciful heart, one will be reborn in the House of Good Fortune, and live peacefully without anything to do."

Zhao Tai replied, "I did neither anything good, nor anything evil."[16]

After all the trials had finished, Zhao Tai was assigned to work as the inspector of waterworks, taking more than 1,000 people to transport sand and shore up river banks. He worked assiduously day and night and wept with regret, saying, "I did not do good things, yet now I fell into this place."

Later he was transferred to the position of Supervisor of Waterworks, in charge of the affairs of various hells. He was given a horse and sent east to inspect the hells.

Further he arrived at the *Nili* hell,[17] where lived 6,000 people. There was a fire tree, 50 paces in circumference and 10,000 feet tall. All around the tree were swords, and fire was burning on the tree. Beneath it people in tens or in fives fell onto the fire swords, which pierced through their bodies. [The prison official] said, "These people cursed others, robbed others, and by doing so hurt those who are good and kind."

Tai saw his parents and a younger brother weeping in this hell and also saw two men come with documents in hand. They ordered the prison officials, saying, "There are three people, whose families serve Buddha. On their behalf,[18] their families hung streamers and canopies in the temple, burned incense, chanted the *Lotus Sutra*, and promised to redeem the sins they committed when they were alive. Let them go out to live in the Houses of Good Fortune."

Having already dressed in ordinary clothing, they headed to a gate named "Great House of Opening Light." It was a black gate of three layers,[19] each of which consisted of white walls and red pillars. Those three men then entered the gate, and they saw in the palace the precious treasures dazzling under the sun. In front of the hall stood the statues of a pair of crouching lions, shouldering a bed made of gold and jade.[20] It was called "The Seat of Lions."

They saw a great man, ten feet tall, whose face was golden-colored and whose neck radiated sunlight, sitting on the bed. Numerous Buddhist monks were standing by to wait on him. Noted Daoist priests and bodhisattvas sit all around him. The Governor of Mount Tai came to greet him.

Zhao Tai asked an officer, "Who is this great man?"

The officer said, "He is the Buddha, master of converting and saving people in heavens and this world."

Then he heard the Buddha say: "Now I want to save beings in the evil paths of existence as well as those in various hells and let all of them out of the hells to accept salvation."

It was said that at that moment nineteen thousand people were able to come out, and then the hells became empty.[21] It was seen that ten people who should go up to the heaven were summoned while the carriages and horses waited for them, and they rose into the void and left.

Further, Zhao Tai saw another city which was more than two hundred *li* squared, and its name was City of Receiving Transformation. It was said that those who had never heard of the teaching of Buddha and whose interrogation in hell was finished would receive their karmic retribution through transformation in this city.

Zhao entered this city from the northern gate and saw that there were hundreds and thousands of earthen buildings. In the middle there was a tiled house, its width was more than fifty steps. Under the house there were more than five hundred officials who faced each other and recorded people's names and the good or bad deeds they did.

The kind of transformations they would receive followed what each person did: Those who killed living creatures were said to become mayflies, which are born in the morning and die in the evening;[22] if they were to become human beings, they would die young. Those who stole and robbed were to become pigs or sheep, to be slaughtered and given to people. Those who had committed acts of sexual wantonness were to become cranes, ducks or snakes. Those who had instigated trouble between people were to become owls that make evil cries; people who hear them all curse them and wish that they would die. Those who refused to pay their debts were to become species such as donkeys, horses, oxen, fishes, or turtles. Under this big house there was a basement facing north with one door facing south. People were summoned and entered through the northern door. All those who went out of the southern door had their shapes transformed into those of animals.

He saw another city, which was one hundred square *li*. In it, there were peaceful and pleasant tiled houses. It was said that people who, while alive, did not do evil things nor good things would stay in this ghost realm, and after 1,000 years they would be able to go out and become human beings.

He saw another city, which was five thousand steps wide and was called "Center of the Earth." Those who were punished there could not bear the suffering. There were around 50 or 60,000 men and women, all naked; they helped each other in hunger and fatigue. Seeing Zhao Tai, they *kowtowed* to him and cried.

Having finished inspecting the hells, Zhao Tai returned. The supervisor asked him, "Aren't the hells like what the dharma says? You committed no sins, so you were invited to be Supervisor of Waterworks. Otherwise, you and the others in this hell would be treated in the same way."

Tai asked, "What should a person do while he was alive in order to be happy after his or her death?"

The supervisor replied, "Only the followers of Buddha who make great efforts in practice and never violate the precepts would be happy."

Tai asked further, "If the piled up sins committed by a person before he believed in Buddha are as high as a mountain, but then he begins to follow the dharma, would those sins be wiped out?"

The supervisor replied, "All of the sins would be wiped out."

The supervisor again summoned the Emissary of Record Keeping and asked, "What was the cause of Zhao Tai's death?"

The emissary opened a rattan box and examined the old records, saying, "He still has another thirty years to live. His life was absurdly taken by an evil ghost. Now he should be sent back home."

From then on, Zhao's family, old and young, determined to serve Buddha. To seek good fortune on behalf of his grandparents, his parents,[23] and his two younger brothers, Zhao Tai hung streamers and canopies, and he chanted the *Lotus Sutra* as well.

(from Liu Yiqing, *Youminglu*)

Notes

1　For the depiction of such court trials in Buddhist sutras, see Zhu Tanwulan 竺曇無蘭 (Dharmarājan), trans., *Fo shuo tiecheng nili jing* 佛說鐵城泥犁經 (*Buddha Preached Sutra on Iron City Hell*): https://www.fojingzaixian.com/86.html

2　Zhenjun Zhang, *Buddhism and Tales of the Supernatural in Early Medieval China*, pp. 126–37.

3　舉 "從地獄出、受畜牲身" 諸例，吾國稗官、院本承之而細密. See Qian Zhongshu 錢鐘書, *Guan zhui bian* 管錐編, Vol. 2 (Beijing: Zhonghua shuju, 1979), p. 795.

4　This is one of the noted "Netherworld Adventure" narratives, in which many aspects of the Chinese netherworld have changed to reflect the Buddhist assumptions. The trial and physical tortures described here, for example, are not at all indigenous. Sacrificial offering in traditional Chinese culture was also challenged.

5　Baqiu 巴丘 County, modern Xiajiang 峽江, Jiangxi.

6　*Mingsi* 冥司 (the netherworld) is added from *TPGJ*.

7　佞神殺生，其 (flattered spirits by killing living creatures, so) are added from *TPGJ* (283. 3254).

8　Pingyi 馮翊 Commandery, seat was in present-day Dali 大荔, Shanxi, during the Jin dynasty.

9　Dulu Zhuzhe 都錄主者, Supervisor of Record Keeping, sometimes called simply zhu-zhe 主者, Supervisor, is the head of the department that keeps records of people's life spans.

10　This is one of the earliest "Netherworld Adventure" narratives, which shows a heavy influence of Buddhist concepts of hells with great detail. In addition, the depiction of the "City of Transformation" is creative and could not be found anywhere else, including Buddhist sutras.

11　Beiqiu 貝邱, southeast to the modern city of Linqing 臨清, Shandong. During the Jin, it belonged to the Qinghe State at the border of modern Hebei and Shandong. See Tan Qixiang, 3: pp. 39–40.

12　The "Song Taishi" (465–471) in *TPGJ* (190. 740) is a mistake of "Jin Taishi," since it was much later, even after the death of Liu Yiqing (d. 444), the compiler of this collection. *Bianzheng lun* reads "Jin" for "Song." *Mingxiang ji* (quoted in *TPGJ* 377. 2996) also reads "Zhao Tai of the Jin."

13　For 六師督錄使者, *BZL* note reads 六部都錄使者 (Emissaries of Record Keeping from the six ministries), which is what I follow here.

14　The three bad realms for the dead are ghosts, animals, and hell. Hell is considered the worst.

15　"Five Precepts" refer to the first five of the "Ten Commandments," that are against killing, stealing, adultery, lying, and intoxicating liquors. The observance of these five ensures rebirth in the human realm. "Ten Good Characteristics" is defined as the non-committal of the ten evils – killing, stealing, adultery, lying, double-tongue, coarse language, filthy language, covetousness, anger, perverted views.

16　For 上不犯惡, *BZL* reads 亦不犯惡.

17　*Nili* is the Sanskrit pronunciation of hell. It has been translated as hell as well as Taishan 泰山, Mount Tai.

18　According to *Mingxiang ji* and the note in *Bianzheng lun,* "weiyou" 為有 here should be "weiqi" 為其, "for them" or "on their behalf."

19　*Hei* 黑 (black) here is added from *BZL*.

20 *Xiang* 象 (resembling) is replaced by *fu* 負 (shouldering) according to the hand copy version.
21 *Jishi* 即時 is replaced by *jihong* 即空 (then became empty) according to the Ming dynasty hand copy version.
22 For *shazhe* 殺者 (killers), *BZL* reads *shashengzhe* 殺生者 (those who killed living creatures).
23 *Fumu* 父母 (parents) is added according to *BZL*.

Further Readings

Campany, Robert Ford. "Return-from-Death Narratives in Early Medieval China." *Journal of Chinese Religions* 18 (Fall 1900): 91–125.
Matsunaga, Daigan and Alica Matsunaga. *The Buddhist Concept of Hell*. New York, NY: Philosophical Library, 1972.
Zhang, Zhenjun. "From Mount Tai to Buddhist Hell: Changing Concepts of Netherworld." In *Buddhism and Tales of the Supernatural in Early Medieval China*. Leiden and Boston, MA: Brill, pp. 106–37.

15 Buddhist Saviors

In traditional Chinese culture, heaven has been described as an omnipotent high god who supervises and dominates the world of creatures. It responds to the affairs of human beings by sending down calamities, bestowing good fortunes, as well as acting as savior.

Along with the transmission and spread of Buddhism in China, new saviors appeared. Central to popular Mahayana doctrine was the idea that salvation could be obtained through worship and invocation of the name of the Buddha(s) or bodhisattvas – those who achieved enlightenment but choose to remain in the human world to save others. As a tale in the *Signs from the Unseen Realm* (Mingxiang ji) suggests: "Since the Jin, Song, Liang, Chen, Qin, and State of Zhao, Avalokiteśvara, Ksitigarbha, Maitreya, and Amitābha have had their names chanted, and people who have been saved in that way are numerous."[1]

Avalokiteśvara, Guanshiyin or Guanyin in Chinese, is a minor figure in some major Mahayana scriptures such as *Vimalakirti Sūtra* and *the Langer Sūtra*. He becomes prominent in the *Avataṃsaka-sūtra* (*Huayan jing: the Flower Adornment Sutra*) and the *Saddharma-puṇḍarīka-sūtra* (*Fahua jing*: Lotus Sūtra). In the *Lotus Sūtra* and *Amitāyurdhyāna Sūtra* (*Guan wuliangshou jing: The Sūtra of Visualization on Amitayus Buddha*), he assumes the role of a savior,[2] and gradually became the dominant savior.

It is noteworthy that the Guanshiyin in the stories of early medieval China is a man (generally a monk), but in order to adapt to Chinese culture (precisely, kind mother [*cimu*]), this image was later transformed into a goddess in a white gown – the most popular image of Guanyin to appear in later Chinese Buddhist scriptures and popular culture.[3]

The saviors in the miraculous tales here include the Buddha and the Avalokiteśvara.

Raksasa

During the Song reign there was a state that was close to *raksasa*.[4] The *raksasa* entered its territory several times, eating countless people.

The king of the state made an agreement with the *raksasa*, which said, "From today each of the families in this state will have a special day of duty. On that day,

DOI: 10.4324/9781003490821-18

the family on duty should send a boy to you. Please do not kill people randomly anymore."

A family of Buddha devotees had an only son at the age of 10, who was the next boy should be sent to the *raksasa*. At the time of his departure, his parents wailed bitterly, and then chanted the name of Buddha wholeheartedly. Because Buddha's power was great, the *raksasas* could not get close to the boy.

The next morning, the parents found that their son was still alive and they returned together happily.

From then on, the calamity of the *raksasa* ceased completely. Lives of people in the state had indeed relied on this family.

(Liu Yiqing, *Youming lu*)

The Monk Daojiong

In the eighteenth year of the Hongshi reign period (399–416), the monk Daojiong 道冏 from Later Qin was sent by his master Daoyi to Mount Huo in Henan to gather stalactites.[5] Daolang and three other men went together with him. They entered a cave with a torch in hand and went three *li* when they encountered a deep stream which could be crossed only a board that was laid over it. Daojiong passed first, but then all the younger ones fell off and drowned. In addition, the torch went out, so it was extremely dark.

Losing all hope, Daojiong cried loudly. But still he set his mind on calling *Guanyin* (Avalokiteśvara) and pledged that if he could find the way going out, he would gather a hundred of people in gratitude to the powerful god.

When the night passed, he saw a light glimmering like a firefly. Suddenly everywhere in the cave became bright. In this way, he was able to make his way out of the cave.

Because of this, his belief in Buddhism became even deeper, and he saw the miracles repeatedly. In the twentieth year of Yuanjia reign of Song (443), the Prince of Linchuan and Kang[6] garrisoned in Guangling. He invited Daojiong to live with him. In the ninth month of that year, he held a ten-day fast on behalf of Avalokiteśvara.

(From Shi Daoshi 释道世, *Fayuan zhulin*法苑珠林, Chapter 76)

Dou Fu

Dou Fu was a native of Henei. During the Yonghe reign period (346–356) of Eastern Jin, the governor of Bingzhou, Gao Chang, and the governor of Juzhou, Lü Hu, each controlled his own troops. The two did not get along well. Dou Fu was an official under Gao Chang. Lü Hu sent troops to attack and seized him. He was imprisoned together with six or seven of his companions. They were all fettered tightly and were to be executed soon.

The monk Zhi Daoshan was at the time in the camp of Lü Hu. He happened to be acquainted with Dou Fu. Hearing that Dou Fu was imprisoned, he went to see him and talked with him outside of the door. Fu told Daoshan, "I'm now in dire straits and will lose my life any day now. How can you save me?"

The monk replied, "There is nothing humanly possible I can do to save you. But the Bodhisattva Avalokiteśvara saves people from calamities. If you sincerely pray, something will happen."

Dou Fu had heard of Avalokiteśvara. On hearing these words, he concentrated on him and took refuge in him for three days.[7] Looking at his fetter, it seemed looser than usual. When he tried to push and shake it, he found it was broken and dropped off.[8]

So he sincerely said, "Now, because of your pity and protection, my fetters fell off of their own accord. But I still have several companions with me. There is no way I can leave them here. Your divine power will save everyone, so please let all of us be free of our fetters."

After he finished speaking, he pulled the arms of his companions; the fetters all broke and dropped off one by one, as if being cut by someone.

Thereupon they rushed out the door and walked among the patrols. But nobody noticed them. Then they climbed over the city wall and fled. The sky was just growing light. After walking four to five *li*, it was daybreak. They dared not go forward. So they hid in the shrubs.

A while later, Lü Hu's army found that the prisoners had disappeared. They came out searching in all directions, burning grass and trees. They searched everywhere. But nobody reached the place about one acre squared, where Dou Fu and his companions were hidden. Thus they were able to escape.

After returning home, Dou Fu worshipped and sincerely believed in Avalokiteśvara. All of his companions became devoted to Buddhism.

Later, Daoshan crossed the river and told Xie Qingxu the story in detail.

(Fu Liang 傅亮, Guang Shiyin yingyan ji 光世音應驗記)

Sir Tang

Sir Tang, named Pin, was a Presented Scholar of the *xinchou* year. Having been bed-ridden for some time, his end was drawing near. Suddenly, he felt a thread of hot air inside the lower part of his body gradually rise upward. When it reached his thighs, his feet lost sensation; when it reached his stomach, his legs lost sensation; when it reached his heart – the most difficult part to lose sensation – all the trivial things that had happened when he was a child and had already been forgotten came back along with blood to his heart one by one like a rising tide. If it was a good deed, he felt tranquil and at ease; if it was an evil deed, he felt annoyed and upset, resembling being boiled in boiling oil – the intolerable suffering was beyond depiction.

He recalled that when he was seven or eight years old, he took out a young sparrow from its nest and killed it. This single incident caused hot blood to rush through his heart like a tide. The feeling did not pass until a long while, perhaps the time it takes to finish a meal.

It was not until all events in his life were reviewed one by one that he felt the heat rush through his throat, enter his brain, and gush out from the top of his head, rising up like cooking smoke to the sky. After almost half a day, his soul escaped his body.

After discarding his dead human shell, Sir Tang became homeless and drifted over the road on the outskirts of town. Suddenly there came a giant, a few dozen feet tall, who picked Tang up and put him into its sleeve.

After going in the sleeve, Tang found a crowd of people with their limbs folded and compressed, which made them stuffy and upset – almost intolerable. Suddenly it occurred to him that the Buddha could alleviate his distress, so he chanted the name of Buddha. After chanting only three or four times, he floated out of the sleeve. The giant then put him into his sleeve again. After he dropped out of its sleeve three times, the giant gave up and left.

Standing there, Sir Tang hesitated, not knowing where to go. He recalled that the Buddha was in the West, so he walked to the West. In a moment, he saw a monk sitting cross-legged on the side of the road. He approached him, bowed, and then asked him for directions.

The monk said, "The records about the life and death of all scholars are kept by the Lord Wenchang and the sage Confucius. You must go to those two places to remove your name so that you can go elsewhere." Sir Tang asked the location of their residences, so the monk showed him the road. He ran in that direction.

After a short while, he arrived at the Confucian Temple and saw Confucius sitting there, facing the south as an emperor does. Sir Tang bowed and prayed as he did before. Confucius said, "To remove your name, you still have to go to the Lord and Emperor [Wenchang]." He then guided him in the right direction.

Sir Tang hurried off again. Seeing a palace like the one where a king lives, he lowered his head and entered. As expected, there was a holy man resembling the legendary lord and emperor. Sir Tang knelt and prayed.

The emperor checked his name and said, "You have a sincere and upright heart, so you can live longer. But your flesh and bones have rotted, and nobody but the Bodhisattva Guanyin can make you revive." So he urged him to hurry off to find the Bodhisattva.

Following the instructions, Sir Tang suddenly saw a lush forest, some tall and slender bamboo, and a magnificent temple. Walking into the main hall, he saw the Bodhisattva sitting with a tall and dignified spiral-shaped coil on her head and golden light on her moon-like round face. The slender drooping willow branches were soaked in the jade vase, resembling green smoke.

Sir Tang respectfully kowtowed and retold what Lord Wenchang had said. Hearing that, the Bodhisattva felt it would be hard to deal with. Sir Tang pleaded sincerely and repeatedly. A monk next to the Bodhisattva suggested, "If the Bodhisattva applies great magical power, she can take up the soil with her fingers to make it flesh and break off the willow branch to make it bone."

The Bodhisattva approved the request. She broke a willow branch, poured a little water from the vase, and mixed it with earth to make the mud and attached the mud to Tang's body. Then she sent a boy to bring Tang back to his home and pushed him into the rotted body. Then there was a buzz and some movement in Tang's coffin, and he was suddenly healed.

The family gathered in surprise and helped Tang out. After calculating the time, they found that Sir Tang had been dead for seven days.

(Pu Songling, *Liaozhai zhiyi*, Chapter 3)

Notes

1 自晉、宋、梁、陳、秦、趙國, 觀音、地藏、彌勒、彌陀, 稱名念誦, 得救者不可勝紀. See "Sun Jingde" 孫景德, in Li Fang, *Taiping guangji* (Beijing: Zhonghua shuju, 1961), Vol. 111. p. 765.
2 See Chün-Fang Yü, *Kuan-yin: The Chinese Transformation of Avalokiteśvara* (New York: Columbia University Press, 2001), pp. 93–150.
3 For a detailed description of this interesting transformation, see Chün-Fang Yü, *Kuan-yin: The Chinese Transformation of Avalokiteśvara (New York: Columbia University Press, 2000)*, pp. 293–499.
4 *Raksasas* is one of the most noted Buddhist demons, which was transmitted into China along with Buddhist teachings. See Huilin's 慧琳 (fl. 5 century) *Yiqiejing yinyi* 一切經音義 (Pronunciation and Meaning of All the scriptures) says, "*Raksasas* are evil demons. They eat the flesh of people. Some of them fly in the air while some walk on the ground. Both types are nimble, quick, and terrible." "*Raksasa* is the name of violent and evil demons, which are extremely ugly as males and extremely beautiful as females. But both of them eat people. In addition, there is a state of female *raksasas* that is located on an island in the ocean" (Cf. *Taishō Tripitaka*, 54: p. 464).
5 Mount Huo 霍山 is in Linfen City, Shanxi province.
6 Liu Yiqing (403–444) was the compiler of *Shishuo xinyu* 世説新語 and *Youming lu* 幽明錄.
7 Guanyin 觀音 in the Six Dynasties period was still a monk instead of a goddess – the most popular image of Guanyin to appear in later Chinese Buddhist scriptures and popular culture.
8 One of Guanyin's powers in the *Lotus Sutra* is to break chains.

Further Readings

Yü, Chün-Fang. *Kuan-Yin: The Chinese Transformation of Avalokiteśvara*. New York, NY: Columbia University Press, 2001.
Zhang, Zhenjun. "From Heaven to Buddha: Changing Concepts of Savior." In *Buddhism and Tales of the Supernatural in Early Medieval China*. Leiden and Boston, MA: Brill, pp. 166–72.

16 Receivers of Current-Life Retribution

Retribution is an important notion in both Buddhist and Chinese culture. The concept of retribution, or *bao* 報, is found in the *Laozi* and *The Classic of Odes* (*Shi jing* 詩經) as a moral concept, ethical retribution. It can be traced back to the Shang (c. 1554–1045 BCE) and the Western Zhou (c. 1045–771 BCE) as a religious concept of heavenly retribution. However, they are fairly different. Based on Karmic retribution in Buddhism, the retribution one receives in his or her next incarnation depends solely on his or her own moral deeds (karma) in the current life, namely, the status one receives in the next life depends completely on what one does in this life.

In Chinese ethical retribution, the retribution one receives depends solely on how one treats others. That is to say, one is responsible for the reward or revenge one receives from other people. In Chinese heavenly retribution, the retribution one receives is also related to what one did, but a third party, heaven, is involved in it; namely, heaven judges what one did and then sends down award or punishment to that person.

In addition, stories of demonic retribution appeared as early as the *Zuo zhuan*. These stories come from an ancient belief that when ordinary men or women die violent deaths, their souls and spirits are able to become avenging ghosts and take revenge on their murderers, rectifying the wrongs done to them. Obviously, these avenging ghosts, like heaven, are incarnations of "justice." In the case of heavenly retribution, heaven acts as an external force to supervise and interact with human behaviors, while in demonic retribution, the ghost is no longer an external force, but acts on behalf of its host, the once-living person from whom it came. A demonic retribution is a divine retribution into which components of ethical retribution have been incorporated. In other words, a demonic retribution is a combination of heavenly retribution and ethical retribution.

As this kind of story continuously spread in orthodox historical writings, demonic retribution became a popular theme in the *zhiguai* (records of strange happenings). While an agent or repayer (heaven, ghost, or man) often appears in indigenous Chinese retribution stories, such a figure cannot be found in Buddhist stories of karmic retribution. Besides, in Indian Buddhism, karmic retribution occurs when one's next life begins. But in Chinese Buddhism retribution is divided

DOI: 10.4324/9781003490821-19

into three categories: retribution in this life (*xianshi bao*), retribution in the next life, and retribution in later lives.[1]

The theme of traditional Chinese retribution in the stories here is blurred because a demonic figure is not directly evident, showing a tendency of intermingling with the Buddhist notion of retribution, "retribution in current life."

An Old Fisherman

During the Yuanxi reign (304–308) of the Jin, there was an old man who lived in the Guiyang Commandery and had always taken fishing as an occupation.[2] Once he went out fishing in the early morning; he encountered a huge fish eating the bait. He pulled the fishing line so quickly that both the man and the boat suddenly fell into the water. His family looked for his corpse at the fishing site and saw that both the old man and the fish were dead and entangled in the fishing line. On the belly of the fish there were some red words, which read,

> I heard that Zeng Pool is a delightful place,
> therefore I came here from Yan Pool.
> I killed this old man,
> who bullied me with a fishing pole several times.
> He liked to eat red carp,
> and today he got what he deserves.
> (Liu Yiqing, *Youming lu*)

Mao Bao

In the middle of the Xiankang reign period of the Jin (335–342), Mao Bao, the Governor of Yuzhou,[3] was defending Zhucheng.[4] A soldier in the army bought a white turtle in the market of Wuchang. It was four to five inches long. He placed it in a jar and fed it. The turtle grew bigger and bigger before he released it in the Yangzi River.

Later [the troops in] Zhucheng were defeated by Shi [Le], and all the people who ran into the river drowned. The person who had nurtured the turtle entered the water with his armor on, and felt as if he had fallen onto a stone. In a moment he saw that it was the white turtle that he previously released.

After he was able to land on the opposite bank, he looked back, but the turtle had left.

(Liu Yiqing, *Youming lu*)

The Sons of Mr. Zhou

Mr. Zhou of the state of Pei had three sons. All of them were dumb – not able to speak at all. One day, a man came to his house to beg for drinking water. Hearing his sons' voices, the guest asked him why. Mr. Zhou told him all about the malady of his sons.

The guest said, "You are sinful. You should go inside to think about it."

Feeling that his words were strange, Zhou knew he was not an ordinary man. After a long while, he replied, "I cannot recall any wrongdoings that I have done."

"Please think about the events when you were young," the guest said.

Zhou entered his house. After the time it takes to eat a meal, he came out, saying, "I recalled that when I was a child, there was a swallow nest above a [gate] frame in which there were three fledglings. After returning to feed them, their mother would leave to find food for them. Since I could reach the nest if I reached up high, I put my fingers into the nest and the young birds held them in their beaks. Then, I picked up three caltrops and put one in the beak of each fledgling. Then they all died. When their mother returned, she could not find her young, so she flew away crying sadly. Since then, I have constantly felt regret and condemned myself."

Suddenly, the guest transformed into a Buddhist monk, saying, "Since you felt regret of your own accord, your sin is now removed!"

Right then Zhou heard his sons speak perfectly. The monk though had already disappeared.

(Liu Yiqing, *Xuanyan ji* 宣驗記)

Wang Yao

During the Huichang reign period (841–846) of the Tang dynasty, there lived Wang Yao who claimed that his ancestors were natives of Qingzhou.[5] One ancestor served under the military commissioner of Pinglu;[6] he was surnamed Li but his name was forgotten. Once this military commissioner had a deep-rooted ulcer on his back, which no doctors could cure. With sacrifice and paper money, Wang's ancestor prayed at the shrine of Mount Tai. The deity manifested himself, talked, and stayed with him.

Wang's ancestor kowtowed to him and shed tears with blood, pleading with the deity to take pity on his master. The deity of Mount Tai said, "Your commander is in the position of a regional earl, whose duty was to support commoners. But he maltreated living creatures, did numerous things out of the right way, and applied excessive tortures and punishments, causing the wronged souls to launch lawsuits against him in the court of the netherworld. The back ulcer is the mark of flogging, which is not curable. Whatever the heavenly law may reach is unforgiveable." So Wang's ancestor kowtowed and begged to see his master just once.

When he returned to Qingzhou, his master had already died. So Wang's ancestor told his master's wife what he saw and heard at Mount Tai.

His master's wife asked, "How can you verify it?"

Wang's ancestor said, "My master is still in the netherworld. I also worried that you would not believe me when I come back, so I requested to see my master. I briefly saw him in jail; he had been fettered for quite a while. He tore off part of the sleeve from his clothes, about an inch in diameter, gave it to me and said, 'After you return home, please give this to my family.' Here is that piece of sleeve."

When his wife got the patch of sleeve, she checked the cloth with what her husband wore when he died and found part of it was torn off. The blood of the ulcer was still there. Thus she knew the words of Wang's ancestor were not false.

(From *Ermu ji* 耳目記, quoted in Li Fang, *Taiping guangji*, Chapter 126)

Notes

1 See Huiyuan, Sanbao lun 三報論 [On the Three Types of Retribution], in *Zhongguo Fojiao sixiangshi ziliao xuanbian* 中國佛教思想史資料彙編 [Collected Materials on the History of Chinese Buddhist Thought] (Beijing: Zhonghua shuju, 1981), pp. 87–89.
2 Guiyang 桂陽 Commandery, the region centered in the modern city of Chenzhou 郴州, Hunan.
3 Mao Bao's 毛寶 biography is found in *Jin shu*, 81. 2122. Being defeated by Shi Jilong 石季龍 (r. 335–349) of the Later Zhao (328–351), Mao Bao fell into the river and drowned.
4 Zhucheng 邾城 was located 20 *li* northwest of modern Huanggang 黃崗, Hubei.
5 In the Tang dynasty Qingzhou 青州 covered seven counties, including Yidu 益都 (modern Qingzhou City in Shandong).
6 The Pinglu 平盧 District was established in the seventh year of Kaiyuan period (719); its seat was Yingzhou 營州 (modern Chaoyang City in Liaoning).

Further Readings

Kao, Karl S. Y. "Bao and Baoying: Narrative Causality and External Motivations." *Chinese Literature Essays Articles Reviews* 11 (1989): 115–38.
Zhang, Zhenjun. "From Demonic to Karmic Retribution: Changing Concepts of Bao in Early Medieval China as Seen in the Youming Lu." *Acta Orientalia* 66 (3) (2013): 267–87. (*Buddhism and Tales of the Supernatural in Early Medieval China*, pp. 82–106).

17　Legendary Monks and Nuns

Lu Xun remarks in his *A Brief History of Chinese Fiction* that "from the time of the Wei and Jin dynasties onward, more and more Buddhist scriptures were translated until Indian stories spread throughout China. Since scholars enjoyed these strange tales they adopted them consciously or unconsciously, until these stories became Chinese."[1]

Of the strange tales from India, the prominent ones are stories about Buddhist monks with unique and marvelous magic abilities. The following tales demonstrate the magic arts and characteristics of Buddhist monks that are different from those of Daoist masters.

A Foreign Monk

In the twelfth year of the Taiyuan reign period (387), there came a Buddhist monk from abroad who was able to swallow knives and spit fire, pearls, jade, gold, and silver from his mouth. He said that the master from whom he learned his techniques was a Brahman, not a Buddhist.

One day as he was traveling he met a man carrying goods on a shoulder-pole. Among the load there was a cage just large enough for a peck or so of grain. The monk said to the bearer, "I'm truly tired of walking, could you carry me?"

Marveling at his request, the bearer thought that he must be crazy. He then responded, "As you wish. But where do you want to sit?"

The monk replied, "If you agree, I will just go in your cage."

Marveling at him even more, the carrier said, "If you can truly enter the cage, you'll be a divine man!"

He then put his load down, and the monk entered the cage. Yet the cage did not grow larger nor the monk smaller. Furthermore, the bearer didn't find his load any heavier.

After walking several dozen *li*, the bearer stopped to eat under a tree and invited the monk to eat together.

The monk said, "I have food for myself." He was reluctant to get out of the cage.

Staying inside the cage, the monk displayed utensils for eating and drinking as well as a splendid feast. Then he asked the carrier to join him.

DOI: 10.4324/9781003490821-20

In the middle of their dining, the monk said, "I want to eat with my wife." Thus he took from his mouth a woman around 20 years old, and both her appearance and her clothes were beautiful; then they had their meal together.

When she was about to finish her meal, her husband went to sleep. The woman said to the bearer, "I have a lover who wants to eat with me. Don't tell my husband when he wakes." So the woman spat out a young man, and they ate together. So now there were three people in the cage, yet the matter of being spacious or narrow remained the same.

In a little while, her husband turned around as if about to wake, thus the woman put her lover in her mouth. When her husband woke, he said to the bearer, "We should go." Right then he put the woman back into his mouth first and then put the food and vessels back as well.

When they arrived at a city, there was a rich man who had accumulated a large fortune but was stingy by nature and had never done anything kind to others. The monk told the carrier, "I'll try to let the miser take out money from his stingy pocket." Then they went to the rich man's home.

The rich man had a nice steed that he cherished very much. It was always tied to a pillar in his courtyard. Suddenly, the steed disappeared and was nowhere to be found.

The next day, the steed was found in an earthenware jar, which was big enough for only half a bushel of grain. Since there was no way to break the jar, nobody knew how to take the steed out.

At this point, the monk went to the rich man's home and told him, "If you cook meals for one hundred people and thereby to help out the poor around you, your horse will be able to come out of the jar."

The owner of the steed hurriedly cooked the food. After everything was done, the horse returned to its original place.

The next morning, while staying in the main hall, the rich man's parents suddenly disappeared. The whole family was terrified, but they didn't know where to find them. After opening a lady's dressing case, they found the aged couple in a rouge bottle. Nobody knew how to take them out.

When they went to the monk to seek help, he said, "You should cook food enough for one thousand people and give it to the poor, then your parents will be able to come out."

After the rich man had the meal made, his parents returned and sat on their bed.

(From Mr. Xun 荀, *Linggui zhi* 靈鬼志)

Fotu Cheng

Fotu Cheng 佛圖澄 (232–348) was a native of the Western Regions.[2] His original surname was Bo. When he was young, he became a monk. He purified his mind, devoted himself to learning, and could chant several million words of sutras. He was especially good at explaining the meaning of texts. Although he did not read the Confucian classics and history, while debating on unsettled ideas with a variety of scholars, what he said was as if in accord with the classics and history so that nobody could best him. He said to himself, "I'll go back to Jibin [in the West] to learn from famous masters." But people in the West all said that he had attained the Dao.

In the fourth year of Yongjia reign (311) of Emperor Huai of Jin 晉, he came to Luoyang, intending to carry forward the grand dharma. He was good at chanting incantations and able to enslave demons. When he mixed sesame oil and rouge on his palm, events that occurred 1,000 miles away could be seen clearly within his palm, as if they were occurring in front of him. He could also allow those who practiced abstinence to see them. In addition, he could foretell events by listening to the sound of bells. None of his predictions failed.

Fotu Cheng intended to build a monastery at Luoyang, but the capital was in an uproar because Liu Yao had rebelled and attacked Luoyang. With his plan thwarted, he hid in the countryside to wait for a change. At that time, Shi Le (274–333) was garrisoned by the Ge Lake and tried to establish his power by indiscriminate kill-ing, including many Buddhist monks.[3] Taking pity on the common people, Fotu Cheng intended to change Shi Le with the Dao. He went to the gate of the garrison. The grand general of Shi Le, Guo Heilue 郭黑略, had worshiped the Dharma all along, so Fotu Cheng lodged at his home. Heilue treated him with courtesy as a Buddhist disciple who officially accepted the five precepts. From then on, when Heilue followed Shi Le to fight, he could always predict the result of the battle.

Suspicious, Shi Le asked him, "I haven't found your wisdom outstanding, but you always know if a battle is going to go well or not. Why?"

Heilue replied, "Your divinity and might are endowed by Heaven and even the spirits are helping you. Now there is a Buddhist monk with exceptional techniques and wisdom who said you are likely to govern China. I have already accepted him as my mentor. What I said previously are all his words."

Shi Le was pleased and said, "It is Heaven who sent me this man."

So he summoned Fotu Cheng and asked him, "How can the way of Buddha be made effective?"

Knowing that Shi Le didn't know the subtle reasoning and so magic arts would work as verification, Fotu Cheng thus said, "Although the Dharma is distant and intangible, it can also be verified by things close to us." Then he poured water inside an earthenware bowl, burned incense, and chanted magic spells. In a moment, a green lotus grew out in the bowl; its color was dazzling. That convinced Shi Le.

Thereupon, Foyu Cheng began to remonstrate with him, "It is the case that when the moral transformation of a ruler fills everywhere within the four seas, the Four Auspicious Beings will appear to manifest auspiciousness; when governing fails and the Way vanishes, shooting stars will be seen in the sky. The appearance of constant astronomical phenomena is followed immediately by good fortune or dis-aster. This is the constant omen from ancient times until today and the clear warn-ing from heaven to man."

Shi Le was pleased with it. Of the rest who were supposed to be executed, eight to nine out of ten benefited from Fotu Cheng. Thereupon, almost all people in cen-tral China, Chinese or foreigners, worshiped Buddha.

At that time, those who suffered from illnesses that could not be treated in the human world were treated by Fotu Cheng, and their illnesses gradually healed. Those who practiced Buddhist Dharma and benefited from it were numerous.

(Huijiao 慧皎 [497–554], *Gaoseng zhuan* 高僧傳, Chapter 9)

A Buddhist Nun

Huan Wen (312–373), whose style name was Yuanzi, was the commander-in-chief of Jin.[4] In his later years an anonymous Buddhist nun from afar suddenly came to Wen and took him as a benefactor. The nun's talent and behaviors were outstanding. Wen treated her with much respect and allowed her to live inside his inner gate.

Each time the nun bathed, it would take at least a couple of hours.[5] Suspicious, Wen spied on her. He saw the naked nun cut open her belly with a knife, then take out her viscera; she then cut her head off and divided them all into parts, and sliced them up.

Shocked and fearful, Wen retreated. Yet when the nun left the bathroom, her body was normal. Wen asked her what was going on.

The nun replied, "If you remove or bully the supreme ruler, your body should end up like that."

At that time, Huan Wen had plans to "inquire about the tripods."[6] Hearing what the nun said, he felt very unhappy. Yet Wen was on guard and fearful so that he maintained his integrity as a subject [without usurping the throne] in the end.

Later the nun bid farewell and left; nobody knew where she went.

(Tao Qian, *Soushen houji*, Chapter 2)

Notes

1 Yang Hsianyi and Gladys Yang, trans., *A Brief History of Chinese Fiction* (Beijing: Foreign Languages Press, 1964), p. 59.
2 Xi yu 西域 (areas of the West) refers to India and some small states between China and India, such as Qiuci 龟兹, Shule 疏勒, and Yutian 于阗.
3 Shi Le 石勒 was the founder of the Later Zhao 後趙 (319–351) in the Sixteen State period.
4 Huan Wen was the son-in-law of Emperor Ming 明帝 of Jin. At first he was the Governor of Jingzhou and later wielded power arbitrarily as the Da Sima 大司馬 (Commander-in-chief). He has secret plans to overthrow the Jin dynasty, but died before he succeeded. His biography can be found in *Jin shu*, 98: pp. 2568–2583.
5 In ancient China time was recorded by the system of Tiangan 天干 (Heavenly Stems) and Dizhi 地支 (Earthly Branches). A day was divided into 12 periods which were matched with the 12 Earthly Branches: 子 (23:00–1:00), 丑 (1:00–3:00), 寅 (3:00–5:00), 卯 (5:00–7:00), 辰 (7:00–9:00), 巳 (9:00–11:00), 午 (11:00–13:00), 未 (13:00–15:00), 申 (15:00–17:00), 酉 (17:00–19:00), 戌 (19:00–21:00), and 亥 (21:00–23:00). So the change of a time period indicates more than two hours.
6 The *ding* vessel, or tripod, is a symbol of the power of a country. Wending 问鼎 (inquiring about the tripods) is a metaphor for wanting to usurp the throne.

Further Readings

Kieschnick, John. *The Eminent Monk: Buddhist Ideals in Medieval Chinese Hagiography*. Honolulu, HI: University of Hawaii Press, 1997.
Poo, Mu-Chou. "The Images of Immortals and Eminent Monks." *Numen* 42 (1995): 172–96.
Zhang, Zhenjun. "Buddhist Imagery in Early Medieval China as Seen in the Youming Lu." In *Buddhism and Tales of the Supernatural in Early Medieval China*. Leiden and Boston, MA: Brill, pp. 148–73.

18 Dream Adventurers

Along with the wide dispersal of Buddhist teachings, dream adventure stories became popular from the Six Dynasties to the Tang. Since the stories were developed in the Buddhist milieu, they bear obvious Buddhist coloring.

"Dream adventure inside a microcosmic world" is a well-known motif in Chinese narrative. While the extant prototype of this motif is found in the Six Dynasties *zhiguai*, the representative work of this motif is Shen Jiji's (740–800) "The World inside a Pillow" (*Zhenzhong ji*). In the tale, scholar Lu is a Confucian scholar who longs for success. But a dream he experiences completely changes his worldview. What Lu realizes at the end of the story seems fairly clear: human life is a short and transient phenomenon, resembling an illusion or a dream; all honor, fame, and gains are unreliable. The sense of the transitory and illusory nature of life comes precisely from Buddhism.[1] Though such a sense of life is also found in Daoist classic *Zhuangzi*, but it did not become popular in literary works until the Six Dynasties, especially the Tang dynasty, when Buddhism became popular in China. In the "Introduction" to his *Classical Chinese Tales of the Supernatural and the Fantastic*, Karl Kao claims that Shen Jiji's "Record of Being in a Pillow" "preaches the Taoist outlook by showing the ephemeral and illusory nature of worldly successes in officialdom." Victor Mair criticizes him immediately in a book review, "Kao tends to overlook the powerful impact of Buddhism upon the development of Chinese classical fiction" (CLEAR v.8. n.1/2: 99–102).

The other two tales are also related to Buddhist thought. "Xue Wei Becomes a Fish" obviously promotes the idea of refraining from killing living creatures, while "Old Man Du" intends to give a warning against greed (here the erotic), one of the "Three Poisons" that cause sufferings in Buddhism, by Du's experience of almost becoming a pig in his next incarnation in a dream.

The World Inside a Pillow

In the seventh year (719) of the Kaiyuan reign (713–742) [of the Tang dynasty], an old Daoist priest with the surname Lü, who had acquired the arts of divine immortality, stopped at an inn on his way to Handan.[2] Taking off his cap and loosening his belt, he sat there leaning against his pack. Soon afterward, he saw a young traveler – he was Scholar Lu. Wearing a short coat of coarse cloth and riding a

DOI: 10.4324/9781003490821-21

black pony, Lu was going to the fields [to farm] and also stopped at the inn. He and the old man were seated next to each other, and their conversation and laughter were particularly hearty.

After a long while, Scholar Lu looked at his shabby clothes, heaved a deep sigh, and said, "As a man born in a world that he is discordant with, I'm so distressed!" The old man said, "Observing your face and figure, you look like you suffer neither pain nor illness. We have just talked and laughed merrily together. Yet you sigh and claim you are distressed. Why?" Scholar Lu said, "I'm just eking out a shameful existence, how can that be called content?" The old man said, "If this cannot be called content, what can be called content?" Scholar Lu said, "A man living in the world should do good deeds and gain renown, be a general outside and a prime minister inside the court, to have caldrons arrayed to eat from and select good sounds to listen to, making his clan more prosperous and his family more wealthy. Only then can he talk of being content. I had once set my will on learning, enriched myself by roaming in the arts, and I thought in those years that I would be able to put on the green and purple official garments easily. Now I have reached the prime of my life, I am still farming away in the fields. If this is not distress, what is?" After saying this, his eyes became blurry and he was sleepy.

At that time, the owner of the inn was steaming yellow millet. The old man took out a pillow from his bag and handed it to Scholar Lu, saying, "Sleeping on my pillow should make you glorious and content, just as you wish you were." The pillow was made of green porcelain, with small holes at both ends. Scholar Lu laid his head on it and saw that the hole gradually become larger and brighter. He lifted his body and entered, so he arrived at his home.

Several months later, he married a girl from the Cui family from Qinghe (in Hebei).[3] The girl was exceptionally beautiful, and the scholar became richer and richer. The scholar was greatly pleased. After that, his clothes and equipage became increasingly brighter and more luxurious. In the following year, he passed the imperial examination and ascended the rank as an Advanced Scholar. He took off his coarse clothes and became an Imperial Library Editor. Then he took a special exam hosted by the emperor and was transferred to be the magistrate of Weinan County. Soon he was promoted to investigating censor and then moved to be a diarist of imperial activity and repose, as well as the director of decrees. Three years later, he was appointed as the prefect of Tongzhou and was soon transferred to be the prefect of Shaanzhou. Scholar Lu was by nature enthusiastic about construction projects. He cut through the river 80 *li* from Shaanxi to help the area in its lack of transportation. The people benefited from it and established an engraved stone monument to commemorate his merit. Later, he moved to be prefect of Bianzhou, was then appointed as the investigating commissioner of Henan Circuit, and then summoned to be the governor of the capital.

In that year, the Spiritual and Martial Emperor was fighting against the western barbarians (*rong* 戎) and northern barbarians (*di* 狄) and thereby expanding his territories. By chance Tubo's 吐蕃[4] generals Ximoluo (Stagra [Konlog]) and Zhulong Mangbuzhi (Cogro Manpoci) captured Guazhou and Shazhou,[5] and the military governor Wang Junchuo (d. 727) was killed. All the people in the area between the

Yellow River and the Huang River were shocked. The emperor, craving for a talented commander, appointed Scholar Lu as vice censor-in-chief and military commissioner of west of the Yellow River. He crushed the western barbarian troops, beheading 7,000 soldiers and occupying 900 *li* of land. He also constructed three large cities, thus laying a solid defense in the key areas. The people living along the border set up a carved stone at Mount Juyan to praise him.

When he returned to the court to have his merits be recorded, the favor and courtesy the emperor offered him were exceptionally splendid. After being appointed as vice director of the ministry of personnel, he was promoted to minister of revenue and the censor-in-chief at the same time.

While his fame was pure and dignified and he was admired and loved by everyone, he was greatly envied by the prime minister at the time. The prime minister slandered him, and as a result, he was relegated to the post of prefect of Duanzhou.⁶ Three years later, he was recruited as a policy adviser to the emperor and, shortly afterward, jointly served as manager of affairs and the secretariat-chancellery. Together with Xiao Song (c. 667–749), the secretariat director, and Pei Guangting (676–733), the director of the chancellery, he jointly controlled the major policy for more than a decade. In order to offer excellent plans or receive secret orders, he often met with the emperor several times a day; by offering alternative policies and enlightening the emperor, he was recognized as a worthy prime minister. But his colleagues envied him and, furthermore, falsely accused him of conspiring with the border generals. An imperial edict ordered to have him imprisoned. The officials of the capital led their followers to the gate of Lu's house in haste to arrest him.

Scholar Lu panicked at this unexpected event and said to his wife, "In my home in Shandong, I have five hundred acres of fertile fields that are enough to withstand our hunger and the cold. Why bother to pursue emolument as an official? Now I have reached such a point that even if I wanted to wear a short coat of coarse cloth, ride a black pony, and talk on the road to Handan, it is impossible!" He drew a knife out to kill himself, but his wife stopped him. All of his accomplices who were involved were executed. Only Scholar Lu was sheltered by the eunuch, and his death sentence was reduced to being banished to Huanzhou 驩州.⁷

A few years later, the emperor learned of his grievances and once again appointed him as Director of the Department of State Affairs and enfeoffed him the title of Duke of Yan. The favor he received from the emperor was exceptional. He had five sons, named Jian, Chuan, Wei, Ti, and Yi; all of them were talented and capable. Jian ascended the rank of Advanced Scholar by passing the imperial examination and became an auxiliary secretary in the Bureau of Evaluations; Chuan was an attendant censor; Wei became assistant minister in the Court of Imperial Sacrifices, and Ti the magistrate of Wannian County. The youngest son, Yi, was the worthiest of them all and was made a rectifier of omissions at the age of 28. Lu's in-laws were all famous noble families. Lu had more than a dozen grandchildren.

Twice banished to the wild borderlands, he reassumed his position each time as prime minister. Traveling between China and foreign countries and being in and out of the imperial court for more than 50 years, his life was grand and glorious. By nature he was extravagant and was fond of leisure and entertainment. Both the music and the dancing girls in his harem were the most beautiful in the world. Fine lands, houses, beautiful women, and celebrated steeds that the emperor sent him over the years were too many to count.

Later, while growing gradually weaker and older, he repeatedly requested to retire but it had not been approved. When he was sick, the eunuchs came to visit him one after another; famous doctors and the best medicines all made their way to him. When he was about to die, he submitted a memorandum which read as follows:

This humble vassal was originally a student from Shandong, who enjoyed farming. By chance he encountered a sagely fate and was able to rank among the officials. He has received many honors, special posts, and mighty imperial grace. Going out of the court, he was thronged by banners of an imperial envoy; entering the court, he was elevated to be the Chief Bulwark of the State. In dealing with people inside and outside of China, he has passed so many years. He felt ashamed by receiving the imperial favor as he did not help your sagely education. An incapable man serving in a gentleman's post, he bequeathed only plunder. As treading on thin ice, his worry increased day by day, not knowing that old age had come. Now he is over eighty, but his post is still among the highest, the Three Dukes. Just like the bell and the clepsydra that eventually stop working, his muscles and bones are all aged and decayed. Lingering in exhaustion, his time is out soon. Considering that he has no merit to repay your goodness and sageliness, he failed to live up to your great favor. He now bids farewell to this sagely dynasty. With unbearable emotions and nostalgia, he respectfully offers this memorandum to express his gratitude.

An imperial edict replied:

Relying on your eminent virtue, my Excellency, you served as prime minister. Going out of the court, you held the hedge and pillar to protect us; entering the court, you helped in achieving harmony and prosperity. The peace of the world in the past several decades has come because of you. Since you have contracted this illness, we heard daily that you are healing. How come it is such a chronic one? We are truly taken with sympathy and sorrow. Now we send General Gao Lishi,[8] the Calvary General-in-chief, to visit your residence and ask after you. I hope you will make an effort to accept stone needle treatments, taking care of yourself for our sakes. We still hope no mishap will befall you and expect your recovery.

That very night, he died.

With a yawn Scholar Lu stretched and woke up. He found himself still lying in the inn. The old man Lü sat beside him, and the owner's steamed yellow millet was not yet cooked. Everything looked the same as before. He suddenly sat up and said, "Is this a dream?" Old Lü said to him, "The content of a man's life is also like that!" Scholar Lu appeared disappointed for a long time, then he thanked Lü, saying, "Now, the ways of favor and disgrace, the fate of distress and success, the reasoning of gains and losses, the feelings of life and death, I have completely known! This is how you, sir, put my appetite in check. How dare I not accept this lesson?" He kotowed to Lü twice and left.

(By Shen Jiji; from Li Fang, *Taiping guangji*)

Xue Wei Becomes a Fish

Xue Wei assumed the post of assistant magistrate of Qingcheng County in Jingzhou[9] during the first year of Qianyuan period (758–761), together with the vice magistrate, Zou Pang, and district defender, Lei Ji, and Pei Liao. In the autumn, Xue Wei was bedridden for seven days. Suddenly he seemed to have stopped breathing. His family called to him several times but received no response. Yet the pit of his stomach was still slightly warm. His family could not bear to encoffin him right away, so they just sat around him and waited.

Twenty days later, he suddenly sat up with a long sigh, asking, "How many days have passed in this world?"

"It has been twenty days," they answered.

"Go to the officials for me to see if they are about to eat fish. Tell them that I have awakened, and I have a wonder to tell them. Just ask them to stop eating and come to listen."

His servant boy went to the officials and found they were indeed about to eat minced fish. So he told them what had happened. All of them stopped eating and followed him.

Xue Wei asked, "Did you all order the revenue manager's servant, Zhang Bi, to buy fish?"

"Yes!" they answered.

Then he asked Zhang Bi, "The fisherman Zhao Gan hid a big carp and gave you a small one, but you found the hidden one in the reeds and brought it back. When you entered the gate of the county seat, a clerk of the revenue manager sat west of the gate while the clerk of the deputy magistrate sat east of the gate. The two were playing chess. When you stepped on the stairs, Zou Pang and Lei Ji were gambling, and Pei Ji was eating a peach. When you reported that Zhao Gan hid the big fish, Pei Ji ordered that he be flogged. When you gave the fish to the cook, Wang Shiliang, he was pleased and killed it. Is all of this correct?"

Then he asked each of them one by one, all responded that his narration was accurate. In surprise, they all asked, "How do you know?"

"I was the fish that you all just had killed!" Xue Wei replied.

Astonished, all of the officials said, "We would like to hear the details."

Xue Wei stated, "When I was first ill, I suffered from an unbearable fever. Suddenly, I felt couped up. So tired of being hot was I that I went in search for fresh cool air despite being sick. I left with a walking stick in hand, not knowing that I was in a dream.

"After passing through the outer city wall, I was so happy. Surely even a bird released from a cage or a beast escaped from his pen would not be happier than I was. Slowly I entered the mountain but found it oppressing walking there. So I walked down to the side of the river. I found the river was deep and tranquil, the autumn was lovely, and light ripples were almost motionless, reflecting the distant sky like a mirror.

"Suddenly I had the desire to bathe, so I put my clothes on the bank and jumped into the river. I was good at swimming when I was a child, but after growing up I never went. Having this opportunity to enjoy myself in the water felt like I was fulfilling a long-held wish. I thought also, 'A man swims slower than a fish. How could I pretend to be a fish so as to swim faster?' A fish by my side said, 'There is a way, but I'm afraid might not be willing. To become a real fish is easy, why do you want to pretend to be one? I'll help you.' Then it left quickly.

"A short while later, a fish with a human body, several feet long, came on the back of a young female whale, with several fish ahead of it as guards. The human body fish announced a decree from the God of the Yellow River,[10] saying,

The way of living in a city and floating in the river differs: one is floating while the other sinking. If it is not to one's strong liking, one would be confused by roaming the river. Xue Wei admires swimming idly in the deep and enjoys floating at will in the boundless blue river; he is tired of the feeling of climbing hills and threw himself into this illusory dreamland while casting his official hairpin. He is permitted to join the scaled crowd instead of being accepted rashly as a permanent member. For the time being, he will be a red carp in the East Pool. Alas! If you take the advantage of the waves to turn over a boat, you will be guilty in this hidden realm; if you ignore a hook and covet the bait, you will be hurt in the visible world. Be careful not to lose your self-possession and thereby bring disgrace to your kind. Try your best, please!

"As I listened, I looked around and found my body had already been covered with fish scales. I plunged into the water and swam to wherever I wanted. I swam leisurely on top of the waves as well as at bottom of the pool, and jumped and danced all over the three rivers and five lakes.

"However, I was assigned to stay in the east pool so I had to return every day in the evening. At one point, I was very hungry but failed to find any food. Following a boat, I found Zhao Gan's fishing hook, on which was fragrant bait. I was alarmed in my mind, but I was unaware when it got close to my mouth. I thought, 'I am a man who became a fish temporarily. Since I failed to find food, I am just going swallow the fishhook?' Thus I changed my mind and swam away.

"A while later, my hunger became intense. I thought, 'I am an official who amuses himself by wearing fish scales. Even if I swallow the hook, how could Zhao Gan kill me? He should surely send me back to the county office.' Thereupon I swallowed the hook.

"Zhao Gan pulled the line and brought me out. While Zhao's hand was about to touch me, I called him repeatedly. But he ignored me. He put a string through my gills and hung me among the reeds.

"Soon Zhang Bi came by, saying, 'Lieutenant Pei wants to buy a fish, but it must be a big one.' Zhao Gan said, 'I haven't gotten any big fish. I have more than ten catties of small ones though.' Zhang Bi said, 'I was ordered to get a big fish, what is the use of small ones.' Then he found me in the reeds and picked me up in his hand. I told Zhang Bi, 'I am the assistant magistrate of your county who was transformed into a fish to swim in the river. How dare you not bow to me?' Zhang Bi would not listen to me; instead he left with me in his hand. I didn't stop cursing him, but he didn't care at all.

"Entering the gate of the county government, I saw the clerks sitting there playing chess. I yelled at them, but none responded. They just said, 'Terrible! This fish is more than three or four catties!'

"Then Zhang Bi stepped on the stairs. I saw Zou and Lei were gambling, and Pei was eating a peach. All of them liked the big fish and urged Zhang to send me to the kitchen. When Zhang Bi mentioned that Zhao Gan hid the big fish and gave him small ones instead, Pei became angry and flogged him. I told all of you, 'I am your colleague and now I am caught. Instead of releasing me, you want to have me killed. Is this human?' I yelled until I was in tears. But the three of you ignored me and sent me to the cook.

"Wang Shiliang, holding a kitchen knife, threw me onto the short table. I told him in a loud voice, 'Wang Shiliang, you are my fish cook. Why are you going to kill me? Why don't you hold me and tell the officials?' It seemed that Wang heard nothing. Holding my neck firmly on the chopping board, he lopped off my head. As my head fell, I came back to my senses. Then you were summoned here."

All of the officials were amazed, and a sense of love and pity for all creatures grew in their minds. However, when Zhao Gan caught him, when Zhang Bi grabbed him, when the clerks were playing chess in front of the county government, when the three men approached the stairs, and when Wang Shiliang killed him, they all saw his mouth moving but heard no sound.

After that, the three gentlemen all gave up minced fish and never ate it again for the rest of their lives. Xue Wei fully recovered. He was repeatedly promoted, and the last post before his death was deputy magistrate of Huayang County.[11]

(From Li Fuyan 李復言 (fl. 831), *Xu xuanguailu* 續玄怪錄)

The Old Man Du

An old man surnamed Du was a native of Yishui County.[12] Once he came out of a market and sat on the ground by the wall to wait for his companions. Feeling a bit tired, he suddenly fell asleep and started dreaming. He dreamed a man took him away with a certificate in his hand. While arriving at a prefectural court he had never seen, a man wearing a commoner's hat with indentations in the middle came out. It was his old friend – a man surnamed Zhang from Qingzhou.

Upon seeing Du, the man was surprised. "Older Brother Du, what brings you here?"

Du replied, "I don't know; all I know is that the man [who led me here] held a certificate."

Suspecting that there was a mistake, Zhang was going to check it for him, so he advised him, saying, "Stand here and don't go anywhere else! If you happened to get lost, I'm afraid there is no way to save you." Then he left, but didn't come out for a long time. However, the man holding a certificate came, admitted his mistake, and let him go.

Du said goodbye and left. On his way back he met six or seven beautiful girls. Engrossed in their beauty, Du followed them. When he got off the main road and walked on a small pass for dozens of steps, he heard Zhang yelling behind him, "Brother Du, where are you going?" But Du was still infatuated with the girls and could not stop following them.

In a moment, he saw the girls enter a moon gate. He recognized that it was a bar owned by the Wang family. He could not help but stretched his head into the gate and stole a glance at the inside. Then he felt his body was in a pigsty and that he was prostrated on the ground together with many piglets. He suddenly realized that he had already become a little pig. Yet he still heard Zhang calling after him.

Terrified, Du rammed the wall with his head. Then he heard someone saying, "This pig is mad!" Looking around, he had already become a man again. He rushed out of the gate and saw Zhang was waiting on the way.

"I told you don't go anywhere!" Zhang scolded. "Why didn't you listen to me? You almost got yourself in deep trouble!"

Holding his hand tightly, Zhang accompanied him to the gate of the market and then left.

Du suddenly awoke and found his body was still against the wall. He went to Wang's family to inquire what had happened. He learned there was actually a little pig that rammed the wall with its head and died.

(Pu Songling, *Liaozhai zhiyi*, Chapter 6)

Notes

1 Zhenjun Zhang, *Buddhism and Tales of the Supernatural in Early Medieval China*, pp. 175–191.
2 In Hebei province.
3 One of the seven noble clans during the Tang dynasty.
4 A Tibetan empire that lasted from 618–842.
5 Both are in modern Gansu province.
6 In modern Guangdong province.
7 In modern Vietnam.
8 A famous eunuch of Emperor Xuanzong (r. 712–756).
9 Jingzhou 荆州 was a prefecture covering modern Hunan and Hubei provinces; its seat was Jiangling (in modern Jingzhou city in Hubei).
10 The principal river in northern China and the second-longest river in China, after the Yangzi River.

11 Huayang 華陽 County in Sichuan province.
12 Yishui 沂水 County in Shandong province.

Further Readings

Knechtges, David. "Dream Adventure Stories in Europe and Tang China." *Tamkang Review*
    4 (2) (October 1973): 101–19.
Zhang, Zhenjun. "The Motif of Dream Adventure inside a Microcosmic World." In *Bud-
    dhism and Tales of the Supernatural in Early Medieval China*. Leiden and Boston, MA:
    Brill, pp. 175–91.

Part IV

Topics Beyond the Three Teachings

The popular image of traditional Chinese society in the West has been a monolithic one, in which everyone conforms to a Confucian code of behavior. In recent decades, more and more Western scholars have come to realize the inadequacy of such an image. Interest has thus turned towards "abnormal" practices and phenomena.

Just like modern China's population is diverse with 56 ethnic minority groups, the world of Chinese culture is a colorful one. In the field of philosophy, Daoism and Buddhism as presented previously have already shown this without mentioning the hundred schools.

We have seen that Daoism has a unique paradigm of the role of man in this world and the way of dealing with things. This includes governing, the ideal man, and the ideal society. All these differ from the views of Confucianism.

As a foreign religion introduced in China, Buddhism had completely new ideas, such as karmic retribution and multiple lives, all of which enriched Chinese culture.

Obviously, however, the "Three Teachings" cannot cover all the beliefs and practices in Chinese culture. Nonconformities in Chinese society include not only Daoism and Buddhism but also other phenomena outside of the "Three Teachings."

The prominent examples presented in this section include the knights-errant and brave warriors, ungrateful men and faithless lovers, dedicated lovers and predestined couple, and ghost wives and spiritual maidens, providing us with a splendidly colorful and variegated cultural landscape.

DOI: 10.4324/9781003490821-22

19   The Knight-Errant

The knight-errant first appeared during the Warring States period against the background of political instability, social unrest, and intellectual ferment – a wandering chivalrous warrior (*youxia* 游侠). Legalist Hanfeizi criticizes such warriors along with Confucian scholars: "The Confucian scholars confuse the law with their writings, while the knights-errant violate the prohibitions by force" (儒以文亂法，而俠以武犯禁).

Sima Qian (145–86 BCE) lays out a more objective view, "Now the knights-errant: their behavior may not follow 'righteousness,' but they always meant what they said, always accomplished what they set out to do, and always fulfilled their promises; they neglected the safety of their own bodies to save people from distress and relieve people from want."[1]

The Chinese knights-errant share many similar features with their Western counterparts: altruism, justice, aiming at high courage and fame, preferring death to dishonor, and mutual faith and truthfulness. Their differences, as James J. Y. Liu has observed, include the following: Western knights-errant formed a definite class and were the backbone of the feudal system, while the Chinese ones came from different classes and represented a disruptive force; Western knights-errant had religious sanction (Christian soldiers) while the Chinese did not; love of the Western knights-errant was honorable and something to aim for but taboo for the Chinese knights-errant.[2]

The stories presented here are all about such Chinese knights-errant.

The Biography of Yu Rang

Yu Rang 豫讓 (?–c.445 BCE) was a native of Jin. In the past, he served the Fan clan and Zhonghang clan, but he was unknown. After leaving them he started to serve Zhibo,[3] who highly respected and favored him. When Zhibo attacked Zhao Xiangzi, Zhao plotted together with the clans of Han and Wei to annihilate Zhibo. After killing him, they divided his territory up equally. Zhao Xiangzi hated Zhibo so much that he painted his skull and used it as a drinking cup.

Yu Rang fled into the mountain, saying, "Alas! A man should die for the one who understands him well, just as a woman makes up for the one who loves her. Now Zhibo was the one who knew me well, I must avenge him at the risk of my

DOI: 10.4324/9781003490821-23

life to repay his favor. Only then can my soul be free of regret." Then he changed his name, tattooed his face to pretend to be a slave, and entered the palace to paint the toilet. He hid a dagger in his clothing, intending to assassinate Zhao Xiangzi.

When Xiangzi went to the privy, his heart started beating quickly, so he detained the slave who was painting the toilet. It turns out that he was Yu Rang and had a knife in his hidden on his person.

"I want to avenge Zhibo," he said.

The attendants wanted to kill him, but Xiangzi said, "He is a dutiful man. All we can do is be careful to avoid him. The fact is that Zhibo died without an heir, so his subject intends to avenge him. This makes him a worthy man under Heaven." Later he let Yu go.

A short while later, Yu Rang painted his body with lacquer to make it look leprous, then swallowed red charcoal to make his voice harsh. In this way, he was unrecognizable. When he begged in the market, even his wife did not recognize him. While walking he met his friend, his friend recognized who he was, asking, "Aren't you Yu Rang?"

He answered, "Yes, I am."

His friend wept for him, saying, "With your talents, if you serve under Xiangzi, he would certainly bring you in close and favor you. When he becomes close with you, you can then do whatever you want. Isn't that much easier? Why did you torture your own body to assassinate Xiangzi? Aren't you making things harder than they should be?"

Yu Rang replied, "After one has already served under someone then he seeks to kill him, that is called harboring disloyalty to serve one's lord. What I am doing is indeed extremely difficult. But the reason why I chose to is that I will make those in future generations who harbor disloyalty in serving their lords feel shameful." Then he left.

Soon afterward, when Xiangzi went out, Yu Rang hid under the bridge where Xiangzi would pass. When Xiangzi reached the bridge, his horse was startled. Xiangzi said, "It must be Yu Rang." He asked his attendant to search the area. It was Yu Rang that startled the horse. Xiangzi began to berate Yu Rang, saying, "Did you not serve the Fan clan and the Zhonghang clan? Zhibo annihilated both of them but you do not avenge them. On the contrary, you offered to be a subject of Zhibo. Now Zhibo has already died. Why do you only single-minded want to avenge him?"

Yu Rang said, "When I served the Fan and Zhonghang, both treated me as a commoner. Therefore, I also repay them as a commoner. As for Zhibo, he treated me as an eminent man of the state. Therefore, I should repay him as an eminent man of the state."

Xiangzi sighed deeply and said through tears, "Alas, Master Yu! To avenge Zhibo, you have achieved your name. But I forgave you; that too should be enough. You should begin to think about your own life. I will not release you today." Then he ordered his soldiers to encircle him.

Yu Rang said, "I heard that a sage lord does not hide other's merits, and a loyal subject is duty-bound to die for his fame. Previously, you pardoned me. All people under Heaven praised your kindheartedness. For what I did today, I will be killed. But I would like to request the chance to strike at your clothing and thus to show my desire for revenge. This way I can die without regrets. I do not expect you grant my wish, but I ventured to voice it anyway."

Considering him a man of honor, Xinangzi ordered someone to give his cloak to Yu Rang. Drawing his sword, Yu jumped up three times to slash at the cloak, saying, "Now I can face Zhibo in the world below!" Then he cut his throat with the sword. On the day of his death, the men of integrity in the State of Zhao heard of this and all wept for him.

(Sima Qian, *Shiji*, Chapter 86)

Feng Yan

Feng Yan 馮燕 was a bold and unrestrained man from Wei.[4] Both his father and grandfather were unknown. When he was young, Yan was willful and given to playing ball and cockfighting. Once, a fight over property occurred in a market-place in Wei. Hearing of this, Yan rushed there, hitting and killing someone in an effort to help the victim. He then hid in a field. As the authorities began searching for him, he fled to Hua,[5] where he became acquainted with the youth in the local army and continued enjoying playing ball and cockfighting with them.

At the time, Prime Minister Jia Dan 賈耽 (730–805) was at Hua. He recognized Yan's talents and kept him to serve in the army. When he was passing by a village one day, Yan saw a woman in front of a house watching him while veiling her face with her sleeve. Her looks appeared extremely seductive. Yan sent someone to ask about her and learned that she had an interest in him. So he took her as his mistress. Her husband was Zhang Ying, the general of the Hua garrison. Hearing of this affair, Ying beat his wife many times. The members of his wife's family all resented Ying.

When Ying was drinking with his friends, Yan found the opportunity to sleep with his wife again. They shut the door of the bedroom. When Ying returned, his wife opened the door to let him in, covering Yan with her skirt. Yan bent down and tiptoed while looking for cover. He found it behind the door. But he left his handkerchief under the pillow near his sword. Ying was drunk, and he lay there with his eyes closed. Pointing at the handkerchief, Yan asked Ying's wife to fetch it. But the woman took the sword and handed it to Yan. Staring at her for quite a while, Yan cut off the woman's head, then grabbed his handkerchief as he left.

The next morning, Ying awoke and saw that his wife was dead. Astonished, he intended to go plead his innocence. His neighbors thought that Ying had indeed killed his wife, so they tied him up and rushed to tell his wife's relatives.

When they had all arrived, they said, "He hated and often beat our daughter, then he slandered her saying she was guilty and deserved it. Now he killed her. How could it be anyone else that killed her? Even if she was killed by others, how could Ying be able to live alone?" They grabbed Ying together and whipped him more than a hundred times. This rendered him unable to speak at all.

The authorities arrested Ying for murder. Nobody came forward to defend him, so he was forced to plead guilty. The law enforcement officers, along with dozens of soldiers holding knives, escorted Ying to the execution market. The onlookers numbered one thousand.

Suddenly, a man came by pushing the crowd away, yelling, "Don't let the innocent die! I stole his wife and then killed her as well. You should arrest me!"

The officials detained the man who pleaded guilty. It was none other than Yan. The law enforcement officers all met Lord Jia and told him everything. Lord Jia sent a memorial to the emperor detailing the case and requested to hand over his official seal to redeem Yan's life. The emperor considered it proper and sent down an edict, which granted clemency to prisoners guilty of death.

Yazhi says: I value the words of the Grand Scribe and also like the narratives about justice. His friends and colleagues told me what they had witnessed and heard. During the Yanhe reign (within 712), Liu Yuanding, the Auxiliary Secretary, told me that during the Zhenyuan period (806–820) these things involving Feng Yan occurred. All of these made it possible for me to write this biography about him. Alas! The desire to commit adultery is more destructive than flood and fire. How can we not be afraid of it? But Yan killed the woman who behaved improperly and exonerated the innocent man. He was truly the hero in ancient times!

(Shen Yazhi 沈亞之 (781–832), *Shen Xiaxian wenji* 沈下賢文集)

An Upright Assassin

Not long ago, there lived an official who was a local county defender near the capital. He often served in the police department. A thief was jailed and fettered, yet his case was not yet concluded. Once when the official sat alone in the court, the thief suddenly told him, "I am not a thief, and I am not an ordinary man. If you exonerate me from the charge, I will certainly repay you handsomely someday in the future."

Seeing that the thief's appearance was distinguished and his wording forceful, the official had already accepted his offer in his mind but pretended not to. At midnight, he secretly asked a clerk to release him and then made the clerk flee.

The next day, a prisoner was missing and the clerk had fled. The official received merely a minor punishment.

After his term of service was finished, the official traveled around for quite a few years. When he arrived at a certain county, he heard that the name of the magistrate was the same as the thief he had released. He went to visit the magistrate and notified the magistrate of his name before their meeting. The magistrate was startled and terrified; he came out to personally welcome and bow to his guest. It was the same man that had been released.

The magistrate put him up in the hall, sleeping on the beds next to each other. They stayed together happily for around ten days. The magistrate did not go home once.

One day when he finally returned home, the guest went to the privy, which was next to the magistrate's residence. The guest heard the wife ask, "What kind of guest is this who kept you away from home for ten days?"

The magistrate replied, "This man did me a great favor in the past. My life was in his hands then. Now I am in this position, I do not know how to repay him."

His wife said, "Have you not heard that a great favor needs no repayment. Why don't you find an opportunity to let him leave?"

The magistrate kept silent for a long while, and then said, "What you said is correct."

Hearing this, the guest returned to tell his servants, then fled on the back of his horse, leaving all of his clothes in the hall.

When night arrived, they had gone fifty to sixty *li* and settled in a village inn in another county. His servants felt it odd that he asked them to flee but did not know why. After everyone was settled, the guest then told them all about how the thief was ungrateful. After he had finished talking, he let out a long, sorrowful sigh.

As his servants wept, a man suddenly came out from under the bed and stood there with a dagger in his hand. The guest was terrified.

Then the man said, "I am a man of principle. The magistrate asked me to take your head, but hearing what you said, I realize that he is ungrateful. If it were not for your explanation, I would have wrongly killed a worthy man. For the sake of righteousness, I will not pardon the magistrate. Please do not go to sleep just yet. I will bring back his head in short order and clear you of the evil you are charged with."

While the guest was terrified, regretful, and grateful at the same time. The man dashed out of the room in a flash, with his dagger in hand.

It was about the second watch when someone yelled, "The head of the evil man has come!"

When they lit a torch to see, they saw that it was the head of the magistrate. The swordsman bid them farewell and left. Nobody knew where he went.

(Huangfu Mi 皇甫謐 (215–282), *Yuanhua ji* 原化記)

Zhang Hui

Zhang Hui, whose courtesy names were Yujun and Caishu, was a native of Wu County.[6] He was well versed in poetry, good at playing the zither, and enjoyed heavy drinking. By nature, he was fond of making friends and strictly keeping his promises, even if calamities came as a result.

At the age of 18, he visited the capital with his father. Hearing that Fa Bao, a Manchurian bannerman, was talented and fond of associating with scholars, he called on him by presenting a poem. As soon as they met, they became fast friends. Fa Bao invited him to live in his home as a guest, treating him with the utmost courtesy. They interacted with each other through poems for half a year.

When his father urged Zhang to return home, Fa Bao presented him with 500 taels of gold as a gift. Zhang Hui refused the gift, saying, "When a gentleman pledges to be brothers with a friend, he will be a lifelong friend. Those who associate with gold are vulgar people in the world and of course not what one expects." He bid farewell with a wave and left.

Taking advantage of being a relative of the royal house, Fa Bao behaved arrogantly several times when composing poems together with his peers. He would do things without strictly following the rules. After hearing of this, the emperor became upset. To avoid repercussions, Fa Bao fled with his wife and around a dozen servants. He purchased a boat and went directly to Huguang to visit his old friend who was a regional commander, but it turned out that he had already died.[7]

Helpless, Fa Bao thought of his old friend Zhang Hui, the knight-errant living in Tiger Hill in Suzhou. He still remembered the words Zhang said when they parted in the past, and he assumed that if he went to him to seek refuge, he would certainly accept him. With this resolve, he started his journey on the Yangzi River and secretly arrived in Gusu[8] from Piling.[9]

One day when the evening market by the Shantang River had ended, Zhang Hui was drinking with his father when someone knocked on his door. Zhang Hui walked out and found Fa Bao standing there.

After inviting Fa Bao to sit in the guest room, Zhang Hui entered and said to his father, "Gentleman Fa is my true friend. He fled the capital because of a crime that is unforgivable by law; anyone who keeps him at home will have to share the punishment of his crime. Now he has nowhere to go. If we fear the punishment, we can hold him and report him to the authorities; but that means he will die. In the past Kong Rong protected Zhang Jian with the support of his mother, and their fame of righteousness has shone through the ages. I venture to ask you, my father, should I betray my friend to protect our family or sacrifice my life for righteousness' sake?"

Opening his eyes widely, Zhang's father said, "What kind of person was Kong's mother? How could I be more of a coward than a woman? Of course, have him stay!" Thereupon Zhang Hui arranged for Fa Bao to live in his home.

Previously, when Fa Bao fled the capital, the emperor was enraged. He issued an imperial edict to search for him throughout the kingdom.

Having stayed at Zhang Hui's home for a long time, Fa Bao was afraid that he might be discovered causing Zhang's family to be implicated. After talking with his friend, Scholar Zou, he moved to Huishan in Wuxi.

In the twenty-fourth year of Kangxi, the emperor visited the south. A servant of Fa Bao reported to the authorities that Fa Bao was planning a rebellion and made known the place where Fa Bao was living. Fa Bao was arrested then along with Zhang Hui and Zhang's father.

Zhang Hui spoke in defense of his father and was able to get him exonerated, but he was sentenced to death. Later, his capital punishment was degraded to being exiled to Qin.[10]

The officials in Qin all praised Zhang Hui's morality and were willing to befriend him. None viewed him as an exiled criminal. They also built a house for him in Chang'an. Upon approaching the house, one could see it was surrounded by a fence, with elegant flowers and trees planted sparingly around it. When a guest arrived, he would lead them to the small multistoried house and set out wine. After drinking, he would play a song on his zither, or compose an eight-line regulated poem with four rhymed lines, as if forgetting that he was in a foreign land.

I assumed that since Zhang Hui had a high opinion of himself and never compromised himself just to avoid calamity, there must be some heroic spirit seen between his eyebrows, just like Zhu Kai, Guo Xie, and the others.[11] However, when I observed him, he was modest and elegant, playing music all day. He is a Confucian scholar as well a hero of high merit! This means his father was also not an ordinary man.

(Niu Xiu 钮琇 (1644–1704), *Gu Sheng* 觚剩)

Notes

1 今遊俠，其行雖不軌於正義，然其言必信，其行必果，已諾必誠，不愛其軀，赴士之阨困，既已存亡死生矣，而不矜其能，羞伐其德，蓋亦有足多者焉 Sima Qian, *Shiji*, Vol. 124 (Beijing: Zhonghua shuju, 1959), p. 3181.
2 Cf. James J. Y. Liu, *The Chinese Knight-Errant* (University of Chicago Press, 1967), pp. 195–208.
3 Zhibo 智伯, named Zhi Yao 智瑶 and Xun Yao 荀瑶 (506–453 BCE), was a minister Jin 晉 during the Spring and Autumn period.
4 Weizhou 魏州 is a prefecture 15 miles east of present-day Wei County in Hebei.
5 Huazhou 滑州 was near modern Hua County in Henan.
6 Wu County is located in present-day Suzhou in Jiangsu province.
7 Huguang 湖廣 is the combined area of Hunan and Hubei.
8 Gusu 姑蘇 is an old name for Suzhou.
9 Piling 毗陵 is located in present-day Changzhou.
10 Qin is located in present-day Shanxi.
11 Both Zhu Kai and Guo Xie are noted knights-errant in the "Biographies of the Knight-errant" in Sima Qian's *Shiji*.

Further Readings

Altenburger, Roland. *The Sword and Needle: The Female Knight-Errant (xia) in Traditional Chinese Narrative*. Bern and New York, NY: Peter Lang, 2009.
Liu, James J. Y. *The Chinese Knight-Errant*. University of Chicago Press, 1967.

20   The Brave Warrior

Along with the knight-errant, which mainly features chivalrous actions to make true one's promises, another group of heroic figures presented here is the courageous warriors recognized for their bravery and mighty strength. These resemble Wu Song and Lu Zhishen in the famous novel *Water Margins* (*Shuihu zhuan* 水滸傳) as well as Zhang Fei and Xu Chu in another classic novel, *Romance of the Three Kingdoms* (*Sanguo yanyi* 三國演義).

Three stories are presented here; it is worth noting that the warrior in the first story, Li Ji, is actually a brave and smart young girl.

Li Ji Slays the Serpent

In the area of East Yue and Minzhong[1] stands the Yong Ridge, towering dozens of *li* into the air. In the swamp northwest of the ridge, there lived a giant serpent 70 or 80 feet long and more than five feet around.[2] Local folks lived in constant terror. The commandant of the capital city Dongye[3] and many officials of its subordinate towns were killed by it. Oxen and sheep were offered to it as a sacrifice, so further calamities were avoided for a time.

By sending messages through dreams or notifying the shaman directly, the serpent stated that it wanted to eat young girls about 12 or 13 years old. Both the commandant and the magistrate were beside themselves with this matter, but the tone of its demand was getting severer.

They decided to try and find a girl among the daughters born to slaves or criminals and raised her at home first. When the first day of the eighth month arrived, the little girl would be sent as a sacrifice to the entrance of the cave in which the giant serpent was living. The serpent would swallow the little girl as soon as it came out of the cave. This had been the case for many years. Up to that point, nine girls had been eaten by the creature.

This year, their search did not result in a suitable girl. Li Dan, a native of Jiangle County, had six daughters but not a single son. His youngest daughter, named Ji, intended to go as a volunteer, but her parents would not allow her.

"My parents," Li Ji said, "your fate is not good. You have begotten six daughters but not a single son. Although you have descendants, it is the same as having none. I have done no meritorious deeds for you as Tiying did to her father.[4] Furthermore,

DOI: 10.4324/9781003490821-24

I also cannot support you, so I am just wasting food and clothes. Rather than living uselessly, it is better for me to die early. By selling myself, I can get a little money to support you. Isn't that a good thing?"

Her parents were kind and truly loved her, so they did not allow her to go. But Li Ji secretly went to the recruiters herself so that nobody could stop her.

Li requested a sharp sword and a hound dog. On the first day of the eighth month, she arrived at the shrine and sat down with the sword hidden in her clothes and the dog by her side. She had prepared a few bushels of cooked glutinous rice balls mixed with honey and cooked flour, which she placed at the mouth of the cave.

Then the serpent slithered out of its lair, with a head as large as a grain basket and eyes as big as two feet wide bronze mirrors.

When the serpent smelt the fragrant smell of the rice balls, it ate them first. This gave Li Ji a chance to release the hound. The dog rushed forward to bite the serpent. Li Ji hacked at the snake with her sword, resulting in a few wounds on its back.

Not being able to stand the severe pain, the serpent slithered out of the cave, then dashed to the hall and died there.

Li Ji entered the cave to look around. She saw the skulls of the nine girls. She gathered them all up and said with regret, "You were too weak and timid and so you were eaten by the serpent. What a pity!" Thereupon, Li Ji walked out slowly and returned home.

Hearing of this incident, the king of East Yue chose Li Ji as his queen and appointed her father the magistrate of Jiangle. Her mother and sisters were all rewarded.

From then on, there was no monster in Dongye; a ballad about Li Ji is still sung there until today.

(Gan Bao, *Soushen ji*, Chapter 19)

Zhong Fu Fights the Tiger

In Anlu commandery[5] there lived a reclusive scholar surnamed Ma, whose name was unknown. He said that he was a native of Jiangxia. He also claimed he visited Lake Dongting and the Xiang River when he was young and lived in Zhongling as a visitor for more than ten years.[6]

Ma once spoke of Zhong Fu, a native of Yu Zhang, who was unrestrained when he was young and widely known for his bravery and persistency among the locals. He never made a living by farming; instead, he was constantly found hunting. None of the bears, deer, or other animals could escape when they came across Zhong Fu.

One day, his relatives gathered for a feast. While Zhong Fu had a great capacity for liquor, he was drunk that day. He did not set forth to return home until it was about dark. He left with only one servant boy. Two or three *li* away from his home, there was a large mountain with streams. A greenish-blue tiger with black patterns and white fur on its forehead came out of the forest, rushing toward him from a distance of one hundred paces.

The servant saw the tiger, causing his thighs to shake with terror; he told Zhong Fu, "Climb up a big tree quickly!"

With the help of the strength of the liquor, Zhong Fu was much more audacious. With the servant's white stick in hand, he stood there like a mountain to ward off the tiger.

The tiger rushed toward Zhong Fu. Zhong Fu jumped left and right to avoid it, hitting it with the stick as he did so. When the tiger crouched down, Zhong Fu also squatted down. In a moment, they attacked each other again. This occurred several times. Then the tiger got its front paws on Zhong Fu's shoulders while Zhong Fu tightly held the tiger's neck with his arms. This lasted for a long time. The ferocious tiger had nowhere to use its claws and teeth, and the brave Zhong Fu had nowhere to attack. They just held onto each other, with the servant screaming next to them.

Zhong Fu's family wondered why he didn't return after dark, so they went to look for him with swords in hand. When they saw Zhong Fu was fighting the tiger, they hacked at the tiger with swords. They broke the tiger's spine, and Zhong Fu was saved from the fight.

Several years later, there was a disturbance south of the Yangzi River. A variety of robbers had gathered together. All of them were persuaded by Zhong Fu because of his fame of fighting the tiger. So he was elected to be their head. Later he was given the post of commander. By controlling Zhongling, he suppressed and pacified the district and cleared up the six commanderies.

During the time under Emperor Xi and Emperor Zhao of Tang, Zhong Fu enjoyed fleeting fame in Jiangxi. His official title reached Secretariat Director.

(Zhang Zhuo 張鷟, *Ermu ji*)

Yu Jiang Kills the Wolves

Once there was a villager named Yu Jiang. His father once slept in a field and was eaten by a wolf. Yu Jiang was 16 years old then. When he found the lost shoes of his father, he was so sad and angry that he wanted to die. After his mother went to bed that night, he secretly left home with an iron hammer in hand, lay down at the place where his father had slept, hoping to avenge his father by killing the wolf.

A while later, a wolf came, hesitantly sniffing around him. Jiang did not move. In a moment, the wolf slightly touched his forehead with its tail; then, it gradually lowered its head to lick his thigh. Jiang still did not move. Then the wolf moved to bite his neck. Jiang suddenly hit the wolf's head with his hammer, killing it on the spot. Yu Jiang stood up and put the dead wolf onto the grass.

In a short while, another wolf arrived and acted like the first one. Yu Jiang killed it as well. But after that, no wolf came until midnight.

During a short nap, he dreamed of his father, who told him, "Killing these two creatures is enough to quench my hatred toward the wolf, but the one that killed me had a white nose – neither of these two is it."

After awaking, Jiang lay again resolutely to wait for the other wolf.

When daybreak arrived, nothing had happened. He wanted to drag the wolves back home but was afraid that they would terrify his mother. Therefore, he threw them into a dry well and returned home. When night fell, he went to the same place again, but again nothing happened.

After three or four nights had passed like that, suddenly a wolf came, pulling Yu Jiang away with one of his legs in its mouth. After the wolf walked a few steps, thorns pierced Jiang's flesh and a stone bruised his skin. Jiang looked as if he were dead. The wolf then dropped him onto the ground, intending to tear open his belly.

Suddenly, Yu Jiang stood up and whacked it with the hammer. The wolf fell; he hammered it again and again until it died. Yu Jiang looked at it carefully and found it was truly the wolf with the white nose.

Greatly pleased, Yu Jiang lifted the wolf on his shoulder and returned home. At that moment, he told his mother everything. His mother followed him to the dry well where they pulled out the other two wolves.

Commentary: Among the farmers is there really such a heroic man? Though his dutifulness and staunchness came from his sincere love for his family, he was not only brave but also exceptionally clever.

(Pu Songling, *Liaozhai zhiyi*, Chapter 3)

Notes

1 Dongyue 東越 was an old state, covering the southern part of Zhejiang and the northern part of Fujian. Minzhong 閩中 refers to the area of present-day Fujian.
2 *Wei* 圍 is half a foot or five *cun*.
3 Dongye 東冶 was an old city located in present-day Fuzhou in Fujian.
4 Tiying was a brave girl in the Han dynasty who extricated her father from physical punishment by offering herself as a slave to the court.
5 Anlu 安陸 was a prefecture of the Tang dynasty that covered six counties; its seat was located at what is currently Anlu city in Hubei.
6 Zhongling 鍾陵 was an old county established in the Tang; its seat was located northwest of present-day Jinxian County is Jiangxi.

21　The Ungrateful Man

Ungrateful men are notorious in many cultures of the world but are much more so in ancient China where a common maxim – "a man cognizant of a kindness must repay it" (*zhi'en bibao* 知恩必報) was a strong ethical code. This was shown in "The Biography of Yu Rang" and "Wu Bao'an Ransoms His Friend" in part one of this book.

Surprisingly, the most popular name for an ungrateful man in Chinese is an animal, the "Zhongshan Wolf," taken from an allegorical story that is included herein.

Another name for an ungrateful man is that of a fictional figure, Wang Kui. A story about him is included under the theme of "The Heartless Lover" next. In fact, the protagonists in all three stories under that theme are ungrateful men. The only difference between those stories and the stories presented here is that the victims of the ungrateful men in those stories are women, instead of men.

The Zhongshan Wolf

Led by hunting managers and followed by falcons and hounds, Zhao Jianzi 趙簡子[1] hunted in Zhongshan 中山.[2] Numerous swift birds and ferocious beasts fell as soon as the arrows hit them.

A wolf, standing upright like a man and howling at him, blocked the way.

Ascending the chariot leisurely, Zhao Jianzi pulled his Craw-crying bow and shot a Sushen-made arrow that sank completely into the beast. The wolf fled with a terrified cry.

Enraged, Jianzi drove his chariot after it. Flying dust veiled the sky and the horses' hooves sounded like thunder. Outside of ten steps, one could not distinguish a man from a horse.

At that same moment, a Moist,[3] Sir Dongguo 東郭, was going to Zhongshan to seek a position as an official. Driving a crippled donkey with his sack of books on its back, Sir Dongguo walked on the road in the morning but had lost his way. Seeing the dust, he was startled.

The wolf suddenly appeared. Stretching its head, it stared at him and asked, "Sir, do you have the will to save creatures? In the past, Mao Bao released a turtle and was later able to survive by crossing the river with its help, and the Marquis of Sui once saved a snake and received a pearl in return. A turtle or a snake is not

DOI: 10.4324/9781003490821-25

necessarily more numinous than a wolf. For now, why don't you let me enter your bag to stay? If I can escape today's danger, your favor is akin to gaining me a second life. How could I not follow the example of the turtle and the snake and repay you sincerely?"

"My!" Sir Dongguo said. "If were I shelter you, wolf, I would offend the minister and nobleman, and disaster will likely befall me. How could I expect you to repay me? Yet the way of Mohism is based on impartial love. So regardless I should find means to save your life. I cannot refuse to do so even if the results are bad."

So he took out his books to empty his bag and tried to slowly put the wolf into the bag. Since he was afraid to press the wolf's dewlap too hard in front and fold its tail too hard in the back, he repeatedly failed to put it in. As he hesitated to find the best way, the hunter drew closer and closer.

"This is truly urgent!" the wolf begged him. "Sir, would you still be courteous while saving people from a fire and from drowning or would you ring bells while escaping from robbers? Please figure out what to do quickly!"

Thus the wolf folded its four legs to let Dongguo tie them up and bent its head and tail to hide its snout, shrinking like a hedgehog, curling like an inchworm, coiling like a snake, holding its breath like a turtle, and gave itself completely over to Sir Dongguo.

Following the wolf's instruction, Sir Dongguo placed it into the bag. He tied the bag, lifted it onto the back of the donkey, and withdrew to the left side of the road, waiting for Zhao's people to pass by.

After a moment, Jianzi arrived. Unable to find the wolf, he was enraged. He drew his sword, cut the shaft tip of his carriage, and showed it to Sir Dongguo, cursing, "Anyone who dares to hide the trace of the wolf will be treated like this shaft."

Sir Dongguo prostrated himself on the ground, crawled forward, and knelt while keeping his body upright, saying, "I am a humble man and not smart. I am traveling far from home to seek a post as an official, but I am lost. How can I trace the wolf and point it out to your falcons and hounds? But I have often heard that 'there are many forks in the road so it is easy to lose a goat.' A goat can be easily controlled by a boy; it is so docile, but can still be lost because of the forks in the road. A wolf is not comparable with a goat, but how many forks are in the road in the Zhongshan area, where a goat may be lost? Now, you search for the wolf only on the broad road, isn't this like 'waiting by a tree to catch a dead rabbit' or 'climbing a tree to catch fish?'

"Furthermore, hunting is the affair of the officer in charge of parks and hunting. Thus, you should go to ask them. How could you blame a man passing by? In addition, although I am not smart, how could I not know the wolf? It is covetous and ferocious by nature and colluded with the jackal to do evil things. Since you can kill it, I would of course help you with what I can; how could I hide its tracks and not tell you?"

Zhao Jianzi said nothing; he turned his chariot around and left. Sir Dongguo drove his donkey to go forward at double speed.

A long while later, the traces of hunting banners gradually receded, and the sound of chariots and horses faded away. Assuming that Jianzi had gone quite far, the wolf spoke up in the bag, "Good sir! Please take me out of the bag, untie the string, and pull the arrow out of my leg. I'm dying."

Lifting his hand, Sir Dongguo took the wolf out. The wolf roared towards him, saying, "Before I was chased by the hunting manager, who was very fast. Luckily, you saved me. Now I am extremely hungry. If I have no food, I will die. Rather than die of starvation on the way and be eaten by beasts, it would be better to be killed by the hunting manager and become food for the noble family. Since you are a Moist who shaves his head and wears out his heels solely to benefit the world, how could you begrudge feeding me with your body to keep my humble life?"

Thus the beast bared its teeth and claws, rushing toward him.

Sir Dongguo hastily fought against it with his hands. While fighting, he withdrew, hiding behind and circling around the donkey. As Sir Dongguo strived to protect himself, the wolf could not bite him. Exhausted, they panted on opposite sides of the donkey.

Sir Dongguo said, "You, wolf, are ungrateful! You are so ungrateful!"

The wolf said, "I don't intend to be ungrateful, especially since you and your kind are purposely created by Heaven to be eaten by my kind."

Having been locked in a stalemate for a long time, Sir Dongguo thought, "It is getting late. If more wolves arrive, I will surely die." Thus, he told the wolf, "According to folkways, to settle a dispute, we must inquire with three seniors. If they say I can be eaten, then you can eat me; if not, you must give up."

The wolf was greatly pleased, so it walked together with him.

As it was late, they passed no travelers on the way. The wolf became deadly hungry.

Seeing an old tree standing by the road, the wolf said, "Sir, you can ask this senior."

"Grass and trees have no emotions," Sir Dongguo replied. "What good will asking the tree do?"

"Just ask," the wolf said. "It must tell you something."

Left with no choice, Sir Dongguo bowed to the tree with his hands clasped before him and told it everything, asking, "This being the case, should the wolf eat me?"

A rumbling sound came from the tree, saying, "I am an apricot tree. When the old gardener seeded me in the past, he used only one apricot seed. One year later, I blossomed; two years later, I bore fruit; three years later, my trunk could be measured with hands; and ten years later, my trunk could be measured with arms. Now, it has been twenty years. The old gardener ate my fruit, his wife and children ate my fruit, and his visitors and servants all ate my fruit. Furthermore, they sold my fruit at the market to make money. I have performed great and meritorious services to the old gardener. Now, I am old and cannot blossom or bear fruit anymore. This made the old gardener mad at me. He cut off my larger branches, trimmed my small branches and leaves, and is about to sell me to the carpenter's shop for what I'm still worth. Alas! Now I'm aged and have become a piece of useless timber; still,

I cannot avoid being cut down by his ax. What favor have you done for the wolf? How could you expect to avoid being eaten? It should devour you."

After the old tree finished its words, the wolf extended its snout and claws, rushing again toward Sir Dongguo.

Sir Dongguo said, "Wolf, you are breaking the rule! We pledged to inquire with three seniors. We have only met an apricot tree. Why are you so hasty?"

Again, they set off together. But the wolf grew more impatient.

Seeing a cow was exposed to the sun due to some collapsed walls, the wolf said, "Ask this senior."

Sir Dongguo answered, "Previously, the senseless tree troubled us with its absurd words. The cow is but a beast. Why should we ask him?"

"Just ask it!" the wolf said. "Otherwise, I'll bite you."

Left with no choice, Sir Dongguo bowed to the old cow with his hands clasped before him, told his story from beginning to end, and asked his question.

The cow knitted its brows, opened its eyes wide, licked its nose, opened its mouth, and said, "The old apricot tree is right. When I was young and my horns just started to grow, I was fairly strong and energetic. The old farmer traded a knife for me. He put me among other oxen to plow the land. When I was in the prime of my life, the other oxen grew old and weak; I did everything for him. When he hunted, I drew the hunting carriage and rushed along shortcuts; when he plowed, I got rid of the carriage to walk in the fields to open up virgin soil. The old farmer cared dearly for me as if I were his left and right hands. By relying on me, he got clothes and food, took a wife, paid taxes, and filled his storehouse with grain. I assumed that I would be sheltered with a canopy and a mat, as a dog or a horse would.

"In the past, the grain in his storehouse was no more than a couple of bushels, but now he harvests more than ten bushels of wheat each year. In the past, he lived poverty-stricken and felt bored, but now he often strolls in the village. In the past, his lips were always dry and his dust-covered cups and jars were rarely filled with wine, but now he has distilled wine with grain, possesses many cups and jars filled with wine, and pampers his wife and concubines. In the past, he wore a short-sleeved shirt woven from coarse cloth, accompanied with wood and stone, he did not know how to clasp his hands while bowing to someone, and his mind never thought of learning; now he holds a book, wears a bamboo cap, a leather belt, and a large robe. Every single thread of cloth and every single grain of wheat that he possesses was acquired by my strength.

"Taking advantage of my old age, however, he drove me into this place. The cold wind blows hard against my eyes, and the wintry sun shines over my lonely form; my skinny body is like the craggy mountains, and my old tears flow like rainwater; my drooping saliva cannot be held, and my spastic legs cannot be lifted; my skin and fur are both gone, but the sores and wounds do not heal.

"The old farmer's wife is jealous and fierce, and she says all day long, 'There is nothing useless in the body of a cow. Its flesh can be made into dry meat, its skin can be tanned into leather, and the bones and horns can be polished and fashioned into utensils.' Pointing at her eldest son, she said, 'You have apprenticed as a butcher for so many years, why don't you sharpen your knife and wait?' With such talk, things do not bode well for me. I do not know the place where I will be killed. The case is that though I have merits, my owners are heartless. So I will come to a bad end. What kindness have you done the wolf in hopes of avoiding death?"

As soon as these words were finished, the wolf extended its snout and claws, rushing toward Sir Dongguo again.

Sir Dongguo cried, "Stop being in such a hurry!"

In the distance came an old man with a wooden stick. His beard and eyebrows were both white, his gown and hat refined and elegant. He appeared to be a Daoist.

Sir Dongguo was pleased and startled. He left the wolf, went forward, and kowtowed while crying, "I beg you to speak fairly to save my life!"

The old man asked the reason. Sir Dongguo said, "This wolf was cornered by hunters when it asked me for help. I saved its life. Unexpectedly, it wants to eat me now. I begged it not to, but I can't get rid of it. I will likely be killed by it today. To delay it a little while, I agreed to let three seniors judge this matter. We first met an old apricot tree and the wolf forced me to ask it, but the tree's ignorance almost killed me; we then met an old cow and the wolf forced me to ask it, and the beast's ignorance almost killed me again. Now I have run into you, isn't it Heaven who will spare this scholar? So I beg you to save me with one word." Thus he kowtowed under the old man's cane, resigning himself to his fate.

Hearing this, the old man sighed repeatedly. He thumped the wolf with his cane and said, "You are wrong! After one has done you a favor, you betray him; nothing is more inauspicious than this! Confucians believe that one who is done a favor and cannot bear to betray it must be a filial son; they also believe that the tiger and wolf know the feelings between father and son. Now you are ungrateful like this, indicating you have lost even the feeling between father and son." Then he said sternly, "Wolf, go away now! Otherwise, I will kill you with this stick!"

The wolf said, "You only know one side of the coin. Please, let me tell you the truth. I hope you will listen to the end. When the gentleman rescued me, he tied my legs, sealed me in the bag, and pressed his books against me. I was compressed and couldn't breathe. He also made up a lie to trick Janzi, by which he meant to let me die in the bag and enjoy the gains alone. How could I not eat him?"

The old man looked at Sir Dongguo and said, "If this was so, you are also sinful."

Sir Donguo thought this unfair, so he described more details about how he took pity on the wolf. The wolf also cleverly argued his case. The old man said, "Neither of your stories is enough to convince me. Put the wolf in the bag again. I will see if it is in pain."

The wolf happily followed what he said and extended its legs to the gentleman. Sir Dongguo tied the wolf into the bag and placed it onto the donkey's back, and the wolf was oblivious to what was happening.

The old man whispered in Sir Dongguo's ear, "Do you have a dagger?"

The gentleman said, "Yes." So he unsheathed the dagger.

The old man winked at Sir Dongguo, indicating he should stab the wolf with the dagger.

The gentleman asked, "Wouldn't that wound the wolf?"

The old man said with a smile, "The beast betrayed you like this, yet still you can't bear to kill it. You are indeed benevolent, but you are also too stupid! Jumping into a well to save others or taking off your own clothes to save others in cold weather is quite good to the ones being saved, but isn't this killing yourself? Are you that kind of man? It is unbecoming of a gentleman to push benevolence to the point of stupidity."

After finishing his words, the old man laughed loudly. Sir Dongguo also laughed. Then the old man gave Sir Dongguo a hand in killing the wolf. After that, they discarded its body by the side of the road and left.

(From Ma Zhongxi 馬中錫 [1446–1512], *Dongtian ji* 東田集)

Shi Yeguang

Shi Yeguang 師夜光 of the Tang dynasty was a native of Jimen.[4] When he was young, he was clever and fond of learning, especially about Buddhism. Consequently, he became a Buddhist monk and lived in his own commandery. Within ten years, he mastered the mysteries of the inner Buddhist scriptures. There was a monk called Huida, whose family was very rich and possessed sizable wealth. Because he admired Yeguang's learning, he became friends with him.

At that time, Emperor Xuanzong was fond of immortality and Buddhism, and he was searching for and recruiting noted monks and magicians (*fangshi*) from all over the country. However, Yeguang was stricken by poverty, so he could not go west to Chang'an; because of this, he was always in a foul mood.

After learning about his situation, Huida gave him 70,000 coins to pay for his travel, and said to him, "I believe that your knowledge and talent are without compare. When the emperor selects eminent men from all over the world, you will certainly stand out among them and receive imperial favor. From then on, you will shed the title of monk and become a minister of the sagacious emperor. For you, this will be as easy as lifting your foot. By then, you will surely have many visitors. I hope you will not forget a friend like me who knows you right before you leave."

Yeguang thanked him and said, "I'm so fortunate to receive your generous support, which enables me to go west to Chang'an. If I can become an official of the fifth rank in the court, that would be a reward for your favor."

When Yeguang arrived in Chang'an, he bribed those around the Princess of the Ninth Fairy[5] to be summoned to bathe in the warm springs. The emperor ordered the eunuch to select ten erudite monks to debate with the magicians. Yeguang was among them. His eloquent remarks on profound Buddhist teachings and explanations of the contentious points were beyond compare. Nobody among the monks dared compete with him.

Amazed by his eloquence, the emperor granted Yeguang a silver seal and red ribbon, appointing him academician of the Four Gates to serve by the emperor's side every day. The emperor also granted him a residence and thousands of gold coins as well as colored silk. He was called "Fortunate Minister."

Consequently, Huida went to Chang'an from Jimen to visit him. Hearing of Huida's arrival, Yeguang felt fairly unhappy, thinking he came to collect the debt. Huida realized what he thought, so he said goodbye to him and returned home.

More than a month after Huida returned, Yeguang was worried that he would come back asking again for the debt to be repaid. So he sent a secret letter to the commander of Jiman, Zhang Tinggui, which said, "Recently, Master Huida arrived in the capital. He slandered you, saying you have been preparing military supplies and have plans to start a revolt. Many people know this. Your loyalty to the court is known to everyone in the realm, but accumulated slander can dissolve gold, so you must be cautious." Tinggui was startled and enraged after reading the letter; immediately he summoned Huida and flogged him almost to death.

A few days later, Yeguang saw Huida suddenly coming into his courtyard, cursing, "I gave you seventy thousand coins to help you to go west to Chang'an. Why did you slander me so that I would be killed unjustly? Why did you wrong me so?" Upon finishing his words, he jumped up to grab Yeguang; after quite some time he disappeared. The children of the Shi family all saw it.

A few days later, Shi Yeguang died.

(Zhang Du 張讀 [fl. 853], *Xuanshi zhi* 宣室志)

The Tradesman of Shanxi

Once, a businessman from Shanxi lived at the Xincheng Inn in the capital. His clothes, servants, and horses were all gorgeous. He also said he would be appointed to a post by donating silver according to the official governmental policy.

One day, a poor old man came to visit him, but the servants refused to inform their master. The old man waited by himself by the gate until he was finally able to see him.

Treating the old man coldly, the businessman offered no courtesy of exchanging greetings except for a cup of tea.

When the old man eventually made known his intention to seek his help, the businessman became angry, saying, "I currently do not even have enough money for my donation; where can I find extra money for you?"

Feeling that he would be treated unfairly, the old man publicly revealed that in the past, when the businessman was poor, he relied on the old man's help to live for ten years.

The old man said, "I also helped him do business with one hundred pieces of gold, and thus he gradually became a wealthy man. Now my term as an official is done, and I wander about destitute. After hearing of his coming, I was so pleased, thinking I would have a new life. I have no extravagant hopes, but only wish to get back the amount that I previously gave him, to help reduce my burden and help me retire to my hometown – that is all I want."

After finishing his words, the old man wept unceasingly. But the businessman looked as if he heard nothing.

Suddenly, a man who also lived in the same inn and who was surnamed Yang bowed to the businessman of Shanxi with his hands folded in front and asked him, "Is what this old man said true?"

Blushing with shame, the businessman said, "It is indeed true; unfortunately, however, I have no money to repay him."

Yang said, "You are going to be an official. You have no worries about where to borrow money from. If someone is willing to lend you one hundred pieces of gold for a year with no interest, would you repay this old man all his money?"

The businessman said reluctantly, "I'm willing to."

"Then just write a receipt for the loan," Yang said, "I have the money."

Forced by the public, the businessman had no choice but to write the receipt.

Upon receiving the receipt, Yang opened a very old box, took out one hundred pieces of gold, and gave them to the businessman from Shanxi. The businessman unhappily handed the gold to the old man.

Further, Yang set up a feast and invited the old man and the businessman to drink together. The old man was very happy, but the businessman left the gathering early.

The old man bid Yang farewell and expressed his gratitude as he was leaving. Yang also left after a few days without a parting message or trace.

When the businessman checked his boxes later, he found he had lost one hundred pieces of gold, but the lock and seal were both untouched – thus, he could not investigate who did it. Furthermore, he lost a sweater made of fox fur, and in his box he also found a pawn ticket worth 2,000 cash, roughly the amount for the cost of the feast. Thus, he realized that Yang was a magician who was just making fun of him.

All the guests who lived in the same inn secretly showed their gratification, leaving the businessman ashamed and depressed. He moved out of the inn, but no one knows where he went.

(Ji Yun 紀昀 [1724–1805],
Yuewei caotang biji 閱微草堂筆記, Chapter 4)

Notes

1 He was a grand master of the state of Jin during the Spring and Autumn period.
2 Zhongshan is located near present-day Ding County in Hebei.
3 Mohists were followers of Mozi 墨子 (400–300 BCE), an ancient philosopher who advocated for impartial love.
4 Jiming was also known as Jizhou 冀州, located where Ji County is today in Hebei.
5 Her name in Chinese is Jiuxian gongzhu 九仙公主; she was the sister of Emperor Xuanzong.

Further Reading

Yang, Lien-Sheng. "The Concept of Pao as a Basis for Social Relations in China." In *Excursions in Sinology*. Cambridge, MA: Harvard University Press, 1969, pp. 3–23.

22 The Heartless Lover

During the Tang dynasty, a large number of young scholars traveled to the capital, Chang'an, to take the imperial examination. As brothels were prevalent in the capital, visiting them became a popular practice of the young scholars. Some of them wasted their money and energy in the brothels and thereby ruined their careers (such as scholar Zheng in the first half of "The Tale of Li Wa"), while some abandoned their lovers after the examination changed their social status (as did Scholar Li in "Prince Huo's Daughter").

Interestingly, all of the heartless Chinese lovers since the Tang are in love stories featuring young scholars and courtesans, reflecting serious concerns over the social issues of the new environment and the morals of the literati.

Of the three tales presented here, two were written during the Song dynasty and one in the Ming dynasty. Yet all share the same theme.

The Tale of Wang Kui

Wang Kui failed in the imperial examination and arrived at Laizhou in Shandong. His friends invited him to visit the Northern Market, wherein a deep alley an extremely beautiful woman poured him a cup of wine, saying, "My name is Guiying. Wine is Heaven's venerated blessing. If you associate with Guiying and drink Heaven's blessing, this is a propitious omen for your passing next year's spring exams."

She then took off her silk scarf and asked Wang Kui to compose a poem which read as follows:

At the feast of Ms. Xie I heard elegant singing,[1]
Who is clinking jade behind the curtains?[2]
A sound has pierced the azure autumn sky,
Several wisps of floating clouds dare not fly.

Guiying said, "Now, you may dedicate yourself wholly to studying every day. As for the expenses of paper, brushes, and your clothing for the four seasons, I will prepare them for you."

DOI: 10.4324/9781003490821-26

After more than a year, there was an imperial edict issued seeking men of worth and ability. Guiying prepared for him the cost of traveling to the capital and brought him to a holy temple overlooking the sea north of the prefecture. Kui vowed, "This man, Kui, and Guiying love each other. I pledge to never betray her. If we are separated while I am still alive, as a god you should kill me."

After arriving at the capital, Kui sent a letter to Guiying which read:

In carving the moon and grinding the clouds I am matchless;[3]
Picking flowers and breaking off willow branches are the affairs of a real man.[4]
Next spring if I leave here with success,
A pair of Mandarin ducks will be raised in one pond.[5]

When the list of the finalists was announced at the imperial palace, he was declared first under Heaven. Kui thought privately, "With such a rank, I will immediately ascend to a distinguished position. But now I am dishonored by a prostitute. Furthermore, I have a strict father at home who will certainly not tolerate my relationship with her." Consequently, he sent no letters to Guiying.

Guiying sent a letter to Kui, which read as follows:

A husband becoming noble and his wife glorified, this is a celebrated matter to last for a thousand years,
Your talent and my beauty are properly matched.

Another letter read:

A girl combs and washes her hair in the capital following trends of fashion,
On seeing this, I suppose, my husband will think of me.
Sooner or later, when you come back to our secluded chamber,
I must let you, following Zhang Chang, draw my new eyebrows.[6]

Another letter read as follows:

The capital is an embroidered place full of music and songs;
My talented husband is now happy and unruly.
Who knows of this haggard woman in her secluded quarter,
Feeling the belt of her spring gown lengthening day by day.[7]

Coincidentally, Kui's father had arranged his marriage with the daughter of the Cui family, and Kui dared not refuse. Consequently, Kui was offered the position of Notary of Administrative Assistant in Xuzhou. Guiying felt happy; she said, "Xuzhou is not far from here, he will certainly send someone to pick me up." She sent her servant to deliver a letter to Kui.

Kui was sitting in the government office and surrounded by officials. He became enraged and refused to accept the letter.

Guiying said, "Now Wang Kui has broken our oath, I should kill him in return." Then she cut her throat with a knife.

When Wang Kui was in the exam office, a person came out beneath a candle – she was Guiying.

Kui asked, "Are you okay?"

Guiying replied, "You have belittled my favors, discarded righteousness, and betrayed your pledge; you made me act like this!"

Kui said, "It was my sin! I will call for a Buddhist monk to recite sutras to release your soul and burn lots of money. Could you spare me?"

Guiying replied, "I only want your life, what good are Buddhist sutras and paper money!"

Kui again stabbed himself with a knife.

"Why are you acting so crazy?" his mother asked.

Kui replied, "I come across my adversary every day. She has been urging me to die."

So Kui's mother called him over to set up an altar and pray. The Daoist Priest Ma Shousu arrived in a dream at an official court at night, where Kui stood beside a woman, their hair tied together. Someone warned him, "Now that you know what has happened, you should not try any further to save him."

Several days later, Kui died.

(From Zeng Zao 曾慥 [1091–1155], *Lei shuo* 類說)

Chen Shuwen

Chen Shuwen was a native of the capital.[8] By specializing in a particular Confucian classic, he passed the national imperial exam and was appointed assistant magistrate of Yixing County in Changzhou. Since his family was poverty-stricken, with no savings for the expense of even a few days, he could not go to assume his post. Shuwen was handsome and graceful, but depressed.

Once, sitting idly at the home of a courtesan, Cui Lanying, Shuwen mentioned that he was appointed to a position but he couldn't assume it because of his poverty. Lanying said to him, "Although I am not your old friend, I have saved one thousand strings of cash and intended for a long time to marry a man. If you don't have a wife, I would like to marry you." Shuwen said, "I am still single. If you truly do marry me, it would be nice." Thus, after only one conversation, their marriage was confirmed.

Shuwen returned home and lied to his wife, "Because of our poverty, we have no expense for traveling, so we cannot live together anymore. I am going to assume the post myself, and from time to time I will support you with my salary." His wife agreed.

Shuwen and Wenying traveled by ship eastward along the Bian River. They were happy to be together, and Shuwen often sent his wife money and souvenirs.

Three years later, his term was out, and they were returning home. While the boat sailed upstream on the Bian River, Shuwen thought himself: Lanying had more than 1,000 strings of cash in her box, and thus she did me a favor. However, she does not know that I have a wife, and my wife does not know she is my new wife. When we return and these two women who have never seen each other meet at my home, they will not only refuse to accept each other but also sue me in court.

Shuwen tried to find a good solution, scheming day and night. Realizing there were no good choices, he thought, if I don't kill her, she will be trouble for me. Thus, he drank wildly with Lanying until they were both drunk. After the first watch, he pushed Lanying into the river together with her servant maiden. Shuwen cried, "My wife fell into the Bian River by accident. Our servant maiden tried to save her but fell in as well." It was dark, and the currents in the Bian River flowed as swift as arrows. The boatmen tried to rescue them from along the riverbank but found neither.

When Shuwen arrived at the capital, he met his wife and discussed their future. Shuwen said, "Our family was originally very poor, but now luckily we have accumulated two to three thousand strings of cash, so I will not be an official anymore." Then he opened a pawnshop. After a year, his family had more than enough to spend, and both he and his wife were well-fed and well-clothed.

When the Winter Solstice Festival arrived, Shuwen visited the Daoist temples with his wife. When they arrived at the Xianguo Temple, two women from among the crowd followed them. Looking back, Shuwen found they strikingly resembled Lanying and her servant maiden. A moment later, the woman approached and greeted Shuwen. With an excuse, Shuwen asked his wife to go home first.

When Shuwen and Lanying sat on the stairs under the corridor side by side, Shuwen asked, "Are you okay?"

Lanying replied, "When I fell into your trap, both of us fell into the river. We embraced each other and were swept about for a couple of *li* before colliding with driftwood. We yelled for help and were saved, so we were able to survive."

Ashamed and regretful, Shuwen wept, "You were very drunk. While standing on the ship, you fell in by accident. The servant maiden tried to save you, so she fell in as well."

Lanying said, "Don't mention what happened in the past, which makes me hate you very much. But now I am alive, so I won't resent you for what you did. I have lived here for a long time in a lane near the fish market by the city wall. You should come to visit me urgently tomorrow. If you don't come, I'll press charges in court and put you in jail, grinding you into pieces and powder."

Shuwen dishonestly promised her, and they parted.

After returning home, Shuwen was worried and terrified. At the entrance of the lane where he lived was a man named Wang Zhenchen, who gathered kids to teach. Shuwen told him everything and asked him what he should do. Zhenchen said, "If you don't go, there will be a lawsuit. You won't benefit from that."

So Shuwen purchased some mutton, fruit, and a jug of wine. Fearful that his family would learn what was going on, he rented a room in another lane to live in and had a child bring his food there.

When he arrived at the lane by the city wall, the woman and her servant maiden were already waiting for him. Shuwen entered her room, but by sunset he had still not come out.

His carrier stood by the door with his carrying pole but heard no words from him. Someone asked him, "Why are you staying here for so long? It is sunset but you still have not left." The carrier said, "I was hired by someone, who is inside this residence and has not yet come out. I'm waiting for him."

Those who lived nearby said, "This is an empty house!" Thereupon, they lit a candle and entered the house together. They found there some cups and plates on the ground, and Shuwen laid face up, with his two arms tied against his back, like an executed prisoner.

When the case was brought to court, Shuwen's wife was summoned to recognize his corpse, but there was no wound on the body. So the judge ordered her to bring the corpse back for burial.

Comments: This occurrence was heard of by everyone in the capital. When you wrong others, if you are not sentenced to death by law, you will be killed by a ghost. The reasoning is crystal clear. However, this is still a wonder!

(Liu Fu, *Qingsuo gaoyi*)

The Faithless Lover

During the Wanli period (1573–1620),[9] Scholar Li of Eastern Zhe 浙, the son of a regional governor,[10] became a visiting student at the Northern Imperial Academy through a donation,[11] where he fell in love with Du Shiniang 杜十娘, a girl from a brothel.[12]

They associated intimately for years until Li's wealth was depleted. The girl's mother became fairly tired of his frequent visits, but the girl and the young man's affections for each other grew even deeper.

The girl's beauty was without compare in all the brothels,[13] and she was also famous for her skills in playing musical instruments, singing, and dancing. Thus, the youth of the capital all regarded her as the symbol of amorous affairs and a life of gaiety.

Vexed by Li's affection for her daughter, the mother tried to provoke him with course speech, but the young man was as polite as before. Later, the mother became harsh in her tone and severe in her expressions. Unable to bear her mother's behavior, the girl pledged to marry Scholar Li.

The mother thought to herself: This girl was not given birth by me, and based on the regulation expunging her name from the list of brothels requires at least several hundred *liang* of gold. Furthermore, I know very well that the young man is now penniless. If I find a way to stump him, making him feel embarrassed, he will probably run away himself. Thus she smacked her palms and told the girl, "If you can urge your man to raise three hundred *liang* of gold for me, I'll let you go anywhere you want."

The girl replied frankly, "Although Mr. Li lives at the inn in poverty, it is still possible for him to raise three hundred *liang* of gold. Considering that it is not easy to collect the gold, if the gold is ready but you break your promise, what can we do?"

Intending to drive Scholar Li into a dead end, the mother insulted them by pointing at the candle wick and saying with a laugh, "As long as Mr. Li can return with the gold in his hand, you can go with your man right away. The candle producing a charred wick predicts that Mr. Li will obtain a girl."

Thereupon, they made their promises to each other and parted.

At midnight, the girl wept in grief. She said to Li, "The cash you have on hand is of course not enough to ransom me. But are you willing to borrow money from your friends and relatives for this urgent situation?"

Pleasantly surprised, Li replied, "Yes, of course! It is not that I was unwilling to do so previously. I just dared not tell you."

The next day, Li intentionally bundled himself up, bidding farewell to his relatives and friends and begging for loans from everyone he visited. His relatives and friends all knew that he had indulged in visiting prostitutes for quite a long time. Now his sudden desire to journey southward to his home seemed doubtful and dubious. Moreover, Li's father, angered at his wandering, had sent letters to cut off his return. Thus, if anyone loans him money, they would neither please his father nor be able to collect the debt. Therefore everyone prevaricated with excuses. Li continued to beg for loans for a month, but in the end he returned to Shiniang with empty hands.

At midnight, the girl sighed, saying, "You could not raise any money? Inside my cotton-padded mattress, there are one hundred and fifty *liang* of gold. They are wrapped in cotton toward the edge. Tomorrow let's ask the servant to secretly take them and give them to my mother respectively. Beyond this, I cannot raise any more money. What should we do?"

Pleasantly startled, the scholar cautiously took the cotton cloth from inside the mattress and left. He took out the gold from the mattress and talked with his relatives and friends. Taking pity on the girl who had set her mind on marrying Li, his relatives and friends resolutely raised gold and gave it to the scholar. However, it was only one hundred *liang*.

The scholar told the girl while weeping, "I have exhausted all my resources. Where can I find the remaining fifty *liang* of gold?"

The girl jumped with joy, saying, "Don't worry! Tomorrow morning I'll get it from my sisters next door."

At the appointed time, she indeed obtained fifty *liang* of gold. She put all the gold together and delivered it to her mother.

When her mother intended to break her pledge, the girl wept with grief, saying, "Previously you ordered my lover to raise three hundred *liang* of gold. Now the gold is ready yet you broke your promise. I'll let the man leave with the gold, and I will kill myself right now!"

Afraid of losing both the girl and the gold, her mother said, "I'll do whatever I promised; however, from your head to your heel, neither an inch of earring nor a foot of silk belongs to you." The girl happily accepted her mother's request.

The next morning, following the young scholar, Shiniang walked out of the door of the brothel in commoner's clothes, with her hair unpinned.

Touched by her situation, all her sisters wept, saying, "Shiniang has been the head of us courtesans, but now with her lover she leaves our courtyard in rags. Isn't this a shame upon us?"

Each of them then gave Shiniang whatever they brought with them. After a moment, she was bedecked in all-new accouterments: hairpins, rings, clothes, and shoes.

The sisters said to each other, "Our older sister and her lover will travel for thousands of *li*, yet they have little luggage." So they jointly gifted them a suitcase. Neither the scholar nor the girl knew what was in it.

At sunset, each of her sisters bid her farewell and parted in tears.

The girl reached the inn where the scholar stayed, but within the four walls it was empty. Being at a loss, the scholar merely stared at his tablet. The girl took off the raw silk fabric from her left arm and tossed him twenty *liang* of Zhuti silver,[14] saying, "Take this as payment for the boat and cart."

The next day, the scholar hired a carriage. They left the town through the Chongwen Gate, reached the Lu River,[15] and paid for a boat. They spent all the silver when the boat arrived. Again, the girl exposed the raw silk fabric on her right arm, took out thirty *liang* of silver, and said, "This can be used for food."

The scholar had experienced frequent mishaps, but he was delighted by his encounter with Shiniang. It was late autumn. He laughed at the flying wild geese for not being coupled and belittled the swimming fish for lacking companionship. As white dews became frost, they pledged to be together until their hair turned gray; they pointed to flaming red maples and likened them to their sincere hearts. How happy they were!

When they reached Guazhou,[16] they left the big ship, rented a small boat, and planned to cross the Yangzi River the next day. That night, the whole river glowed with moonlight, like fluttering white silk reflected in a bright mirror.

The scholar told the girl, "Since we walked out of the gate of the capital, you have never shown your face to the outside world. Tonight we are in our own boat; what do you worry about? Moreover, how can the wind and smoke north of the fortress compare with the river and moon south of the Yangzi River? Why do you keep silent?"

The girl had long covered herself. Now, touched by the interflowing of the river and moon, she felt sad for being distant. Hand in hand, she and the scholar sat at the head of the boat in the moonlight.

The scholar became excited. Raising a wine cup, he asked the girl to sing a song to toast the moon on the river. The girl gently chanted with her sweet and soft voice and suddenly started singing. Even the caw of a crow and the cry of an ape could not be more sorrowful than her song.

In a neighboring boat, there was a young man who was accumulating salt at Weiyang and would be back in Xin'an by the end of the year.[17] He was only about 20 years old and was esteemed as the leader of the frivolous brothel-gang youth. Drunk, he heard the song. He felt that he could fly, but the song stopped suddenly, causing him to be unable to sleep the rest of the night.

At dawn, strong winds and heavy snow blocked the ferry. The man of Xin'an saw the scholar's boat, knowing that inside was the beautiful woman. So he donned a mink cap and a down jacket, acted flirtatiously, and admired his reflection. Upon seeing any movement, he would knock on the side of the boat and sing.

When the scholar lifted the canopy to look around, he saw the thick snowfall. The man from Xin'an suggested to the scholar that he take precautions, and then invited him ashore to have a heart-to-heart talk in a restaurant.

When they drank to their hearts' content, the man of Xin'an asked the young master, "Who sang yesterday night?"

The scholar told him the truth.

Then the man asked further, "After crossing the river, are you going to go home?"

The scholar looked sad and told the man why it was hard for him to return home. Lingering over the wine cup, he disclosed all the truth without reason, "The beauty invited me to wander around the mountains and rivers in the Wu and Yue."

The man of Xin'an sternly said to the young master, "What you are doing is like traveling through fragrant grasses while carrying peaches and plums. Yet didn't you hear that when bright pearls fall upon the ground, men of strength will vie with each other for them? Besides, men south of the Yangzi River are extremely good with romantic affairs: whenever one loves a woman, he dares not begrudge his life. Even in my mind, this idea emerges from time to time. Furthermore, while a beauty like her is talented, her conduct is unpredictable. How do you know that she is not merely using you like a ladder to secretly make some upcoming appointment? In that case, the mist-covered waves of Zhenze,[18] the wind and waves of Qiantang,[19] and fish bellies and shark teeth would all form your tomb. I have also heard the saying: Who is dearer between your father and a beauty? What is more urgent between pursuing pleasure and avoiding calamity? I hope you will think about these questions carefully."

With a worried frown, the scholar asked, "Then what can I do?"

The man of Xin'an said, "I have a perfect plan, which fits your case extremely well. But I do not think you will be able to do it."

The young master asked, "What is the plan?"

The man replied, "If you can part with your lover, of whom you are now tired, I would willingly offer a thousand *liang* of gold for your birthday, though I'm not smart and capable. After obtaining a thousand *liang* of gold, you can return home to report to your respected father; you would have no worries on your way by getting rid of this beauty. I hope you will seriously consider this proposition!"

The scholar had been wandering alone for years. Though the companionship of lovers should last until death, his situation resembled a swallow nesting on a curtain, and it pushed him into a dilemma. Like a goat whose claws are hitched in a fence or a fox whose tail dipped into the water before crossing a river, he doubted what he was doing. Thinking of Flying Swallow, Empress Zhao of Han, who killed numerous princes with her sister,[20] and Baosi, the consort of Emperor You of Zhou, who was said to be born of dragon saliva and ruined the Zhou dynasty, he felt as if he was a forlorn soul, crying in a dream. Thus he lowered his head, contemplated for a while, and then declined the suggestion by saying that he would go back to talk with the woman. Hand in hand, he disembarked with the man of Xin'an, and both returned their boats.

Having trimmed the wick, the girl was waiting for the scholar to have a few drinks. Turning away his eyes several times, the scholar intended to talk to her but kept silent instead. They slept together, sharing the same quilt. At midnight, the scholar cried sadly.

The girl sat up suddenly, held him in her arms, and said, "I have lived together with you for nearly three years. We have traveled several thousand *li* yet have never been sad. Now we are crossing the Yangzi River, and we should be happy for our long-lasting harmonious union. I don't understand why you suddenly show me a face like this. Perhaps this means that you are going to part with me, but why?"

The scholar poured out his words together with his tears, and he became saddened by his deep feelings for her. Having poured out everything that was on his mind, the scholar continued to shed tears.

The girl let go of him and asked, "Who made such a plan for you? This person is a great hero! You get a thousand *liang* of gold and can see your parents; I would follow a man and not be a burden upon you. An affair derives from feelings and yet stops within the bounds of ritual and righteousness.[21] This is great! Both of us would get what we want. But where is the gold?"

The scholar replied, "Since I did not know what you would think, the gold is still in that man's possession."

The girl said, "Tomorrow, please go quickly to promise him that you agree to the arrangement. But transferring a thousand *liang* of gold is no small event. I will not go into that man's boat until the gold is in your box."

Midnight had just passed, but she arose to apply formal makeup, saying, "Today's makeup is for seeing off the old and welcoming the new, it cannot be informal." When her makeup was done, it was almost dawn.

The man of Xin'an had already moved his boat next to the scholar's. Hearing of the message from the girl, he was greatly pleased and said, "Please show me your box as proof."

The girl delightedly said to scholar Li, "Give it to him." Then she asked the man of Xin'an to transfer the betrothal fee to Li's boat and weigh it to make sure it is the exact amount.

Thereupon the girl walked out from the middle of the boat. Standing by the side of the boat, she told the man of Xin'an, "In the box you previously took there is Scholar Li's passport. Please bring it back and return it to him immediately."

The man of Xin'an followed her order.

The girl asked Scholar Li to pull out a box that was filled with colorful jade phoenixes worth several hundred *liang* of gold. The girl threw them all into the river. Scholar Li, the frivolous man from Xin'an, and the people on both boats, all started yelling loudly at her.

The girl asked the scholar to pull out another box, filled with jade bird feathers, bright earrings, jade flutes, and gold pipes worth several thousand *liang* of gold. Again she cast them into the river.

Then she asked Scholar Li to take out a leather bag, filled with antiques of old jade and purple gold, all invaluable rare treasures. She also cast them into the river.

Finally, she asked the scholar to pull out a flat case filled with a handful of luminous pearls. At this moment everyone in both boats was terrified, and the sounds of yelling disturbed and attracted people of the city.

When the girl was about to cast away the pearls, Scholar Li felt great regret. He embraced the legs of Shiniang and tried to stop her while weeping. Even the man of Xin'an came to persuade her.

The girl pushed the scholar away and spat in the face of the man of Xin'an, cursing, "The song you heard stirred your lust, and then you wagged your tongue like a warbler. Despite the spirits and Heaven, you made the bottle drop into the well by cutting the rope, causing me to die unjustly.[22] I hate that I am merely a weak woman and cannot draw my knife to fight you, you crude man.

"However, by coveting money, you came to hold me by force. How can your behavior be differentiated from a dog vying for bones after foolishly following others? After I die, if my soul is numinous, I'll sue you before the spirits and deprive you of your mortal life in no time.

"Moreover, by hiding my tracks and trusting my sisters to store rare treasures, I intended to help Scholar Li return to see his parents. Now he is unable to be with me in the end.[23] I now expose everything publicly because I want everyone to know that Scholar Li has eyes, yet fails to see.

"For the sake of Scholar Li, I had shed tears until my eyes were dry and my united souls were scattered numerous times.[24] Luckily, we achieved some success. Unexpectedly, however, he quickly forgot our joining hands[25] and neglected the harmony between us and suddenly succumbed to the glib tongue.[26] Like being afraid of walking because of too much dew on the road,[27] he suddenly abandoned me, as if I was nothing but leftovers. Seeing that he covets the remnant jewelry and intends to gather the water that has been poured out, how can I not feel ashamed if I allow him again to lead me by the nose?

"My life is over! The brightness of the East Sea coast comes from the gathering of sands, and the height of Huashan, the sacred mountain of the west,[28] owes itself to the accumulation of tiny particles of earth and stone. What a pity that our accumulated love stopped in such a way! When will it end if I am tangled in it?"

Thereupon, the spectators on the boats and the riverbank all shed tears, cursing Scholar Li as an ingrate. The girl, holding the bright pearls, threw herself into the water and died.

At that time, all the witnesses intended to beat the man of Xin'an and Scholar Li. Both Scholar Li and the man of Xin'an hoisted their sails and fled. Nobody knew where they went.

Alas! This young lady deserves to be called an unyielding woman by Zizheng.[29] Even a virgin deep inside the boudoir could not be more chaste than her!

(Song Maocheng 宋楙澄 [1569–1622], *Jiuyue ji* 九籥集)

Note: This is from my 2022 rendition in Victor Mair and Zhenjun Zhang, *Ming Dynasty Tales* (London: Bloomsbury Academic, 2022), 143–52.

Notes

1 *Xie shi* 謝氏, also known as *Xie niang* 謝娘, refers to sing-song girls (courtesans) in traditional Chinese literature, especially poems. *Xie niang* also refers to talented women.
2 *Jia yu* 戛玉, or "clinking the jade," refers to clear and sweet singing.
3 *Zhuoyue moyun* 琢月磨雲, or "carving the moon and grinding the clouds," refers to writing, which is associated with using an inkstone. Both *yue* and *yun* were considered raw materials for inkstones.
4 For *panhua zheliu* 攀花折柳, "picking flowers and breaking off willow branches," and *Zuiweng tanlu* reads *duhua zhanliu* 都花占柳, "possessing flowers and occupying willows," both refer to leading a life of debauchery by being given to beautiful women.
5 Mandarin ducks symbolize lovers in Chinese culture. Here they refer to the poet and his lover.
6 Zhang Chang 張敞 (d. 48BC) was the governor of the capital (Jingzhao yin) under Emperor Xuan of Han 漢宣帝. He was noted for drawing eyebrows in the new style for his wife, which became a symbol of marital harmony.
7 This line indicates that because she became thinner, it seemed her belt became longer.
8 The capital referred to here is Bian of Northern Song, where Kaifeng in Henan is located today.
9 The only reign period of Shenzong 神宗 of the Ming, Zhu Yijun 朱翊鈞 (r. 1573–1620).
10 *Fannie* 藩臬, *fansi* 藩司, and *niesi* 臬司 refer to the provincial governor (*buzhengshi* 布政使) and judicial commissioner (*anchashi* 按察使) during the Ming and Qing dynasties.
11 After the capital of the Ming Empire was moved from Nanjing to Beijing in the eighteenth year of Yongle's reign (1420), the Imperial Academy was divided into two. The one in Beijing was called Beiyong 北雍, the Northern Imperial Academy. According to the governmental policy, a scholar could be eligible to study at the Imperial Academy by donating money or grain to the government.
12 Jiaofang 教坊, or the "Institute of Music," also refers to brothels during and after the Song and Yuan dynasties.
13 *Pingkang* 平康, or "ward," in the capital Chang'an of the Tang dynasty was filled with brothels. So much so that in later times Pingkang became another name for brothels.
14 Zhuti 朱提 is known now as Zhaotong 昭通, a city in Yunnan; it was known for producing high quality silver.
15 The Lu 潞 River refers to the northern canal flowing through the east suburbs of Beijing.
16 Guazhou is located on the north bank of the Yangzi River, south of present-day Yangzhou in Jiangsu.
17 Weiyang 維揚 is located in a part of what is present-day Yangzhou. Xin'an 新安 was located where She County 歙县 in Anhui is today.
18 Zhenze 震澤, or Lake Tai, lies between Jiangsu and Zhejiang.
19 The Qiantang River springs from the borders of Anhui and Jiangxi and passes Hangzhou before flowing into the East Sea.
20 Empress Zhao refers to the second empress of Emperor Cheng 成 of Han 漢 (r. 32 BC–7 BC). Zhao was known for her beauty and skilled dancing, and she was so skinny that when she walked in small steps, it seems like she shook like a soft, weak branch in one's hand. The biography of Empress Zhao states that both Empress Zhao and her sister were childless even though they had monopolized the favor of the emperor for over ten years. Both history and legend have a long record detailing her and her sister Zhao Hede's 趙 合德 (d. 7 BC) persecution of palace women impregnated by the emperor and of the babies born to them. See *Han shu*, 97b.3988–99; "Zhao Feiyan biezhuan" (Supplementary Biography of Empress Zhao). My English translation of this tale can be found in Zhenjun Zhang and Jing Wang, *Song Dynasty Tales: A Guided Reader* (Singapore: World Scientific Publishing, 2017), pp. 1–31.

21 *Fahu qing, zhihu liyi* 發乎情，止乎禮義, meaning "it derives from feelings and yet stops within the bounds of ritual and righteousness," is a saying from the "The Great Preface" (*Shi daxu* 詩大序) on the "Changed Airs" (*bianfeng* 變風) of *The Classic of Odes* (*Shijing* 詩經). The preface was written during the late Western Han dynasty. It later became a Confucian moral code for people. The translation here is from Victor H. Mair, ed., *The Columbia Anthology of Traditional Chinese Literature* (New York: Columbia University Press, 1994), p. 122.

22 Guyinxuebi 骨殷血碧 (dark red bone and blue blood) indicates an unjust or wrongful death.

23 Xuwobuzu 慉我不卒 is from the "Riyue" 日月 poem in the "Beifeng" 邶風 section of *The Classic of Odes*; it means, literally, "loving me but not to the end."

24 Chinese believe that in one's body there are three souls, which will all be scattered when one is startled.

25 Xieshou 携手, meaning "join hands," is from "Beifeng" poem of the "Beifeng" section in *The Classic of Odes*: "Ye who love and regard me, let's join hands and go together" 惠而好我，携手同行. See James Legge, ed., *The Chinese Classics* (Hong Kong: Hong Kong University Press, 1960), p. 67.

26 *Shenghuang* 笙簧, or "reeds of a panpipe," refers to a glib tongue or cunning talk. The "Qiaoyan" 巧言 poem in the "Xiaoya" 小雅 section of *The Classic of Odes* says, "Their artful words, like organ-tongues/Show how unblushing are their faces" 巧言如簧，顏之厚矣. Legge, *The Chinese Classics*, p. 342.

27 *Wei xing duolu* 畏行多露, or "being afraid of walking because of too much dew on the road," is from "Xing lu" 行露 in the "Zhaonan" 昭南 section of *The Classic of Odes*. It states, "Might I not have walked there in the early dawn? But I said there was too much dew on the path" 岂不夙夜？谓行多露. Legge, *The Chinese Classics*, p. 27.

28 Huashan is located 120 kilometers west of Xi'an, Shaanxi.

29 Zizheng 子政 is the courtesy name of Liu Xiang 劉向 (77–6 BCE), a Han dynasty scholar and the author of the *Lienüzhuan* 列女傳 (Biographies of Exemplary Women).

Further Reading

Zhang, Zhenjun and Jing Wang. *Song Dynasty Tales: A Guided Reader*. Singapore: World Scientific, 2017.

23   The Dedicated Lover

Contrary to the heartless lovers, the dedicated lover is another popular theme in Chinese literature and culture.

The great playwright Tang Xianzu (1550–1616) says in the preface to his masterpiece, *Peony Pavilion*,

> Love is of source unknown, yet it grows ever deeper. The living may die of it, [but] by its power the dead live again. Love is not love at its fullest if one who lives is unwilling to die for it, or if it cannot restore to life one who has so died.

(Cyril Birch)

Although Tang was only talking about love in the play, his words accurately summarize the characteristics of devoted lovers in Chinese love stories. All of the devoted lovers presented here are from love stories depicting a marriage of life and death.

Han Ping and His Wife

Han Ping, an attendant of Prince Kang of Song (420–479), took Miss He as his wife. She was beautiful, so Prince Kang took her by force. Han Ping held a grudge. Then Prince Kang imprisoned him and sentenced him to be a city wall builder with guard duty.

Ping's wife secretly sent him a letter with an abstruse message: "The rain pours, the river is broad, and the water deep. Take special care when the sun rises!" Not long afterward, the prince obtained the letter and showed it to the people around him. But nobody understood it. Su He, one of his vassals, answered, " 'The rain pours' indicates that she is worrying and misses her husband; 'the river is broad and water deep' means that they cannot contact each other; 'take special care when the sun rises' indicates that she is determined to die."

A little while later, Han Ping committed suicide. Then his wife secretly made her clothes rotted. When the prince climbed to a terrace together with her, she threw herself down from the terrace. The attendants tried to hold her back, but her clothes could not bear her weight; thus she fell to her death. She had left a letter attached to her belt, which read, "Your Majesty benefits from my life, yet I benefit from my death. I wish for my corpse to be buried together with Ping's." The prince

DOI: 10.4324/9781003490821-27

became angry. He had their neighbors bury them separately, their tombs facing each other.

The prince said, "As husband and wife you loved each other constantly. If you can let your tombs join together, I will not stop you." Just overnight, big trees grew on top of both tombs; after ten days, they became so big that they could fill the span of a man's arms. The trunks of the trees bent close to each other, the roots crossed below, and branches crossed above. A pair of Mandarin ducks, male and female, always perched on the trees from morning to night. They crossed their necks and sang with grief. Their songs were so moving.

Taking pity on them, the people of the state of Song named the trees "lovesick trees." The word "lovesick" originated here. In modern Suiyang, there is a place named after Han Ping, and the song about him and his wife is still sung today.

(Gan Bao, *Soushen ji*, Chapter 11)

The Girl Who Sells Face Powder

There was once a very wealthy family that had only a single son. The parents doted on the boy and were excessively indulgent with him.

Once, when the boy was wandering in the market, he saw a beautiful young girl selling face powder. He fell in love with her but found no means to express his feelings. Pretending to buy face powder, he went to the market every day. Upon purchasing the powder, he would leave without a word.

Gradually, the girl became deeply suspicious.

The next day, when the boy came again, she asked, "After buying this powder, what are you going to do with it?"

The boy replied, "I love you, and I didn't dare tell you, but I always want to see you. By buying this powder, I can see your lovely face. That is all."

The girl became somewhat upset but was also deeply touched. Thus, she promised him a private meeting the following evening.

That evening, the boy laid quietly in his room, waiting for the girl. Once it was dark, the girl arrived as expected. The boy was extremely overjoyed. He held the girl's arm and cried, "My long-cherished wish will now be fulfilled!" He jumped in excitement – and died.

The girl was seized with anxiety and fear, not knowing what to do. She fled, returning the next morning to the powder store.

At breakfast time, the boy's parents were surprised that he still had not risen. When they went to have a look, they found him dead. As his corpse was about to be placed in a coffin and brought to the graveyard, they opened his bamboo suitcase and found more than one hundred packets of face powder in different sizes, all piled together.

The mother of the boy exclaimed, "It must be this face powder that killed my son!" Then they went to the market and purchased face powder everywhere they found it.

Upon reaching the girl, they found that her method of tamping the powder into packets matched what they had seen previously at home. Thus, they seized the girl, demanding, "Why did you kill our son?"

The girl sobbed and told them what had happened. The parents did not believe her, so they brought a lawsuit against her in court. The girl said, "Why should I still care to continue living! I beg to let me see his body once more to mourn for him." The magistrate granted her request.

She went directly to the boy's home. Embracing the corpse, she wailed, "I'm so unlucky that things turned out like this! If after death your soul is still numinous, what regret could I possibly have!?"

Suddenly, the boy revived. The girl told him everything that had happened. They subsequently became husband and wife, and their sons and grandsons proved very prosperous.

(Liu Yiqing, Youming lu)

Cui Hu

Cui Hu,[1] a native of Boling,[2] was highly intelligent and had great features. However, he was withdrawn and lofty by nature and did not get along easily with others.

He traveled to the capital to participate in the imperial civil service examination but failed.

On the day of the Qingming Festival,[3] he went sightseeing alone in the capital's southern suburbs. There, he noticed a family's country estate which encompassed approximately one *mu* of the surrounding land. Flowers, grass, and trees grew dense and luxuriant within, so tranquil and quiet as if no one lived there.

Cui Hu knocked for quite a while before a girl peered out through the crack in the door, asking, "Who is it?"

Cui Hu told her his name, and added, "I came here on a spring tour of the outskirts by myself. Having drunk some wine, I am very thirsty. Would you please give me a cup of water to drink?"

The girl retreated inside and shortly after returned carrying a cup of water. She opened the door, brought out a couch, and then invited him to sit. Yet she leaned against the slanted branch of a small peach sapling and remained on her feet for a long time. Her attitude towards Cui Hu was very solicitous. Her appearance was charming, and her demeanor bewitching, much more attractive than he expected.

Cui Hu spoke to and teased her. She did not reply. The two of them stared at each other for a long, long time.

Afterward, Cui Hu rose and took his leave. She saw him off to the gate seeming unable to control her emotions, then turned and went back inside. Cui Hu also reluctantly parted and returned home.

From then on, Cui Hu did not go there again for a long time.

During the Qingming Festival the following year, Cui Hu suddenly missed the girl. Unable to suppress his feelings, he went there directly to search for her.

The door and courtyard appeared the same as they had the year before, but the door was padlocked. So Cui Hu wrote a poem on the left door panel:

On this day last year, through this very door,
Peach blooms augmented one rosy face;

The face has now vanished – I know not where,
Blossoms laugh in spring's breeze as before.

A few days later, he found himself in the capital's southern outskirts by chance and accordingly went to seek the girl again. There, he heard someone crying behind the door and knocked on the door to inquire about it.

An old man walked out and demanded, "Are you Cui Hu?"

Cui Hu answered, "I am."

Weeping, the old man cried, "You have murdered my daughter!"

Cui Hu, shocked and frightened, did not know what to say.

The old man went on, "My daughter had already reached the age to have her hair pinned up – fifteen – and was further learned in literature. However, she had not yet been betrothed to anyone. Since last year, she has frequently been distracted, seeming as if she had lost something. Over the last few days, I went out with her and upon returning discovered characters on the left panel of the door. After she read the poem, she went inside and not long after fell ill. She did not eat for several days and just died. I am advanced in age and have only this one daughter. I hadn't married her off previously because I had planned to find a good son-in-law so that I would have someone to rely on in my old age. But now she has unfortunately died. Thus, is it not you who killed her?" He tugged at Cui Hu, weeping in anguish.

Cui Hu was also grief-stricken. He asked to be allowed into the room to mourn for her.

After entering the room, he beheld the girl laying on the bed, who looked as if she was still alive. Cui Hu lifted up her head, rested his head on her thigh, and weeping while chanting, "I am here. I am here!"

Soon, the girl opened her eyes. After quite some time, she revived.

Ecstatic, the elderly man married her to Cui Hu.

(From Meng Qi 孟棨, *Benshi shi* 本事詩)

Notes

1 *Cui Hu* 崔护 (772–846) was a Tang dynasty poet.
2 Boling 博陵 was located where present-day Dingzhou is in Hebei.
3 This is also known in English as Tomb Sweeping Day.

Further Readings

Hsieh, Daniel. *Love and Women in Early Chinese Fiction*. Hong Kong: The Chinese University Press, 2008.
Li, Wai-Yee. *Enchantment and Disenchantment: Love and Illusion in Chinese Literature*. Princeton, NJ: Princeton University Press, 1993.

24　The Predestined Couple

Predestination, or *mingding* 命定, is an old Chinese religious concept originating from the idea of *tianming* 天命 (the Mandate of Heaven) and expressed by *ming* 命 (fate) and *dingshu* 定數 (fixed number). As a theme, it appeared in the Six Dynasties *zhiguai* but became much more popular in the Tang dynasty tales and is exemplified in the romantic context by the predestined couple.

The reason why this theme became prevalent was, as Karl Kao points out, very likely due to the complementary Buddhist doctrine of karma. Predetermined marriage is often described with Buddhist terminology, such as *yuan* 緣 (a predestined relationship).[1] As a later proverb goes, "If *yuan* exists, two people who live one thousand *li* apart will meet each other; but without *yuan*, even if brought face-to-face, they will never know one another" 有緣千里來相會，無緣對面不相識.

The three stories here depict such marvelous marriages.

The Inn of Betrothal

Wei Gu of Duling[2] lost his father when he was very young. He wanted to marry as early as possible but efforts had come to naught numerous times; he was always turned down each time he proposed marriage to someone.

During the second year of the Yuanhe period (806–821), he was on his way to visit Qinghe,[3] and lodged in an inn south of Songcheng,[4] where a guest proposed that he marry the daughter of Pan Fang, the prior adjutant of Qinghe. They arranged to meet in front of the gate of the Longxing Monastery west of the inn before daybreak the next day.

Eagerly anticipating the meeting, Wei Gu arrived while the slanting moon was still bright. He found an old man sitting on the stairs leaning against a bag, facing the moon while reading a book.

Wei Gu stepped forward while glancing at the book and found he could not understand the words in it, which were not in Chinese in any style, nor Sanskrit. Therefore, he said, "Uncle! What kind of book are you perusing? I studied very hard when I was young. I thought that I know all the words in the world, and I can even read the Sanskrit of the western states. But I have never seen this book. What it is?"

DOI: 10.4324/9781003490821-28

The old man replied, "This is not a book of this world. How are you able to read it?"

"It is not a book of this world?" Wei Gu asked, "What book is it?"

"A book of the netherworld," the old man answered.

"Why is a man of the netherworld here?" Wei Gu asked.

"You came too early. It is not me who should not be here. All the officials of the netherworld are in charge of human affairs. How could they not walk among them? Of all the passersby at this moment, half are men and the other half are ghosts. Naturally, it is hard for one to differentiate them."

Wei Gu asked, "Then, what affairs are you in charge of?"

"The records of all the marriages under the world," the old man replied.

Pleased, Wei Gu said, "I was orphaned when I was a child and hoped to marry early to beget more children. Over the last ten years, I have tried in many ways to find a wife but never had my wish fulfilled. Today, I have an appointment with someone here to propose a marriage with the daughter of Adjutant Pan. Will I succeed?"

The old man answered, "Not yet. If you are not matched by fate, you will not succeed even if you remove your official cap and sash to seek marrying with the daughter of a butcher or a gambler, let alone marrying the daughter of an adjutant of a prefecture! Your wife is now only three years old. At the age of seventeen, she will enter the gate of your home."

Wei Gu asked, "What is in your bag?"

The old man replied, "Only red strings that are used to tie the feet of a couple. When they are born, I will secretly tie their feet with this string. Even if they are from feuding families, or if one is noble and the other of humble birth, or if one serves as an official in the far corners of the earth, or if their homes are as far apart as Wu and Chu, after being bound with this string, none of them will escape the other in the end. Your foot has been tied together with hers. What good is there in seeking another woman?"

Wei Gu asked, "Where is my wife? What is the profession of her family?"

The old man replied, "She is the daughter of a vegetable vendor, the old lady Chen, who lives north of this inn."

Wei Gu asked, "May I see her?"

The old man answered, "Lady Chen often comes with the girl in her arms to sell vegetables in the market. If you follow me, I'll show you."

After daybreak, the matchmaker Wei Gu was expecting did not show up. The old man rolled up his book, took his bag, and left.

Wei Gu ran after the old man and arrived at the vegetable market. There came an old lady with one eye blinded, holding her three-year-old daughter. Both of them looked extremely shabby. The old man pointed at them and said, "This is your wife."

"Can I kill her?" Wei Gu asked angrily.

The old man said, "This girl is destined to enjoy the emolument of office and the title as an honorable lady because of her son. How could you kill her?"

Suddenly, the old man disappeared.

Wei Gu cursed, "You damned old ghost! How are you so absurd? I'm from a noble family, so I must take a wife from a proper family. Even if I do not, I can still choose a beauty from among the courtesans as my concubine, or as my wife if I deign to give her the status. How could I marry the humble daughter of an old blind lady?"

He sharpened a dagger and gave it to his servant, saying, "You are always capable. If you kill that girl for me, I'll give you ten thousand coins."

The servant replied, "Sure."

The next day, the servant went to the market with the dagger hidden up his sleeve. He stabbed the little girl in the crowd and then ran away. The whole market erupted in chaos. Wei Gu and his servant fled.

Wei Gu asked, "Did you get her?"

The servant replied, "I tried to stab her heart, but unfortunately only hit the middle of her eyebrows."

Afterward, Wei Gu repeatedly attempted to find a wife but never succeeded.

Fourteen years later, benefiting from the privilege of his late father, he was appointed the administrative adjutant of Xiangzhou. The governor, Wang Tai, assigned him to be the substitute revenue manager, dealing exclusively with the legal cases. Wang considered him decent and had his daughter marry him.

The governor's daughter was 16 to 17 years of age and was very beautiful. Wei Gu was very pleased with her, but she always put a beauty mark between her eyebrows, which she never removed even when bathing or sitting leisurely.

After a year, Wei Gu grew suspicious. Suddenly recalling the servant's words about his hitting the middle of the little girl's eyebrows, he urged her to tell him the truth.

His wife said in tears, "I am not the governor's daughter, but his niece. My father was the magistrate of Songcheng but died before his term was over when I was still an infant. Soon, my mother and brother died respectively, too. I then lived with my wet nurse, Lady Chen, in a village south of Songcheng. The village was close to the market, so she supported us two by selling vegetables. Lady Chen loved me. She could not bear leaving me even for a moment. When I was three years old, she was walking in the market with me in her arms. Suddenly, I was stabbed by a crazy bandit. The scar is still there, so I cover it with a beauty mark. Seven to eight years ago, my uncle assumed his post in Lulong, so I was able to go live with him. It was an act of kindness to let me marry you as his daughter."

Wei Gu asked, "Was Lady Chen one-eyed?"

His wife said, "Yes. Why did you know?"

"I sent the man who stabbed you," Wei Gu said. He then exclaimed, "What wonder! This is our fate."

Then he told his wife everything, and they respected each other even more.

Later, his wife gave birth to a son they named Kun, who was subsequently appointed governor of Yanmen, and she was granted a title by the emperor as the Grand Lady of the Taiyuan Commandery. By this, they understood that the hidden fate is unalterable.

When the magistrate of Songcheng heard of their story, he named the inn "The Inn of Betrothal."

(Li Fuyan, *Xu Xuanguai lu*)

Li Xingxiu's Second Marriage

Li Xingxiu, the late grand master of remonstrance, married the daughter of Wang Zhongshu, the investigation commissioner of Jiangxi, who was chaste and virtuous. Xingxiu respected her as if she were his guest. Lady Wang had a little sister, whom she often brought with her even after marrying Li. Xingxiu also loved her dearly and treated her like his own sister.

During the Yuanhe period (806–820), a nobleman proposed marriage with Li Yong, the area commander of Huainan, while their clansmen were all gathered in Luoyang, the eastern capital. At that time, Xingxiu had just resigned from the post of retainer of Xuanzhou and had lodged in Luoyang. When the wedding day was set, the Li family insisted that Xingxiu be the master of ceremonies.

After the ceremony finished in the evening, Xingxiu fell lightly asleep. He dreamed of his second wedding, in which the bride was the younger sister of his wife. He awoke with a startle and was fairly disgusted. He ordered his servants to quickly drive him back home.

Upon entering the gate of his house, he found his wife had just risen, weeping with her arms around her knees. Since their old servant was harsh and unreasonable by nature and thus often disobeyed Lady Wang, Xingxiu assumed that his wife was displeased again by the old servant.

"Is it that old slave again?" he cursed, intending to flog him.

As he traced the causes of Lady Wang's displeasure, everyone in his family said, "In the kitchen, the old servant said that he had a dream at dawn in which his master married another girl from the Wang family."

Since the old servant's dream matched his own, Xingxiu felt even more disgusted. So he comforted Lady Wang, saying, "How could you believe in a dream of that old servant?"

Not long afterward, Lady Wang died of illness. Sir Wang was the governor of Wuxing at the time. When news of his daughter's death arrived, he grieved and sent a letter to Xingxiu, advising him to consider remarrying. With his deep sorrow for his deceased wife fresh, Xingxiu resolutely refused his father-in-law's proposal.

Wei Sui, the assistant of the Palace Library, was the son of the deceased governor of Jiangling, Wei Boyu. He could recognize talented men. Because of this he often predicted things correctly. Once, he told Xingxiu out of the blue, "Palace Censor Li, why are you thinking so deeply of your deceased wife? If you want to see your wife, why don't you ask the old Wang at Chousang?"

For the two to three years afterward, Sir Wang repeatedly and tactfully entrusted his little daughter to Li Xingxiu. But Xingxiu resolutely refused.

The year that Xingxiu was appointed censor of the East Censorate, Li Jie from Bian removed his commander, so the emperor dispatched the troops in Xuzhou and

Haozhou to attack Li Jie. Messengers rushed back and forth on the roads, and many horses were looted.

Xingxiu got out of the Tongguan Pass slowly on a horse and stopped at the Chousang Inn. Hearing that several imperial envoys had arrived earlier, he decided to lodge there.

It grew dark outside as he reached the inn. There he saw an old man approach from the east as people grabbed his clothes, not allowing him to leave. Xingxiu asked the reason for their clamoring. The innkeeper said, "Old Wang is good at fate books and face-reading, so he is respected by the locals."

Suddenly, Xingxiu realized what Wei Sui's words meant. So he secretly summoned the old man and told him what had been on his mind. The old man said, "If you, the eleventh child of Li family, want to see your deceased wife, tonight is fine." He asked Xingxi to dismiss his attendants and wear a pair of sandals. Led by him, Xingxiu walked along a path, entered an earthen mountain, and climbed a hill several dozen feet high. From there he faintly saw the forest.

The old man stopped by the roadside and told Xingxiu, "Eleventh child, call Miaozi under the trees, and someone will respond. When they do, say, 'Tell the ninth lady, tonight I'll bring Miaozi to see my deceased wife.'"

Following the old man's instructions, Xingxiu called for Miaozi in the forest. A voice answered as expected. Then he repeated the old man's words.

After a while, a girl about 15 came out. "The Ninth Lady sent me to accompany you." She then broke a bamboo reed to ride on, which Xingxiu saw was swift as a horse. In a moment, she broke another bamboo reed for Xingxiu. He galloped side by side with the girl, so close they seemed to touch each other.

After going southwest for several dozen *li*, they suddenly reached a place with a splendid palace. After they went forward and passed a gated hall, the girl said, "Just go straight north along the west porch. The second yard from the south is the residence of your worthy wife. No matter what you see inside, you must pass quickly and do not be scared." Xingxiu kept that in his mind.

Walking along the west porch, he saw the bright light under the orange canopy with red lining, and inside it, several hundred eyeballs an inch or so in diameter were scattered about. Following the girl's instructions, Xingxiu rushed to the north porch. When he arrived at the second yard, Xingxiu saw what he lost over ten years before. A maiden came out, bowed to Xingxiu, and offered him a couch, saying, "Please sit. The lady will be with you shortly."

Xingxiu was suffering from an illness in his lung. Lady Wang prepared boiled honey locust soup for him. He had rarely seen this soup since the death of Lady Wang. Now the maiden held the soup for Xingxiu to drink. It tasted the same as when his wife made it. Before he finished speaking, the lady walked out quickly. They looked at each other through their tears.

When Xingxiu was about to express how much he had grief during their long separation, Lady Wang stopped him and said, "Now I'm going on a different path than you – one is dark; one is bright. I am truly reluctant to do so and bring calamity upon you. If you have not forgotten our past marriage, marry my little sister and take good take of her. Then everything you could do for me is done. The only reason why I want to meet you is for this request."

Immediately after Lady Wang finished her words, they heard a girl urgently call from outside, "Li the Eleventh, come out quickly!"

Xingxiu hurriedly walked out, but the girl started berating him anyway. "You down-at-heel stupid pedant! Hurry up and go back!" They returned together by riding on the bamboo reeds again.

After a moment, they arrived where they had departed from, they found the old man slept using a stone as a pillow. Hearing Xingxiu's arrival, he quickly stood up and asked, "Are you unhappy with the meeting?" Xingxiu answered, "Yes." The old man said, "You should thank the Ninth Lady for sending someone to accompany you." Xingxiu also did as he was told.

Exhausted, Xingxiu asked, "What is this place?"

The old man said, "On this hill there is a temple to the divine and effective Mother of Nine Sons."

The old man walked ahead and led Xingxiu to the inn where he was staying, where the light was bright upon the wall and the horses chewed grasses as they did before. The servants were exhausted and quickly fell asleep, while the old man bid him farewell and left. Muddleheaded, Xingxiu vomited the honey locust soup that he had drunk.

Sir Wang had by then moved to garrison Jiangxi. Xingxiu continued his bond with the Wang family by marrying their youngest daughter, and later he was appointed grand master of remonstrance.

(Wen Yu 温畬, *Xu Mingding lu* 續命定錄)

The Record of the Drifting Red Leaf

During the Xizong reign period (874–888) of the Tang dynasty,[5] a Confucian scholar named Yu You was once taking an evening stroll along a broad road in the imperial city.[6] The season was late fall, when all things on earth were withering and falling in the autumnal wind; it was about sunset, increasing his sorrow as a traveler.

Watching the Royal Canal, Yu You saw drifting leaves continuously flowing down. He approached the canal to wash his hands.[7] A while later, he saw one fallen leaf a little larger than the others. From a distance, it appeared that there were traces of ink on it. The floating red leaf drifted leisurely and seemed to bear endless affection from afar. Yu You picked it up, examined it, and found a quatrain written on it, which read,

Why does the water flow so fast?
In the deep palace I am leisurely all day long.
Ardently I bid farewell to this red leaf,
and wish you safe arrival to the human world.

Yu You took the leaf and hid it in a bookcase, reciting and savoring the poem all day long. He liked the novelty and beauty of the lines but wondered who composed and inscribed them on the leaf. Considering that the water in the Royal Canal flows out from the imperial palace, the poem must have been composed by a palace beauty. Yu You treasured the leaf merely as a souvenir, yet from time to time he also spoke of it to those who had nothing better to do. Thenceforth, Yu You always ruminated over the anonymous author of the poem, exhausting both his energy and spirit.

One day, a friend saw him and said, "Why are you so thin? There must be a reason. Tell me please!" Yu You said, "I have lost both my appetite and sleep for several months." Then Yu told his friend about the red leaf and the lines on it.

His friend laughed loudly at him, saying, "Why have you become so stupid? It's not as if the lady wrote this poem especially for you. You obtained it by chance. Why do you care so much? Though you have been secretly loving her for so long, she is deep in the imperial palace. Even if you had wings, you would not dare venture there. Your stupid enthusiasm is ridiculous."

Yu You said, "Though Heaven is high above, he is aware of everything below. If one has a will, Heaven will certainly grant his wish. I have heard the story of Niu Xianke encountering Liu Wushuang.[8] In the end they obtained a clever strategy from Scholar Gu古and married. Things are intrinsically unpredictable; the only thing one needs to worry about is not having ambition."

Yu You still could not stop ruminating and worrying, so he further composed two lines and wrote them on a red leaf, which read,

> I have learned of the sorrow of a beauty, written on a leaf,
> After writing the poem on the leaf, to whom did you intend to send it?

He placed the red leaf on the flowing water of the upper reaches of the Royal Canal, enabling it to drift into the palace. Some laughed at him for this, but he was also praised by some enthusiastic ones. Someone presented a poem to him as a gift, which read,

> The imperial favor did not stop the east-flowing water,
> The grief of a palace girl flowed through this ditch.

Afterward, Yu You took the imperial examination several times but never passed. He became tired of the life he lived, so he sought refuge with Han Yong, a noble of the Hezhong prefect,[9] and lodged in his guest room. Having earned barely enough money and silk to support himself, he had no intention to seek an official rank anymore.

Quite a while later, Han Yong called Yu You in and told him, "In the imperial palace more than three thousand women have had some demerits. The emperor allowed all of them to marry. Lady Han, who shares a surname with me, was in the palace for a long time. Now she has left the imperial palace and lives at my residence. Currently, you are not married and have passed the prime of your life. You have been suffering from privation, achieving nothing and living alone. I feel extremely sorry for you. Now Lady Han has no less than a thousand strings of cash in her suitcase; besides, she was originally from a good family, now is only thirty years old, and she is extremely beautiful. I'll talk with her and convince her to marry you. How does this sound?"

Yu You left his seat, knelt down onto the ground, and said, "As a poverty-stricken scholar, I have sponged off you under your roof. In the daytime I have enough food to eat and at night I have a warm place to sleep. It has been quite a long time since I have received your favor. I regret that I have no special skills and therefore cannot repay your kindness. I feel ashamed and terrified from morning to evening, not knowing what to do. How could I dare have such an absurd hope?"

Han Yong ordered that the marriage be proposed in a message through a matchmaker. He aided Yu You in purchasing and forwarding betrothal gifts, such as a lamb and a swallow, completing the process of the six marriage rites and intertwining the happiness of the two families.[10] On the evening of his wedding day, Yu You was extremely delighted. The next morning, he found that the dowry in Lady Han's boxes was handsome, and her appearance gorgeous. As Yu You had never dared to have such an extravagant hope, he thought that he had entered the land of immortals by accident, and he went into ecstasies.

A short while later, Lady Han saw the red leaf in Yu You's bookcase. She said with astonishment, "This is the poem I composed. How did you acquire it?" Yu You told her what happened. Lady Han said further, "I also received a red leaf. I wonder who wrote the poem on it." Then she opened her suitcase and took the red leaf out; it was exactly the poem composed by Yu You. Face to face, they sighed in astonishment and wept emotionally for quite a while. Both asked, "How could this have happened by accident? Is it possible that it was destined?"

Han said, "When I first got the leaf, I composed a poem, which is now still in my suitcase." She took it out and showed Yu You. The poem read,

Walking alone on the bank of the Royal Canal,
It was then I approached the flowing water and acquired the leaf.
Such a feeling, who could understand?
Simply a poetic couplet that broke my heart!

Those who heard their story all sighed in wonder and amazement.

One day, Han Yong held a banquet in honor of Yu You and Lady Han. Yong said, "Today you two may want to say thanks to your matchmaker."

Lady Han replied with a smile, "The marriage of You and I was made by Heaven, not a matchmaker."

Han Yong asked, "Why do you say that?"

Lady Han asked for a brush and composed a poem, which read:

A good couplet was written for [dropping into] the flowing water,
Ten years' secret feeling satisfied my long-cherished wish.
Today we have become husband and wife,
Thus I know the red leaf was a good matchmaker.

Han Yong said, "Now I know that nothing in the world happens by chance."

Later when Emperor Xizong visited Shu,[11] Han Yong ordered Yu You to lead a hundred servant boys to march out front. Because she used to be a palace girl, Lady

Han was able to see the emperor and told him the whole story about her marriage with Yu You. The emperor replied, "I have also heard a bit of it." Then he called Yu You in and said with a smile, "You have been an old guest of mine." Yu You prostrated himself on the ground and kowtowed, apologizing for his offense.

When the emperor returned to the Western Capital,[12] and because he accompanied the emperor, Yu You obtained a position as an official and became an inspector in the Army of Inspired Strategy. Lady Han gave birth to five sons and three daughters. Their sons all became officials because of their diligent studying, and their daughters all married into famous families. Because Lady Han had regulated her family well, she was given a title as a woman by the emperor that she retained all her life. The Prime Minister Zhang Jun (?–904) composed a poem for the couple,[13] which read,

> In Chang'an there are millions of households,
> Day by day the imperial river flows eastwards.
> On the river there are numerous red leaves,
> You were the only one who got the good lines.
> Then you wrote on the fallen leaf,
> Let it flow into the imperial residence.
> Deep in the palace, where the women numbered thousands,
> The leaf drifts only to Lady Han.
> Three thousand ladies leaving the forbidden city,
> Lady Han is recorded as one of them.
> Recalling the past, she thanks the imperial favor,
> Shedding tears like a rain of rouge.
> Lodging in the home of a nobleman,
> Thereupon she met you.
> Communicating through a matchmaker and completing the six rites,
> You become husband and wife forever.
> Sons and daughters crowd before your eyes,
> Men in green and purple robes fill your home.[14]
> Such a thing has never happened in the past,
> It can be spoken of for thousands of years.

Commentary: Flowing water is unfeeling, and red leaves are unfeeling too. Absurdly, [Lady Han's] entrusting an emotionless substance onto another emotionless substance to seek for enchanted ends with the emotionless substance being obtained by the enchanted, and further, she married the enchanted. This is indeed something I have never heard of. Those who follow the principles of heaven can love each other and be wed, even if they live far apart, but those who reject these principles can do neither, even if they are close neighbors. After reading this story, those who rejoice in what they have and those who crave to gain more should draw a lesson from it.

(By Zhang Shi 張實; from Liu Fu, *Qingsuo gaoyi*)

Note: This is from my 2017 rendition in my *Song Dynasty Tales: A Guided Reader* (Singapore: World Scientific, 2017), 33–42.

Notes

1 Karl S. Y. Kao, ed., *Classical Chinese Tales of the Supernatural and the Fantastic* (Bloomington: Indiana University Press, 1985), pp. 15–16.
2 Duling is located to the southeast of present-day Xi'an in Shaanxi.
3 Qinghe county was where Xingdai in Hebei is now; another Qinghe county, which was changed to Huaiyin in 1914, was in Jiangsu.
4 Songcheng was located where Shangqiu, Henan, is today.
5 Xizong 僖宗, named Li Xuan 李儇 (r. 874–888), was an emperor of the late Tang.
6 Information about Yu You's life is not available.
7 During the Tang dynasty, water was drawn from Mount Zhongnan 終南山 to Chang'an, flowing through the royal palace. It was called *yugou* 御溝 (the Royal Canal) or *jingou* 禁溝 (Forbidden Canal).
8 Niu Xianke 牛仙客 is a mistake for Wang Xianke.
9 Hezhong, also known as Puzhou 蒲州. Its seat was located in present-day Yongji 永濟 County, Shanxi province.
10 *Liu li* 六禮, six rites, see footnote 17, page 76.
11 Xizong fled from the capital, Chang'an, to Shu (present-day Sichuan) in 880 because the rebels led by Huang Chao 黃巢 had seized the capital.
12 The Western Capital refers to Chang'an 長安, while the Eastern Capital refers to Luoyang 洛陽.
13 Zhang Ri, styled Yuchuan 禹川, a native of Hejian 河間 commandery. During the Xizong reign, he was the *Tong zhongshu menxia pingzhangshi* 同中書門下平章事 (Jointly Manager of Affairs with the Secretariat-Chancellery).
14 *Qingzi* 青紫, Green and purple: colors of the ribbons attached to the seals held by high-ranking officials of Han, and the colors of clothing worn by high-ranking officials of Tang.

Further Readings

Kohn, Livia. "Counting Good Deeds and Days of Life: The Quantification of Fate in Medieval China." *Asiatic Studies/Etudes Asiatiques* 52 (1998): 833–70.
Zhang, Dainian. "Destiny." In Zhang Dainian and Edmund Ryden, ed. *Key Concepts in Chinese Philosophy*. New Haven, CT: Yale University Press, 2002, pp. 125–39.

25 The Ghost Wife

The term "ghost" (*gui* 鬼) is derived from the belief that a person becomes a ghost after death.[1] While in early texts the ghosts always seem to have supernatural powers and therefore inspire awe in people, the portrayal of ghosts in the Six Dynasties *zhiguai* is quite different: the ghosts are not only shown in their divine aspect but are also full of human emotions.

The ghost wife motif portrays a man who interacts and marries a ghost girl. A variant of it involves a girl who cannot marry her lover until she dies. The early stories featuring this motif are about a sex dream with the following structure: (1) a beautiful young girl appears in a man's dream; (2) the girl has died young and now is from the other world; (3) the girl comes to the man on her own initiative; (4) the dream occurs in the daytime. What is emphasized in these stories is not the lust of the man, but the desire of the woman who has died young without experiencing marriage. In later stories, the focus of the motif switches from sex to a real marriage. As a result, the wife coming back to life becomes a new plot element. In certain stories, the ghost wife lives with her man like a living woman, so coming back to life becomes unnecessary.

As I have observed elsewhere, although the ghost wife is as beautiful as the descended goddess in the stories between human beings and goddesses, the tone of the motif in ghost wife stories is always somewhat sad. While the descended goddess symbolizes the ideal women in the mind of tale authors or Chinese literati, the ghost wife represents the ugly fact in how women were treated as inferior compared with men for thousands of years in Chinese history; if we say that the goddess is the incarnation of beauty, then the ghost wife is the incarnation of resentment. This is closely related to the lowly social status of women in traditional China as well as the hardships and tragedies of women under Confucian rituals.[2]

The King of Wu's Little Daughter

The little daughter of 夫差 Fu Chai, the King of Wu 吳 (r. 495–473 BCE), named Purple Jade 紫玉, was 18 years old and was talented and beautiful. A boy named Han Zhong 韓重 was 19 years old and learned Daoist magical arts. Falling in love, Purple Jade secretly associated with him through trysts and exchanging letters and promised to be his wife.

DOI: 10.4324/9781003490821-29

Before going to study in the area of the Qi and Lu, Han Zhong asked his parents to propose marriage. The king became angry and refused. Purple Jade died of depression and was buried outside the West Gate.

Three years later, Zhong returned and asked his parents about Purple Jade. His parents replied, "The king was enraged. Purple Jade died of depression and has already been buried."

Zhong wept in grief. With sacrifices and paper money, he went to offer his condolence in front of her tomb. The soul of Purple Jade emerged from the tomb to meet Zhong. In tears she said, "After you left in the past, your parents came to my father, the king, to propose marriage. I supposed that our wish would be fulfilled. Unexpectedly, however, it was not and now this is my fate. What can I do?"

Looking to the left and bending her neck, she sang,

On the southern hill was the crow,
Over the northern hill a net was set.
The crow flew up in the sky,
What is the use of the net?
I have wished to follow you,
But slanderous words were too much.
Contracting illness because of grief,
I ended my life under the Yellow Spring.
My fate is such an unfair one,
To whom can I express my resentment?
The queen of birds is the phoenix,
Losing her mate, she was saddened for three years.
Though varied birds are numerous,
None could be her match.
Showing up with my humble appearance,
I met the brilliant looks of you.
Away from each other, our hearts are close,
I never forgot you even for a moment.

After finished singing, she sighed in tears and invited Zhong to her tomb.

Zhong said, "The ways of the dead and the living are different. Fearing calamities, I dare not accept your invitation."

"I also know that the ways of the dead and the living are different," Purple Jade replied, "but after parting today we will never be able to meet again. Are you afraid that, as a ghost, I will harm you? I intended to sincerely present my offer, how could you disbelieve me?"

Touched by her words, Zhong accompanied her back to her tomb. Purple Jade feasted with him, kept him there for three days, and fulfilled the courtesy of a couple. While Zhong was about to leave, Purple Jade took out a bright pearl one inch in diameter to give him as a gift, saying, "Now my fame has been spoiled and my wish has been refused as well, what else can I say? Should you pass by my home, please greet the king on my behalf."

After leaving the tomb, Han Zhong went to see the king of Wu and told him what had happened. The king was enraged, saying, "My daughter has already died. Now you still defame her soul with this slander! You must have dug up her tomb for the pearl thereby pretend that her spirit has given you a gift."

The king ordered that Zhong be captured. But Zhong escaped and went to Purple Jade's tomb to tell her.

"Do not worry!" Purple Jade said, "I'll return home to tell His Majesty."

The king was dressing when Purple Jade appeared. Startled with grief and joy, he asked, "How could you be revived?"

Purple Jade knelt and said, "In the past, the scholar Han Zhong proposed to marry me, and Your Majesty refused him. Your daughter's fame was spoiled and thereby she died. When Zhong returned from afar and heard that I died, he brought sacrifices and paper money to mourn me in front of my tomb. Touched by his utmost sincerity, I met him and thereupon gave him my pearl. He did not rob my tomb. I hope you will not punish him."

Hearing this, the queen came out to embrace her. But Purple Jade became a wisp of smoke.

(From Gan Bao, Soushen ji, Chapter 16)

Xu Xuanfang's Daughter

During the Jin dynasty, Feng Xiaojiang of Dongping was the governor of Guangzhou.[3] His son was called Mazi and was a little over 20. One night while sleeping alone in the stable, he dreamed of a girl about 18 or 19 years old. The girl told him, "I am the daughter of Xu Xuanfang, the previous governor of this state and a native of Beihai.[4] Unfortunately, I died young. It has been four years since I was unjustly killed by a ghost, but according to the record of lifespans, I should live to be more than eighty years old. Now I have been permitted to come back alive, but only if someone called Mazi allows me to be his wife. Can you trust me and bring me back to life?" Mazi answered, "Yes." She then told Mazi the time of her next appearance.

When the appointed day arrived, hair appeared on the floor in front of Mazi's bed. He ordered someone to sweep it away, but it became more distinct. It was only then Mazi realized that this was the girl he had dreamed of. He ordered everyone out, and gradually a forehead emerged, then the head and face, and finally the neck, shoulders, and the entire body appeared all at once. Mazi had her sit on the couch in front of him. She talked to him, and her words were wonderful. Consequently, the girl slept together with Mazi, but frequently warned him, "Be careful. I'm still weak."

He then asked when she could finally come out. She answered, "I should come out on the birthday of my zodiac year, but that day has not yet come." She then went to the stable. Her words and voices were heard by everyone.

As her birthday soon approached, the girl taught Mazi the way to resurrect her in detail. After finishing giving instructions, she said goodbye and left.

Following her instructions, when the day arrived Mazi prepared a scarlet cock, a plate of cooked millet, and a liter of clear wine; he displayed the cock and millet, and poured the wine in front of her grave, which was a little more than ten paces from the stable. Having finished offering the sacrifice, he dug up her coffin, opened it, and looked inside; he found her body and appearance were the same as before. He gently took her out with his arms and placed her inside a felt curtain. There was only a faint warmth near her heart. Breath came from her mouth. Mazi ordered four maidservants to watch over and take care of her. They kept her eyes moist with the milk of a black goat; gradually she was able to open them. She could also eat some porridge. Shortly afterward, she could talk.

After 200 days, she got up and walked with a walking stick. A year later her color, flesh, skin, and strength were all recovered to normal. Thus, Mazi sent a message to Mr. Xu, and everyone in the family, honorable or lowly, all came. An auspicious day was chosen, and they officially became man and wife.

(Tao Qian, Soushen houji, Chapter 4)

Teng Mu's Drunken Excursion to the Scenic Viewing Park[5]

At the beginning of Yanyou reign period [1314–1320] of the Yuan dynasty (1279–1368), scholar Teng Mu, a native of Yongjia,[5] was 26 years old. He was endowed with a graceful bearing, well versed in composition of poetry, and esteemed by everyone.

Having heard of the beauty of the landscape of Lin'an[7] many times, he longed to visit there. During the year of *jiayin* [1314],[8] the imperial edict regarding the imperial examination was announced.[9] Thus, with a letter of recommendation from his own village, Teng went to Lin'an for the exam.

Upon his arrival, he lodged outside the Yongjin Gate.[10] Every day, he traveled between the northern and southern mountains, or among the monasteries such as Lingyin, Tianzhu, Jingci, and Baoshi.[11] As for the most notable sites, such as Jade Spring, Tiger Run Temple,[12] Heavenly Dragon Mountain, Holy Eagle Peak, the Stone-room Cave, the Pavilion of Cold Spring, the secluded valleys and deep forests, and the steep precipices and cliffs, there was nowhere that he didn't leave his footprint.

On the fifteenth day of the seventh month, he enjoyed the lotus flowers at Quyuan,[13] and thus spent the night on West Lake,[14] mooring his boat under the Leifeng Pagoda.[15] That night, the moon made it as bright as daytime, and his body was filled with the fragrance of lotus. From time to time, he heard the sound of large fishes splashing up and down in the waves, and birds flying and chirping over the bank.

The scholar had drunk so much that he could not sleep. Throwing on his clothes, he got up, roaming and looking around by the dike. Arriving at the Scenic Viewing Park, he strolled in aimlessly. It had been 40 years since the fall of the Song dynasty, so the terraces and buildings such as the Gathering Fragrance Palace, the Clear Light Tower, and the Green Light Pavilion had all been deserted. Only the western wing of the Jade Ford Veranda still stood lofty there. Scholar Teng walked to the foot of the veranda, resting briefly as he leaned against it.

Suddenly, he saw a beauty enter the park, following by another maiden. With hair windblown and fog-moistened, she looked so graceful, as if a goddess descended there. Holding his breath, Scholar Teng remained under the veranda to observe what she was doing.

The beauty said, "The lake and mountain remain the same and the scenery isn't different than it was before, but time has passed and the world has changed. These provoke sorrow over losing one's country and family!" When she walked to the water-smoothed rocks from Taihu Lake[16] at the northern section of the park, she composed a poem, which read:

> The garden and pavilion on the lake are so nice,
> Coming again, I recall my previous visits.
> Selecting songs, matching the tones of "Jade Tree,"[17]
> Watching dances performed in the Liangzhou style.[18]
> On the narrow pass, flowers welcomed the imperial carriage,
> In the deep lake, willow branches brushed our boat.
> People of the past have all gone –
> With whom can I discuss romantic affairs?

Scholar Teng was an unrestrained man. When he first saw her appearance, his emotions were stirred; having heard the poem, he couldn't stop himself from showing off his own skills. Thus he stood under the veranda and recited the following poem in response to hers:

> The garden and pavilion on the lake are so nice,
> I met a beauty who is matchless.
> Is she Chang'e from the Moon Palace?[19]
> Or the Waving Maid descended from the Milky Way?[20]
> Having not yet understood the thoughts in her mind,
> I suspect I am simply dreaming.
> I wish to play the magic music of Master Zou,[21]
> Bringing spring sunlight into a dark valley.

After finishing, he rushed toward her. Not at all startled, the beauty said slowly, "I knew you were here, so I came to look for you."

When Scholar Teng asked her name, she replied, "It has been a long time since I left this mortal world. I have something I intend to tell you, but I'm truly afraid that you'll be scared."

Hearing this, Scholar Teng realized that she was a ghost. But he was unafraid and reiterated his question.

Thus she replied, "My name is Fanghua, surname Wei, a palace lady of the deceased emperor Lizong of Song (r. 1225–1264).[22] I died at the age of twenty-three and was buried beside this park. This evening I went to the Yanfu Temple to visit Lady Jia. I was asked to stay a bit longer and unwittingly came back late, therefore causing you to wait here for so long."

Then she directed her maiden servant, "Qiaoqiao, please go bring a mat and some wine and fruit from our home. Tonight the moonlight is so nice, and the scholar has also arrived, so we must not waste our time. We will take pleasure in the moon right here." The maiden left with her orders.

In a little while, she brought back a purple wool blanket and set up flower-patterned white jade cups and green glass plates; the wine was fragrant, not like anything seen in the mortal world.

The beauty then talked, bantered, laughed, and recited poems together with the scholar; the tone of her words was limpid and graceful. Furthermore, she asked Qiaoqiao to sing to encourage their drinking. Qiaoqiao proposed to sing Liu Yong's lyric "Wang haichao."[23] The beauty told her, "It's not proper to sing an old song before a new friend." On the spot she herself composed a lyric to the tune of "Mulanhua Man"[24] and ordered Qiaoqiao to sing it:

Recalling bygone events of the previous dynasty,
This was the place of gathering the goddesses.
Facing the cloudy stairs under moonlight,
We join our green sleeves again,
Come to pick the delicate floral pendants.[25]
Prosperity goes always with the flowing water,
Alas! So hard for the dream of spring to come true.
In the deserted port, dew drops on the lotus,
On the broken dike, crying willow branches are like smoke.

The northern and southern peaks remain the same,
Grasses grow luxuriant over the pass for the imperial carriage.
How sad that by the villa and temporary palace,
Smoke conceals the phoenix-patterned banner,
And waves threaten the dragon boat.
Previously, this was a golden house with jade screens;
Now, facing a dark lamp, the night is so long.
At sunset, oxen and sheep fill the field,
On the west wind, bramble finches fly by the forest.

After the song was finished, the beauty shed sorrowful tears. While consoling her with good words, Scholar Teng also flirted with her through veiled allusion, wishing to see how she would respond.

The beauty stood up just then and thanked him, saying, "It's been so long since I died and turned back to earth. If I could serve you with my body, I'd have no regrets, even if I were to die again. And from your poem, I could tell what you have already promised me. You wish to play the magic music of Master Zou, bringing spring sunlight into a dark valley."

Scholar Teng said, "That poem was composed rashly and there was no special meaning in it. Who knew that such a casual prophecy would be fulfilled!"

After quite some time, the moon went down behind the western wall, and the star Altair sank beneath the eastern mount. The beauty asked Qiaoqiao to clear off the dinner mat, then said to the scholar, "My residence is shabby and out of the way, not a proper place for you to be. But this western veranda will serve just fine for us." Then, hand in hand, they entered and slept together under the veranda. They made love just as human beings do. When it was nearly dawn, they parted in tears.

After daybreak, Scholar Teng revisited the park. He found beside it there was truly the tomb of Wei Fanghua, a palace lady of the Song. To the left of the tomb there was a small mound, in which Qiaoqiao was buried. Scholar Teng sighed for a long while.

At dusk, he went to the western veranda again, where the beauty had already arrived. She welcomed him, remarking, "I was touched by your visit today, but I had only prepared for the night, not the daytime, and therefore I dared not meet you. In a few days more, we should be able to meet at any time."

From then on, they were together every night. Ten days later, they could also meet during the daytime, thus the scholar brought her back to where he lived.

In a short while, Scholar Teng failed the imperial examination and was about to return eastward. The beauty was willing to accompany him. He asked her, "Why isn't Qiaoqiao going with us?"

The beauty replied, "Since I will be serving you as your wife, my old residence will be empty. I'm just letting her stay as a doorkeeper."

Scholar Teng returned home with the beauty where he was met by his relatives and friends. He lied to them, "My wife is from a good family in Hang commandery." Seeing that she behaved gently and spoke wisely, everyone trusted and liked her. The beauty lived as his wife in Scholar Teng's home, served the seniors with courtesy, treated the servants with favor, and got along well with all of her neighbors. Furthermore, she was diligent in running the home and chaste as a woman – she even rarely went out through the inner door. Everyone congratulated Scholar Teng for his obtaining a capable and virtuous wife.

Three years passed swiftly. In the early autumn of the *dingsi* year [1317],[26] Scholar Teng prepared his baggage again so he could participate in the provincial examination in Zhe[jiang]. A few days before his departure, the beauty pleaded, "Lin'an is my hometown, and it has been three years since I came here with you. I'd like to travel with you in order to see Qiaoqiao."

Scholar Teng approved her request. He rented a boat, went aboard together with her, traveled directly to Qiantang, and secured lodging there.[27] The next day, precisely the fifteenth day of the seventh month, the beauty said to him, "I met you three years ago on the night of this very day. I want to go to the Scenic Viewing Park with you again to renew our old visit. How does this sound?"

Scholar Teng accepted her suggestion, and they went there with wine.

At night, the moon rose above the eastern wall, lotus flowers blossomed at the southern edge of the lake, dew-bearing willows and misty bamboos swayed on the embankment – just like the scenery from the past. When they arrived at the park, Qiaoqiao welcomed them by prostrating herself on the ground by the road, crying, "My lady, you have accompanied your man to visit the inside and outside of the city walls for three years, enjoying all the happiness of the mortal world. Have you forgotten your old residence?"

The three of them entered the park, arrived at the west veranda, and sat down there. The beauty suddenly shed tears, explaining to Scholar Teng, "I appreciate your acceptance, so I could serve you within your own home. But before we've even fulfilled our deep love, we have to bid farewell for good."

Scholar Teng asked, "What is the matter?"

The beauty replied, "This humble concubine belongs to the dark world by nature, but she has lived in the bright world. That is rather improper for her. Because she has an affinity with you that was predestined from a previous incarnation, she violated the regulations to accompany you. Now that the affinity is out in the open, she should of course part with you."

Astonished, Scholar Teng asked, "When will the parting take place?"

"This very night!" she answered.

Scholar Teng became very anxious and could not bear the thought of parting. The beauty said, "It isn't that I'm not willing to serve you and live in happiness forever, but my time is limited and I cannot violate it. If I continue staying, punishment will result. It would hurt not only me, but also you. Don't you know the story of Yueniang?"[28]

Scholar Teng gradually realized what was happening, but still felt sorrow and was unable to sleep at all that night.

When the bell of the mountain temple rang and the roosters of the water village crowed, the beauty hurriedly got up and bid Scholar Teng farewell. She took off her jade ring, tied it to Teng's belt, and said, "When you see this in the future, please don't forget your former love." Then she took her leave of him. She looked back repeatedly, and then eventually vanished.

Scholar Teng tearfully wailed for a long time, and then returned home.

The next day, he displayed dishes and wine, burned incense in front of her tomb, and composed some verses to mourn her:

She was born virtuous, beautiful, and matchless;
Endowed with wonderful bearing among the goddesses,
And gathered the essence of both Heaven and Earth.
Brightly were her looks as beautiful as flowers,
Purely was her nature as warm as the jade.
In her prime, she lived in the heavenly golden house,
In frustration, she stayed in a secluded tomb by the road.
Living together with the pine trees,
Facing foxes and hares running in groups.
Her lost love is like falling flowers on flowing water,
Rain that stopped and clouds that scattered.

The Central Plains had encountered much turbulence,
Her motherland suffered from having no lord.
Time flew like a horse jumping over a ditch,
The sun and the moon moved swiftly as running wheels.

Yet her spirit could not perish,
Her virtues could exist forever.
No need to rely on the magic arts of Li the Youthful Old Man,[29]
I myself could bring Qiannü's soul back from wandering.[30]

Holding a fan patterned with a jade box and a simurgh being ridden,[31]
Wearing a skirt embroidered with golden threads and a swarm of butterflies.
Clinking was the sound of her pendant jade rings,
Fragrant was the perfume of the orchid she was wearing.
Intending to enjoy our life together while growing old,
We had no choice but to part after we had joined!

Stepping on the sock by which the Goddess of Luo River walked on the
    waves,[32]
Reaching the cup used for the Queen Mother of the West's Jade Pool feast.[33]
Approaching the sock, nothing is seen,
Knocking on the cup, no sound is heard.
It is sad that we cannot continue our tryst;
To whom can I express my sorrow about our past?
Shutting up the yard with its willows in the spring wind,
Closing the door while night rain falls onto pear blossoms.

When love ended, the sky was misty,
Sadness accumulated like dark clouds.
Your voice and appearance is nowhere to be heard and seen,
My mind is confused and disorderly.
Restraining my sorrow, I respectfully offer my mourning,
And hope you will be touched by this writing.
Alas, what a shame!
I beg you to partake of this sacrifice!

From then on, their relationship was finished. Scholar Teng lodged in an inn, behaving as though he'd lost his wife. When the date of the examination arrived, he was in no mood to enter the exam yard and returned home downheartedly. His relatives and friends asked him the reason, so he told them everything. Everyone sighed and marveled at it.

Scholar Teng didn't marry for the rest of his life. One day he entered Mount Yandang to gather herbs and never returned home.[34]

(Qu You 瞿佑 [1347–1433], *Jiandeng Xinhua* 剪燈新話, Chapter 2)

Notes

1 The saying in Chinese is *Ren si yue gui* 人死曰鬼, as seen in the "Jifa" 祭法 chapter of *Liji*. See *Liji zhengyi,* in Ruan Yuan 阮元 (1764–1849), ed., *Shisanjing zhushu* 十三經 註疏, Vol. 46 (Beijing: Zhonghua shuju, 1980), p. 1588.

2 See Zhenjun Zhang, *Chuantong xiaoshuo yu Zhongguo wenhua* (Nanning: Guangxi daxue chubanshe, 1996), pp. 99–102.

3 Dongping was a state in the Jin dynasty. Its capital was located at Wuyan 無鹽, where Dongping, Shandong is today. Guangzhou in the Jin period was comprised of what is now Guangdong and Guangxi provinces.

4 Beihai was where modern Yidu 宜都 County is in Shandong today.

5 Jujing yuan 聚景園, literally "Gathered Scenes Park." Outside of the Qingbo 清波 Gate of Hangzhou, the park has been a place where Xiaozong 孝宗 of the Song 宋 (r. 1163–1189) nurtured his foster father, Gaozong 高宗 (r. 1131–1162), but was neglected later on.

6 Present day Wenzhou, Zhejiang.

7 Present day Hangzhou, Zhejiang.

8 According to the Chinese Stem-Branch 干支 Cycle of dates system, each year is named by a pair of one of the 10 Heavenly Stems 天干 and one of the 12 Earthly Branches 地支. The *jiayin* 甲寅 year is the 51st year of the 60-year cycle of dates (e.g., 1974, 2034, etc.).

9 The imperial Civil Service Examination stopped after the Yuan destroyed the Song dynasty in 1279, and it was restored in the early years of Yanyou.

10 Western gate of Lin'an.

11 All are famous monasteries in Hangzhou.

12 It is said that in the 14 years of the Yuanhe 元和 reign (819) of the Tang, a Buddhist master decided to leave Mount Daci 大慈 because there was no water. Suddenly he saw two tigers climb the mountain with their claws, and then sweet spring water poured out. Thus he not only stayed, but also built a temple there and named it "Tiger Run Temple."

13 "Wind-Facing Lotus in Quyuan 曲院" is one of the ten famous sites on West Lake.

14 West Lake is one of the most famous lakes in China, located in Hangzhou. There are numerous monasteries, pagodas, and gardens built within or around the lake.

15 A five-story tower located on Sunset Hill south of West Lake, which was originally built in 977 by the King of Wu Yue 吳越, collapsed in 1924, and was rebuilt in 2002. Leifeng Pagoda is also related to a popular love story, in which a white snake spirit transforms into a beautiful girl and falls in love with a young man named Xu Xian 許仙 but is finally imprisoned beneath the pagoda by Fa Hai 法海, a hideous Buddhist monk.

16 Taihu 太湖, the third largest freshwater lake lies in Jiangsu with its southern shore borders Zhejiang, is famous for its water-smoothed rocks.

17 Yushu 玉樹, "Jade Tree," refers to Yushu houtinghua 玉樹后庭花 (Jade Tree with Backyard Blossom), a tune composed by the last emperor (Chen Shubao 陳叔寶, r. 583–89) of the Southern Chen Dynasty.

18 Liangzhou 梁州 should be 涼州, the area of modern Gansu and Ningxia.

19 Chang'e 嫦娥, the Moon Lady in Chinese legend. It is said that she was originally the wife of Houyi 后羿, the lord of Youqiong 有窮 State during the Xia 夏 (21st–17th century BCE) period. After stealing and partaking of the elixir that Houyi got from Queen Mother of the West, she flew to the moon palace.

20 Zhinü 織女, "Weaving Maid," is the name of a star [Vega]. Based on *Jing Chu suishi ji* 荊楚歲時記, "East of the Milky Way there lived the Weaving Maid, who was the daughter of the God of Heaven. After many years' diligent work, she finished weaving the cloudy-silk heavenly garment. Having pity on her for living alone, the God of Heaven allowed her to marry the cowherd who lived west of the Milky Way. She gave up weaving after their marriage. The God of Heaven was enraged, and he ordered the Weaving Maid to go back to the east of the Milky Way and allowed her to meet the cowherd only once a year." 天河之東有織女，天帝之子也。年年機杼勞役，織成雲錦天衣。帝憐其獨處，許嫁河西牽牛郎，嫁後遂廢織紝。天帝怒，責令歸河東，但使一年一度相會。

21 Zouzi 鄒子, Master Zou, refers to Zou Yan 鄒衍 (ca. 305–240 BCE), a philosopher of the Warring States period (475–222 BCE). It is said that when he visited the state of Yan 燕,

there was a piece of fertile land in a severely cold location. When Zou Yan played his magic music, the land became warm, and grain seedlings grew luxuriantly.

22 The fifth emperor of the Southern Song, named Zhao Yun 趙昀.

23 Liu Yong 柳永 (987–1053): Song dynasty poet. "Wanghaichao" 望海潮 ("Observing the Tide") is one of his meditations upon the realities and costs of urban living.

24 Mulanhua 木蘭花: The flower of the lily magnolia.

25 Floral pendant: translation of *huadian* 花鈿. It is here a kind of hair ornament, or hair-pin, instead of a flower-shaped decoration on the temples.

26 The *dingsi* 丁巳 year is the 54th year of the 60-year cycle of dates.

27 Qiantang: another name of Lin'an.

28 A story in Liu Fu's (fl. 1073f) *Qingsuo gaoyi* in which a ghost lady named Yueniang is punished by a Daoist priest because of her lingering with the man she loved.

29 Li Shaoweng 李少翁, Li the Youthful Old Man, a master of occult arts of the Western Han dynasty who was said to be able to summon and make visible the dead. He was summoned to bring back the spirit of Lady Wang for Emperor Wu but was killed later on when his magic failed.

30 Qiannü 倩女 is a girl whose soul detached in a Yuan dynasty drama titled *Qiannü lihun* 倩女離魂, "Qiannü's Soul Detached."

31 "Record of a Jade Box" (玉匣) is a book about divination such as choosing an auspicious date by Lord Xu, Xu Jingyang 許旌陽 (239–374) of Eastern Jin; riding the simurgh (驂鸞) – a mythological creature similar to the phoenix – is a metaphor for ascending to heaven to become immortal.

32 Luo fei 洛妃, Goddess of the Luo River, is also known as Fufei 宓妃, Consort Fu, the daughter of the mythical emperor Fuxi 宓犧 (伏羲).

33 Wangmu 王母, Queen Mother of the West, is the queen of immortals living in the Kunlun mountain in the far west in Daoist mythology, whose Jade Pool Feast was famous for its food, including the peaches that ripened every 3,000 years.

34 Mount Yandang 雁蕩, 90 *li* east of Yueqing 樂清 County.

Further Readings

Campany, Robert Ford. "Ghosts Matter: The Culture of Ghosts in Six Dynasties Zhiguai." *Chinese Literature: Essays, Articles, Reviews (CLEAR)* 13 (1991a): 15–34.

Yu, Anthony. "Rest, Rest, Perturbed Spirit! Ghosts in Traditional Chinese Fiction." *Harvard Journal of Asiatic Studies (HJAS)* 47 (2) (1987): 397–434.

Zeitlin, Judith T. *The Phantom Heroine: Ghosts and Gender in Seventeenth-Century Chinese Literature*. Honolulu, HI: University of Hawai'i Press, 2007.

Zhang, Zhenjun. "The Motif of Revival of a Ghost Girl Through Sexual Dreams." In *Buddhism and Tales of the Supernatural in Early Medieval China*. Leiden and Boston, MA: Brill, pp. 191–205.

26 The Spirit Maiden

In Chinese tales of love between men and supernatural beings, the spirit maiden is another type in addition to the descended goddess and the ghost wife presented previously.

Differing from ghosts, supernatural beings here refer to monsters (*yao* 妖) and goblins (*jing* 精) which belong to animistic phenomena. As Ge Hong (283–343) says in *The Master Who Embraces Simplicity*, "As for all the old creatures, their spirits can change into the form of a person, so as to dazzle and delude men's eyes."[1] In some tales from early and medieval China, monsters, male or female, appear frequently to harm human beings. But in many tales since the Six Dynasties and the Tang, especially in Qing dynasty tales such as Pu Songling's *Strange Tales from Liaozhai*, spirit maidens became more and more popular as lovers of men. This indicates the evolving development of Chinese tales of love between men and supernatural beings. The successful creation of the images of flower spirits and fox girls brought new brilliance into the field of Chinese love stories.

The most popular spirit maidens include the spirits of the fox and snake. *Xuanzhong ji* says that "a fifty-year-old fox can become a woman and a hundred years old one can become a beautiful girl." The spirit maiden in the three tales selected here includes a tiger spirit, a fox, and a flower spirit.

Shen Tucheng's Wife

In the ninth year of the Zhenyuan period (785–805), Shen Tucheng, a commoner, was appointed as the district defender of Shifang 什邡 County in Hanzhou 漢州.[2] On his way to assume the post, he encountered a snowstorm and bitter coldness around ten *li* east of the Zhenfu 真符 district.[3] His horse could not continue onward.

Seeing that in a thatched cottage by the road there was a fire spreading smoke and warmth, he walked toward it. Around the fire, an old couple and a young girl were sitting. The girl was about 14 or 15. Her hair was a mess and her clothes shabby, but her skin was snow white, her appearance was flower-like, and her manner bewitching.

Seeing Cheng was approaching, the old couple stood up and said, "You must feel very cold after being in the storm, please come forward to warm yourself by the fire." Cheng thanked them and sat down.

DOI: 10.4324/9781003490821-30

A long while later, it became dark; but the storm still had not stopped. Cheng asked, "Isn't the county seat to the west far? Could I stay here for the night?"

The old couple replied, "If you do not mind our humble house, how could we refuse your request!"

Thus Cheng untied his saddle, spread his quilt, and set up his curtain there. Since there was a guest, the girl dressed again and put on some make-up. When she came out from the inner room, she looked much more beautiful and charming.

In a moment, the old lady entered from outside with a jug of wine in hand and warmed the wine by the fire. She said to Cheng, "You have been in the cold too long; drink this to warm yourself up."

Cheng stood up, bowed to the old lady, and said, "Please start with the host, then you drink, and I will drink last." Accordingly, he said, "I notice that there is no seat for your daughter at the table."

The old couple laughed, "How can a girl born in a cottage be a host?"

Turning her head back, the girl cast a sidelong glance at them, saying, "Isn't the wine too expensive so that you say it is not proper for me to join you?"

The old lady tugged her daughter's skirt and had her sit next to her.

Intending to test her capability, Cheng proposed to play the drinker's forfeit game to observe her response. Holding a cup, he said, "Please cite lines from a book to describe what you are now experiencing." He started with

"Quietly drinking wine at night,
I will not return home before I am drunk."

Lowering her head, the girl said with a smile, "With the weather so bad where are you going back to?"

Soon, it was the girl's turn. She chanted,

"The dawn is darkened by the storm,
The rooster's crowing never stops."

Astonished, Cheng sighed deeply and said, "Your daughter is so clever! Fortunately, I still have not married. I would venture to be my own matchmaker. What do you think?"

The old man said, "Although I am poor and humble, I have pampered and loved her dearly. Quite a few guests have proposed marriage and sent us gold and silk as betrothal gifts. I refused them because I could not bear to part with her at that time. But now with an honorable guest like you asking for her hand, how dare I begrudge anymore?" Then he entrusted his daughter to Cheng.

So Cheng performed the rite of a son-in-law and gave him all he had. The old lady did not take anything. "You don't mind that she is from humble origins – that is enough for us. What use do we have for money and gifts?"

The next day, the old couple said to Cheng again, "This place is remote and isolated, with no neighbors. It is also low-lying and not worth staying for long. Now that my daughter has married you, you can leave."

The next day, they bid farewell with much reluctance. Cheng then left with his wife on the horse.

After assuming his post, Cheng found his emolument was fairly meager. His wife tried her best to make ends meet and associate with guests and friends. Within ten days or so, Cheng gained good fame, and their love as husband and wife became deeper as well. She treated Cheng's relatives kindly and nurtured his nephews as well. Even their servants were all happy.

When his term was ended and he was about to return home, his wife gave birth to a son and a daughter, both of whom were smart. Cheng respected her even more. He once composed a poem titled "For My Wife," which read,

As a defender, I am ashamed of mentioning Mei Fu,
Within three years, I am ashamed to face a wife as nice as Meng Guang.
What can be a metaphor for our deep feelings?
A pair of mandarin ducks on the river.

His wife chanted it, and it seemed that she silently composed one in response to it, but she never mentioned it to anyone. She often said to Cheng, "The way of a wife is that she must study the classics. But if she composes poems, she would look like a singing girl."

After Cheng resigned from his post, he set off right away with his family back to Qin.[4] Having passed through Lizhou, they reached the bank of the Jialing River and took a rest on the grass. In melancholy, his wife suddenly told Cheng, "When I read your poem previously, I composed one in response to it, but I did not want to show you. But now I cannot keep silent facing such beautiful scenery." She chanted,

Although the love between husband and wife is deep,
My propensity towards mountains and forests is intense.
I am constantly worrying that when the season changes,
I will be unworthy of the wish to be together for a hundred years.

After she finished, she became saddened and shed tears, as if longing for something. Cheng said, "The poem is indeed beautiful, but mountains and forest should not be longed for by a woman. If you are missing your parents, we will be arriving there soon. Why do you cry in grief? As for marriage and karmic manifestation in one's life, they are all destined."

More than 20 days later, they arrived again at his wife's home. The cottage was still there, but nobody was in it. Cheng lodged there with his wife and children. Thinking of her parents, his wife wept tears all day long.

Suddenly they found under some old clothes a piece of tiger pelt covered with dust. On seeing it, his wife suddenly laughed out loud. "I didn't know it was still here!" As soon as she put it on her body, she transformed into a tiger, rushed forward with a roar, broke the door open, and disappeared into the forest.

Startled, Cheng barely avoided her. Leading his two kids, he searched for her on the way and called for her in the forest for several days. In the end, however, he did not know where she had gone.

(Xue Yusi 薛漁思, *Hedong ji* 河東記)

Qingfeng

The Geng family of Taiyuan was of nobility and lived in a splendid, spacious mansion. Later, the family declined, and half of their linked storied buildings were left desolate. Thus, strange things such as the hallway door opening and closing by itself frequently occurred. The family was always startled and screamed in terror at midnight. Mr. Geng was so annoyed that he moved with his family to a country villa and left only an old man to guard the door. Since then the residence became even more desolate, and some heard the sounds of laughter, talk, song, and music coming from there.

Mr. Geng had a nephew named Qubing who was wild and unruly. He urged the old man to inform him promptly when he saw or heard anything abnormal. One night, the old man saw a twinkling bright light on the storied building, and he rushed to tell the scholar. The scholar went to enter the building to have a look. The old man attempted to stop him, but he would not listen.

The scholar had long been familiar with the residence, but this time he had to push the thickets of mugworts away and enter through a winding way. After ascending the building, he found nothing abnormal. While passing through it, he heard people talking in whispers. When he peeped in secretly, he found a pair of big candles burning and the room was as bright as daytime. An old man wearing a scholar's cap sat towards the south, and on his opposite side was an old lady; both of them were in their forties. On the east side, there was a young man around 20; on his right was a girl who had just reached 15. They were seated around a table full of meat and wine, talking and laughing.

The scholar entered suddenly, laughed, and shouted, "An uninvited guest has come!"

Startled, all of them fled to hide. But soon the old man came out alone and questioned him in a scolding voice, "Who are you that you dare enter a private inner room of others?"

The scholar replied, "This is the inner room of my family. It is occupied by you, and now you are drinking such good wine yourselves without inviting the owner of the house. Is not that a little stingy?"

Staring at his face, the old man said, "You are not the owner of the house."

The scholar said, "I am the wild scholar Geng Qubing, nephew of the owner of this house."

"I have long admired your fame!" exclaimed the old man. He bowed to the scholar with hands clasped and invited him to join them, and then he asked his family to replace the dishes. The scholar stopped him. So the old man poured wine to toast his guest.

The scholar said, "We are both from the two families tied with friendship, no guests seated should evade the feast. I beg you to call them all back to have a drink."

"Xiao'er!" called the old man.

In a moment, the young man came back from outside. The old man said, "This is my humble son." After bowing to the scholar with hands clasped, the young man sat down.

The scholar asked about their family. The old man said, "My name is Hu Yijun."

The scholar had long been a forthright man, and his talk was cheerful and humorous. Xiao'er, too, was unrestrained. While unbosoming themselves in the conversation, they became fairly close to each other. The scholar was 21, two years older than Xiao'er, so he called him "my younger brother."

The old man said, "I heard that your grandfather had compiled 'An Unofficial Biography of Tushan Clan,' Do you know that?"

The scholar replied, "Yes, I do."

The old man said, "I am among the offspring of the Tushan clan. I can still remember our family tree since the Tang Yao reign, but before the five dynasties nothing was passed down.[5] I'd be fortunate if you can tell me something about it."

The scholar then talked briefly about the merit of Tushan's daughter who assisted Yü as his wife. He peppered the story with good words. His witticisms were pouring like a spring.

Greatly pleased, the old man said to his son, "It is so lucky that I have heard what I have never heard before. This gentleman is not an outsider. Please ask your mother and Qingfeng to come out to listen together, allowing them to know the merits of our ancestors." Then Xiao'er entered the curtain.

In a moment, the old lady came out with the girl. Glancing at the girl, the scholar found that her delicate figure gave rise to charm, her bright eyes were like the autumn water, and her beauty was matchless in the human world.

"This is my humble wife," the old man said while pointing to the lady; then he pointed to the girl, saying, "This is my niece, Qingfeng, who is smart and never forgets things after hearing them. That is the reason why I asked her to listen to you talk."

After finishing his talk, the scholar drank wine again, and he stared at the girl nonstop. The girl noticed so she lowered her head. The scholar then gently stepped on her lotus-like slipper. The girl drew her foot back quickly, but she did not become angry. Delighted, the scholar could not control himself. Slapping the table, he said, "If I can get such a wife, I would not exchange her even for the throne of a king!"

Seeing that the scholar was gradually becoming drunk and wild, both the old lady and the girl stood up, lifted the curtain, and left. The scholar was disappointed. He bid the old man farewell and walked out. But affection lingered in his mind all the time – he had no way to stop thinking of Qingfeng.

When night befell the next day, the scholar went to the room again. Although the fragrant smell remained, he did not hear even a cough of hers during the whole night when he waited. After returning home, he talked with his wife and intended to live there with his family, hoping to meet the girl again.

After his wife refused him, he went there himself and read books downstairs. When he leaned against a short table reading, a ghost entered with disheveled hair and a face as black as lacquer, staring at him with wide-open eyes. The scholar laughed, smeared his face with newly-rubbed black ink, and fixed his shining eyes at the ghost. The ghost felt ashamed and left.

Late the next night, the scholar extinguished the candle and was about to sleep, when he heard a loud sound of the door bolt being pulled out behind the building. He got up quickly and stealthily went for a look. He found the door was half open. Soon he heard the sound of quick and gentle steps. Candlelight was coming from the room. Looking inside, he found Qingfeng.

When she suddenly saw the scholar, Qingfeng drew back in terror and closed the door quickly. The scholar knelt upright in front of the door and said, "I did not avoid any danger because I wanted to see you. Luckily, no one else is here now. If I can hold your hand with a laugh, I would have no regret even if I die right away."

The girl responded in distance, "How could I ignore your deep feeling for me? But my uncle's moral code for me is very strict, so I dare not accept your wish."

The scholar pleaded with her again, "I dare not expect bodily intimacy. It would be enough to see your lively face."

It seemed the girl agreed. She opened the door and walked out. In ecstasy, the scholar pulled her arms and brought her downstairs, where he embraced her and placed her on his knees.

The girl said, "It is lucky that we have such a destined affinity. After this night, however, it would be in vain even if we still long for each other."

"Why?" The scholar asked.

The girl said, "My uncle was afraid of your wildness, so he became a ferocious ghost to scare you. But you were not affected by him at all. Now he has already found another place and all my family have moved to the new home. Tonight I'm taking care of my home, but tomorrow I will have to leave as well."

After finished speaking, she intended to leave, saying, "I'm afraid my uncle will come back."

The scholar forced her to stay and wanted to make love to her. When they were locked in a stalemate, the old man entered stealthily.

Ashamed and terrified, the girl felt there was nowhere to hide. She lowered her head and leaned against the bed, pinching her sash without a single word.

The old man shouted at her, "You cheap maiden have brought disgrace to our household! If you do not leave here quickly, I'll flog you from behind."

The girl left hurriedly, with her head lowered, and the old man rushed out as well.

Trailing behind them eavesdropping, the scholar heard the old man's vicious criticisms and cursing and Qingfeng's muffled sobbing, which pierced him to the heart.

"I'm the one to be blamed! It has nothing to do with Qingfeng," the scholar shouted. "If you pardon Qingfeng, I'd be willing to bear any punishment, even if it is done with a knife, saw, hatchet, or ax!" Everything went suddenly silent. The silence lasted for quite a while until the scholar returned to sleep.

Since then nothing had happened again. Hearing this, the scholar's uncle marveled at it. He was willing to sell the house to his nephew without bargaining on the price. The scholar was pleased, and he moved in with his whole family. Living there for a year, he felt it was very comfortable, but he had not forgotten Qingfeng even for a moment.

On the day of the Qingming Festival, the scholar was returning home after offering sacrifices to his ancestors in the graveyard. By chance, he saw a dog running after two small foxes. While one fled by dashing into the wild fields, the other one kept running hurriedly on the road. Seeing the scholar, it lowered its head with folded ears. It looked at him while crying, seemingly begging him for help. Taking pity on it, the scholar untied his shirt, held it with his arms against his breast, and returned home. When he closed the door and put the fox on his bed, he found it turned into none other than Qingfeng.

Greatly pleased, the scholar comforted her and asked her what had been going on. The girl said, "I was just playing with the maid when the dog came out of nowhere. If you had not come when you did, I would certainly be in the dog's stomach now. I hope you do not dislike me because I belong to a different species."

The scholar replied, "I have been thinking of you day and night, even in dreams. Seeing you for me is like obtaining a rare gem. How could think I would dislike you?"

The girl said, "This is indeed destined. Without the disaster, how can I be together with you? How lucky I am! The maid must assume that I died, so I can stay with you forever." The scholar was so pleased. He found a separate room for her to live in.

More than two years later, the scholar was reading one night when Xiao'er entered. Startled, the scholar stopped reading and asked where he came from. Xiao'er prostrated himself on the ground and said sorrowfully, "My father is in dire straits. Nobody but you can save him. He should have come to beg you himself, but he was afraid you would not see him, so he asked me to come."

"What is the matter?" The scholar asked.

Xiao'er said, "Are you familiar with the Third Son of Mo?"

"He is the son of a man who took the imperial examination the year I did," the scholar replied.

Xiao'er said, "Tomorrow he will pass by here. If he brings a newly hunted fox with him, I hope you may keep it."

The scholar said, "The disgrace your father gave me in this building still lingers in my mind, so I dare not deal with anything related to him. If you really want me to serve you with my meager capability, nobody but Qingfeng has to come."

Xiao'er responded in tears, "It has been three years since Qingfeng died in a wild field."

Shaking his sleeves in displeasure, the scholar said, "In that case, my resentment is even deeper." He held a book and chanted loudly, ignoring Xiao'er. Xiao'er stood up and left, wailing while covering his face with his sleeve.

The scholar went to Qingfeng's room and told her the story. The color on the girl's face changed in astonishment, she asked, "You won't save him, will you?"

"I will," the scholar said, "I did not promise him because I want to get him back for his overbearing manner toward you."

The girl was delighted, saying, "I became an orphan when I was young, so I had to rely on my uncle to survive. Though he offended you in the past, it was because he must follow our family discipline."

The scholar said, "It is indeed true, but I still feel unhappy with him. If you had truly died, there is no way I would help him."

The girl said with a laugh, "How could you be so hard-hearted?"

As expected, the next day there came the Third Son of Mo on a horse bearing an engraved harness, ornaments, and a tiger skin bowcase, followed by splendid servants. The scholar found Mo had caught many birds and beasts, among which there was a black fox, its pelt and fur matted with dark red blood. When the scholar touched it, its skin and flesh were still warm. Then, using his worn-out fur coat as an excuse, he begged for the fox to repair it with its pelt. Mo untied it and generously presented it to him as a gift. The scholar gave it to Qingfeng right away and then drank wine with his guest.

After the guest left, the girl held the fox in her arms. Three days later, it woke up and, through multiple stages, changed into the old man. Seeing Qingfeng, he suspected that he was not in the mortal world. The girl told him everything. The old man kowtowed and regretfully gave an apology for his past offense. Turning to Qingfeng, he said joyfully, "I assumed you did not die. Now, you see, I was correct!"

The girl told the scholar, "If you still care for me, I beg you let us live in this building so that I can satisfy my wish to care for my uncle as a filial child."

The scholar promised her, and the old man, blushing, bid them farewell and left. At night, their whole family moved in.

From then on, they lived together as close as father and son, with no suspicion and jealousy at all. The scholar lived in the studio, where Xiao'er talked and drank with him from time to time. When his sons born to his wife gradually grew older, he asked Xiao'er to teach them; Xiao'er taught them systematically and patiently, serving well as a mentor.

(From Pu Songling, *Liaozhai zhiyi*, Chapter 1)

The Fragrant Jade

By the Pure Palace at the foot of Mount Lao,[6] there was a common camellia tree, 20 feet high and dozens *wei* around, and there were also peonies 10 feet high and as dazzling as a brocade while they were in full bloom.

Scholar Huang from Jiaozhou lived and studied in the Pure Palace. One day, looking through the window, he saw a girl in white in the flowers. Puzzled, Huang rushed out of the study to have a look, but the girl had already fled.

After that, Huang frequently saw her. So he hid in the bushes to wait for the girl to come. After a little while, the girl came with another girl in a red skirt. Gazing at them from a distance, Huang saw that both girls were incredibly beautiful. As they drew closer, the girl in red suddenly stepped back and whispered, "There is a stranger here!"

When Huang rushed, the two girls dashed back in terror, with their sleeves and skirts flying in the air and fragrant aroma spreading everywhere. Huang chased them over the short wall, but the girls had vanished without a trace. Huang's love and admiration of the girl became even more intense, so he wrote a quatrain under the tree, which read,

My infinite longing for her is bitter,
Harboring love, I face the short window.
I fear that she is taken by Shatuoli,
Where can I find my Peerless?[7]

After returning to his study, he was thinking of her when the girl in white entered the room. Shocked and pleased, Huang greeted her. The girl smiled and said, "You have been as fierce as a robber and looked so scary before. I did not realize that you are a romantic and talented scholar. Now it won't hurt to meet you."

When Huang asked about her family, the girl said, "My courtesy name is Fragrant Jade. I previously lived in Pingkang Alley. But later a Daoist priest shut me in this mountain. What happened was truly against my will."

"What is the name of this Daoist priest?" Huang said. "I would like to right this wrong for you." The girl said, "No need to do that. He also dared not force me. And it is not that bad if I have an opportunity to frequently meet up with a romantic man like you." Huang asked who the red girl was. Xiang Yu said, "Named Crimson Snow, she is my older foster sister." Then the two became intimate in his studio.

When they woke up, the light of early dawn had already reddened in the sky. The girl hurriedly got up and said, "Indulging in carnal passion, we overslept!" After putting on her clothes and shoes, she said, "I also put together a poem in response to yours, but please do not laugh at my abilities:

A good night ends so easily,
The morning sun has been on the window.
I wish to be the swallow on the beam,
Always flying and perching in pairs.

Holding her wrist, Huang said, "You have a beautiful appearance and clever mind, making me love you until it hurts! If I have to be apart from you for one day, it would be like leaving on a one thousand *li* trip. You must manage to find time to come. Don't wait until the evening!" Fragrant Jade promised him.

From then on, they stayed together day and night. But each time Huang invited Crimson Snow, she would not come. Huang felt it was unfortunate he could not meet her. Fragrant Jade said, "My older sister is arrogant and lofty by nature, not as infatuated as me. It will take some time to persuade her. Don't be impatient!"

One night, the girl suddenly broke into the study and said, "If you can't keep even me, how can you expect her? Now I bid you farewell for good."

Huang was shocked, he asked, "Where are you going?"

The girl wiped her tears with her sleeves and said, "This is God's will; it's hard to tell you. Anyway, the previous verse has become a prophecy now. The lines 'I fear that she is taken by Shatuoli, Where to find a chivalrous man like Guard Gu?' seem to be composed for me."[8]

Huang repeatedly asked her what was going on; she said nothing but sobbed all night and left at dawn. Huang felt something was not right.

The next day, a native of Jimo County surnamed Lan went to visit the Pure Palace. Seeing the white peony, he loved it. He dug it up and took it away. It was only then that Huang realized Fragrant Jade was a peony flower demon. This brought him no small amount of sadness and regret. After a few days, Huang heard that after Mr. Lan had transplanted the peony flower at his house, but that it withered more each day. Huang was much bothered by the news. He composed 50 poems entitled "Mourning the Flower." He wept bitter tears by the original spot of the white peony every day.

One day after mourning, Huang was returning home. In the distance, he saw the girl in red weeping tears by the side of the hole. He slowly walked over, but the girl did not flee. Huang pulled on her sleeves. There they stood, face to face with tears flowing freely. A while later, Huang invited her to his room, and the girl followed.

She said with a deep sigh, "We have been sisters since childhood, now our tie has been cut off. Hearing your sorrowful crying, I felt much more saddened. When your tears flow down to the Yellow Spring, maybe she will be resurrected by your sincerity; but then again the soul of the deceased might have dissipated, so how can she talk and laugh with us soon?"

Huang said, "Born under an unlucky star, I hindered the life of my lover; I should also have no fortune to enjoy double beauty. In the past, I conveyed my enthusiasm through Fragrant Jade many times. Why did you not come again?"

Crimson Snow replied, "I think that young scholars are mostly frivolous. Little did I know you are one of the sincerest of men. However, I will associate with you through emotion instead of lust. If you expect bodily intimacy all day and night, you will be disappointed." Then she went to take her leave.

Huang said, "Fragrant Jade has left me forever, making me unable to sleep and eat. Your short stay will comfort me a little bit. Why do you refuse so resolutely?" So the girl stayed overnight before leaving, but then did not show up for several days.

Facing the cold rain and the dark window, Huang bitterly missed Fragrant Jade. He tossed and turned in bed at night, and his tears wet the pillow and mat. Draping his clothes, he got up and picked up a candle to write a poem based on the rhyme scheme of the previous one:

Rain is falling on the mountain courtyard at dusk,
With curtain hung, I sit by the small window.
Longing for my love but not seeing her,
I shed tears at midnight.

After writing it, he chanted it to himself when someone outside the window said, "A poet should have someone to respond to his poem!" Hearing the voice, he realized that it was Crimson Snow. Huang hurriedly opened the door and let her in. The girl looked at the poem and then added a poem below it:

Where are you, my sleeve-joining sister?
A lonely light shines in the night window.
In the empty mountain lives one man,
Facing his shadow they become a pair.

After reading the poem, Huang wept more; he also asked her why she rarely came to visit. Crimson Snow responded, "I can't be as enthusiastic as Fragrant Jade; instead, I can only comfort you a little bit." When Huang wanted to be intimate with her, Crimson Snow refused, saying, "Why must the pleasure of our meeting be bodily intimacy?"

From then on, whenever Huang was lonely, Crimson Snow would visit him once. When she arrived, they would have a feast and compose poems together. Sometimes she left without spending the night, and Huang would let her take her liberty. He said, "Fragrant Jade was my beloved wife and Crimson Snow my good friend."

Huang always asked Crimson Snow, "Which peony in the yard are you? I hope you can show me as early as possible so I can move you into my home. I do not allow the same thing that happened to Fragrant Jade happen to you – being stolen by a wicked man, leaving behind nothing but long-lasting regret."

Crimson Snow said, "It is hard for one to leave one's hometown. It is no use telling you. Even your beloved wife could not follow you forever, let alone a friend!"

Huang did not listen to her. He grabbed her arm and led her to the courtyard. Each time when they arrived at a peony flower, he would ask, "Is this you?" Crimson Snow responded with no words, she merely laughed at him, covering her mouth with her sleeve.

Soon, it was the end of the twelfth lunar month, and Huang returned to his hometown for the New Year.

One night in the second month, he suddenly dreamed of Crimson Snow who came to him and said sadly, "Something bad is going to happen. If you hurry you will be able to see me; otherwise, it would be too late!"

After awakening, he was surprised. He hurriedly ordered his servants to prepare a horse and rushed at night to Mount Lao, where he found the Daoist priests building a house, and the carpenter was about to cut the common camellia tree which hindered the construction. Huang hurriedly stopped him.

At night, Crimson Snow came to the study to express her gratitude. Huang smiled and said, "Since you did not tell me where you lived, you deserve this bad turn of events! Now I know which tree you are. If you do not come to visit, I will scorch you with a moxa cone."

Snow said, "Because I knew that you would react like this, I dared not tell you before."

The two sat talking for a long while. Huang said, "Facing a good friend now makes me think of my beautiful wife more intensely. It has been a long time since I mourned Fragrant Jade. Can you mourn her with me?" So they went to the peony hole and wept for her. When more than two hours had passed, Crimson Snow stopped crying to comfort Huang. Another night a few days later, Huang was sitting alone in his study when Crimson Snow suddenly walked in with a smile and said, "I have good news for you! Moved by your sincere affection, the goddess of flowers let Fragrant Jade be born again to this temple!"

Huang asked, "When?"

Crimson Snow replied, "I don't know. My guess is it won't be too long!"

Early in the morning, when Crimson Snow got off the bed to leave, Huang told her, "I have come back to the Pure Palace for you this time. Please don't keep me lonely!" Crimson Snow smiled and promised him.

After Crimson Snow had not shown up for two nights, Huang went to hug, sway, stroke, and repeatedly whisper the name of the tree, but there was no echo. So Huang ran back to the study and made a moxa cone under the lamp. He was about to cauterize the tree. Suddenly, Crimson Snow entered the room, grabbed the moxa cone and threw it away, and said, "If your prank hurt me, I will break things off with you!" Huang smiled and hugged her.

They just sat down. Fragrant Jade sneaked in. Seeing her, Huang began crying. He got up quickly, grabbed her with one hand, and held Crimson Snow's wrist with the other hand. Face to face, the three of them sobbed in grief.

After sitting down, Huang felt that his palm was empty as if he held nothing. When he asked Fragrant Jade with amazement, she tearfully replied, "In the past, I was the spirit of the flower, so I was solid; now I am a ghost of the flower, so I am not. Although we can meet today, please do not think that it is true. Just think of it as a dream."

Crimson Snow said, "It is great that my sister has come. I have been annoyed almost to death by your man!" Then she left.

Fragrant Jade laughed and talked as lovely as before. When Huang touched or leaned against her body, however, she was just like a shadow. Huang felt fairly uncomfortable. Fragrant Jade also felt regret. She told him, "You can mix ampelopsis japonica power with some sulfur and put them in water, then pour a cup on me every day. I will repay your kindness a year from today." Then, she also left.

The next day, Huang went to the white peony pit and saw that the peony sprouts had already grown out. He cultivated it every day and also built a fence to protect it. When Fragrant Jade came, she was very grateful.

Huang intended to transplant the peony to his hometown. Fragrant Jade dissuaded him, "No, I am too weak to be damaged again. Furthermore, everything grows in its own place. I do not want to grow in your home. If you do anything against my will, my lifespan will be shorter. As long as we love each other, our good days will come naturally."

When Huang was upset that Crimson Snow rarely came, Fragrant Jade said, "I must urge her to come. I can do it." Then she led Huang to the winter tree, with a lamp in hand. She picked up a grass stem, measured the tree with her palm, found the place four feet and six inches from the bottom of the trunk, and then had Huang tickle the tree with his two hands.

Soon they saw Crimson Snow coming out from behind, cursing with a smile, "You bad maiden! How can you be an accomplice in evil?"

Hand in hand, they entered the study together. Fragrant Jade pleaded, "My dear sister, please do not be upset with me. I just want to trouble you to accompany my husband temporarily. In a year I will not bother you again!" After that, Crimson Snow often came to be with Huang.

Looking at the peony bud, Huang found it was growing day by day. When the spring passed, it has grown to two feet high. Before returning to his hometown for New Year, he gave the Daoist priest some money and asked him to care for it every day.

When Huang came back in the fourth month of the following year, he found the peony budding blossom was waiting to burst forth. Huang stood a long while by the flower. As it swayed slightly, he saw it open as big as a huge disc. Seated in the stamen was a beautiful figure only three or four inches high; she floated down and turned into Fragrant Jade. With a smile, she asked, "I have been waiting for you through the wind and rain. How come you have come so late!" Then they entered the study.

Crimson Snow also arrived, and she joked with a smile, "I have been a wife on behalf of others, luckily now I can retreat to being a friend." They talked and feasted until midnight. then Crimson Snow left, and Huang and Fragrant Jade slept together, continuing their harmonious intimacy as they did before.

Later, Huang's wife died. He entered the mountain and never returned. At that time, the stem of the peony was as thick as an arm. Huang often pointed to the peony and pledged, "In the future, I will entrust my soul here, right on your left!" The two laughed, saying, "Don't forget your promise!"

After more than a decade, Huang suddenly was dying. His son arrived and cried in grief. Huang smiled and said, "This is the time of my birth, not death. Why are you crying!" Then he turned to the Taoist and said, "On a certain day in the future, a red bud will grow quickly from the bottom of the peony and split into five leaves. That will be me." Then he spoke no more. His son drove him home in a carriage, and he soon passed away.

One day in the second year, under the peony flower a large bud truly grew out, with five leaflets. The Daoist priests marveled at it and carefully watered it. In three years, it grew to a few feet high, and its stem could be measured by two hands. However, it never blossomed.

After the old Daoist priest died, his disciple did not cherish the peony and cut it off. Then the white peony withered and died; soon, the evergreen tree died as well.

Commentary: When one's emotion reaches the extreme, one can truly connect with ghosts and spirits. The ghost of the peony was attached to the flower, and the soul of the man was entrusted to the flower as well. Isn't this the result of both engaging with deep feelings? When one was cut off, the other two died soon afterward. Even if it cannot be considered chastity, it could be said to be dying for love. If one cannot keep chastity, it is only that his or her love is not deep. Confucius read the poem "Tang Di" and remarked, "He did not really think of her."[9] How true this is.

(from Pu Songling, *Liaozhai zhiyi*, Chapter 11)

Notes

1 萬物之老者, 其精悉能假託人形, 以眩惑人目. See Wang Ming 王明, ed., *Baopuzi neipian jiaoshi* 抱朴子內篇校釋 [The Master Who Embraces Simplicity with Collations and Explanations] (Beijing: Zhonghua shuju, 1980), p. 300.
2 Shifang County is located in what is present-day Sichuan province.
3 The seat of the Zhenfu district was where Mao County in Sichuan is today.
4 Qin is located in what is now Shaanxi.
5 The five dynasties here refer to the Tang (Yao), Yu (Shun), Xia (Yü), Shang, and Zhou.
6 The Pure Palace is a Daoist temple. Mount Lao 嶗山 is on the southeastern coastline of the Shandong Peninsula.
7 Shatuoli is a foreign general who took the girl scholar Han loved in the "Tale of Lady Liu," while the Peerless is a lovely girl in another Tang dynasty tale, "Wushuang the Peerless."
8 Guard Gu is the knight-errant who helped scholar Wang to marry his lover Peerless in the tale "The Peerless."
9 D. C. Lau, trans., *Analects*:

The flowers of the cherry tree,
How they wave about!
It is not that I do not think of you,
But your home is so far away."

The Master commented, "He did not really think of her. If he did, there is no such thing as being far away." (Penguin Books, 1979), 9: p. 100.

Further Readings

Allen, Sarah M. *Shifting Stories: History, Gossip, and Lore in Narrative from Tang Dynasty China*. Cambridge, MA: Harvard University Asia Center, 2014.
Huntington, Rania. *Alien Kind: Foxes and Late Imperial Chinese Narrative*. Cambridge, MA: Harvard University Asia Center, 2003.
Zeitlin, Judith T. *History of the Strange: Pu Songling and the Chinese Classical Tale*. Stanford, CA: Stanford University Press, 1993.

Bibliography

Ban Gu 班固 (32–92). *Han shu* 漢書. Beijing: Zhonghua shuju, 1962.

Bianzheng lun 辨證論. Cited in Lu Xun's Guxiaoshuo gouchen 古小説鉤沉. In *Lu Xun quanji* 魯迅全集 v. 8. Beijing: Renmin wenxue chubanshe, 1973.

Campany, Robert. *Making Transcendents: Ascetics and Social Memory in Early Medieval China*. University of Hawai'i Press, 2009.

Chen Qiyou 陳奇猷, ed. *Hanfeizi jishi* 韓非子集釋. Daibei: He Luo tushu chubanshe, 1974.

Dai Wangshu 戴望舒. *Xiaoshuo xiqu lunji* 小説戲曲論集, Beijing: Zuojia chubanshe, 1958.

Dong Zhongshu 董仲舒 (179–104 BCE). *Chunqiu fanlu* 春秋繁露, in Shanghai guji chubanshe, *Ershi'er zi* 二十二子. Shanghai: Shanghai guji chubanshe, 1986.

Duan Chengshi 段成式 [803–863]. *Youyang zazu* 酉陽襍爼. Beijing: Zhonghua shuju, 1981.

Fan Ye 范曄 (398–445) and Sima Biao 司馬彪 (?–306), ed. *Hou Hanshu* 後漢書. Beijing: Zhonghua shuju, 1962.

Fang Xuanling 房玄齡 (579–648) et al. *Jin shu* 晉書. Beijing: Zhonghua shuju, 1974.

Feng Menglong 馮夢龍 (1574–1646). *Qingshi* 情史. *Feng Menglong quanji* 馮夢龍全集, vol. 7. Nanjing: Jiangsu guji, 1993.

Feng Menglong. *Jingshi tongyan* 警世通言. Beijing: Renmin wenxue chubanshe, 1956.

Fu Liang 傅亮 (374–426), Zhang Yan 張演 and Lu Gao 陸杲. *Guang Shiyin yingyan ji* 光世音應驗記. Beijing: Zhonghua shuju, 1994.

Gan Bao 干寶 [fl. 335–349]. *Soushen ji* 搜神記. Ed. Wang Shaoying 汪紹楹. Beijing: Zhonghua shuju, 1979.

Gao Ming 高明. *Da dai li jinzhu jinyi* 大戴禮今注今譯. Taibei: Taiwan shangwu yinshuguan, 1975.

Ge Hong 葛洪 (284–344). *Shenxian zhuan* 神仙傳. Beijing: Zhonghua shuju, 2010.

Gou Daoxing 句道興. *Soushen ji* 搜神記 in Wang Zhongmin 王重民 etc., ed., *Dunhuang bianwen ji* 敦煌變文集 [Beijing: Renmin wenxue chubanshe, 1984.

Hannan, Patrick. The Chinese Vernacular Story. Cambridge, Mass: Harvard University Press, 1969.

He, Huaihong. *Social Ethics in the Changing China: Moral Decay or Ethic Awaking?* Washington, D.C.: Brookings Institution Press, 2015.

Hegel, Robert E. and Richard C. Hessney. *Expressions of Self in Chinese Literature*. New York: Columbia University Press, 1985.

Holzman, Donald. "The Place of Filial Piety in Ancient China." *Journal of the American Oriental Society*, vol.118, no.2: 185.

Huang, Martin W. "Male Friendship in Ming China: An Introduction." *Nan Nü* 9 (2007): 14.

Huangfu Mi 皇甫謐 (215–282). *Gaoshi zhuan* 高士傳. Shanghai: Shanghai guji chubanshe, 1987.

Huangfu Mi. *Yuanhua ji* 原化記. In Jiu xiaoshuo 舊小說. Shanghai: Shangwu yinshuguan, 1921.

Huijiao 慧皎 (497–554) et al. *Gaoseng zhuan heji* 高僧傳合集. Shanghai: Shanghai guji chubanshe, 1991.

Huilin 慧琳 (fl. 5 century). *Yiqiejing yinyi* 一切經音義. Taibei: Datong 大通 shuju, 1970.

Huiyuan 慧遠 (334–416). "Sanbao lun 三報論." *Zhongguo fojiao sixiangshi ziliao xuanbian* 中國佛教思想史資料彙編. Beijing: Zhonghua shuju, 1981.

Ji Yun 紀昀 (1724–1805). *Yuewei caotang biji* 閱微草堂筆記. Beijing: Zhongguo wenlian chuban gongsi, 1996.

Kao, Karl S. Y. ed. *Classical Chinese Tales of the Supernatural and the Fantastic*. Bloomington: Indiana University Press, 1985.

Lau, D. C. trans. *Mencius*. Penguin Books, 1970.

Lau, D. C. trans., *The Analects*. Penguin Books, 1979.

Legge, James, trans. *The Chinese Classics IV: The She King or Book of Poetry*. Hong Kong: Hong Kong University Press, 1960.

Li Fang 李昉 (925–996) et al., ed. *Taiping guangji* 太平廣記. Beijing: Zhonghua shuju, 1961.

Li Fengmao 李豐楙. *Xianjing yu youli: shenxian shijie de xiangxiang* 仙境與游歷：神仙世界的想象 (Beijing: Zhonghua shuju, 2010.

Li Fuyan 李復言(fl. 831). *Xu xuanguailu* 續玄怪錄. Shanghai: Shanghai guji chubanshe, 1985.

Liezi 列子. *Liezi*. Beijing: Zhanghua shuju, 2005.

Liu Fu 劉斧 [fl. 1073]. *Qingsuo gaoyi* 青瑣高議. Shanghai: Shanghai guji chubanshe, 1983.

Liu, James J. Y. *The Chinese Knight-Errant* (University of Chicago Press, 1967

Liu Xiang 劉向 (79–8 BCE). *Shuo yuan* 說苑. Taibei: Taiwan Zhonghua shuju, 1965.

Liu Xiang, *Lienü zhuan* 列女傳. Taibei: Taiwan Zhonghua shuju, 1965.

Liu Yiqing 劉義慶 (403–444), *Youming lu* 幽明錄. In *Guxiaoshuo gouchen* 古小説鈎沉. *Lu Xun quanji* 魯迅全集 v. 8. Beijing: Renmin wenxue chubanshe, 1973.

Liu Yiqing. *Shishuo xinyu* 世説新語. Taibei: Yiwen yinshuguan, 1964.

Liu Yiqing. *Xuanyan ji* 宣驗記. Beijing: Beijing chubanshe, 2000.

Lynn, Richard John, trans. *The Classic of Changes: A New Translation of the* Yijing *as Interpreted by Wang Bi*. New York: Columbia University Press, 1994.

Ma Zhongxi 馬中錫 [1446–1512]. *Dongtian ji* 東田集. Jinan: Qi Lu shushe, 1997.

Mair, Victor H. ed. *The Columbia Anthology of Traditional Chinese Literature*. New York: Columbia University Press, 1994.

Mair, Victor H. trans. *Wondering on the Way: Early Taoist Tales and Parables of Chuang Tzu*. Honolulu: University of Hawaii Press; Revised edition, 2002.

Mair, Victor H. and Zhenjun Zhang, *Anthology of Tang and Song Tales: The* Tang Song cuanqi ji *of Lu Xun*. Singapore: World Scientific, 2020.

Meng Qi 孟棨. *Benshi shi* 本事詩. Shanghai: Shanghai guji chubanshe, 1991.

Nienhauser, William H. Jr. ed. *The Grand Scribe's Records* v. 5. 1. Bloomington: Indiana University Press, 2006.

Niu Sengru 牛僧孺 (779–848), *Xuanguai lu* 續玄怪錄. Shanghai: Shanghai guji chubanshe, 1985.

Niu Su 牛肅 (fl. 804). *Jiwen* 紀聞. Beijing: Beijing chuban she, 2000.

Nie Xiu 钮琇 (1644–1704). *Gu Sheng* 觚剩. Shanghai: Shanghai guji chubanshe, 1986.

Pei Xing 裴铏 (fl. 860). *Chuanqi* 裴铏傳奇. Zhou Lengjia 周楞伽 ed. Shanghai: Shanghai guji chubanshe, 1986.

Pu Songling 蒲松齡 (1640–1715). *Liaozhai zhiyi* 聊齋志異. Shanghai: Shanghai guji chubanshe, 1979.

Qian Zhongshu 錢鐘書. *Guan zhui bian* 管錐編. Beijing: Zhonghua shuju, 1979.

Qu You 瞿佑 [1347–1433]. *Jiandeng Xinhua* 剪燈新話. Beijing: Zhonghua shuju, 1962.

Ren Fang 任昉 (460–508). *Shuyi ji* 述異記. Taipei: Taiwan shangwu yinshuguan, 1983.

Ruan Yuan 阮元 (1764–1849), ed. *Shisanjing zhushu.* Beijing: Zhonmghua shuju, 1980.

Ruan, Yuan, ed. *Shisanjing zhushu* 十三經註疏. Beijing: Zhonghua shuju, 1980.

Shen Deqian 沈德潛, ed. *Gushi yuan* 古詩源 (Taipei: Taiwan shangwu yinshuguan, 1966.

Shen Yazhi 沈亞之(781–832). *Shen Xiaxian, wenji* 沈下賢文集. Shanghai: Shanghai shu-dian, 1994.

Shi Daoshi 释道世. *Fayuan zhulin* 法苑珠林. Shanghai: Shanghai guji chubanshe, 1991.

Sima Qian 司馬遷 (145–86? BCE). *Shiji* 史記. Beijing: Zhonghua shuju, 1959.

Song Maocheng 宋楙澄 [1569–1622]. *Jiuyue ji* 九籥集. Shanghai: Shanghai guji chubanshe, 2002.

Sun Xidan 孫希旦. "Hunyi" 婚儀 in *Liji jijie* 禮記集解. Beijing: Zhunghua shuju, 1989.

Tan Fengliang 譚鳳梁, ed. *Lidai wenyen xiaoshuo jianshang cidian* 歷代文言小說鑒賞詞典. Nanjing: Jiangsu wenyi, 1991.

Tao Qian 陶潛 (365–427). *Soushen houji* 搜神後記. Beijing: Zhonghua shuju, 1981.

Uchiyama, Chinari 内山知也. *Tangdai xiaoshuo xuanzhu* 唐代小說選注, Tokyo: Mokuji-sha, 1973.

Wang Ming 王明, *Taiping jing hejiao* 太平經合校. Beijing: Zhonghua shuju, 1960.

Wang Ming, ed. *Baopuzi neipian jiaoshi* 抱朴子内篇校釋. Beijing: Zhonghua shuju, 1980).

Waley, Arthur. trans., *The Analects of Confucius.* George Allen & UNWIN LTD, 1938.

Wen Yu 温畬. *Xu Mingding lu* 續命定錄.

Xiao Tong 蕭統 (501–531), ed. *Wen Xuan* 文選. Shanghai: Shangwu yinshuguan,1936.

Xue Yusi 薛漁思. *Hedong ji* 河東記. Beijing: Beijing chubanshe, 2000.

Xun 荀, Mr. *Linggui zhi* 靈鬼志. Taibei: Yiwen yinshuguan, 1968.

Yang, Hsianyi and Gladys Yang, trans., *A Brief History of Chinese Fiction.* Beijing: Foreign Languages Press, 1964.

Zeng Zao 曾慥 [1091–1155]. *Lei shuo* 類說. Beijing: Beijing tushuguan guji zhenben con-gkan, 1988.

Zha Changguo 查昌國. "You yu lian Zhou junchen guanxi de yanbian" 友與兩周君臣關係的演變. *Lishi yanjiu* 5 [1998]: 94–109.

Zhang Chang 張萇. "Luelun Zhongguo gudai xiaoshuo zhong de renshenlian gushi" 略論中國古代小說中的人神戀故事. *Xinan shida xuebao* 西南師大學報 1 (1991): 94–99.

Zhang Du 張讀 [fl. 853]. *Xuanshi zhi* 宣室志. Taibei: Taiwan shangwu yinshuguan, 2012.

Zhang Jian 張薦 [774–804]. *Lingguai ji* 靈怪集. Beijing: Beijing chubanshe, 2000.

Zhang Tingyu 張挺玉 (1672–1755). *Ming Shi* 明史. Beijing: Zhonghua shuju, 1974.

Zhang Zhenjun 張振軍. *Chuantong xiaoshuo yu Zhongguo wenhua* 傳統小說與中國文化. Nanning: Guangxi daxue chubanshe, 1996.

Zhang Zhenjun. "Lun Daojiao dui chanting xiaoshuo zhi gongxian" 論道教對傳統小說之貢獻." in *Daojia wenhua yanjiu* 道家文化研究 9 (1996): 332–46;

Zhang, Zhenjun. *Buddhism and Tales of the Supernatural in Early Medieval China: A Study of Liu Yiqing's Youming lu.* Leiden: Brill, 2014.

Zhang, Zhenjun. *Hidden and Visible Realms: Early Medieval Chinese Tales of the Super-natural and the Fantastic.* New York: Columbia University Press, 2018.

Zhang, Zhenjun and Jing Wang. *Song Dynasty Tales: A Guided Reader.* Singapore: World Scientific Publishing, 2017.

Zhang Zhuo 張鷟. *Ermu ji* 耳目記. https://ctext.org/wiki.pl?if=gb&chapter=541005.

Zhu Tanwulan 竺曇無蘭 (Dharmarājan), trans. *Fo shuo tiecheng nili jing* 佛說鐵城泥犁經. https://www.fojingzaixian.com/42.html

Index

For Product Safety Concerns and Information please contact our EU
representative GPSR@taylorandfrancis.com
Taylor & Francis Verlag GmbH, Kaufingerstraße 24, 80331 München, Germany

www.ingramcontent.com/pod-product-compliance
Lightning Source LLC
Chambersburg PA
CBHW071555110726
47908CB00007B/2110

* 9 7 8 1 0 3 2 7 9 1 6 3 0 *